The Big Book Of Home Plans

500+ Home Designs
In Every Style—Plus Landscape Plans!

The Big Book Of Home Plans

hanley▲wood

Published by Hanley Wood
One Thomas Circle, NW, Suite 600
Washington, DC 20005

Distribution Center PBD
Hanley Wood Consumer Group
3280 Summit Ridge Parkway
Duluth, Georgia 30096

Vice President, Home Plans, Andrew Schultz
Director, Marketing, Mark Wilkin
Associate Publisher, Development, Jennifer Pearce
Editor, Simon Hyoun
Assistant Editor, Kimberly Johnson
Publications Manager, Brian Haefs
Production Manager, Theresa Emerson
Senior Plan Merchandiser, Nicole Phipps
Plan Merchandiser, Hillary Huff
Graphic Artist, Joong Min
Product Manager, Susan Jasmin
Marketing Manager, Brett Bryant

Most Hanley Wood titles are available at quantity discounts with bulk purchases for educational, business, or sales promotional use. For information, please contact Andrew Schultz at aschultz@hanleywood.com.

BIG DESIGNS, INC.
President, Creative Director, Anthony D'Elia
Vice President, Business Manager, Megan D'Elia
Vice President, Design Director, Chris Bonavita
Editorial Director, John Roach
Assistant Editor, Carrie Atkinson
Senior Art Director, Stephen Reinfurt
Production Director, David Barbella
Production Manager, Rich Fuentes
Photo Editor, Christine DiVuolo
Graphic Designer, Billy Doremus
Graphic Designer, Nick Nesser

PHOTO CREDITS
Front Cover Main: Design HPK0600433 by ©Frank Betz Associates, Inc.
Photo by ©Terrebone Photography. For details, see page 367.
Top Left: Photo by ©Home Planners, LLC.
Top Middle: Design HPK0600432 by ©Stephen Fuller, Inc.
Photo by ©Scott W. Moore & Duvaune E. White. For details, see page 366.
Top Right: Design HPK0600285 by ©Larry E. Belk Designs.
Photo by Karen Stuthard. For details, see page 230.
Back Cover: Design HPK0600006 by ©The Sater Design Collection.
Photo by Doug Thompson Photography. For details, see page 10.

10 9 8 7 6 5 4 3

Printed in the United States of America

Library of Congress Control Number: 2004099004

ISBN: 1-931131-36-8

The Big
Of Home Plans

122

Welcome!

The book you're holding is the definitive collection of home plans created by America's most celebrated and trusted designers. The plans are for homes in a broad range of sizes—from cozy starters measuring under 900 square feet, to grand manors spanning over 6,500—in a wide array of architectural styles. In short, *The Big Book of Home Plans* is your best bet for finding a design that fits your taste and respects your needs. As always, our goal is to help you realize what your family is looking for in a new home and to help you find it. *The Big Book* is divided into five sections; each section begins with a tour of a typical home within the designated square-foot range and an overview of the benefits and trade-offs of such a home. Let the sidebars and

check-up questions guide your thinking as you tour our selection of plans.

The final section of the book offers 12 of our most popular landscape plans to complement your home. Remember that choosing a landscape is a decision based on personal taste and your unique sense of home. The hard part's over! Relax and be creative. Consult our product reviews and take a moment to consider what a decorative trim will bring to the foyer or what deck and paving materials will be best for the climate in your region. This is a good chance to bring together the spaces of the home under your personal sense of style.

This is also a good time to think about how you would like to modify a plan to meet the particular needs of your

family. Our customization consultation package (turn to page 456 for details) puts you in touch with a qualified plan designer who can modify the plan you have purchased or are considering for purchase. Does your home need an extra bedroom? Would you like higher ceilings in the great room? Can the plan accommodate a larger garage? The budget-friendly price of a predrawn plan combined with the customization options available through a modification designer equals an affordable and satisfying way to build a brand new home.

Once you find a home and landscape you like, follow the instructions on page 454, which also offers tips, a price schedule, and other useful information you'll need to place an order. If at any point you would like to ask specific questions about a home you see—or would just like a second opinion—our knowledgeable staff is on hand to assist you. ●

You've been warned: A vacation-style home with this much elegance may mean shorter and shorter days at the office.

Plans in this square-foot range are ideal for those looking to build a smart, flexible, cost-efficient, and energy-saving home that is no larger than what the family needs or what the plot allows. Of course, a smaller home should feel snug, not cramped—a challenging balance for designers to attain.

One space-saving strategy is to forgo formal spaces such as separate dining rooms, which can cut up a floor plan into uncomfortable squares. Instead, smartly built smaller homes call for rooms that flow easily between household hotspots and perform "on demand." For instance, the dining area in the featured design faces the peninsula counter of the adjoining kitchen, allowing the space to function flexibly as a dining area, prep space, breakfast bar, and serving buffet for larger meals. Adding another set of doors to the rear porch would introduce attractive possibilities for outdoor dining.

A good principle to remember is that a well-designed small space can create a sense of order through travel paths and visual paths as well as with physical structures such as walls. This will allow areas of the home to retain definition without being closed off. Just as a few pillars can establish a separation between the dining room and great room, the foyer retains its integrity at the bottom of the plan by way of contrast to the great room's soaring height.

In areas where some level of privacy is necessary, consider

With dramatic windows
and a decorative mantel,
soaring great rooms
like this one will alleviate
any fear of heights.

Space-saving cabinets have reclaimed needed floor space for foot traffic and a cozy nook by the window.

building walls that don't reach the ceiling. For instance, in cases where the master suite resides on its own floor, full-height walls are not necessary to ensure privacy. A slightly lower wall can achieve the same effect while also allowing in air and light from surrounding areas.

A budget-friendly way to increase your living space is to maximize outdoor areas that are extensions of interior rooms. In climates that invite outdoor enjoyment for most of the year, homeowners can nearly double living and entertaining spaces by adding porches and decks that can be accessed from the main house.

Judicious placement of porches, such as on the second floor of this plan, adds both character and square footage to the home.

In the end, the choice to build a smaller home may also depend on your vision of home and community. Smaller spaces can more easily nurture

An extra bedroom has been converted into an entertainment space.

a sense of intimacy and connection within a family, keeping children and parents in comfortable reach of one another. Similarly, a neighborhood of smaller homes can evoke a spirit of shared space and local awareness that all too often seems absent in contemporary American communities. ●

The dining room, modestly furnished, takes advantage of the outdoor views.

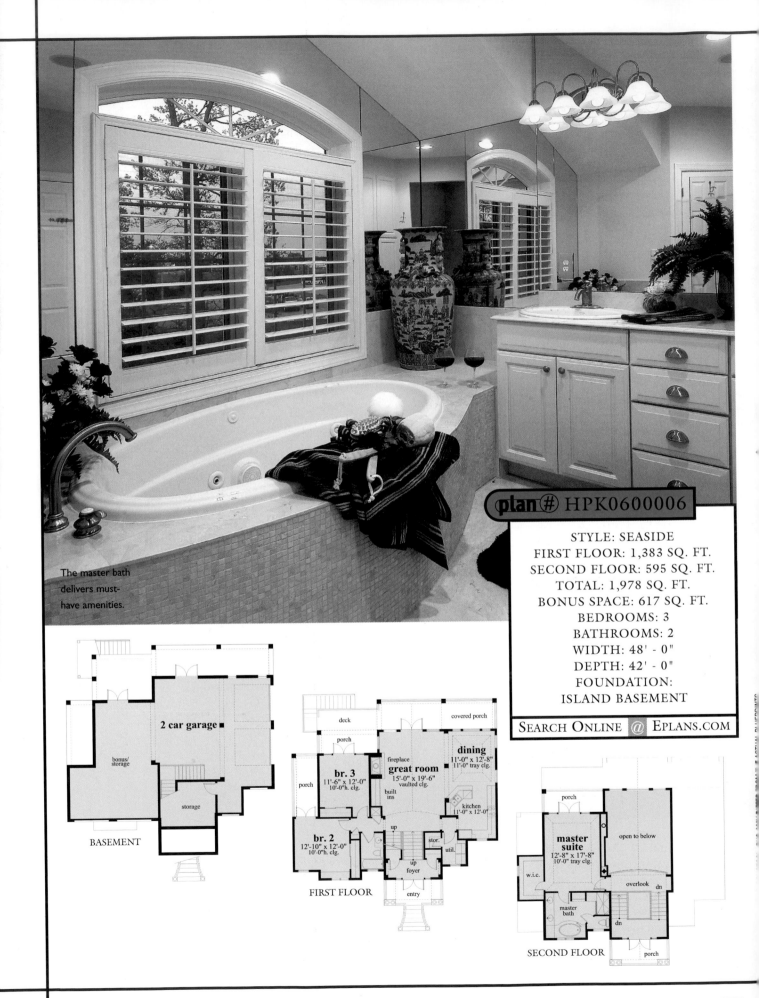

The master bath delivers must-have amenities.

plan# HPK0600006

STYLE: SEASIDE
FIRST FLOOR: 1,383 SQ. FT.
SECOND FLOOR: 595 SQ. FT.
TOTAL: 1,978 SQ. FT.
BONUS SPACE: 617 SQ. FT.
BEDROOMS: 3
BATHROOMS: 2
WIDTH: 48' - 0"
DEPTH: 42' - 0"
FOUNDATION:
ISLAND BASEMENT

SEARCH ONLINE @ EPLANS.COM

2 car garage

bonus/storage

storage

BASEMENT

deck

porch

covered porch

porch

fireplace
br. 3
11'-6" x 12'-0"
10'-0"h. clg.
built ins

great room
15'-0" x 19'-6"
vaulted clg.

dining
11'-0" x 12'-8"
11'-0" tray clg.

kitchen
11'-0" x 12'-0"

br. 2
12'-10" x 12'-0"
10'-0" clg.

up

up
foyer

stor.

util.

entry

FIRST FLOOR

porch

master suite
12'-8" x 17'-8"
10'-0" tray clg.

open to below

w.i.c.

overlook

dn

master bath

dn

porch

SECOND FLOOR

plan# HPK0600007

STYLE: TRADITIONAL
SQUARE FOOTAGE: 1,860
BEDROOMS: 3
BATHROOMS: 2
WIDTH: 85' - 4"
DEPTH: 36' - 8"
FOUNDATION: BASEMENT

SEARCH ONLINE @ EPLANS.COM

Traditional symmetry graces the facade of this charming brick home. The covered entry announces the foyer, which opens to the great room with a vaulted ceiling and corner fireplace. To the right of the foyer is the spacious living/dining room. The island kitchen, with its convenient snack bar, is situated between the dining room and the sunny breakfast bay. Access to the rear porch and the garage as well as the utility room is found just to the right of this area. The left wing holds the master suite, two family bedrooms, and a shared full bath.

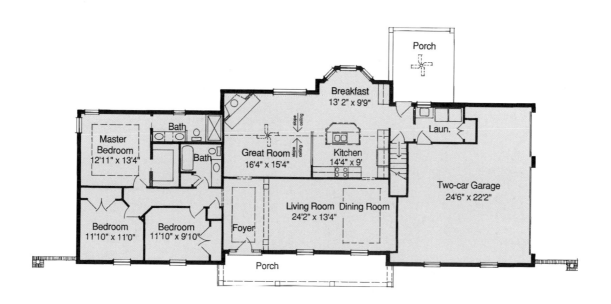

Porch
15-4x5-0

Bedroom
13-9x10-0

Greatroom
15-6x18-11

Dining
10-11x12-7

Owner's
Bedroom
12-11x15-4

Bath
6-0x16-10

Stor.

Bath

Kitchen
10-11x14-1

Garage
19-1x20-4

Basement
Option

Bedroom
13-9x11-0

Porch
26-8x5-8

plan # HPK0600008

STYLE: TRADITIONAL
SQUARE FOOTAGE: 1,643
BEDROOMS: 3
BATHROOMS: 2
WIDTH: 62' - 2"
DEPTH: 51' - 4"
FOUNDATION: CRAWLSPACE,
SLAB, BASEMENT

SEARCH ONLINE @ EPLANS.COM

OPT
BONUS RM
OVER GARAGE
14-0 x 22-0

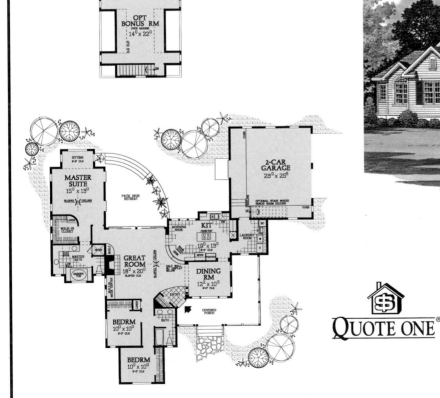

SITTING

MASTER
SUITE
15-0 x 19-0
SLOPED CEILING

WALK-IN
CLOSET

PATIO DECK
RETREAT

2-CAR
GARAGE
23-0 x 25-6

MASTER
BATH

GREAT
ROOM
18-2 x 20-0
SLOPED CLG.

KIT
10-0 x 13-0

MORNING
NOOK

LAUNDRY
ROOM

DINING
RM
12-2 x 10-0

ENTRY

BEDRM
10-0 x 10-0

BATH

COVERED
PORCH

BEDRM
10-0 x 10-0

QUOTE ONE®

plan # HPK0600009 L

STYLE: FARMHOUSE
SQUARE FOOTAGE: 1,937
BONUS SPACE: 414 SQ. FT.
BEDROOMS: 3
BATHROOMS: 2
WIDTH: 76' - 4"
DEPTH: 73' - 4"
FOUNDATION: CRAWLSPACE

SEARCH ONLINE @ EPLANS.COM

plan# HPK0600010 LD

STYLE: FARMHOUSE
SQUARE FOOTAGE: 1,830
BEDROOMS: 3
BATHROOMS: 2
WIDTH: 75' - 0"
DEPTH: 43' - 5"
FOUNDATION: BASEMENT

SEARCH ONLINE @ EPLANS.COM

This charming one-story traditional home greets visitors with a covered porch. A uniquely shaped galley-style kitchen shares a snack bar with the spacious gathering room where a fireplace is the focal point. The dining room furnishes sliding glass doors to the rear terrace, as does the master bedroom. This bedroom area also includes a luxury bath with a whirlpool tub and separate dressing room. Two additional bedrooms, one that could double as a study, are located at the front of the home. The two-car garage features a large storage area and can be reached through the service entrance or from the rear terrace.

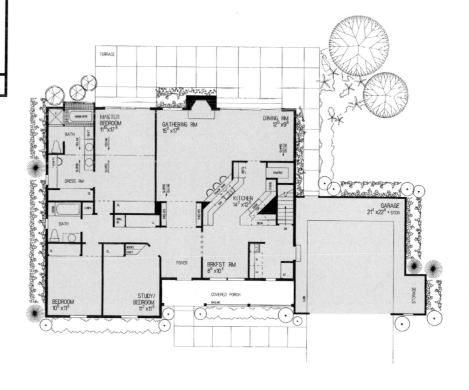

plan # HPK0600011

L

STYLE: FARMHOUSE
SQUARE FOOTAGE: 1,389
BEDROOMS: 3
BATHROOMS: 2
WIDTH: 44' - 8"
DEPTH: 54' - 6"
FOUNDATION: SLAB

SEARCH ONLINE @ EPLANS.COM

FAMILY RM
VAULTED CLG
12⁴ x 12⁰

MASTER BEDRM
VAULTED CLG
13⁰ x 12⁰

MASTER BATH

BAY WINDOW

SNACK BAR

DW

KIT
12⁴ x 10⁰

SINK

REFG

PANTRY

D W

LAUNDRY

BEDRM
VAULTED CLG
10⁰ x 10⁸

PLANT SHELF ABOVE

COVERED PORCH

LINEN

BATH

BEDRM
VAULTED CLG
10⁰ x 10⁸

BAY WINDOW

DINING

PLANT SHELF ABOVE

F.A.U.

W.H.

LIVING RM
VAULTED CLG
13¹⁰ x 19⁰

ENTRY

CURB

HALF WALL

COVERED PORCH

GARAGE
21⁴ x 23⁸

Two exteriors, one floor plan—
what more could you ask? Simple rooflines and an inviting porch enhance the floor plan. A formal living room has a warming fireplace and a delightful bay window. The U-shaped kitchen shares a snack bar with the bayed family room. Note the sliding glass doors to the rear yard here. Three bedrooms include two family bedrooms served by a full bath and a lovely master suite with its own private bath.

QUOTE ONE ®

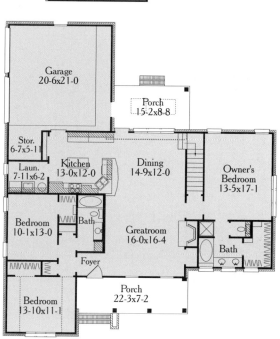

plan # HPK0600012

STYLE: TRADITIONAL
SQUARE FOOTAGE: 1,709
BONUS SPACE: 710 SQ. FT.
BEDROOMS: 3
BATHROOMS: 2
WIDTH: 54' - 6"
DEPTH: 62' - 8"
FOUNDATION: CRAWLSPACE,
SLAB, BASEMENT

SEARCH ONLINE @ EPLANS.COM

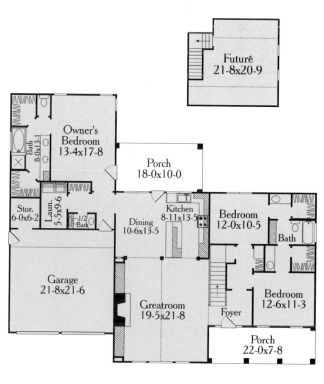

plan # HPK0600013

STYLE: TRADITIONAL
SQUARE FOOTAGE: 1,927
BONUS SPACE: 400 SQ. FT.
BEDROOMS: 3
BATHROOMS: 2½
WIDTH: 64' - 0"
DEPTH: 56' - 0"
FOUNDATION: CRAWLSPACE,
SLAB, BASEMENT

SEARCH ONLINE @ EPLANS.COM

plan # HPK0600014

A covered porch and interesting window treatments add charisma to this cheerful ranch home. The entry opens to a sunny great room with a center fireplace framed by transom windows. Nearby, an efficient kitchen is highlighted by an island snack bar, a corner sink flanked with windows, and access to the backyard. The spacious master suite features a walk-in closet and a pampering master bath with a whirlpool tub and a compartmented toilet and shower area. Two secondary bedrooms—one an optional den designed with French doors—share a full hall bath.

STYLE: TRADITIONAL
SQUARE FOOTAGE: 1,479
BEDROOMS: 2
BATHROOMS: 2
WIDTH: 48' - 0"
DEPTH: 50' - 0"

SEARCH ONLINE @ EPLANS.COM

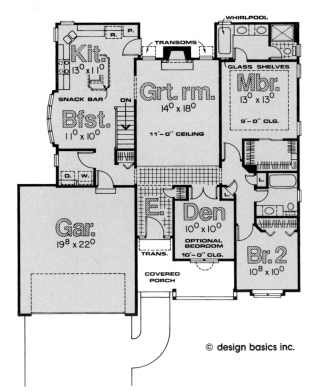

© design basics inc.

OPTIONAL LAYOUT

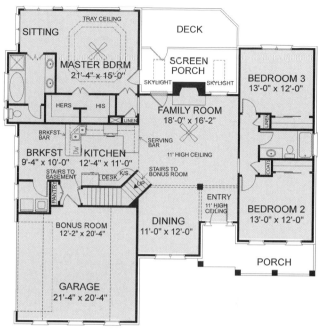

SITTING

TRAY CEILING

DECK

MASTER BDRM
21'-4" x 15'-0"

SCREEN PORCH

SKYLIGHT   SKYLIGHT

BEDROOM 3
13'-0" x 12'-0"

HERS   HIS

LINEN

FAMILY ROOM
18'-0" x 16'-2"

BRKFST BAR

SERVING BAR

11' HIGH CEILING

BRKFST
9'-4" x 10'-0"

KITCHEN
12'-4" x 11'-0"

STAIRS TO BONUS ROOM

BEDROOM 2
13'-0" x 12'-0"

STAIRS TO BASEMENT

DESK   K/S

UP

ENTRY
11' HIGH CEILING

PANTRY

BONUS ROOM
12'-2" x 20'-4"

DINING
11'-0" x 12'-0"

PORCH

GARAGE
21'-4" x 20'-4"

plan # HPK0600015

STYLE: TRADITIONAL
SQUARE FOOTAGE: 1,787
BONUS SPACE: 263 SQ. FT.
BEDROOMS: 3
BATHROOMS: 2
WIDTH: 55' - 8"
DEPTH: 56' - 6"
FOUNDATION: BASEMENT,
SLAB, CRAWLSPACE

SEARCH ONLINE @ EPLANS.COM

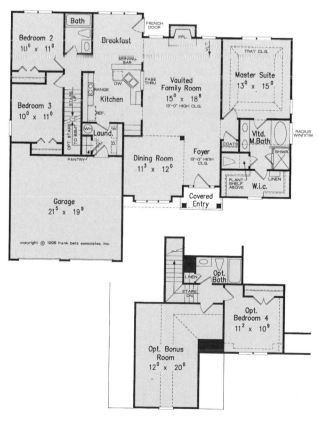

Bedroom 2
10⁰ x 11⁰

Bath

Breakfast

FRENCH DOOR

FPL.

TRAY CLG.

Master Suite
13⁰ x 15⁰

SERVING BAR

PASS THRU

DW.

Vaulted Family Room
15⁰ x 18⁸
13'-0" HIGH CLG.

Bedroom 3
10⁰ x 11⁰

STAIRS UP

RANGE

Kitchen

REF.

Vltd. M.Bath

RADIUS WINDOW

WH

Laund.

W

COATS

SHWR.

PANTRY

Dining Room
11³ x 12⁰

Foyer
13'-0" HIGH CLG.

PLANT SHELF ABOVE

LINEN

W.i.c.

Garage
21⁵ x 19⁹

Covered Entry

copyright © 1996 frank betz associates, inc.

plan # HPK0600016

STYLE: COUNTRY COTTAGE
SQUARE FOOTAGE: 1,583
BONUS SPACE: 544 SQ. FT.
BEDROOMS: 3
BATHROOMS: 2
WIDTH: 54' - 0"
DEPTH: 47' - 0"
FOUNDATION: CRAWLSPACE,
BASEMENT, SLAB

SEARCH ONLINE @ EPLANS.COM

LINEN   Opt. Bath

STAIRS DN.

Opt. Bedroom 4
11² x 10⁹

Opt. Bonus Room
12⁰ x 20⁰

PORCH

DINING
11/2 X 12/8
(9' CLG.)

BUILT-INS

SHELVES

VAULTED
MASTER
12/8 X 15/2

VAULTED
GREAT RM.
16/8 X 17/0

11/4 X 12/10

REF.

MEDIA

LIN LIN

FOYER
(10' CLG.)

BR. 3/
DEN
10/6 X 11/4
(9' CLG.)

GARAGE
20/6 X 21/0

BR. 2
11/0 X 10/0
(9' CLG.)

PORCH

plan# HPK0600017

STYLE: COUNTRY COTTAGE
SQUARE FOOTAGE: 1,580
BEDROOMS: 3
BATHROOMS: 2½
WIDTH: 50' - 0"
DEPTH: 48' - 0"
FOUNDATION: CRAWLSPACE

SEARCH ONLINE @ EPLANS.COM

OPTIONAL LAYOUT

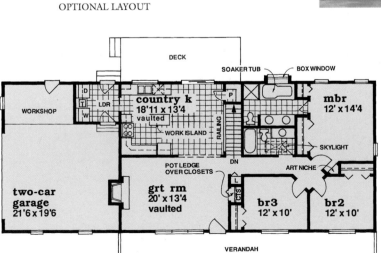

DECK

SOAKER TUB

BOX WINDOW

WORKSHOP

D
T
W

LDR

country k
18'11 x 13'4
vaulted

WORK ISLAND

RAILING

P

mbr
12' x 14'4

SKYLIGHT

POT LEDGE
OVER CLOSETS

DN

ART NICHE

two-car
garage
21'6 x 19'6

grt rm
20' x 13'4
vaulted

L
CTS

br3
12' x 10'

br2
12' x 10'

VERANDAH

RAILING

plan# HPK0600018

STYLE: RANCH
SQUARE FOOTAGE: 1,408
BEDROOMS: 3
BATHROOMS: 2
WIDTH: 70' - 0"
DEPTH: 34' - 0"
FOUNDATION: BASEMENT,
CRAWLSPACE

SEARCH ONLINE @ EPLANS.COM

plan # HPK0600019

STYLE: TRADITIONAL
SQUARE FOOTAGE: 1,615
BEDROOMS: 3
BATHROOMS: 2
WIDTH: 72' - 4"
DEPTH: 32' - 4"
FOUNDATION: BASEMENT,
SLAB, CRAWLSPACE

SEARCH ONLINE @ EPLANS.COM

A front porch and attractive gabled rooflines are both current and historic, fitting today's return to nostalgic styling. The living and dining rooms are wide open, enhancing the visual impression of lots of space. A dramatic cathedral ceiling highlights both rooms. Another highlight is a multi-sided fireplace, which the living room shares with the rear-facing family room. The family room also features a cathedral ceiling, skylight, and rear window wall, which includes a sliding glass door. There is also space for built-ins adjacent to the fireplace. A spacious U-shaped eat-in kitchen works around a center island. The adjacent breakfast area includes a double window to the rear yard. The kitchen also contains a cathedral ceiling and skylight. The master suite includes a walk-in closet, a spacious private bath with a double vanity, and a sloped ceiling with a skylight.

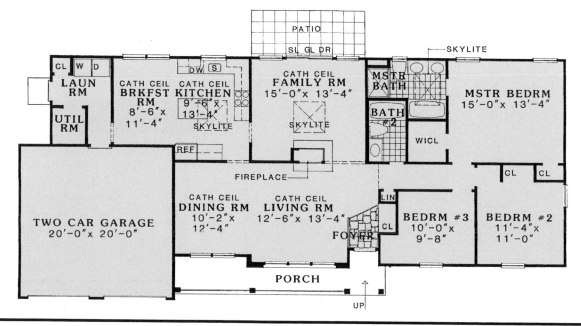

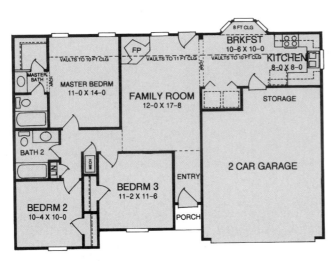

COPYRIGHT LARRY E. BELK

plan# HPK0600020

STYLE: TRADITIONAL
SQUARE FOOTAGE: 1,142
BEDROOMS: 3
BATHROOMS: 2
WIDTH: 48' - 10"
DEPTH: 35' - 8"
FOUNDATION: CRAWLSPACE,
SLAB

SEARCH ONLINE @ EPLANS.com

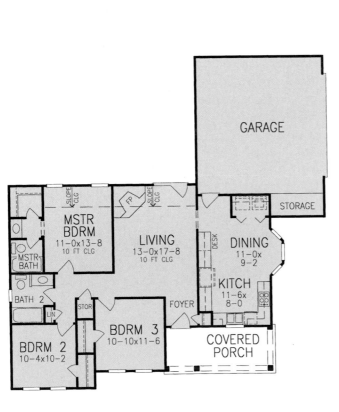

COPYRIGHT LARRY E. BELK

plan# HPK0600021

STYLE: TRADITIONAL
SQUARE FOOTAGE: 1,170
BEDROOMS: 3
BATHROOMS: 2
WIDTH: 51' - 10"
DEPTH: 53' - 6"
FOUNDATION: CRAWLSPACE,
SLAB

SEARCH ONLINE @ EPLANS.com

plan# HPK0600022

LD

STYLE: CAPE COD
FIRST FLOOR: 1,016 SQ. FT.
SECOND FLOOR: 766 SQ. FT.
TOTAL: 1,782 SQ. FT.
BEDROOMS: 3
BATHROOMS: 2½
WIDTH: 33' - 0"
DEPTH: 30' - 0"
FOUNDATION: BASEMENT

SEARCH ONLINE @ EPLANS.COM

Here's an expandable Colonial with a full measure of Cape Cod charm. Salt-box shapes and modular structures popular in Early America enjoyed a revival at the turn of the century and have come to life again—this time with added square footage and some very comfortable amenities. Upstairs, a spacious master suite shares a gallery hall which leads to two family bedrooms and sizable storage space. The expanded version of the basic plan adds a study wing to the left of the foyer as well as an attached garage with a service entrance to the kitchen.

SECOND FLOOR

OPTIONAL SECOND FLOOR

FIRST FLOOR

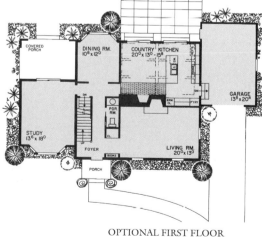

OPTIONAL FIRST FLOOR

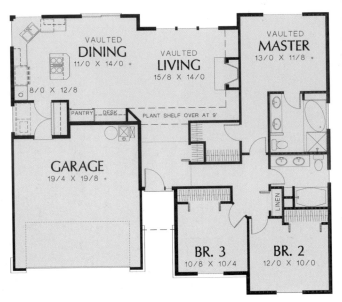

VAULTED
DINING
11/0 X 14/0 +

VAULTED
LIVING
15/8 X 14/0

VAULTED
MASTER
13/0 X 11/8 +

8/0 X 12/8

PANTRY   DESK   PLANT SHELF OVER AT 9'

GARAGE
19/4 X 19/8

LINEN

BR. 3
10/8 X 10/4

BR. 2
12/0 X 10/0

plan# HPK0600023

STYLE: COUNTRY COTTAGE
SQUARE FOOTAGE: 1,467
BEDROOMS: 3
BATHROOMS: 2
WIDTH: 49' - 0"
DEPTH: 43' - 0"
FOUNDATION: CRAWLSPACE

SEARCH ONLINE @ EPLANS.COM

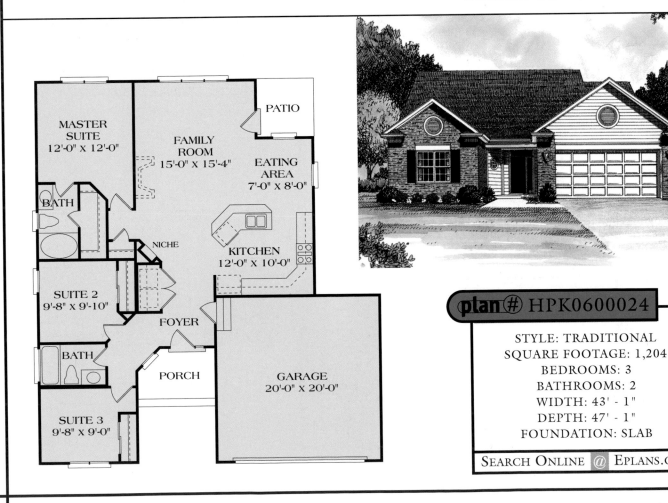

MASTER
SUITE
12'-0" X 12'-0"

FAMILY
ROOM
15'-0" X 15'-4"

PATIO

EATING
AREA
7'-0" X 8'-0"

BATH

NICHE

KITCHEN
12'-0" X 10'-0"

SUITE 2
9'-8" X 9'-10"

FOYER

BATH

PORCH

GARAGE
20'-0" X 20'-0"

SUITE 3
9'-8" X 9'-0"

plan# HPK0600024

STYLE: TRADITIONAL
SQUARE FOOTAGE: 1,204
BEDROOMS: 3
BATHROOMS: 2
WIDTH: 43' - 1"
DEPTH: 47' - 1"
FOUNDATION: SLAB

SEARCH ONLINE @ EPLANS.COM

FOR MORE DETAILED INFORMATION, PLEASE CHECK THE FLOOR PLANS CAREFULLY.

plan # HPK0600025

LD

STYLE: COUNTRY COTTAGE
FIRST FLOOR: 1,137 SQ. FT.
SECOND FLOOR: 796 SQ. FT.
TOTAL: 1,933 SQ. FT.
BEDROOMS: 4
BATHROOMS: 3
WIDTH: 40' - 0"
DEPTH: 28' - 0"
FOUNDATION: BASEMENT

SEARCH ONLINE @ EPLANS.COM

This traditional Cape Cod cottage is updated with an open floor plan that invites easy living. True to tradition, the formal living room sits to the front of the plan, just off the foyer. Comfortable living will surely be centered around the fireplace in the family room with the conjoining spacious kitchen. Enjoy casual dining at the snack bar or sit down for a meal in the formal dining room with a bay window. A study on the main level would also make a nice guest room thanks to the full hall bath nearby. Up the central stairs, you will find the master bedroom with a private bath.

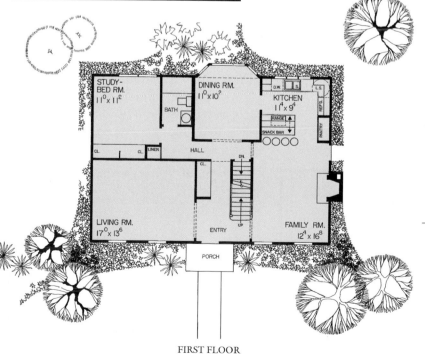

FIRST FLOOR

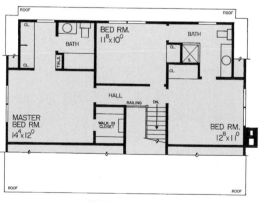

SECOND FLOOR

plan# HPK0600026

STYLE: TRANSITIONAL
SQUARE FOOTAGE: 1,395
BEDROOMS: 3
BATHROOMS: 2
WIDTH: 44' - 11"
DEPTH: 50' - 1"
FOUNDATION: SLAB

SEARCH ONLINE @ EPLANS.COM

Quaint cottage style graces the exterior of this lovely home. The three bedrooms are made up of two familiy suites, which share a hall bath, and a master bedroom on the opposite side of the home. The master suite includes a private bath with two linen closets, a garden tub, and a walk-in closet. A family room with a fireplace is open to a dining area, which overlooks the rear patio deck. The kitchen accesses a laundry room, which conveniently connects to the garage.

PATIO

FAMILY ROOM
14'-0" X 14'-0"

DINING AREA
10'-6" X 14'-0"

MASTER SUITE
12'-0" X 14'-0"

SUITE 3
11'-6" X 9'-6"

W.I.C.

LIN.

KITCHEN
9'-0" X 11'-4"

MASTER BATH

LIN.

BATH

P.

FOYER

LIN.

LAUN.

SUITE 2
11'-6" X 10'-8"

PORCH

GARAGE
20'-0" X 19'-4"

W/H

plan # HPK0600027

STYLE: FARMHOUSE
SQUARE FOOTAGE: 1,787
BONUS SPACE: 326 SQ. FT.
BEDROOMS: 3
BATHROOMS: 2
WIDTH: 66' - 2"
DEPTH: 66' - 8"

SEARCH ONLINE @ EPLANS.COM

Cathedral ceilings bring a feeling of spaciousness to this home. The great room features a fireplace, cathedral ceilings, and built-in bookshelves. The kitchen is designed for efficient use with its food preparation island and pantry. The master suite provides a welcome retreat with a cathedral ceiling, a walk-in closet, and a luxurious bath. Two additional bedrooms, one with a walk-in closet, share a skylit bath. A second-floor bonus room is perfect for a study or a play area.

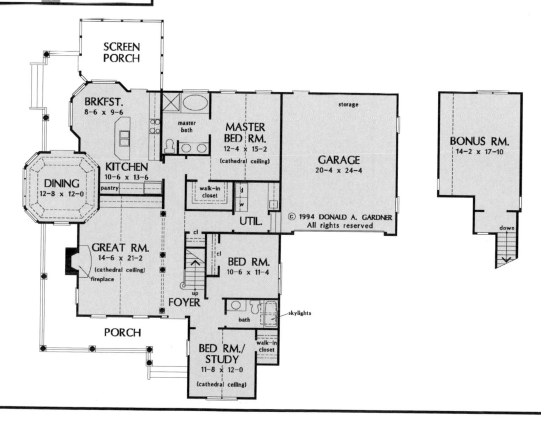

© 1994 DONALD A. GARDNER
All rights reserved

2 CAR GARAGE
21' X 21'

LIVING ROOM
18' X 24'
VAULTED CEILING

POWDER

W.I.C.

MASTER BATH
10' CLG.

DINING ROOM
11' X 13'
VOLUME CEILING

FOYER
VOLUME CEILING

KITCHEN
12' X 12'
9' CLG.

NOOK

MASTER BEDROOM
15' X 19'
10' CLG.

PORCH
18' X 6'

FIRST FLOOR

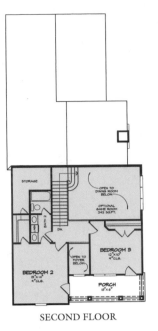

STORAGE

OPEN TO DINING ROOM BELOW

OPTIONAL GAME ROOM 242 SQ.FT.

BATH 2

DN.

BEDROOM 3
13' X 10'
9' CLG.

BEDROOM 2
13' X 13'
9' CLG.

OPEN TO FOYER BELOW

PORCH
18' X 6'

SECOND FLOOR

plan # HPK0600028

STYLE: TRADITIONAL
FIRST FLOOR: 1,347 SQ. FT.
SECOND FLOOR: 537 SQ. FT.
TOTAL: 1,884 SQ. FT.
BEDROOMS: 3
BATHROOMS: 2½
WIDTH: 32' - 10"
DEPTH: 70' - 10"
FOUNDATION: CRAWLSPACE

SEARCH ONLINE @ EPLANS.COM

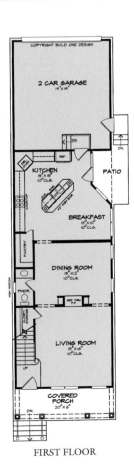

COPYRIGHT BUILD ONE DESIGN

2 CAR GARAGE
18' X 18'

KITCHEN
15' X 15'
10' CLG.

REF.

DN.

PATIO

BREAKFAST
13' X 10'
10' CLG.

PANTRY

DINING ROOM
15' X 12'
10' CLG.

PWDR.

CLOSET STORAGE

LIVING ROOM
15' X 16'
10' CLG.

UP

COVERED PORCH
20' X 6'

FIRST FLOOR

COVERED PORCH

BEDROOM 2
12' X 12'
9' CLG.

DN.

BATH 2

BEDROOM 2
10' X 11'
9' CLG.

MASTER BATH
9' CLG.

HER CLOS.

DN.

MASTER BEDROOM
15' X 16'
9' CLG.

HIS CLOS.

COVERED PORCH
20' X 6'

SECOND FLOOR

plan # HPK0600029

STYLE: TRADITIONAL
FIRST FLOOR: 911 SQ. FT.
SECOND FLOOR: 1,029 SQ. FT.
TOTAL: 1,940 SQ. FT.
BEDROOMS: 3
BATHROOMS: 2½
WIDTH: 20' - 10"
DEPTH: 75' - 10"
FOUNDATION: CRAWLSPACE

SEARCH ONLINE @ EPLANS.COM

FOR MORE DETAILED INFORMATION, PLEASE CHECK THE FLOOR PLANS CAREFULLY.

plan # HPK0600030

STYLE: TRADITIONAL
FIRST FLOOR: 880 SQ. FT.
SECOND FLOOR: 755 SQ. FT.
TOTAL: 1,635 SQ. FT.
BEDROOMS: 3
BATHROOMS: 2½
WIDTH: 36' - 0"
DEPTH: 54' - 4"
FOUNDATION: BASEMENT,
CRAWLSPACE, SLAB

SEARCH ONLINE @ Eplans.com

With a wrapping front porch that just begs for summer's lazy days, this three-bedroom farmhouse is a step back in time. Arches and columns define the foyer, which opens to the hearth-warmed living room and dining room. At the rear, the family room and island kitchen combine to form a casual space, just right for relaxing. Utility rooms line the back of the two-car garage. Bedrooms are located upstairs, including two secondary bedrooms and a spacious master suite. An additional walk-in closet can be found in the hall and gives access to abundant attic space.

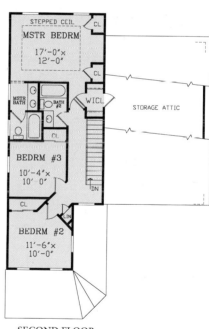

SECOND FLOOR

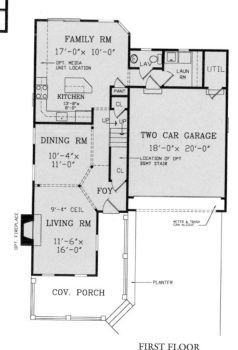

FIRST FLOOR

Country finesse and stylish charm present a lovely siding-and-stone exterior. The rear of the house encourages outdoor relaxation with abundant porches, an elegant bayed turret, and a graceful curved stairway cascading from a second-floor porch to the rear patio. Inside, the family room is warmed by a large fireplace, and the dining room is illuminated by the spectacular turret bay. The first-floor master suite is enchanting with a walk-in closet and a private bath. Upstairs, two family bedrooms share a full hall bath and a study loft area.

plan # HPK0600031

STYLE: COUNTRY
FIRST FLOOR: 1,301 SQ. FT.
SECOND FLOOR: 652 SQ. FT.
TOTAL: 1,953 SQ. FT.
BONUS SPACE: 342 SQ. FT.
BEDROOMS: 3
BATHROOMS: 2½
WIDTH: 58' - 0"
DEPTH: 55' - 0"
FOUNDATION: BASEMENT

SEARCH ONLINE @ EPLANS.COM

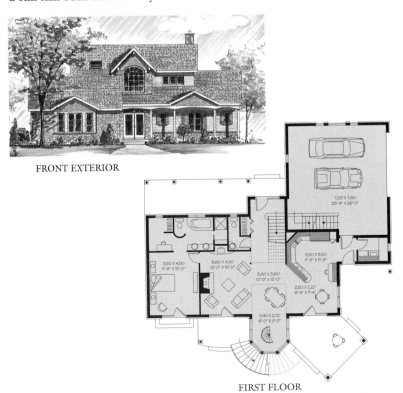

FRONT EXTERIOR

FIRST FLOOR

SECOND FLOOR

plan # HPK0600032 L

STYLE: VICTORIAN
FIRST FLOOR: 911 SQ. FT.
SECOND FLOOR: 861 SQ. FT.
TOTAL: 1,772 SQ. FT.
BEDROOMS: 3
BATHROOMS: 2½
WIDTH: 38' - 0"
DEPTH: 52' - 0"
FOUNDATION: BASEMENT

SEARCH ONLINE @ EPLANS.COM

Victorian houses are well known for their orientation on narrow building sites. Only 38 feet wide, this home still offers generous style and comfort. Beautiful arched glass panels, skylights, and large double-hung windows allow natural light to fill this home, giving a golden glow to oak and maple hardwood floors and trim. From the covered front porch, the foyer leads to the living and dining rooms, with an extended-hearth fireplace and access to both the veranda and screened porch. Sleeping quarters on the second floor include a master suite and two family bedrooms.

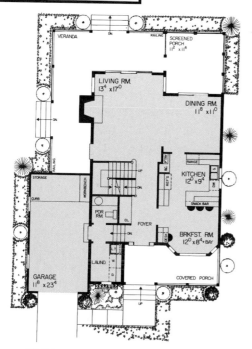

FIRST FLOOR

SECOND FLOOR

QUOTE ONE®

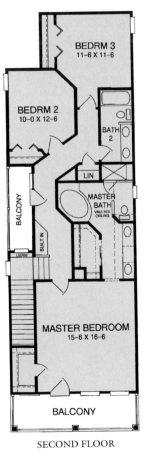

plan# HPK0600033

STYLE: TRADITIONAL
FIRST FLOOR: 904 SQ. FT.
SECOND FLOOR: 1,058 SQ. FT.
TOTAL: 1,962 SQ. FT.
BEDROOMS: 3
BATHROOMS: 2½
WIDTH: 22' - 0"
DEPTH: 74' - 0"
FOUNDATION: SLAB,
CRAWLSPACE

SEARCH ONLINE @ EPLANS.COM

Reminiscent of the popular townhouses of the past, this fine clapboard home is perfect for urban or riverfront living. Two balconies grace the second floor—one at the front and one on the side. A two-way fireplace between the formal living and dining rooms provides visual impact. Built-in book-cases flank an arched opening between these rooms. A pass-through from the kitchen to the dining room simplifies serving, and a walk-in pantry provides storage. On the second floor, the master bedroom opens to a large balcony, and the relaxing master bath is designed with a separate shower and an angled whirlpool tub. Two secondary bedrooms and a full bath are located at the rear of the plan.

Floor plan labels (First Floor):
GARAGE
BRKFST 10-6 X 11-4 10 FT CEILING
PAN
KITCHEN 11-6 X 10-6 10 FT CEILING
PATIO
PASS THRU
DINING ROOM 15-6 X 13-0 TRAYED CEILING
PWDR
TWO WAY FP
ARCH   ARCH
LIVING ROOM 15-6 X 15-0 10 FT CEILING
ENTRY
PORCH

FIRST FLOOR

Floor plan labels (Second Floor):
BEDRM 3 11-6 X 11-6
BEDRM 2 10-0 X 12-6
BATH 2
LIN
BALCONY
BUILT IN
LEDGE
MASTER BATH VAULTED CEILING
MASTER BEDROOM 15-6 X 16-6
BALCONY

SECOND FLOOR

plan # HPK0600034

STYLE: TRADITIONAL
FIRST FLOOR: 1,421 SQ. FT.
SECOND FLOOR: 578 SQ. FT.
TOTAL: 1,999 SQ. FT.
BEDROOMS: 4
BATHROOMS: 2½
WIDTH: 52' - 0"
DEPTH: 47' - 4"

SEARCH ONLINE @ EPLANS.COM

Growing families will love this unique plan. Start with the living areas—a spacious great room with high ceilings, windows overlooking the backyard, a see-through fireplace to the kitchen area, and access to the rear deck. The dining room with hutch space accommodates formal occasions. The hearth kitchen features a well-planned work space and a bayed breakfast area. The master suite with a whirlpool tub and walk-in closet is found downstairs; three family bedrooms are upstairs. A two-car garage and handy laundry room complete the plan.

FIRST FLOOR

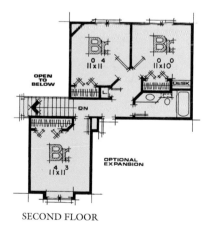

SECOND FLOOR

QUOTE ONE®

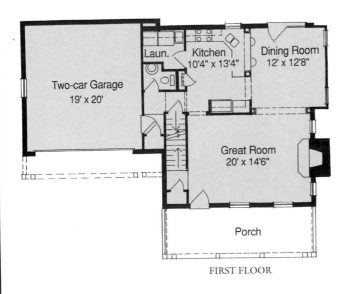

plan# HPK0600035

STYLE: CAPE COD
FIRST FLOOR: 790 SQ. FT.
SECOND FLOOR: 723 SQ. FT.
TOTAL: 1,513 SQ. FT.
BONUS SPACE: 285 SQ. FT.
BEDROOMS: 3
BATHROOMS: 2½
WIDTH: 49' - 8"
DEPTH: 30' - 6"
FOUNDATION: BASEMENT

SEARCH ONLINE @ EPLANS.COM

The nostalgia of a more relaxed time, when neighbors visited and shared evening conversation, is provided with the exterior style of this delightful home. Large rooms and a clean, easy floor plan offer value and efficiency. Upgraded features include a first-floor utility room, a two-car garage, counter space with seating availability, a pantry, and a fireplace. The spacious second floor boasts a generous-sized master bedroom including a private bath and roomy walk-in closet. Two additional bedrooms and a large bonus room that can be finished later complete this comfortable home.

FIRST FLOOR

SECOND FLOOR

plan# HPK0600036

STYLE: FARMHOUSE
SQUARE FOOTAGE: 1,466
BEDROOMS: 3
BATHROOMS: 2
WIDTH: 60' - 0"
DEPTH: 39' - 10"
FOUNDATION: BASEMENT,
SLAB, CRAWLSPACE

SEARCH ONLINE @ EPLANS.COM

This absolutely charming Victorian-style ranch home is warm and inviting, yet the interior is decidedly up-to-date. An assemblage of beautiful windows surrounds the main entry, flooding the entrance foyer and adjoining great room with an abundance of shaded light. An elegant 10-foot stepped ceiling is featured in the great room, as is a corner fireplace and rear wall of French-style sliding doors. The beautiful multisided breakfast room features a 16-foot ceiling adorned with high clerestory windows, which become the exterior "turret." A private master suite includes a compartmented bath, dressing alcove, very large walk-in closet, 10-foot stepped ceiling, and beautiful bay window overlooking the rear.

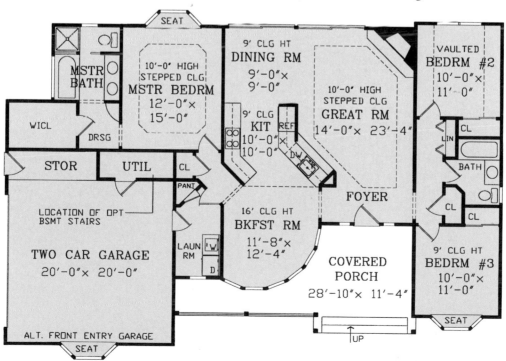

plan # HPK0600037

STYLE: TRADITIONAL
FIRST FLOOR: 905 SQ. FT.
SECOND FLOOR: 863 SQ. FT.
TOTAL: 1,768 SQ. FT.
BEDROOMS: 3
BATHROOMS: 2½
WIDTH: 40' - 8"
DEPTH: 46' - 0"

SEARCH ONLINE @ EPLANS.COM

Multiple gables and different window treatments create an interesting exterior on this plan. A covered porch and Victorian accents create a classical elevation. Double doors to the entry open to a spacious great room and an elegant dining room. In the gourmet kitchen, features include an island snack bar and a large pantry—French doors lead to the breakfast area. Cathedral ceilings in the master suite and dressing area add an exquisite touch. A vaulted ceiling in Bedroom 2 accents a window seat and an arched transom window.

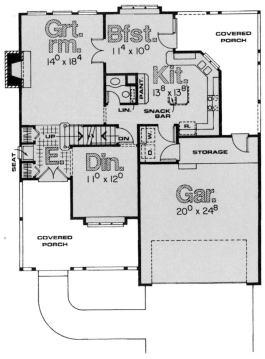

FIRST FLOOR

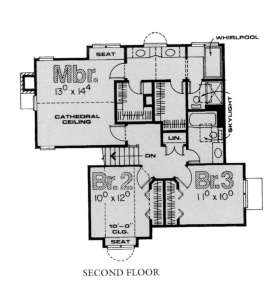

SECOND FLOOR

plan # HPK0600038

STYLE: TRADITIONAL
FIRST FLOOR: 1,467 SQ. FT.
SECOND FLOOR: 513 SQ. FT.
TOTAL: 1,980 SQ. FT.
BONUS SPACE: 340 SQ. FT.
BEDROOMS: 3
BATHROOMS: 2½
WIDTH: 67' - 0"
DEPTH: 51' - 0"

SEARCH ONLINE @ EPLANS.COM

A traditional family home on the outside, this inventive floor plan maximizes living space and is brimming with thoughtful details. From a wide foyer, the dining room and study are flooded with natural light. If you choose to make the study a bedroom, the nearby powder room can easily become a full bath. The living room is crowned with an 11-foot tray ceiling. A warming fireplace here can be viewed from the sunny breakfast nook and deluxe island kitchen. The master suite is tucked away for peace and quiet, with porch access and a soothing private bath. Twin bedrooms share the upper level with a full bath and optional game room.

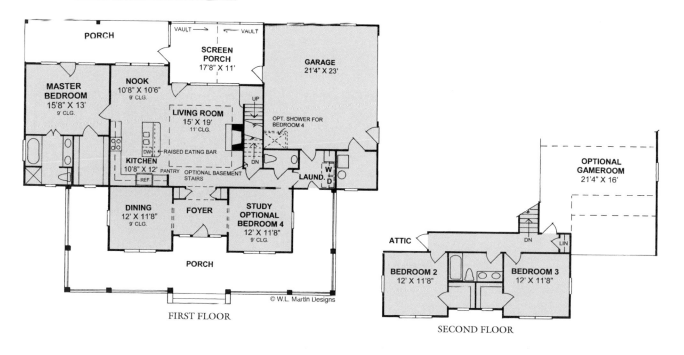

FIRST FLOOR

SECOND FLOOR

© W.L. Martin Designs

This lovely Victorian home has a perfect balance of ornamental features making it irresistible, yet affordable. The beveled-glass front door invites you into a roomy foyer. The open kitchen and breakfast room and abundant counter space make cooking a pleasure. A large family room with a warming fireplace is convenient for either informal family gatherings or formal entertaining. The upper level includes a master suite with a multifaceted vaulted ceiling, a separate shower, and a six-foot garden tub. Two additional bedrooms share a conveniently located bath. A special feature is the large, closed-in storage space at the back of the two-car garage.

plan# HPK0600039

STYLE: COUNTRY COTTAGE
FIRST FLOOR: 812 SQ. FT.
SECOND FLOOR: 786 SQ. FT.
TOTAL: 1,598 SQ. FT.
BEDROOMS: 3
BATHROOMS: 2½
WIDTH: 52' - 0"
DEPTH: 28' - 0"
FOUNDATION: SLAB,
CRAWLSPACE

SEARCH ONLINE @ EPLANS.com

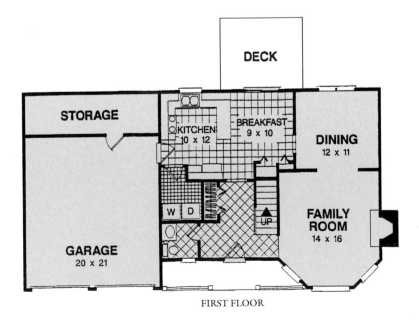

FIRST FLOOR

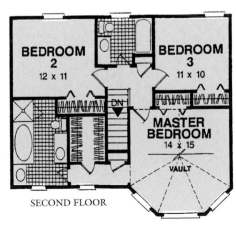

SECOND FLOOR

plan # HPK0600040

STYLE: FARMHOUSE
FIRST FLOOR: 794 SQ. FT.
SECOND FLOOR: 756 SQ. FT.
TOTAL: 1,550 SQ. FT.
BONUS SPACE: 251 SQ. FT.
BEDROOMS: 3
BATHROOMS: 2½
WIDTH: 46' - 11"
DEPTH: 35' - 1"
FOUNDATION: SLAB

SEARCH ONLINE @ EPLANS.COM

The quaint front porch provides the perfect welcome to this farmhouse design. Enter through the foyer to find a formal dining room to the right and a convenient powder room to the left. A practical kitchen sits near the center of the plan with a walk-in pantry and access to the garage. Easily serve the breakfast bar and be included in the goings on in the expansive family room—with a warming fireplace—from the kitchen, as well. Upstairs you'll find three bedrooms and two full baths, as well as bonus space for future development.

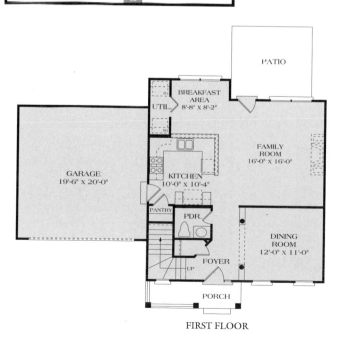

FIRST FLOOR

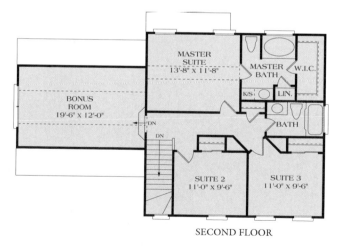

SECOND FLOOR

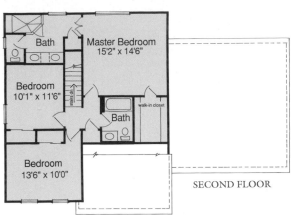

Bath

Master Bedroom
15'2" x 14'6"

Bedroom
10'1" x 11'6"

Bath

walk-in closet

Bedroom
13'6" x 10'0"

SECOND FLOOR

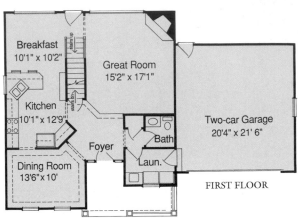

Breakfast
10'1" x 10'2"

Great Room
15'2" x 17'1"

Kitchen
10'1" x 12'9"

Two-car Garage
20'4" x 21' 6"

Foyer

Bath

Dining Room
13'6"x 10'

Laun.

FIRST FLOOR

plan # HPK0600041

STYLE: TRADITIONAL
FIRST FLOOR: 906 SQ. FT.
SECOND FLOOR: 798 SQ. FT.
TOTAL: 1,704 SQ. FT.
BEDROOMS: 3
BATHROOMS: 2½
WIDTH: 29' - 8"
DEPTH: 33' - 10"
FOUNDATION: BASEMENT

SEARCH ONLINE @ EPLANS.com

UNFIN.
BONUS
ROOM
16'-6" x 22'-4"

SUITE 2
10'-0" x 12'-0"

SUITE 3
11'-0" x 12'-0"

BATH

PLANT
SHELF

OPEN
TO
BELOW

WALK-IN
STORAGE

SECOND FLOOR

DECK/
PATIO

plan # HPK0600042

STYLE: CAPE COD
FIRST FLOOR: 1,251 SQ. FT.
SECOND FLOOR: 505 SQ. FT.
TOTAL: 1,756 SQ. FT.
BONUS SPACE: 447 SQ. FT.
BEDROOMS: 3
BATHROOMS: 2½
WIDTH: 50' - 0"
DEPTH: 39' - 0"
FOUNDATION: BASEMENT,
CRAWLSPACE, SLAB

MASTER
BATH

MASTER
SUITE
12'-0" x 16'-0"

BREAKFAST
7'-0" x 12'-0"

KITCHEN
9'-0" x 12'-0"

DINING
ROOM
10'-0" x 12'-0"

W.I.C.

DESK

PANT

LAUN.

GREAT
ROOM
14'-6" x 19'-0"

GARAGE
20'-0" x 22'-0"

PDR.

FOYER

LOGGIA

FIRST FLOOR

SEARCH ONLINE @ EPLANS.com

plan # HPK0600043

STYLE: CAPE COD
FIRST FLOOR: 1,251 SQ. FT.
SECOND FLOOR: 505 SQ. FT.
TOTAL: 1,756 SQ. FT.
BONUS SPACE: 447 SQ. FT.
BEDROOMS: 3
BATHROOMS: 2½
WIDTH: 50' - 0"
DEPTH: 39' - 0"
FOUNDATION: SLAB,
CRAWLSPACE

SEARCH ONLINE @ EPLANS.COM

Ideal for empty-nesters, this economical plan features a main-level master suite that offers convenient living and provides privacy for family or guests on the second floor. The great room includes an expansive, two-story vaulted ceiling with a balcony overlook. Walk through the dining room into the full kitchen, which includes a center work island. A deck/patio is accessible from the breakfast area. The master suite features an ample walk-in closet. In addition to Suites 2 and 3, there is an unfinished bonus room plus generous walk-in storage upstairs.

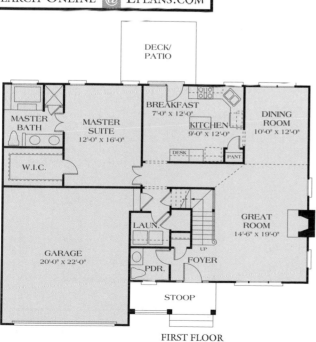

FIRST FLOOR

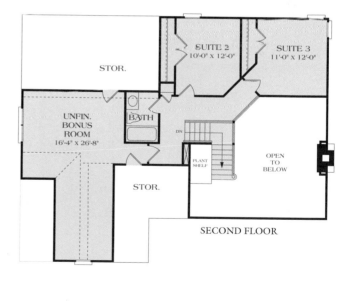

SECOND FLOOR

plan# HPK0600044

Stucco and brick combine with classic styling to give this three-bedroom home plenty of curb appeal. Split-level, with the lower level available for future development, this is a house your family will love to call home. Inside and up a few steps is the living and dining area, with the efficient kitchen nearby. To the right is the sleeping zone, which is complete with two family bedrooms, a full hall bath, and a spacious master bedroom suite. On the lower level, a large room waits for future finishing, and the two-car garage shelters the family fleet.

STYLE: TRADITIONAL
MAIN LEVEL: 1,257 SQ. FT.
LOWER-LEVEL ENTRY: 36 SQ. FT.
TOTAL: 1,293 SQ. FT.
BASEMENT: 476 SQ. FT.
BEDROOMS: 3
BATHROOMS: 2
WIDTH: 48' - 0"
DEPTH: 30' - 0"
FOUNDATION: BASEMENT

SEARCH ONLINE @ EPLANS.COM

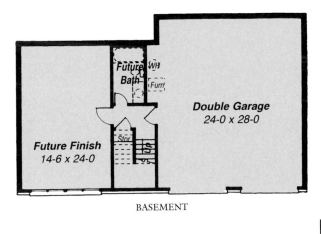

BASEMENT

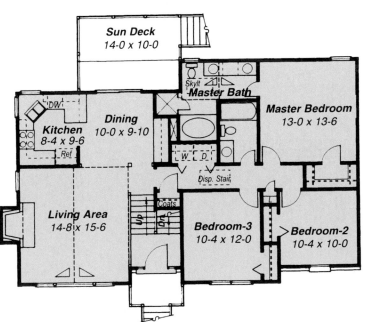

plan # HPK0600045

STYLE: TRADITIONAL
SQUARE FOOTAGE: 1,208
BEDROOMS: 3
BATHROOMS: 2
WIDTH: 48' - 0"
DEPTH: 29' - 0"
FOUNDATION: BASEMENT

SEARCH ONLINE @ EPLANS.COM

Sundeck
10-0 x 10-0

M.Bath

Bedroom 2

Bath 2

Kitchen
8-0 x 10-0

Dining
10-4 x 10-0

Master
Bedroom
11-6 x 14-6

Family Room
18-4 x 13-0

Bedroom 3
11-0 x 10-0

Entry

©1996, Jannis Vann & Associates, Inc.

plan # HPK0600046

STYLE: COLONIAL
SQUARE FOOTAGE: 1,441
BEDROOMS: 3
BATHROOMS: 2
WIDTH: 67' - 0"
DEPTH: 34' - 0"
FOUNDATION: SLAB,
CRAWLSPACE, BASEMENT

SEARCH ONLINE @ EPLANS.COM

Master
Bedroom
13-2x15-3

Greatroom
15-2x19-0

Dining
9-4x10-0

Storage
7-0x5-4

Storage
13-0x5-0

Kitchen
9-0x11-8

Garage
20-4x22-0

Bedroom
13-4x11-8

Bedroom
12-2x13-9

Laun.
9-0x5-5

Porch
16-0x6-5

plan # HPK0630001

A daylight basement provides a walkout to ground level in this charming waterfront cottage. Inside, the family and dining rooms combine for a feeling of spaciousness, heightened by access to a large covered porch. The L-shaped kitchen features an island with seating for quick or casual meals. The first-floor bedroom offers a walk-in closet and access to a full bath. The second floor holds another full bath, a sitting area, and a room that could be used as a study or another bedroom.

STYLE: BUNGALOW
FIRST FLOOR: 1,024 SQ. FT.
SECOND FLOOR: 456 SQ. FT.
TOTAL: 1,480 SQ. FT.
BEDROOMS: 2
BATHROOMS: 2
WIDTH: 32' - 0"
DEPTH: 40' - 0"
FOUNDATION: FINISHED
WALKOUT BASEMENT

SEARCH ONLINE @ EPLANS.COM

FIRST FLOOR

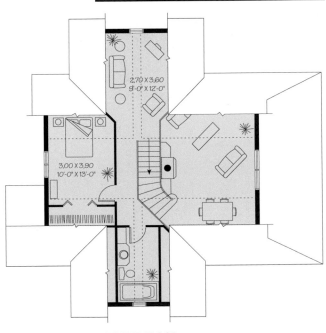

SECOND FLOOR

plan# HPK0600048

L

STYLE: EUROPEAN COTTAGE
FIRST FLOOR: 1,115 SQ. FT.
SECOND FLOOR: 690 SQ. FT.
TOTAL: 1,805 SQ. FT.
BEDROOMS: 3
BATHROOMS: 2
WIDTH: 43' - 0"
DEPTH: 32' - 0"
FOUNDATION: BASEMENT

SEARCH ONLINE @ EPLANS.COM

This quaint Tudor cottage has an open floor plan that is designed for easy living. The gathering room is accented with a cathedral ceiling and a full Palladian window. The dining room is joined to the efficient kitchen, with extra entertaining space available on the deck. The first-floor master suite has a large compartmented bath and bumped-out windows. Upstairs, a lounge overlooks the gathering room and accesses an outside balcony. Two additional bedrooms and a full hall bath complete the second floor.

QUOTE ONE®

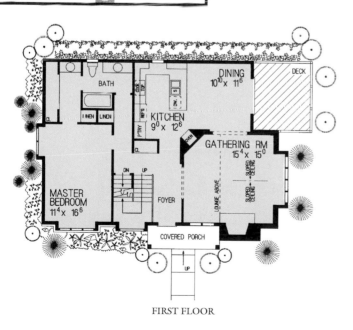

FIRST FLOOR

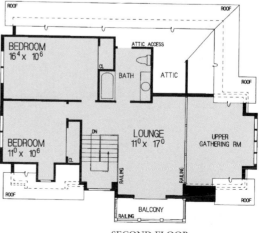

SECOND FLOOR

plan# HPK0600049

D

STYLE: COUNTRY COTTAGE
FIRST FLOOR: 1,113 SQ. FT.
SECOND FLOOR: 543 SQ. FT.
TOTAL: 1,656 SQ. FT.
BEDROOMS: 3
BATHROOMS: 2
WIDTH: 42' - 0"
DEPTH: 28' - 4"
FOUNDATION: BASEMENT

SEARCH ONLINE @ EPLANS.COM

For a lakeside retreat or as a retirement haven, this charming design offers the best in livability. The gathering room with a corner fireplace and wall of windows, a U-shaped kitchen with an attached dining room, and the lovely deck make a complete and comfortable living space. The spacious first-floor master suite offers privacy. Upstairs, two bedrooms with a full bath and a balcony lounge complete the design and provide sleeping accommodations for family and guests.

QUOTE ONE®

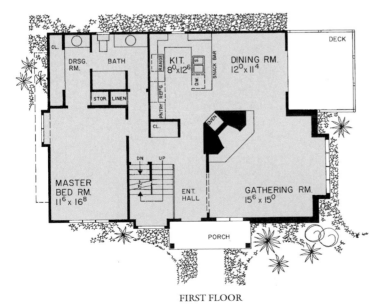

FIRST FLOOR

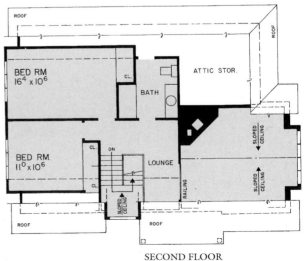

SECOND FLOOR

plan # HPK0600050

STYLE: TRADITIONAL
FIRST FLOOR: 1,282 SQ. FT.
SECOND FLOOR: 541 SQ. FT.
TOTAL: 1,823 SQ. FT.
BEDROOMS: 3
BATHROOMS: 2½
WIDTH: 32' - 0"
DEPTH: 49' - 8"
FOUNDATION: CRAWLSPACE

SEARCH ONLINE @ EPLANS.COM

*This intriguing Northeastern-*style home celebrates unique angles, beautiful details, and a fresh look for a home like no other. Enter from a columned porch to the airy gathering room, warmed by a cozy corner hearth. An open floor plan places the dining room to the left with a clear view of the fireplace. An arched hall leads past a powder room to the wide galley kitchen and sunny breakfast nook. The master suite is located nearby, complete with a box-bay sitting area, massive walk-in closet, and a lavish private bath. A staircase at the front of the home wraps around an open area and presents two generous bedrooms that share a Jack-and-Jill bath. A two-car garage at the rear of the home provides plenty of room for the family fleet, without blocking the home's enchanting facade.

FIRST FLOOR

SECOND FLOOR

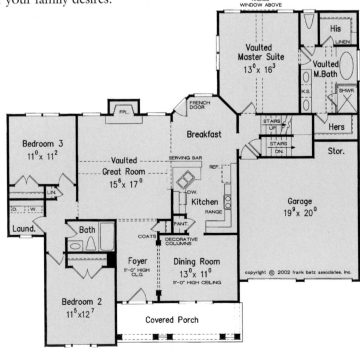

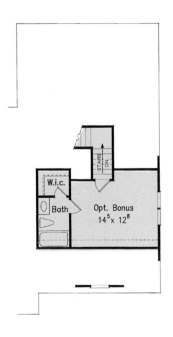

plan # HPK0600051

This inviting Colonial-style home will capture your heart with a lovely facade and flowing floor plan. From the foyer and beyond, raised ceilings visually expand spaces. A vaulted great room is warmed by a cozy hearth and opens to the bayed breakfast nook. A serving-bar kitchen helps chefs prepare marvelous meals for any occasion and easily accesses the columned dining room. Tucked to the rear, the vaulted master suite enjoys light from radius windows and the comforts of a pampering spa bath. Two additional bedrooms are located to the far right, near a full bath and laundry room. Bonus space is available for an extra bedroom, study, or playroom—whatever your family desires.

STYLE: COUNTRY COTTAGE
SQUARE FOOTAGE: 1,725
BONUS SPACE: 256 SQ. FT.
BEDROOMS: 3
BATHROOMS: 2
WIDTH: 58' - 0"
DEPTH: 54' - 6"
FOUNDATION: CRAWLSPACE, BASEMENT

SEARCH ONLINE @ EPLANS.COM

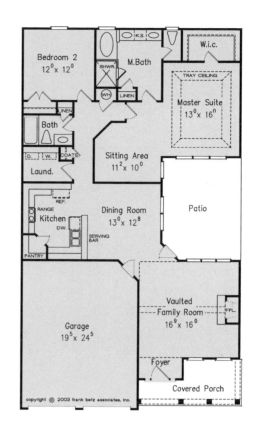

plan # HPK0600052

STYLE: COUNTRY COTTAGE
SQUARE FOOTAGE: 1,546
BEDROOMS: 2
BATHROOMS: 2
WIDTH: 37' - 0"
DEPTH: 64' - 0"
FOUNDATION: SLAB

SEARCH ONLINE @ EPLANS.com

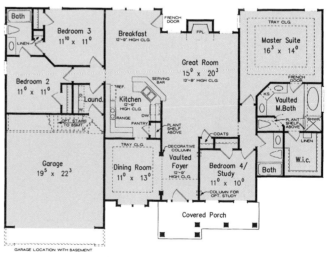

plan # HPK0600053

STYLE: TRADITIONAL
SQUARE FOOTAGE: 1,932
BEDROOMS: 4
BATHROOMS: 3
WIDTH: 63' - 0"
DEPTH: 45' - 0"
FOUNDATION: BASEMENT,
CRAWLSPACE

SEARCH ONLINE @ EPLANS.com

Plan HPK0600054

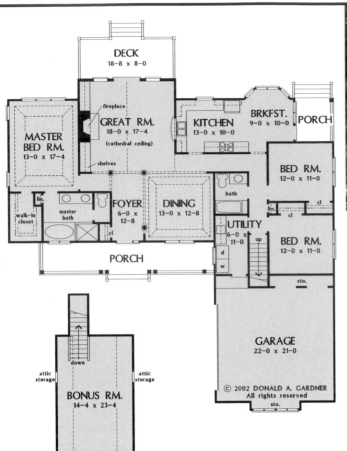

DECK
18-8 x 8-0

GREAT RM.
18-0 x 17-4
(cathedral ceiling)

fireplace

shelves

MASTER
BED RM.
13-0 x 17-4

KITCHEN
13-0 x 10-0

BRKFST.
9-0 x 10-0

PORCH

lin.

master
bath

walk-in
closet

FOYER
6-0 x
12-8

DINING
13-0 x 12-8

bath

UTILITY
6-0 x
11-0

BED RM.
12-0 x 11-0

lin.

cl

cl

up

BED RM.
12-0 x 11-0

d
w

sto.

PORCH

GARAGE
22-0 x 21-0

sto.

down

attic
storage

attic
storage

BONUS RM.
14-4 x 23-4

plan # HPK0600054

STYLE: COUNTRY
SQUARE FOOTAGE: 1,827
BONUS SPACE: 384 SQ. FT.
BEDROOMS: 3
BATHROOMS: 2
WIDTH: 61' - 8"
DEPTH: 62' - 8"

SEARCH ONLINE @ EPLANS.COM

Bedroom 1
11'-10" x 11'-4"
9'-0" Flat Clg.

Bath 2

Porch
39'-6" x 10'-0"
9'-0" Flat Clg.

Nook
9'-4" x 9'-4"
9'-0" Flat Clg.

built-ins

Bedroom 2
11'-10" x 10'-8"
9'-0" Flat Clg.

fireplace

Kit.
9'-4" x
8'-6"
9' Clg.

Master Suite
13'-2" x 15'-2"
Tray Clg.

WIC

Living Room
16'-0" x 14'-8"
Vaulted Clg.

L

WIC

Study/Office
12'-6" x 11'-0"
Tray Ceiling

Foyer

Dining
11'-8" x 10'-4"
Vaulted Clg.

Utility
6'-10" x
10'-10"

WIC

M. Bath

WIC

bench
Dn.

Porch
31'-8" x 7'-0"

2 Car Garage
20'-4' x 23'-10"

plan # HPK0600055

STYLE: FARMHOUSE
SQUARE FOOTAGE: 1,822
BEDROOMS: 3
BATHROOMS: 2
WIDTH: 58' - 0"
DEPTH: 67' - 2"
FOUNDATION: BASEMENT

SEARCH ONLINE @ EPLANS.COM

plan # HPK0600056

STYLE: BUNGALOW
FIRST FLOOR: 1,416 SQ. FT.
SECOND FLOOR: 445 SQ. FT.
TOTAL: 1,861 SQ. FT.
BONUS SPACE: 284 SQ. FT.
BEDROOMS: 3
BATHROOMS: 2½
WIDTH: 58' - 3"
DEPTH: 68' - 6"

SEARCH ONLINE @ EPLANS.COM

Arched windows and triple gables provide a touch of elegance to this traditional home. An entrance supported by columns welcomes family and guests inside. On the main level, the dining room offers round columns at the entrance. The great room boasts a cathedral ceiling, a fireplace, and an arched window over the doors to the deck. The kitchen features an island cooktop and an adjoining breakfast nook for informal dining. The master suite offers twin walk-in closets and a lavish bath that includes a whirlpool tub and a double-basin vanity.

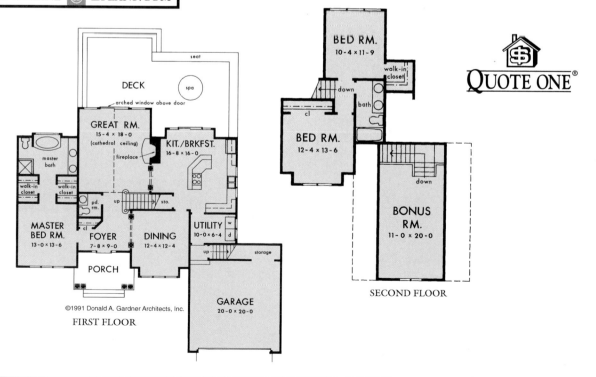

QUOTE ONE®

©1991 Donald A. Gardner Architects, Inc.

FIRST FLOOR

SECOND FLOOR

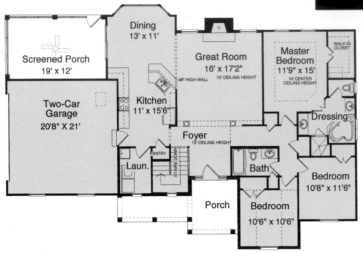

Dining
13' x 11'

Screened Porch
19' x 12'

Great Room
16' x 17'2"
48" HIGH WALL
10' CEILING HEIGHT

Master Bedroom
11'9" x 15'
10' CENTER CEILING HEIGHT

WALK-IN CLOSET

Two-Car Garage
20'8" X 21'

Kitchen
11' x 15'6"

Dressing

Foyer
10' CEILING HEIGHT

Laun.

PANTRY

STAIRS DOWN

Bath

Bedroom
10'8" x 11'6"

Porch

Bedroom
10'6" x 10'6"

plan # HPK0600057

STYLE: CRAFTSMAN
SQUARE FOOTAGE: 1,611
BEDROOMS: 3
BATHROOMS: 2
WIDTH: 66' - 4"
DEPTH: 43' - 10"
FOUNDATION: BASEMENT

SEARCH ONLINE @ EPLANS.COM

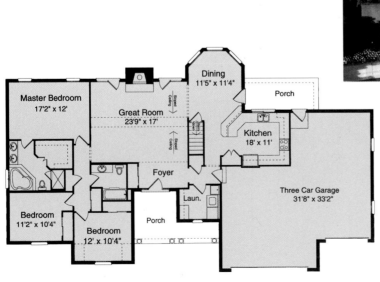

Master Bedroom
17'2" x 12'

Dining
11'5" x 11'4"

Porch

Great Room
23'9" x 17'
Sloped Ceiling

Kitchen
18' x 11'

Foyer

Bedroom
11'2" x 10'4"

Bedroom
12' x 10'4"

Porch

Laun.

Three Car Garage
31'8" x 33'2"

Porch

plan # HPK0600058

STYLE: TRADITIONAL
SQUARE FOOTAGE: 1,755
BEDROOMS: 3
BATHROOMS: 2
WIDTH: 78' - 6"
DEPTH: 47' - 7"
FOUNDATION: BASEMENT

SEARCH ONLINE @ EPLANS.COM

plan # HPK0600059

STYLE: TRADITIONAL
SQUARE FOOTAGE: 1,710
BEDROOMS: 3
BATHROOMS: 2
WIDTH: 53' - 4"
DEPTH: 54' - 10"

SEARCH ONLINE @ EPLANS.COM

Comfort awaits you in this appealing ranch home. Inside, a formal dining room features elegant ceiling details. The volume great room is designed for daily family gatherings with a raised-hearth fireplace flanked by sparkling windows. Outdoor access and a lazy Susan are thoughtful details designed into the kitchen and bowed dinette. For added flexibility, two secondary bedrooms can be easily converted to a sunroom with French doors and an optional den. The secluded master suite is enhanced by a boxed ceiling and deluxe skylit dressing room.

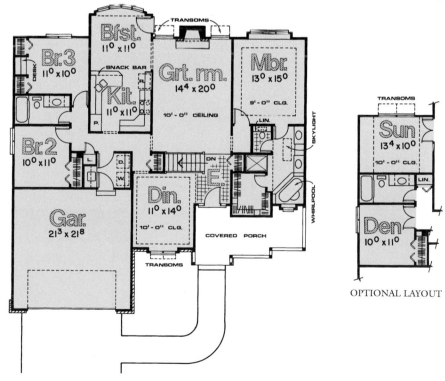

OPTIONAL LAYOUT

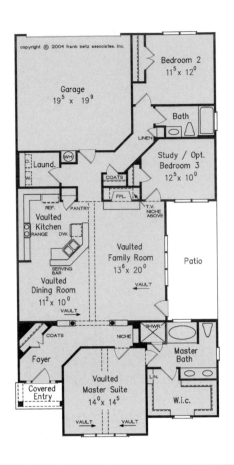

copyright © 2004 frank betz associates, inc.

Garage
19⁵ x 19⁹

Bedroom 2
11⁵ x 12⁰

Bath

LINEN

Study / Opt.
Bedroom 3
12⁵ x 10⁰

Laund.

COATS

FPL

T.V.
NICHE
ABOVE

REF.   PANTRY

Vaulted
Kitchen

RANGE   DW.

SERVING
BAR

Vaulted
Dining Room
11² x 10⁰

Vaulted
Family Room
13⁶ x 20⁰

Patio

VAULT

COATS

NICHE

SHWR.

Master
Bath

Foyer

Covered
Entry

Vaulted
Master Suite
14⁰ x 14⁵

L.N.

W.i.c.

VAULT   VAULT

plan # HPK0600060

STYLE: CRAFTSMAN
SQUARE FOOTAGE: 1,644
BEDROOMS: 3
BATHROOMS: 2
WIDTH: 34' - 0"
DEPTH: 68' - 0"
FOUNDATION: CRAWLSPACE,
BASEMENT

SEARCH ONLINE @ EPLANS.COM

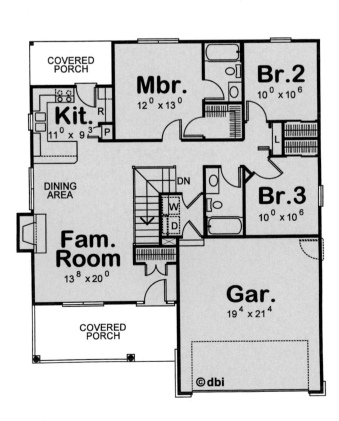

COVERED
PORCH

Kit.
11⁰ x 9³

R

P

Mbr.
12⁰ x 13⁰

Br.2
10⁰ x 10⁶

L

DINING
AREA

DN

W
D

Br.3
10⁰ x 10⁶

Fam.
Room
13⁸ x 20⁰

Gar.
19⁴ x 21⁴

COVERED
PORCH

©dbi

plan # HPK0600061

STYLE: CRAFTSMAN
SQUARE FOOTAGE: 1,195
BEDROOMS: 3
BATHROOMS: 2
WIDTH: 40' - 0"
DEPTH: 48' - 8"

SEARCH ONLINE @ EPLANS.COM

plan # HPK0600062

STYLE: COUNTRY COTTAGE
FIRST FLOOR: 1,407 SQ. FT.
SECOND FLOOR: 472 SQ. FT.
TOTAL: 1,879 SQ. FT.
BONUS SPACE: 321 SQ. FT.
BEDROOMS: 3
BATHROOMS: 2½
WIDTH: 48' - 0"
DEPTH: 53' 10"
FOUNDATION: CRAWLSPACE,
BASEMENT

SEARCH ONLINE @ EPLANS.COM

This captivating three-bedroom home combines the rustic, earthy feel of cut stone with the crisp look of siding to create a design that will be the hallmark of your neighborhood. From the impressive two-story foyer, the vaulted family room lies straight ahead. The extended-hearth fireplace can be viewed from the kitchen, via a serving bar that accesses the breakfast nook. The vaulted dining room is an elegant space for formal occasions. The first-floor master suite includes a pampering bath and dual walk-in closets, one with linen storage. Upstairs, a short hall and family-room overlook separate the bedrooms. Bonus space can serve as a home office, playroom...anything your family desires.

FIRST FLOOR

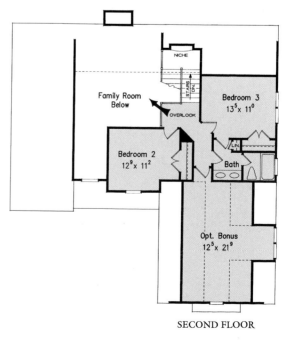

SECOND FLOOR

Floor Plan 1

- **Deck**
- **Master Bedroom** 12' x 14'6" — 10'10" CEILING
- **WALK-IN CLOSET**
- **Dressing**
- **ALCOVE** 3'6" x 6'6"
- **TV ALCOVE**
- **STAIRS DOWN**
- **Great Room** 16'6" x 21'2" — 11'1" CEILING HT
- SLOPED CEILING
- **Breakfast** 12'9" x 13'
- **Porch** 11'8" x 11'
- **Kitchen** 12'6" x 10'11"
- **Laun.**
- HANGING SPACE
- **Hall**
- **Bath**
- **PANTRY**
- **Bedroom** 10' x 12'
- **Bedroom** 11'3" x 11'1"
- **Foyer**
- **Porch**
- **Dining Room** 10'10" x 12'2"
- **Garage** 19'8" x 23'2"

plan # HPK0600063

STYLE: CRAFTSMAN
SQUARE FOOTAGE: 1,860
BEDROOMS: 3
BATHROOMS: 2
WIDTH: 64' - 2"
DEPTH: 44' - 2"
FOUNDATION: BASEMENT

SEARCH ONLINE @ EPLANS.COM

Floor Plan 2

- **SCREENED PORCH** 15'4" x 13'10"
- **DECK** 11'0" x 7'6"
- **SITTING** — 14' CEILING
- **VLT**
- **MASTER SUITE** 21'4" x 15'0"
- **BRKFST** 11'0" x 10'10"
- **BEDROOM 3** 13'0" x 11'0"
- 8' HIGH OPENING
- **FAMILY ROOM** 16'0" x 24'1" — 13'-10" CEILING
- **KITCHEN** 13'8" x 9'6"
- PANTRY
- DW
- **LINEN**
- LINEN COATS
- VLT
- 10' CEILING
- OPTIONAL STAIRS TO BASEMENT
- **DINING** 11'0" x 12'0" — TRAY CEILING
- 9' CEILING
- 13'-4" CEILING
- **BEDROOM 2** 13'0" x 11'0"
- **LIVING** 11'0" x 12'0"
- VLT
- **PORCH** 15'4" x 5'4"
- **3 CAR GARAGE** 21'4" x 29'10"
- 2 CAR GARAGE OPTION

plan # HPK0600064

STYLE: TRADITIONAL
SQUARE FOOTAGE: 1,992
BEDROOMS: 3
BATHROOMS: 2½
WIDTH: 63' - 0"
DEPTH: 57' - 2"
FOUNDATION: SLAB,
BASEMENT, CRAWLSPACE

SEARCH ONLINE @ EPLANS.COM

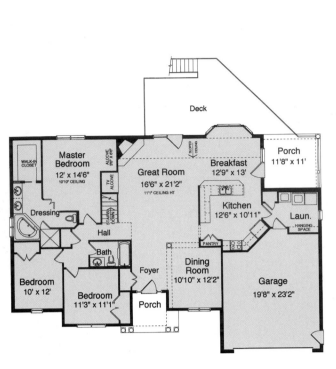

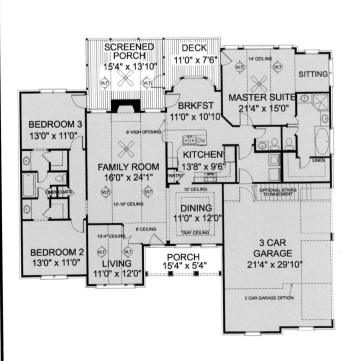

plan# HPK0600065

STYLE: COUNTRY COTTAGE
SQUARE FOOTAGE: 1,979
BEDROOMS: 3
BATHROOMS: 2
WIDTH: 67' - 2"
DEPTH: 44' - 2"
FOUNDATION: BASEMENT

SEARCH ONLINE @ EPLANS.COM

Many fine features mark this one-story country cottage, not least of which are the handsome columns in the front entry and the spacious rear deck. Inside, built-in media centers in the master suite and great room are convenient and attractive. The master suite also boasts a walk-in closet and lavish, amenity-filled bath. The great room, with a corner fireplace, is separated from the kitchen by a curved counter and from the formal dining area by a single column. A handy laundry opens both to the kitchen and the two-car garage.

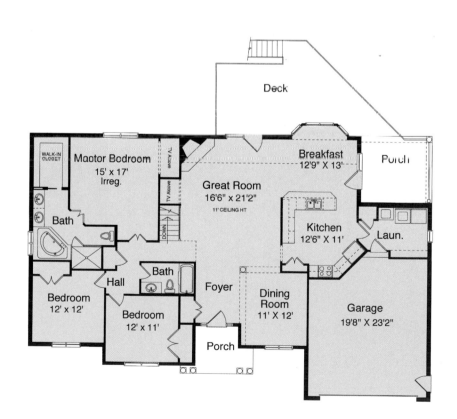

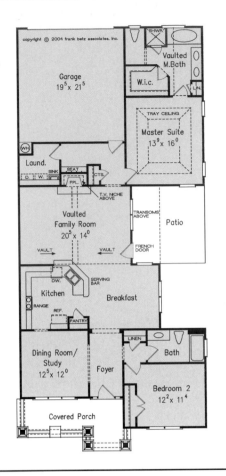

copyright © 2004 frank betz associates, inc.

Garage
19⁵ x 21⁵

Vaulted M.Bath

W.i.c.

TRAY CEILING

Master Suite
13⁹ x 16⁰

WH

Laund.

SEAT

FPL.

T.V. NICHE ABOVE

TRANSOMS ABOVE

Vaulted Family Room
20⁵ x 14⁰

Patio

FRENCH DOOR

VAULT

VAULT

SERVING BAR

DW.

Kitchen

Breakfast

RANGE

REF.

PANTRY

LINEN

Dining Room/ Study
12⁵ x 12⁰

Foyer

Bath

Bedroom 2
12² x 11⁴

Covered Porch

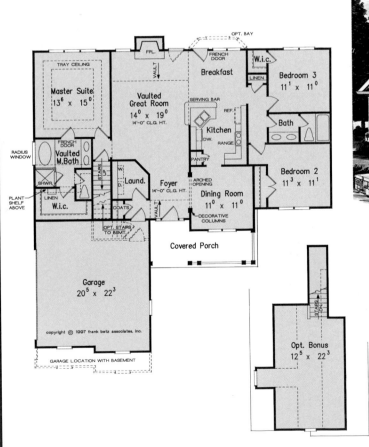

TRAY CEILING

FPL.

OPT. BAY

FRENCH DOOR

VAULT

Breakfast

W.i.c.

LINEN

Bedroom 3
11¹ x 11⁰

Master Suite
13⁶ x 15⁰

Vaulted Great Room
14⁰ x 19⁰
14'-0" CLG. HT.

SERVING BAR

REF.

Kitchen

DW.

RANGE

Bath

RADIUS WINDOW

Vaulted M.Bath

FRENCH DOOR

STAIRS

Laund.

W

D

Foyer
14'-0" CLG. HT.

ARCHED OPENING

PANTRY

Bedroom 2
11³ x 11¹

SHWR.

LINEN

PLANT SHELF ABOVE

W.i.c.

COATS

OPT. STAIRS TO BSMT.

VAULT

Dining Room
11⁰ x 11⁰

DECORATIVE COLUMNS

Covered Porch

Garage
20⁵ x 22³

copyright © 1997 frank betz associates, inc.

GARAGE LOCATION WITH BASEMENT

STAIRS

Opt. Bonus
12⁵ x 22³

plan # HPK0600068

STYLE: COUNTRY COTTAGE
SQUARE FOOTAGE: 1,477
BONUS SPACE: 283 SQ. FT.
BEDROOMS: 3
BATHROOMS: 2
WIDTH: 51' - 0"
DEPTH: 51' - 4"
FOUNDATION: CRAWLSPACE,
BASEMENT

SEARCH ONLINE @ EPLANS.COM

This adorable three-bedroom home will provide a pleasant atmosphere for your family. The communal living areas reside on the left side of the plan. The L-shaped kitchen includes a serving bar, which opens to the dining area. The vaulted family room features a fireplace and leads to the sleeping quarters. A master suite and vaulted master bath will pamper homeowners. Two family bedrooms reside across the hall and share a full hall bath. Upstairs, an optional fourth bedroom and full bath are perfect for guests.

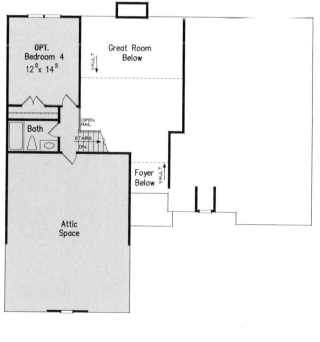

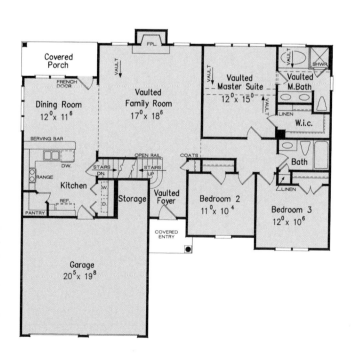

MASTER
14/2 X 14/0
(9' CLG.)

MEDIA CENTER

GREAT RM.
VAULTED
15/0 X 20/4

DINING
12/0 X 12/0
(9' CLG.)

GARAGE/
SHOP
10/0 X 17/6

SPA

NICHE

NICHE

11/0 X 13/0
(9' CLG.)

DESK

REF

BUILT-IN OR CLOSET

FOYER
(9' CLG.)

PANTRY

GARAGE
20/0 X 19/6

BR. 2
10/0 X 11/2
(9' CLG.)

DEN
10/2 X 12/10
(9' CLG.)

plan# HPK0600069

STYLE: COUNTRY COTTAGE
SQUARE FOOTAGE: 1,728
BEDROOMS: 2
BATHROOMS: 2
WIDTH: 55' - 0"
DEPTH: 48' - 0"
FOUNDATION: CRAWLSPACE

SEARCH ONLINE @ EPLANS.COM

MASTER
16/2 X 14/0
(9' CLG.)

BUILT-IN

GREAT RM.
17/6 X 20/6
(12'-4" CLG.)

DINING
11/6 X 13/0
(9' CLG.)

8/6 X 15/0

SHOP /
3RD CAR
12/6 X 19/6

NICHE

PAN.

DEN
11/0 X 10/0
(9' CLG.)

LIN

BR. 2
11/0 X 12/6
(9' CLG.)

BR. 3
11/2 X 12/0
(9' CLG.)

GARAGE
21/0 X 22/6

©Alan Mascord Design Associates, Inc.

plan# HPK0600070

STYLE: TRADITIONAL
SQUARE FOOTAGE: 1,852
BEDROOMS: 3
BATHROOMS: 2
WIDTH: 70' - 0"
DEPTH: 45' - 0"
FOUNDATION: CRAWLSPACE

SEARCH ONLINE @ EPLANS.COM

plan # HPK0600071

STYLE: TRADITIONAL
SQUARE FOOTAGE: 1,971
BONUS SPACE: 358 SQ. FT.
BEDROOMS: 3
BATHROOMS: 3
WIDTH: 62' - 6"
DEPTH: 57' - 2"

SEARCH ONLINE @ EPLANS.COM

This Craftsman cottage combines stone, siding, and cedar shake to create striking curb appeal. The interior features an open floor plan with high ceilings, columns, and bay windows to visually expand space. Built-in cabinetry, a fireplace, and a kitchen pass-through highlight and add convenience to the great room. The master suite features a tray ceiling in the bedroom and a bath with garden tub, separate shower, dual vanities, and a walk-in closet. On the opposite side of the home is another bedroom that could be used as a second master suite. Above the garage, a bonus room provides ample storage and space to grow.

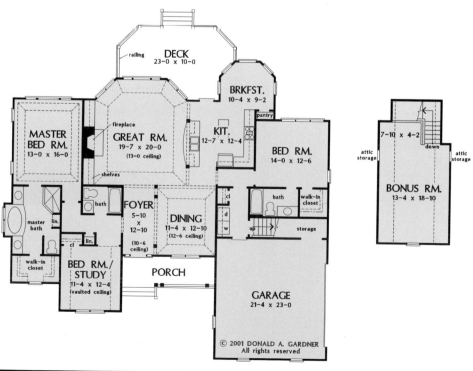

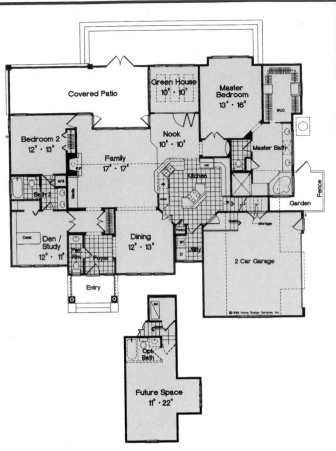

Covered Patio

Green House
10⁰ · 10⁰

Master Bedroom
13⁴ · 16⁰

W.I.C.

Bedroom 2
12⁰ · 13⁰

Nook
10⁰ · 10²

Master Bath

Family
17⁴ · 17⁰

Kitchen

Bath 2

Garden

Fence

Den / Study
12⁰ · 11⁰

Dining
12⁰ · 13⁰

Utility

2 Car Garage

storage

Desk

Pwr. Rm.

Foyer

Entry

©1998 Home Design Services, Inc.

Opt. Bath

Future Space
11⁰ · 22⁴

plan # HPK0600072

STYLE: FARMHOUSE
SQUARE FOOTAGE: 1,997
BONUS SPACE: 310 SQ. FT.
BEDROOMS: 2
BATHROOMS: 2½
WIDTH: 64' - 4"
DEPTH: 63' - 0"
FOUNDATION: CRAWLSPACE,
SLAB, BASEMENT

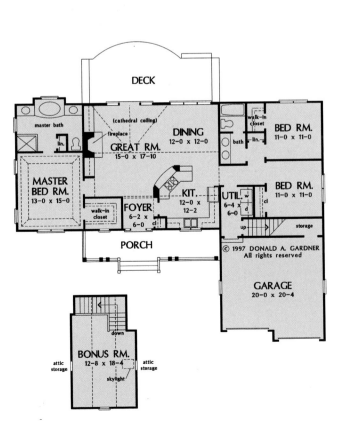

DECK

(cathedral ceiling)

master bath

lin.

fireplace

DINING
12-0 x 12-0

walk-in closet

bath

lin.

BED RM.
11-0 x 11-0

GREAT RM.
15-0 x 17-10

MASTER BED RM.
13-0 x 15-0

walk-in closet

FOYER
6-2 x 6-0

KIT.
12-0 x 12-2

UTIL.
6-4 x 6-0

w d

cl

BED RM.
11-0 x 11-0

up

storage

PORCH

© 1997 DONALD A. GARDNER
All rights reserved

GARAGE
20-0 x 20-4

down

BONUS RM.
12-8 x 18-4

attic storage

attic storage

skylight

© 1997 Donald A. Gardner Architects, Inc.

plan # HPK0600073

STYLE: TRADITIONAL
SQUARE FOOTAGE: 1,517
BONUS SPACE: 287 SQ. FT.
BEDROOMS: 3
BATHROOMS: 2
WIDTH: 61' - 4"
DEPTH: 48' - 6"

plan # HPK0600074

STYLE: TRADITIONAL
FIRST FLOOR: 1,082 SQ. FT.
SECOND FLOOR: 864 SQ. FT.
TOTAL: 1,946 SQ. FT.
BONUS SPACE: 358 SQ. FT.
BEDROOMS: 3
BATHROOMS: 2½
WIDTH: 40' - 0"
DEPTH: 52' - 0"
FOUNDATION: CRAWLSPACE

SEARCH ONLINE @ EPLANS.COM

This home would look great in any neighborhood! From the covered front porch, with a bench to rest on, to the trio of gables, this design has a lot of appeal. Inside, the Craftsman styling continues with built-in shelves in the study, a warming fireplace in the great room, and plenty of windows to bring in the outdoors. The L-shaped kitchen is open to the nook and great room, and offers easy access to the formal dining area. Upstairs, two family bedrooms share a full bath and access to both a laundry room and a large bonus room. A vaulted master suite rounds out this floor with class. Complete with a walk-in closet and a pampering bath, this suite will be a haven for any homeowner.

FIRST FLOOR

SECOND FLOOR

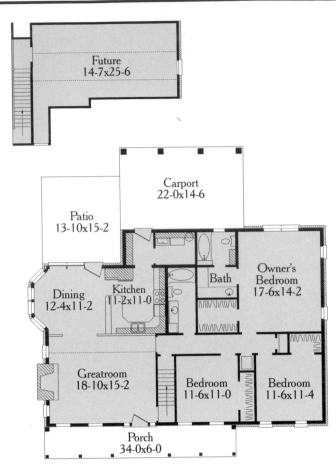

Future
14-7x25-6

Carport
22-0x14-6

Patio
13-10x15-2

Dining
12-4x11-2

Kitchen
11-2x11-0

Bath

Owner's
Bedroom
17-6x14-2

Greatroom
18-10x15-2

Bedroom
11-6x11-0

Bedroom
11-6x11-4

Porch
34-0x6-0

plan# HPK0600075

STYLE: TRADITIONAL
SQUARE FOOTAGE: 1,656
BONUS SPACE: 427 SQ. FT.
BEDROOMS: 3
BATHROOMS: 2
WIDTH: 52' - 8"
DEPTH: 54' - 6"
FOUNDATION: CRAWLSPACE,
BASEMENT, SLAB

SEARCH ONLINE @ EPLANS.COM

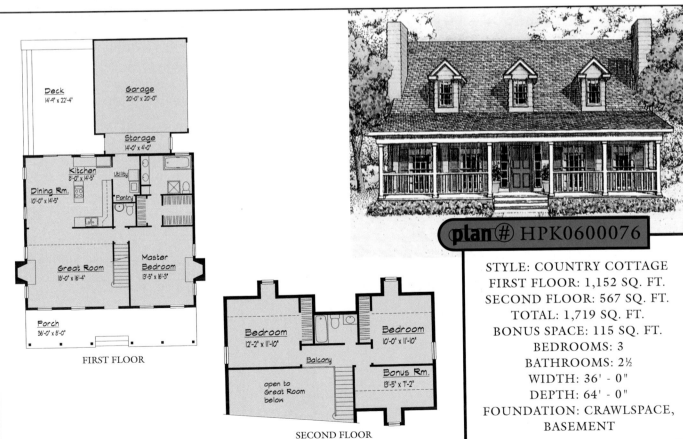

Deck
14'-4" x 22'-4"

Garage
20'-0" x 20'-0"

Storage
14'-0" x 4'-0"

Kitchen
8'-0" x 14'-5"

Utility

Dining Rm.
10'-0" x 14'-5"

Pantry

Great Room
18'-0" x 16'-4"

Master
Bedroom
13'-5" x 16'-3"

Porch
36'-0" x 8'-0"

FIRST FLOOR

Bedroom
12'-2" x 11'-10"

Bedroom
10'-0" x 11'-10"

Balcony

open to
Great Room
below

Bonus Rm.
13'-5" x 7'-2"

SECOND FLOOR

plan# HPK0600076

STYLE: COUNTRY COTTAGE
FIRST FLOOR: 1,152 SQ. FT.
SECOND FLOOR: 567 SQ. FT.
TOTAL: 1,719 SQ. FT.
BONUS SPACE: 115 SQ. FT.
BEDROOMS: 3
BATHROOMS: 2½
WIDTH: 36' - 0"
DEPTH: 64' - 0"
FOUNDATION: CRAWLSPACE,
BASEMENT

SEARCH ONLINE @ EPLANS.COM

plan # HPK0600077

STYLE: COUNTRY COTTAGE
SQUARE FOOTAGE: 1,894
BEDROOMS: 3
BATHROOMS: 2½
WIDTH: 68' - 0"
DEPTH: 56' - 6"
FOUNDATION: BASEMENT, CRAWLSPACE, SLAB

SEARCH ONLINE @ EPLANS.COM

Multiple windows offer insight into this beautiful home

and accent the brilliant design. Entering from the garage, a laundry room is on the left; to the right await a powder room and breakfast room. The kitchen provides plenty of counter space and opens to the dining room. The great room includes a fireplace framed by windows. A lavish master suite is home to two walk-in closets, dual sinks, a separate shower, and a garden tub.

Laun.
7-6x5-5

Basement Stair Location

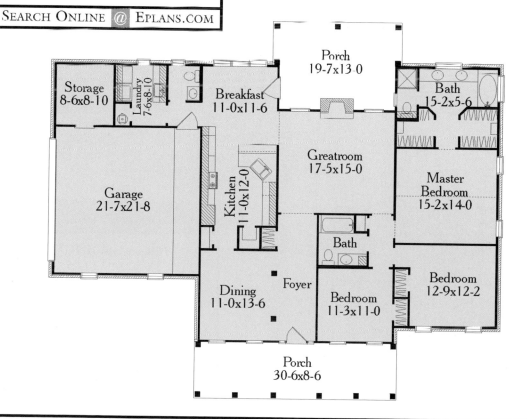

Storage
8-6x8-10

Laundry
7-6x8-10

Breakfast
11-0x11-6

Porch
19-7x13-0

Bath
15-2x5-6

Garage
21-7x21-8

Kitchen
11-0x12-0

Greatroom
17-5x15-0

Master
Bedroom
15-2x14-0

Bath

Dining
11-0x13-6

Foyer

Bath

Bedroom
11-3x11-0

Bedroom
12-9x12-2

Porch
30-6x8-6

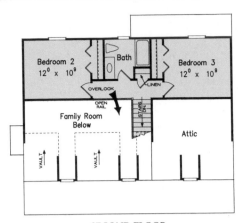

SECOND FLOOR

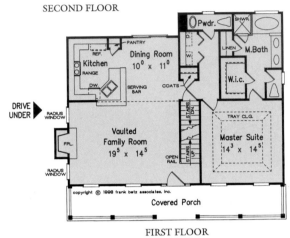

FIRST FLOOR

plan # HPK0600078

STYLE: TUDOR
FIRST FLOOR: 1,061 SQ. FT.
SECOND FLOOR: 430 SQ. FT.
TOTAL: 1,491 SQ. FT.
BEDROOMS: 3
BATHROOMS: 2½
WIDTH: 40' - 4"
DEPTH: 36' - 0"
FOUNDATION: BASEMENT

SEARCH ONLINE @ EPLANS.com

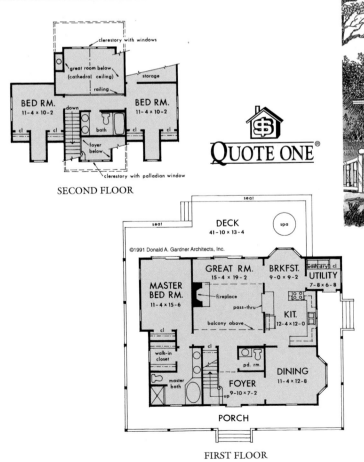

SECOND FLOOR

QUOTE ONE®

FIRST FLOOR

plan # HPK0600079

STYLE: FARMHOUSE
FIRST FLOOR: 1,325 SQ. FT.
SECOND FLOOR: 453 SQ. FT.
TOTAL: 1,778 SQ. FT.
BEDROOMS: 3
BATHROOMS: 2½
WIDTH: 48' - 4"
DEPTH: 51' - 10"

SEARCH ONLINE @ EPLANS.com

plan # HPK0600080

STYLE: FARMHOUSE
FIRST FLOOR: 1,356 SQ. FT.
SECOND FLOOR: 542 SQ. FT.
TOTAL: 1,898 SQ. FT.
BONUS SPACE: 393 SQ. FT.
BEDROOMS: 3
BATHROOMS: 2½
WIDTH: 59' - 0"
DEPTH: 64' - 0"

SEARCH ONLINE @ EPLANS.COM

The welcoming charm of this country farmhouse is expressed by its many windows and its covered wraparound porch. A two-story foyer is enhanced by a Palladian window in a clerestory dormer above to let in natural lighting. The first-floor master suite allows privacy and accessibility. The master bath includes a whirlpool tub, separate shower, double-bowl vanity, and walk-in closet. The first floor features nine-foot ceilings throughout with the exception of the kitchen area, which sports an eight-foot ceiling. The second floor contains two additional bedrooms, a full bath, and plenty of storage space. The bonus room provides room to grow.

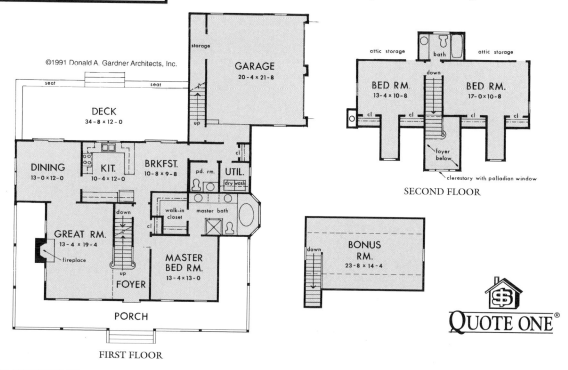

©1991 Donald A. Gardner Architects, Inc.

FIRST FLOOR

SECOND FLOOR

BONUS RM.
23-8 x 14-4

QUOTE ONE®

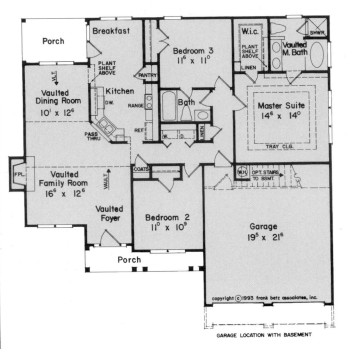

GARAGE LOCATION WITH BASEMENT

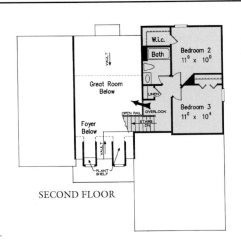

SECOND FLOOR

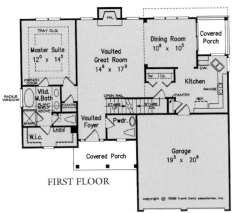

FIRST FLOOR

plan # HPK0600083

STYLE: TRADITIONAL
FIRST FLOOR: 1,160 SQ. FT.
SECOND FLOOR: 540 SQ. FT.
TOTAL: 1,700 SQ. FT.
BEDROOMS: 3
BATHROOMS: 2½
WIDTH: 46' - 0"
DEPTH: 68' - 0"
FOUNDATION: SLAB,
BASEMENT, CRAWLSPACE

SEARCH ONLINE @ EPLANS.COM

This traditional-style home boasts a large receiving porch and free-flowing interior spaces. Five French doors open from the front into the interior, perfect for entertaining a crowd. The spacious living room is open to the adjacent dining room and has a built-in fireplace. The master suite is isolated for privacy and conveniently located only steps away from the kitchen. Upstairs, two bedrooms have dormer windows and access to the attic.

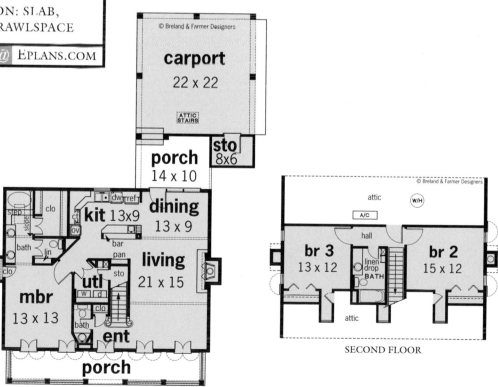

FIRST FLOOR

SECOND FLOOR

plan # **HPK0600084**

This angled, country-style ranch home is designed to fit about any lot. Four bay windows and two dormers distinguish the exterior. A recessed, covered front porch opens to the foyer, which is visually connected to the adjoining great room. The great room features a fireplace and built-ins for media. The great room is a "pavilion-style" area with windows at the front and rear. A dramatic angled kitchen with a snack bar faces the rear porch. A private master suite contains a tray ceiling, a dressing area, two closets, and a compartmented five-fixture bath. Two other bedrooms, one set into an attractive front bay, share a full bath. The unusual-shaped kitchen, which looks out over the covered porch, is easily served by the kitchen. A convenient half-bath is located off the foyer.

STYLE: COUNTRY COTTAGE
SQUARE FOOTAGE: 1,709
BEDROOMS: 3
BATHROOMS: 2½
WIDTH: 70' - 1"
DEPTH: 60' - 7"
FOUNDATION: BASEMENT,
SLAB, CRAWLSPACE

SEARCH ONLINE @ EPLANS.COM

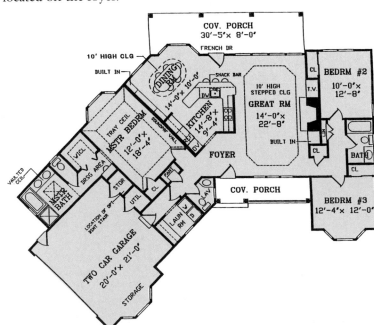

ORDER BLUEPRINTS 24 HOURS, 7 DAYS A WEEK, AT 1-800-521-6797

plan # HPK0600085

STYLE: FARMHOUSE
SQUARE FOOTAGE: 1,793
BONUS SPACE: 779 SQ. FT.
BEDROOMS: 3
BATHROOMS: 2
WIDTH: 69' - 10"
DEPTH: 51' - 8"
FOUNDATION: BASEMENT,
SLAB, CRAWLSPAC

SEARCH ONLINE @ EPLANS.COM

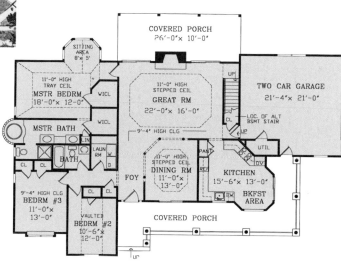

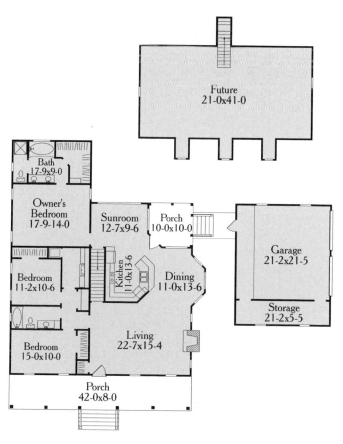

plan # HPK0600086

STYLE: TRADITIONAL
SQUARE FOOTAGE: 1,879
BONUS SPACE: 965 SQ. FT.
BEDROOMS: 3
BATHROOMS: 2
WIDTH: 45' - 0"
DEPTH: 62' - 0"
FOUNDATION: CRAWLSPACE,
SLAB, BASEMENT

SEARCH ONLINE @ EPLANS.COM

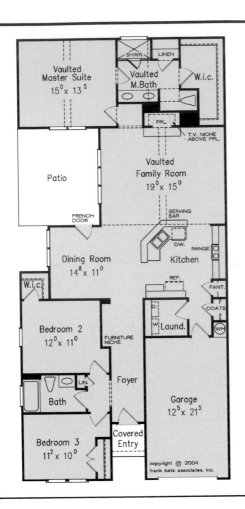

Vaulted Master Suite 15⁰ x 13⁵

SHWR   LINEN

Vaulted M.Bath

W.i.c.

FPL.

T.V. NICHE ABOVE FPL.

Patio

Vaulted Family Room 19⁰ x 15⁰

FRENCH DOOR

SERVING BAR

DW.

RANGE

Dining Room 14⁸ x 11⁰

REF.

PANT.

W.i.c.

COATS

Bedroom 2 12⁰ x 11⁰

FURNITURE NICHE

D.

W.

Laund.

WH

Foyer

Bath

LIN.

Garage 12⁵ x 21⁵

Bedroom 3 11² x 10⁰

Covered Entry

copyright © 2004 frank betz associates, inc.

OPTIONAL LAYOUT

plan # HPK0600087

STYLE: CRAFTSMAN
SQUARE FOOTAGE: 1,634
BEDROOMS: 3
BATHROOMS: 2
WIDTH: 32' - 0"
DEPTH: 68' - 0"
FOUNDATION: CRAWLSPACE, BASEMENT

SEARCH ONLINE @ EPLANS.COM

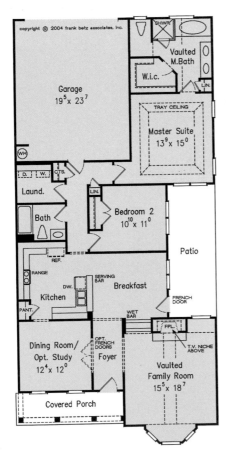

copyright © 2004 frank betz associates, inc.

SHWR

Vaulted M.Bath

W.i.c.

LIN.

Garage 19⁵ x 23⁷

TRAY CEILING

Master Suite 13⁹ x 15⁰

WH

D.   W.   GTS.

Laund.

LIN.

Bath

Bedroom 2 10¹⁰ x 11⁰

REF.

Patio

RANGE

SERVING BAR

Breakfast

Kitchen

DW.

FRENCH DOOR

PANT.

WET BAR

OPT. FRENCH DOORS

FPL.

T.V. NICHE ABOVE

Dining Room/ Opt. Study 12⁴ x 12⁰

Foyer

Vaulted Family Room 15⁵ x 18⁷

Covered Porch

plan # HPK0600088

STYLE: CRAFTSMAN
SQUARE FOOTAGE: 1,610
BEDROOMS: 2
BATHROOMS: 2
WIDTH: 34' - 0"
DEPTH: 72' - 0"
FOUNDATION: CRAWLSPACE, BASEMENT

SEARCH ONLINE @ EPLANS.COM

plan # HPK0600089

STYLE: COUNTRY COTTAGE
SQUARE FOOTAGE: 1,879
BONUS SPACE: 360 SQ. FT.
BEDROOMS: 3
BATHROOMS: 2
WIDTH: 66' - 4"
DEPTH: 55' - 2"

SEARCH ONLINE @ EPLANS.COM

Dormers cast light and interest into the foyer for a grand first impression that sets the tone in this home full of today's amenities. The great room, articulated by columns, features a cathedral ceiling and is conveniently located adjacent to the breakfast room and kitchen. Tray ceilings and circle-top picture windows accent the front bedroom and dining room. A secluded master suite, highlighted by a tray ceiling in the bedroom, includes a bath with a skylight, a garden tub, a separate shower, a double-bowl vanity, and a spacious walk-in closet.

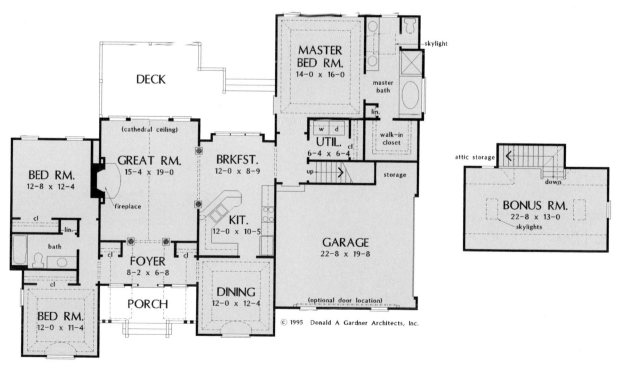

© 1995 Donald A Gardner Architects, Inc.

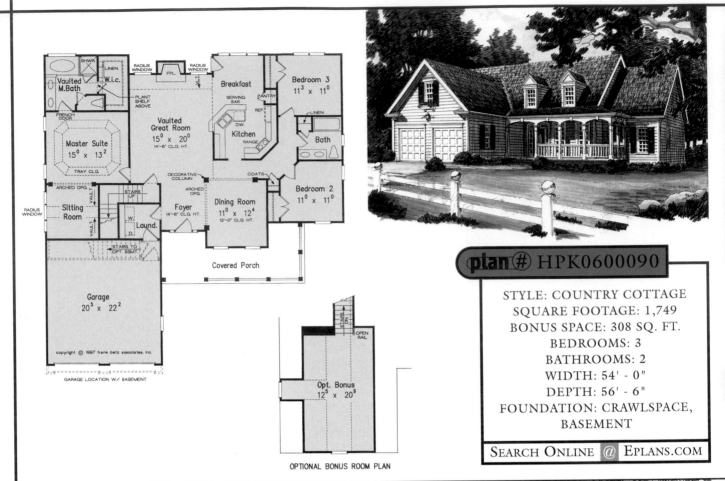

Master Suite 15⁰ x 13²

Vaulted M.Bath

Sitting Room

Garage 20⁵ x 22²

copyright © 1997 frank betz associates, inc.

GARAGE LOCATION W/ BASEMENT

Vaulted Great Room 15⁰ x 20⁰ 14'-6" CLG. HT.

Breakfast

Kitchen

Bedroom 3 11³ x 11⁰

Bath

Bedroom 2 11⁰ x 11⁰

Dining Room 11⁰ x 12⁴ 12'-0" CLG. HT.

Foyer 14'-6" CLG. HT.

Laund.

Covered Porch

Opt. Bonus 12⁵ x 20⁹

OPEN RAIL

OPTIONAL BONUS ROOM PLAN

plan# HPK0600090

STYLE: COUNTRY COTTAGE
SQUARE FOOTAGE: 1,749
BONUS SPACE: 308 SQ. FT.
BEDROOMS: 3
BATHROOMS: 2
WIDTH: 54' - 0"
DEPTH: 56' - 6"
FOUNDATION: CRAWLSPACE,
BASEMENT

SEARCH ONLINE @ EPLANS.COM

MASTER BED RM. 14-8 x 15-4

PORCH

UTILITY 11-8 x 8-4

BRKFST. 10-4 x 8-6

GREAT RM. 17-4 x 19-4 (cathedral ceiling)

KITCHEN 11-8 x 10-6

GARAGE 20-10 x 22-4

BED RM. 12-4 x 11-0

DINING 11-4 x 12-8

FOYER 8-8 x 7-8

BED RM. 10-10 x 12-0

PORCH

© 1994 Donald A. Gardner Architects, Inc.

attic storage

BONUS RM. 20-10 x 17-8

skylights

attic storage

plan# HPK0600091

STYLE: FARMHOUSE
SQUARE FOOTAGE: 1,807
BONUS SPACE: 419 SQ. FT.
BEDROOMS: 3
BATHROOMS: 2
WIDTH: 70' - 8"
DEPTH: 52' - 8"

SEARCH ONLINE @ EPLANS.COM

plan # HPK0600092

STYLE: FARMHOUSE
SQUARE FOOTAGE: 1,864
BONUS SPACE: 420 SQ. FT.
BEDROOMS: 3
BATHROOMS: 2½
WIDTH: 71' - 0"
DEPTH: 56' - 4"

SEARCH ONLINE @ EPLANS.COM

Quaint and cozy on the outside with porches front and back, this three-bedroom country home surprises with an open floor plan featuring a large great room with a cathedral ceiling. A central kitchen with an angled counter opens to the breakfast and great rooms for easy entertaining. The privately located master bedroom enjoys a cathedral ceiling and access to the deck. Two secondary bedrooms share a full hall bath. A bonus room makes expanding easy.

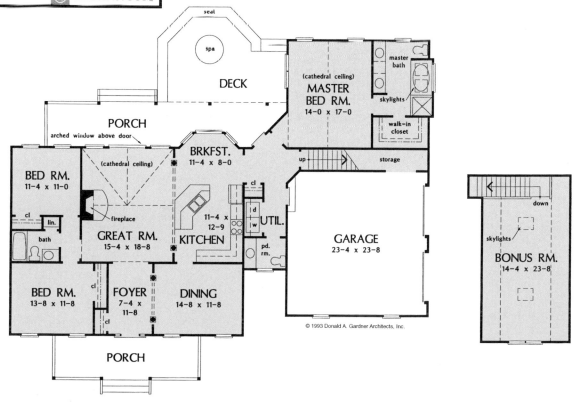

© 1993 Donald A. Gardner Architects, Inc.

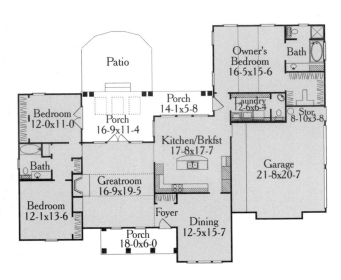

Bedroom
12-0x11-0

Bath

Bedroom
12-1x13-6

Patio

Porch
16-9x11-4

Porch
14-1x5-8

Greatroom
16-9x19-5

Foyer

Porch
18-0x6-0

Kitchen/Brkfst
17-8x17-7

Dining
12-5x15-7

Owner's
Bedroom
16-5x15-6

Bath

Laundry
12-6x6-4

Stor.
8-10x3-8

Garage
21-8x20-7

plan # HPK0600093

STYLE: TRADITIONAL
SQUARE FOOTAGE: 1,974
BEDROOMS: 3
BATHROOMS: 2½
WIDTH: 72' - 0"
DEPTH: 55' - 2"
FOUNDATION: CRAWLSPACE,
SLAB, BASEMENT

SEARCH ONLINE @ EPLANS.COM

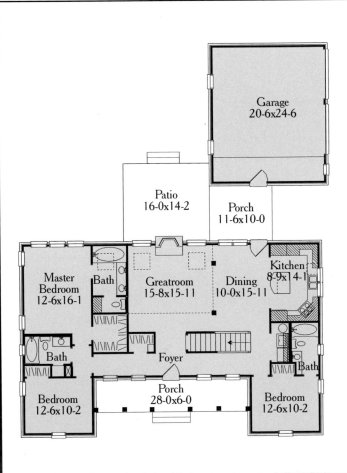

Master
Bedroom
12-6x16-1

Bath

Bath

Bedroom
12-6x10-2

Greatroom
15-8x15-11

Foyer

Porch
28-0x6-0

Dining
10-0x15-11

Kitchen
8-9x14-1

Bath

Bedroom
12-6x10-2

Garage
20-6x24-6

Patio
16-0x14-2

Porch
11-6x10-0

plan # HPK0600094

STYLE: TRADITIONAL
SQUARE FOOTAGE: 1,722
BEDROOMS: 3
BATHROOMS: 3
WIDTH: 57' - 4"
DEPTH: 72' - 0"
FOUNDATION: BASEMENT,
CRAWLSPACE, SLAB

SEARCH ONLINE @ EPLANS.COM

plan # HPK0600095

STYLE: FARMHOUSE
SQUARE FOOTAGE: 1,815
BONUS SPACE: 336 SQ. FT.
BEDROOMS: 3
BATHROOMS: 2
WIDTH: 70' - 8"
DEPTH: 70' - 2"

SEARCH ONLINE @ EPLANS.COM

Dormers, arched windows, and covered porches lend this home its country appeal. Inside, the foyer opens to the dining room on the right and leads through a columned entrance to the great room. The open kitchen easily serves the great room, the breakfast area, and the dining room. A cathedral ceiling graces the master suite, which is complete with a walk-in closet and a private bath. Two family bedrooms share a hall bath.

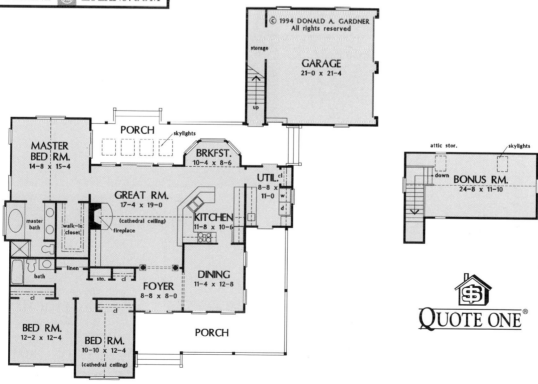

QUOTE ONE®

Laundry
9-0x5-8

Stor.
4-8x3-6

Basement Stair
Location

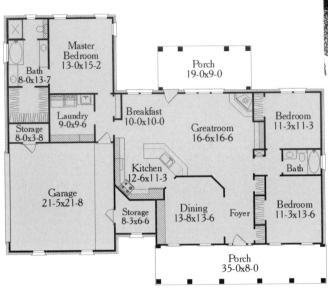

Master
Bedroom
13-0x15-2

Bath
8-0x13-7

Porch
19-0x9-0

Breakfast
10-0x10-0

Bedroom
11-3x11-3

Laundry
9-0x9-6

Storage
8-0x3-8

Greatroom
16-6x16-6

Kitchen
12-6x11-3

Bath

Garage
21-5x21-8

Storage
8-3x6-6

Dining
13-8x13-6

Foyer

Bedroom
11-3x13-6

Porch
35-0x8-0

plan# HPK0600096

STYLE: TRADITIONAL
SQUARE FOOTAGE: 1,836
BEDROOMS: 3
BATHROOMS: 2
WIDTH: 65' - 8"
DEPTH: 55' - 0"
FOUNDATION: CRAWLSPACE,
SLAB, BASEMENT

SEARCH ONLINE @ EPLANS.COM

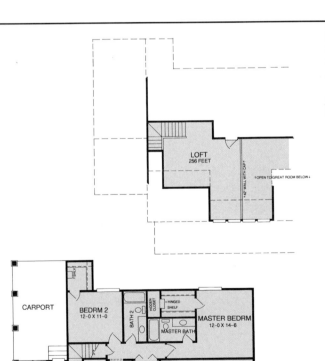

LOFT
256 FEET

OPEN TO GREAT ROOM BELOW

CARPORT

BEDRM 2
12-0 X 11-0

BATH 2

HIDDEN CLOSET

HINGED SHELF

MASTER BEDRM
12-0 X 14-6

MASTER BATH

SCREENED
PORCH
11-0 X 11-0

PANTRY

KITCHEN
10-0 14-8

DINING RM
10-6 X 14-0

GREAT RM
20-0 X 17-6
VAULTED TO 16' CLG

FP

COVERED PORCH
38-0 X 7-0

plan# HPK0600097

STYLE: COUNTRY COTTAGE
SQUARE FOOTAGE: 1,404
BONUS SPACE: 256 SQ. FT.
BEDROOMS: 2
BATHROOMS: 2
WIDTH: 54' - 7"
DEPTH: 46' - 6"
FOUNDATION: CRAWLSPACE

SEARCH ONLINE @ EPLANS.COM

plan # HPK0600098

STYLE: COUNTRY COTTAGE
FIRST FLOOR: 1,244 SQ. FT.
SECOND FLOOR: 636 SQ. FT.
TOTAL: 1,880 SQ. FT.
BEDROOMS: 3
BATHROOMS: 2½
WIDTH: 40' - 6"
DEPTH: 40' - 0"
FOUNDATION: SLAB

SEARCH ONLINE @ EPLANS.COM

The steeply sloping roof of this country home ensures relaxing shade in the summer and a dry view of spring rains. The entry provides access to the second floor via stairs and to the dining room on the right. A butler's pantry connects the galley kitchen and the dining room. A breakfast nook, adjoining the kitchen, features access to the side yard. To the rear of the plan is a hearth-warmed living room with access to the rear deck—a wonderful location for a barbecue grill. Two bedrooms reside on the second floor, each with a private vanity area.

Deck

Bedroom
12'6"x 15'

Living
14'6"x 17'6"

Breakfast
9'8"x 10'6"

Kitch.
9'8"x
11'1"

WIC

Dining
10'8"x 12'

Foyer

Porch

FIRST FLOOR

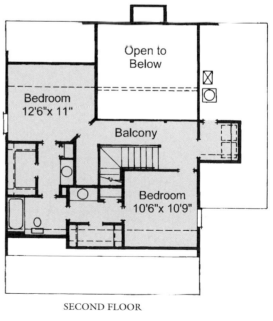

Open to
Below

Bedroom
12'6"x 11"

Balcony

Bedroom
10'6"x 10'9"

SECOND FLOOR

LOFT STUDY
11¹⁰ x 7²

MASTER BATH

WALK-IN CLOSET

MASTER BEDRM
14⁸ x 15⁰

ATTIC ACCESS

SEAT

SECOND FLOOR

QUOTE ONE®

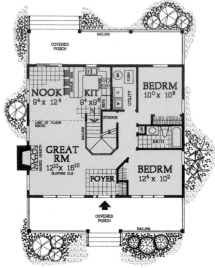

COVERED PORCH

RAILING

NOOK
9⁴ x 12⁴

KIT
9⁴ x 9⁸

BEDRM
10⁰ x 10⁸

UTILITY

STORAGE

GREAT RM
12⁰ x 16¹⁰
SLOPING CLG

BATH

FOYER

BEDRM
12⁴ x 10²

COVERED PORCH

RAILING

FIRST FLOOR

plan # HPK0600099

LD

STYLE: FARMHOUSE
FIRST FLOOR: 1,093 SQ. FT.
SECOND FLOOR: 580 SQ. FT.
TOTAL: 1,673 SQ. FT.
BEDROOMS: 3
BATHROOMS: 2
WIDTH: 36' - 0"
DEPTH: 52' - 0"
FOUNDATION: CRAWLSPACE

SEARCH ONLINE @ EPLANS.COM

kitchen / dining below

master bath

walk-in closet

balcony down

MASTER BED RM.
11-4 x 14-0

great room below

attic storage

SECOND FLOOR

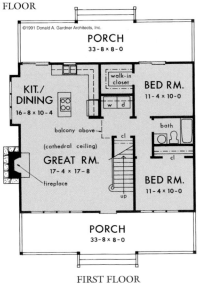

©1991 Donald A. Gardner Architects, Inc.

PORCH
33-8 x 8-0

KIT./ DINING
16-8 x 10-4

walk-in closet

BED RM.
11-4 x 10-0

w d

balcony above

(cathedral ceiling)

GREAT RM.
17-4 x 17-8

fireplace

bath

cl

cl

BED RM.
11-4 x 10-0

up

PORCH
33-8 x 8-0

FIRST FLOOR

plan # HPK0600100

STYLE: COUNTRY COTTAGE
FIRST FLOOR: 1,002 SQ. FT.
SECOND FLOOR: 336 SQ. FT.
TOTAL: 1,338 SQ. FT.
BEDROOMS: 3
BATHROOMS: 2
WIDTH: 36' - 8"
DEPTH: 44' - 8"

SEARCH ONLINE @ EPLANS.COM

plan # HPK0600101

LD

STYLE: FARMHOUSE
FIRST FLOOR: 1,356 SQ. FT.
SECOND FLOOR: 490 SQ. FT.
TOTAL: 1,846 SQ. FT.
BEDROOMS: 2
BATHROOMS: 3
WIDTH: 50' - 7"
DEPTH: 38' - 0"
FOUNDATION: CRAWLSPACE

SEARCH ONLINE @ EPLANS.COM

Split-log siding and a rustic balustrade create country charm with this farmhouse-style retreat. An open living area features a natural stone fireplace and a cathedral ceiling with exposed rough-sawn beam and brackets. A generous kitchen and dining area complement the living room and share the warmth of its fireplace. The master suite with a full bath and a nearby family bedroom with a hall bath complete the main floor. Upstairs, a spacious loft affords extra sleeping space—or provides a hobby/recreation area—and offers a full bath.

SECOND FLOOR

FIRST FLOOR

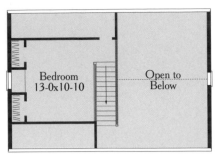

SECOND FLOOR

Bedroom
13-0x10-10

Open to
Below

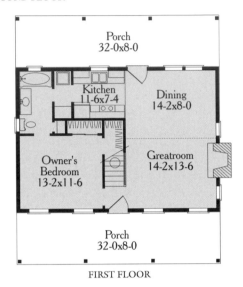

Porch
32-0x8-0

Kitchen
11-6x7-4

Dining
14-2x8-0

Owner's
Bedroom
13-2x11-6

Greatroom
14-2x13-6

Porch
32-0x8-0

FIRST FLOOR

plan# HPK0600102

STYLE: COUNTRY COTTAGE
FIRST FLOOR: 720 SQ. FT.
SECOND FLOOR: 203 SQ. FT.
TOTAL: 923 SQ. FT.
BEDROOMS: 2
BATHROOMS: 1
WIDTH: 32' - 0"
DEPTH: 38' - 6"
FOUNDATION: CRAWLSPACE,
SLAB, BASEMENT

OPEN TO FAMILY
ROOM BELOW

CLO

CLO

BALCONY

BATH
11'5

BATH

BEDROOM 2
12' X 11'

BEDROOM 3
12' X 11'

PORCH 3
10' X 7'

SECOND FLOOR

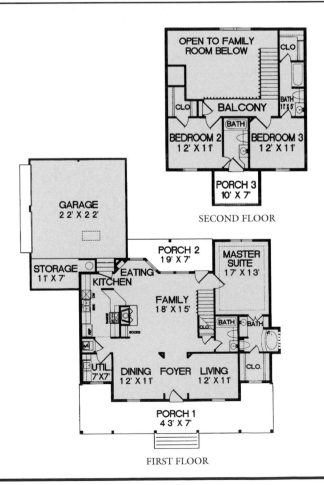

GARAGE
22' X 22'

STORAGE
11' X 7'

PORCH 2
19' X 7'

MASTER
SUITE
17' X 13'

EATING
KITCHEN

FAMILY
18' X 15'

BATH

BATH

UTIL
7'X7'

DINING
12' X 11'

FOYER

LIVING
12' X 11'

CLO

PORCH 1
43' X 7'

FIRST FLOOR

plan# HPK0600103

STYLE: CONTEMPORARY
FIRST FLOOR: 1,320 SQ. FT.
SECOND FLOOR: 552 SQ. FT.
TOTAL: 1,872 SQ. FT.
BEDROOMS: 3
BATHROOMS: 4
WIDTH: 56' - 0"
DEPTH: 61' - 0"
FOUNDATION: BASEMENT,
CRAWLSPACE, SLAB

plan # HPK0600104

D

STYLE: TRANSITIONAL
FIRST FLOOR: 1,112 SQ. FT.
SECOND FLOOR: 881 SQ. FT.
TOTAL: 1,993 SQ. FT.
BEDROOMS: 3
BATHROOMS: 2½
WIDTH: 49' - 0"
DEPTH: 54' - 4"
FOUNDATION: BASEMENT

SEARCH ONLINE @ EPLANS.COM

This classic American homestead is all dressed up with contemporary character and country spirit. Well-defined rooms, flowing spaces, and the latest amenities blend the best of traditional and modern elements. The spacious gathering room offers terrace access and shares a through-fireplace with a secluded study. The kitchen is set between the dining and breakfast rooms. The second-floor master suite shares a balcony hallway, which overlooks the gathering room, with two family bedrooms. Dual vanities, built-in cabinets and shelves, and triple-window views highlight the master bedroom.

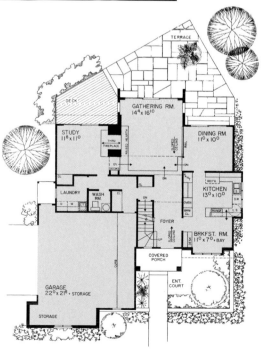

FIRST FLOOR

SECOND FLOOR

Quote One®

OPTIONAL LAYOUT

plan# HPK0600105

STYLE: SOUTHERN
COLONIAL
SQUARE FOOTAGE: 1,688
BEDROOMS: 3
BATHROOMS: 2
WIDTH: 70' - 1"
DEPTH: 48' - 0"
FOUNDATION: CRAWLSPACE,
SLAB, BASEMENT

SEARCH ONLINE @ EPLANS.COM

Dormers and columns decorate the exterior of this three-bedroom country home. Inside, the foyer has immediate access to one family bedroom and the formal dining area. Ahead is the great room with a warming fireplace and ribbon of windows for natural lighting. The master suite is set to the back of the plan and has a lavish bath with a garden tub, separate shower, and two vanities.

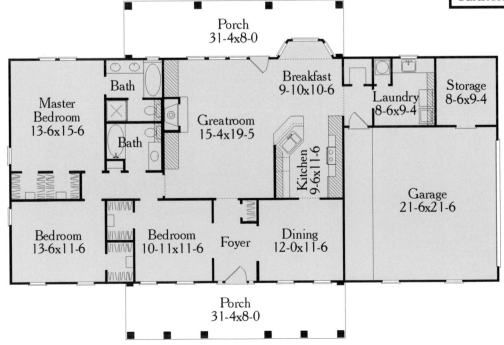

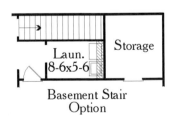

Basement Stair
Option

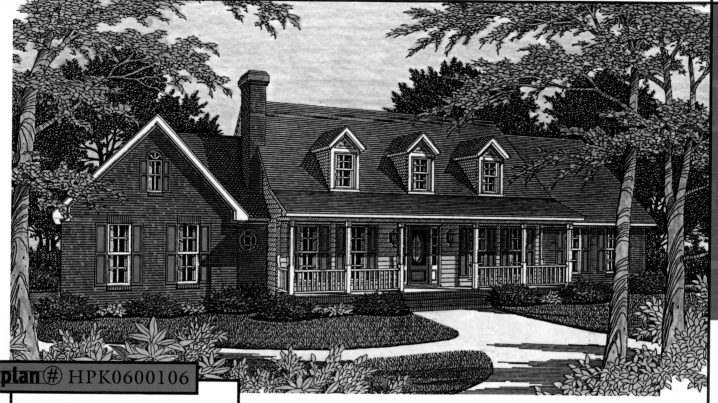

plan # HPK0600106

STYLE: TRADITIONAL
SQUARE FOOTAGE: 1,745
BONUS SPACE: 741 SQ. FT.
BEDROOMS: 3
BATHROOMS: 2
WIDTH: 72' - 0"
DEPTH: 47' 0"
FOUNDATION: BASEMENT,
SLAB, CRAWLSPACE

SEARCH ONLINE @ EPLANS.COM

This charming three-bedroom plan features plenty of amenities. A covered front porch welcomes guests to come inside and visit by the warming fireplace in the great room. The adjoining breakfast room glows with light from the bay window. Nearby, the kitchen includes a snack bar, organizing desk, and access to a porch and deck—a perfect place for an outdoor barbecue. Two family bedrooms reside at the front of the house, shielding the master bedroom from any noise. The master suite enjoys a luxurious bath, walk-in closet, and French door access to a private porch. Two bonus rooms allow for expansion in the future.

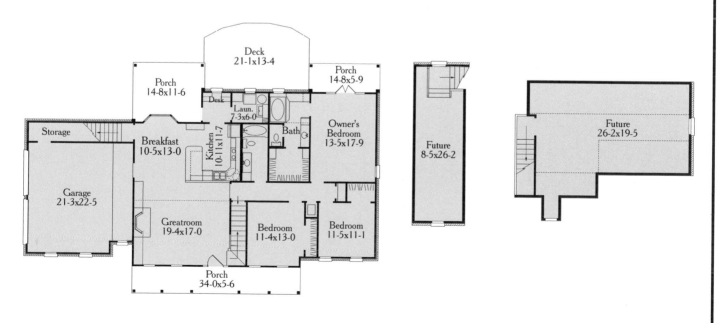

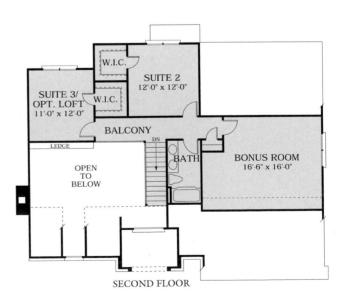
plan# HPK0600107

STYLE: TRANSITIONAL
FIRST FLOOR: 1,383 SQ. FT.
SECOND FLOOR: 546 SQ. FT.
TOTAL: 1,929 SQ. FT.
BONUS SPACE: 320 SQ. FT.
BEDROOMS: 3
BATHROOMS: 2½
WIDTH: 50' - 6"
DEPTH: 42' - 10"
FOUNDATION: SLAB,
CRAWLSPACE

SEARCH ONLINE @ EPLANS.COM

This open, airy design is one that seems much larger than it actually is. A welcoming two-story great room opens into the dining room. The lovely master suite boasts a terrific walk-in closet and a bath with dual sinks. A breakfast area that opens to a deck and corner windows at the kitchen sink help bring the outdoors in. There's plenty of storage, including an ample pantry, a two-car garage, and a bonus room that can double as a fourth suite.

FIRST FLOOR

SECOND FLOOR

plan # HPK0600108

STYLE: TRADITIONAL
FIRST FLOOR: 716 SQ. FT.
SECOND FLOOR: 784 SQ. FT.
TOTAL: 1,500 SQ. FT.
BEDROOMS: 3
BATHROOMS: 2½
WIDTH: 36' - 0"
DEPTH: 44' - 0"
FOUNDATION: CRAWLSPACE

SEARCH ONLINE @ EPLANS.COM

A traditional neighborhood look is accented by stone and decorative arches on this stylish new design. Simplicity is the hallmark of this plan, giving the interior great flow and openness. The foyer, with a coat closet, leads directly into the two-story great room with abundant natural light and a warming fireplace. The island kitchen and dining area are to the left and enjoy rear-porch access. Upstairs, a vaulted master suite with a private bath joins two additional bedrooms to complete the plan.

SECOND FLOOR

FIRST FLOOR

plan# HPK0600109

STYLE: COUNTRY COTTAGE
SQUARE FOOTAGE: 1,432
BEDROOMS: 3
BATHROOMS: 2
WIDTH: 49' - 0"
DEPTH: 52' - 4"
FOUNDATION: CRAWLSPACE,
BASEMENT, SLAB

SEARCH ONLINE @ EPLANS.COM

The beauty of this home lies in its simple yet efficient design and all its extras. Decorative touches include plant shelves, arched openings, and vaulted ceilings. The well-equipped kitchen enjoys a pass-through to the great room, very handy for social get-togethers. It also boasts a walk-in pantry. A tray ceiling, walk-in closet, and a resplendent bath with a separate glass shower and oval tub add splendor to the master suite. The two secondary bedrooms are secluded on the other side of the plan.

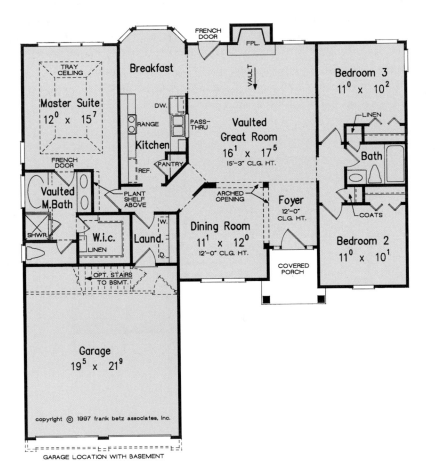

copyright © 1997 frank betz associates, inc.

GARAGE LOCATION WITH BASEMENT

plan # HPK0600110

STYLE: SOUTHERN COLONIAL
FIRST FLOOR: 1,071 SQ. FT.
SECOND FLOOR: 924 SQ. FT.
TOTAL: 1,995 SQ. FT.
BONUS SPACE: 280 SQ. FT.
BEDROOMS: 3
BATHROOMS: 2½
WIDTH: 55' - 10"
DEPTH: 38' - 6"
FOUNDATION: CRAWLSPACE,
BASEMENT, SLAB

SEARCH ONLINE @ EPLANS.COM

Move-up buyers can enjoy all the luxuries of this two-story home highlighted by an angled staircase separating the dining room from casual living areas. A private powder room is tucked away behind the dining room—convenient for formal dinner parties. A bay window and built-in desk in the breakfast area are just a few of the plan's amenities. The sleeping zone occupies the second floor—away from everyday activities—and includes a master suite and two secondary bedrooms.

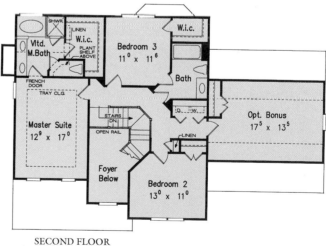

SECOND FLOOR

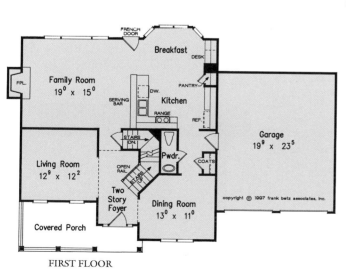

FIRST FLOOR

DECK

GATHERING ROOM
15'-6" x 17'-4"

MASTER SUITE
13'-6" x 16'-2"

GOLF VIEW DINING
15'-0" x 13'-0"

DEN/ SUITE 2
12'-4" x 10'-10"

MASTER BATH

KITCHEN
14'-0" x 12'-8"

W.I.C.

FOYER

BATH

P.

UTIL.

LAN.

SUITE 3
12'-4" x 11'-0"

GARAGE
19'-4" x 22'-0"

plan # HPK0600111

STYLE: TRADITIONAL
SQUARE FOOTAGE: 1,915
BEDROOMS: 3
BATHROOMS: 2
WIDTH: 45' - 10"
DEPTH: 62' - 6"
FOUNDATION: CRAWLSPACE

SEARCH ONLINE @ EPLANS.COM

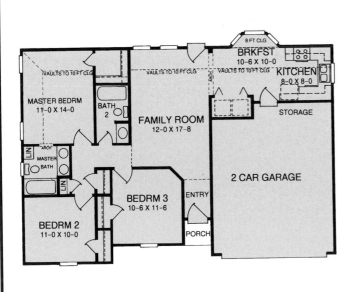

8 FT CLG

BRKFST
10-6 X 10-0

VAULTS TO 10 FT CLG

VAULTS TO 10 FT CLG

VAULTS TO 10 FT CLG

KITCHEN
8-0 X 8-0

MASTER BEDRM
11-0 X 14-0

BATH 2

FAMILY ROOM
12-0 X 17-8

STORAGE

ARCH

MASTER BATH

LN

2 CAR GARAGE

BEDRM 3
10-6 X 11-6

ENTRY

BEDRM 2
11-0 X 10-0

PORCH

COPYRIGHT LARRY E. BELK

plan # HPK0600112

STYLE: TRADITIONAL
SQUARE FOOTAGE: 1,136
BEDROOMS: 3
BATHROOMS: 2
WIDTH: 48' - 10"
DEPTH: 35' - 6"
FOUNDATION:
CRAWLSPACE, SLAB

SEARCH ONLINE @ EPLANS.COM

plan # HPK0600113

STYLE: TRADITIONAL
FIRST FLOOR: 1,032 SQ. FT.
SECOND FLOOR: 743 SQ. FT.
TOTAL: 1,775 SQ. FT.
BEDROOMS: 3
BATHROOMS: 2½
WIDTH: 46' - 0"
DEPTH: 42' - 0"

SEARCH ONLINE @ EPLANS.COM

Sleek rooflines, classic window details, and a covered front porch tastefully combine on the exterior of this three-bedroom home. A bright living room with an adjoining dining room is viewed from the volume entry. Meals will be enjoyed in the bayed breakfast area, which is served by a comfortable kitchen. A raised-hearth fireplace adds warmth to the family room. The second-level hall design provides separation between two secondary bedrooms and the luxurious master suite with a boxed ceiling. Two closets, a whirlpool bath with a plant sill, and double sinks are featured in the bath/dressing area.

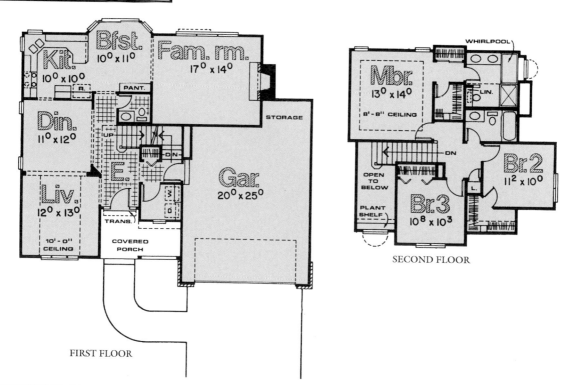

FIRST FLOOR

SECOND FLOOR

SECOND FLOOR

DECK

© 2002 Donald A. Gardner, Inc.

MASTER BED RM. 12-0 x 15-4

shelves fireplace

GREAT RM. 15-4 x 17-10 (vaulted ceiling)

balcony above

BRKFST. 11-0 x 8-4

UTIL. 6-0 x 6-6

storage

walk-in closet

master bath

KIT. 11-0 x 10-0

pd. rm.

FOYER 9-2 x 9-6 (vaulted ceiling)

DINING 11-0 x 12-0

GARAGE 21-0 x 22-0

© 2002 DONALD A. GARDNER All rights reserved

storage

PORCH

FIRST FLOOR

plan # HPK0600114

STYLE: TRADITIONAL
FIRST FLOOR: 1,345 SQ. FT.
SECOND FLOOR: 452 SQ. FT.
TOTAL: 1,797 SQ. FT.
BONUS SPACE: 349 SQ. FT.
BEDROOMS: 3
BATHROOMS: 2½
WIDTH: 63' - 0"
DEPTH: 40' - 0"

SEARCH ONLINE @ EPLANS.COM

SECOND FLOOR

Family Room Below

Bedroom 3 12⁶ x 10¹⁰

Bath

OVERLOOK

OPEN RAIL

STAIRS

Foyer Below

Bedroom 2 11³ x 11⁰

W.i.c.

Opt. Bonus Room/ Bedroom 4 13² x 13¹⁰

Vaulted Family Room 16⁹ x 16⁸

Breakfast

Kitchen ISLAND RANGE

Master Suite 13⁰ x 15⁴

Pwdr

PANTRY

Living Room 11⁰ x 12⁸

Two Story Foyer

OPEN RAIL STAIRS

Dining Room 11³ x 11⁰

Laund. W. D.

M.Bath

W.i.c.

COATS

COVERED ENTRY

copyright © 1999 frank betz associates, inc.

Garage 20⁵ x 19⁸

FIRST FLOOR

plan # HPK0600115

STYLE: TRADITIONAL
FIRST FLOOR: 1,441 SQ. FT.
SECOND FLOOR: 485 SQ. FT.
TOTAL: 1,926 SQ. FT.
BONUS SPACE: 226 SQ. FT.
BEDROOMS: 3
BATHROOMS: 2½
WIDTH: 49' - 0"
DEPTH: 50' - 10"
FOUNDATION: BASEMENT

SEARCH ONLINE @ EPLANS.COM

plan # HPK0600116

STYLE: TRADITIONAL
FIRST FLOOR: 1,314 SQ. FT.
SECOND FLOOR: 458 SQ. FT.
TOTAL: 1,772 SQ. FT.
BEDROOMS: 3
BATHROOMS: 2½
WIDTH: 52' - 0"
DEPTH: 51' - 4"

SEARCH ONLINE @ EPLANS.COM

Handsome detailing and unique windows are hallmarks on the elevation of this two-story design. Triple-arch windows in the front and rear of the great room create an impressive view. Counter space is coordinated in the island kitchen to make it easy to prepare meals. A compartmentalized master bath provides a convenient dressing area and vanity space. In the entry, a U-shaped staircase with a window leads to a second-floor balcony, two bedrooms, and a full bath.

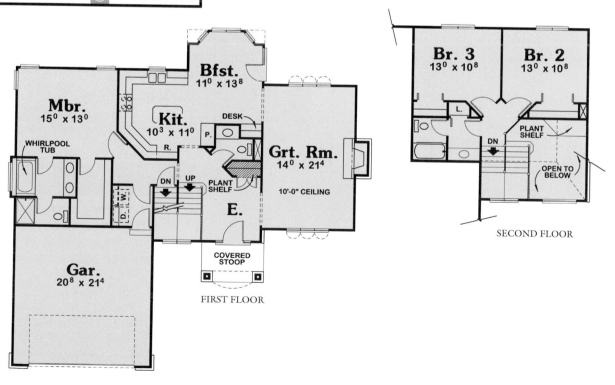

FIRST FLOOR

SECOND FLOOR

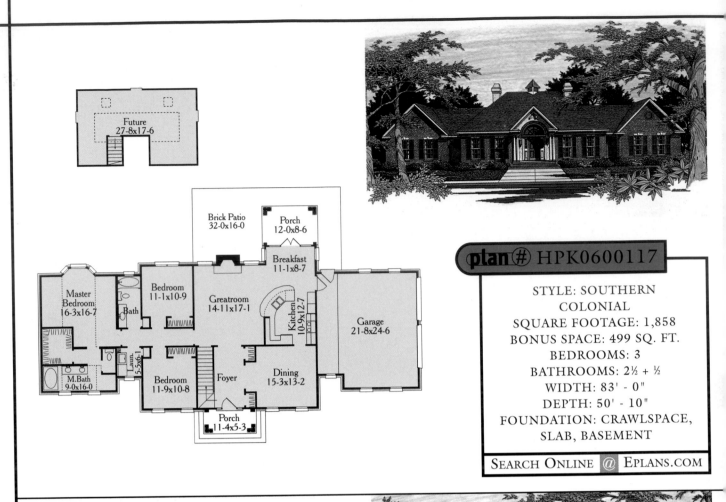

Future
27-8x17-6

Master Bedroom
16-3x16-7

Bath

M.Bath
9-0x16-0

Laun.
5-5x6-1

Bedroom
11-1x10-9

Greatroom
14-11x17-1

Kitchen
10-9x12-7

Bedroom
11-9x10-8

Foyer

Dining
15-3x13-2

Brick Patio
32-0x16-0

Porch
12-0x8-6

Breakfast
11-1x8-7

Garage
21-8x24-6

Porch
11-4x5-3

ptan # HPK0600117

STYLE: SOUTHERN
COLONIAL
SQUARE FOOTAGE: 1,858
BONUS SPACE: 499 SQ. FT.
BEDROOMS: 3
BATHROOMS: 2½ + ½
WIDTH: 83' - 0"
DEPTH: 50' - 10"
FOUNDATION: CRAWLSPACE,
SLAB, BASEMENT

SEARCH ONLINE @ EPLANS.COM

Future
28-9x23-7

Bedroom
10-9x12-9

Bath

Bedroom
13-0x12-0

Patio
15-8x15-0

Porch
15-8x6-6

Greatroom
15-6x19-5

Kitchen
12-3x11-0

Porch
21-11x8-0

Breakfast
14-11x10-0

Laun.
8-4x7-3

Storage
6-5x7-3

Bath

Owner's Bedroom
13-0x15-2

Garage
19-6x23-9

ptan # HPK0600118

STYLE: TRADITIONAL
SQUARE FOOTAGE: 1,730
BONUS SPACE: 520 SQ. FT.
BEDROOMS: 3
BATHROOMS: 2
WIDTH: 61' - 0"
DEPTH: 62' - 0"
FOUNDATION: CRAWLSPACE,
SLAB, BASEMENT

SEARCH ONLINE @ EPLANS.COM

plan # HPK0600119

STYLE: TRADITIONAL
SQUARE FOOTAGE: 1,488
BEDROOMS: 3
BATHROOMS: 2
WIDTH: 51' - 8"
DEPTH: 47' - 0"
FOUNDATION: BASEMENT

SEARCH ONLINE @ EPLANS.COM

This one-level home with a front porch showcases an angled fireplace and sloped ceilings. The great room combines with the dining area, creating an open, spacious effect. A door leads to a raised deck for a favorable indoor/outdoor relationship. The master suite provides a large walk-in closet and deluxe bath with a unique half-moon tub and a separate shower. A bedroom accessed from the foyer creates an optional den.

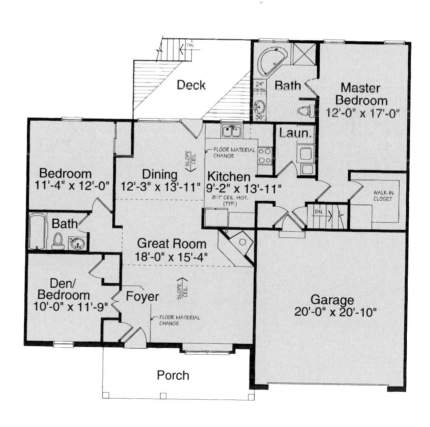

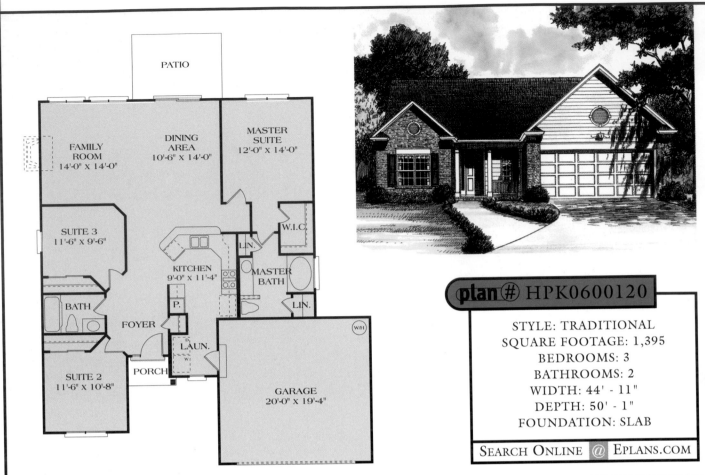

PATIO

FAMILY ROOM
14'-0" X 14'-0"

DINING AREA
10'-6" X 14'-0"

MASTER SUITE
12'-0" X 14'-0"

SUITE 3
11'-6" X 9'-6"

W.I.C

KITCHEN
9'-0" X 11'-4"

MASTER BATH

LIN.

LIN.

BATH

P.

FOYER

LAUN.

W/H

SUITE 2
11'-6" X 10'-8"

PORCH

GARAGE
20'-0" X 19'-4"

plan# HPK0600120

STYLE: TRADITIONAL
SQUARE FOOTAGE: 1,395
BEDROOMS: 3
BATHROOMS: 2
WIDTH: 44' - 11"
DEPTH: 50' - 1"
FOUNDATION: SLAB

SEARCH ONLINE @ Eplans.com

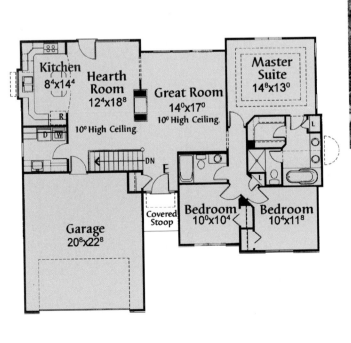

Kitchen
8⁴x14⁴

Hearth Room
12⁴x18⁸

Great Room
14⁰x17⁰
10⁰ High Ceiling.

Master Suite
14⁸x13⁰

10⁰ High Ceiling.

R

D W

DN

E

L

Garage
20⁸x22⁸

Covered Stoop

Bedroom
10⁰x10⁴

Bedroom
10⁴x11⁸

plan# HPK0600121

STYLE: COUNTRY
SQUARE FOOTAGE: 1,558
BEDROOMS: 3
BATHROOMS: 2
WIDTH: 53' - 6"
DEPTH: 47' - 4"
FOUNDATION: CRAWLSPACE,
SLAB, BASEMENT

SEARCH ONLINE @ Eplans.com

plan# HPK0600122

STYLE: TRADITIONAL
FIRST FLOOR: 1,004 SQ. FT.
SECOND FLOOR: 843 SQ. FT.
TOTAL: 1,847 SQ. FT.
ATTIC/STORAGE SPACE:
472/282 SQ. FT.
BEDROOMS: 3
BATHROOMS: 2½
WIDTH: 44' - 4"
DEPTH: 57' - 8"

SEARCH ONLINE @ EPLANS.COM

This home recreates the traditional floor plan into a fresh arrangement of living space. The entry leads to a flex room—make it a study, a living room, or whatever you wish—that shares a see-through fireplace with the eating area. This area accesses the side property and flows right into the island kitchen, complete with a recycling center and a door to the three-season porch in back. Tucked behind the staircase is a spacious gathering room, which you can make formal or casual. A powder room and utility area join forces for convenience; the double garage features a hobby area. The second floor is home to two family bedrooms that share a full bath and a tray ceilinged master suite with its own roomy private bath. Storage options abound with bonus space on the second floor and an attic above.

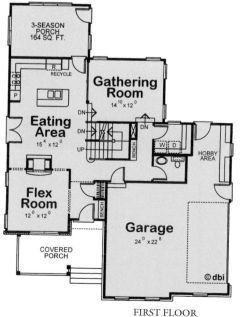

FIRST FLOOR

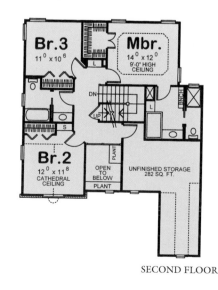

SECOND FLOOR

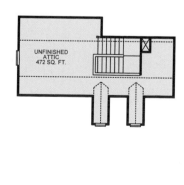

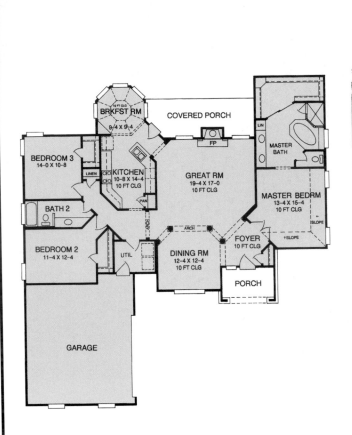

BRKFST RM
9-4 X 9-4

COVERED PORCH

FP

MASTER BATH

LIN

BEDROOM 3
14-0 X 10-8

LINEN

KITCHEN
10-8 X 14-4
10 FT CLG

GREAT RM
19-4 X 17-0
10 FT CLG

MASTER BEDRM
13-4 X 15-4
10 FT CLG

BATH 2

PAN

SLOPE

BEDROOM 2
11-4 12-4

UTIL

DINING RM
12-4 X 12-4
10 FT CLG

FOYER
10 FT CLG

ARCH

SLOPE

PORCH

GARAGE

plan # HPK0600123

STYLE: TRADITIONAL
SQUARE FOOTAGE: 1,955
BEDROOMS: 3
BATHROOMS: 2
WIDTH: 60' - 10"
DEPTH: 65' - 0"
FOUNDATION:
CRAWLSPACE, SLAB

SEARCH ONLINE @ EPLANS.COM

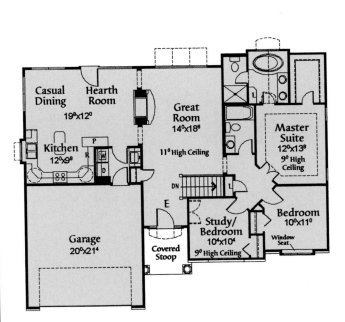

Casual Dining

Hearth Room

Great Room
14⁰x18⁸
11⁰ High Ceiling

Master Suite
12⁰x13⁸
9⁰ High Ceiling

Kitchen
12⁰x9⁸

P
R
W
D

DN

Garage
20⁰x21⁴

Covered Stoop

Study/ Bedroom
10⁴x10⁴
9⁰ High Ceiling

E

Bedroom
10⁰x11⁰

Window Seat

plan # HPK0630002

STYLE: NEW AMERICAN
SQUARE FOOTAGE: 1,486
BEDROOMS: 3
BATHROOMS: 2
WIDTH: 52' - 8"
DEPTH: 44' - 4"
FOUNDATION: UNFINISHED
BASEMENT

SEARCH ONLINE @ EPLANS.COM

plan # HPK0600125

STYLE: TRADITIONAL
SQUARE FOOTAGE: 1,806
BEDROOMS: 3
BATHROOMS: 2
WIDTH: 55' - 4"
DEPTH: 56' - 0"

SEARCH ONLINE @ EPLANS.COM

Beautiful columns and arched transoms are the focal points of this contemporary ranch home. The 10-foot entry opens to the formal dining room and the great room, which features a brick fireplace and arched windows. The large island kitchen offers an angled range, a multitude of cabinets, and a sunny breakfast area with an atrium door to the backyard. Separate bedroom wings provide optimum privacy. The master wing to the right includes a whirlpool bath with a sloped ceiling, a plant shelf above dual lavatories, and a large walk-in closet. The family bedrooms are at the opposite end of the house and share a full bath. The laundry room serves as a mudroom entry from the garage.

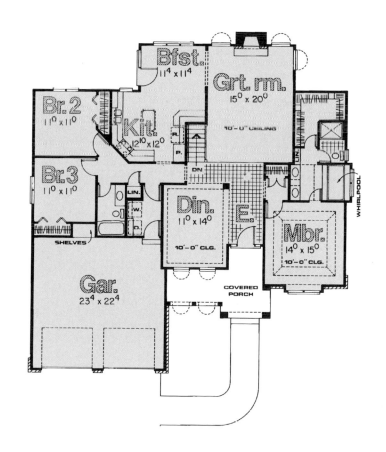

SECOND FLOOR

Great Room Below

Bedroom 2
10⁰ x 12²

Foyer Below

Bath

W.i.c.

Bedroom 3
13⁰ x 10⁰

Opt. Bonus Room
12⁰ x 23⁰

Breakfast

Vaulted Great Room
13⁹ x 16⁷

Master Suite
16⁸ x 12⁰

Kitchen

Two Story Foyer

Pwdr.

Master Bath

Vaulted Dining Room
10⁰ x 11⁰

Covered Porch

W.i.c.

Laund.

Garage
19⁵ x 21²

copyright © 1997 frank betz associates, inc.

FIRST FLOOR

plan# HPK0600126

STYLE: COUNTRY COTTAGE
FIRST FLOOR: 1,179 SQ. FT.
SECOND FLOOR: 460 SQ. FT.
TOTAL: 1,639 SQ. FT.
BONUS SPACE: 338 SQ. FT.
BEDROOMS: 3
BATHROOMS: 2½
WIDTH: 41' - 6"
DEPTH: 54' - 4"
FOUNDATION: CRAWLSPACE,
SLAB, BASEMENT

SEARCH ONLINE @ Eplans.com

Bedroom 2
11⁰ x 11⁹

Great Room Below

W.i.c.

Bath

Opt. Bonus Room
15⁵ x 20⁸

W.i.c.

Bedroom 3
11⁰ x 13²

Foyer Below

SECOND FLOOR

Breakfast

Kitchen

Vaulted Great Room
16⁵ x 16⁶

Master Suite
17⁰ x 13⁰

Stor.

Laund.

Pwdr.

Vaulted M.Bath

Dining Room
11⁶ x 13⁰

Two Story Foyer

W.i.c.

Garage
19⁵ x 19⁹

Covered Entry

copyright © 1998 frank betz associates, inc.

FIRST FLOOR

plan# HPK0600127

STYLE: TRADITIONAL
FIRST FLOOR: 1,433 SQ. FT.
SECOND FLOOR: 546 SQ. FT.
TOTAL: 1,979 SQ. FT.
BONUS SPACE: 293 SQ. FT.
BEDROOMS: 3
BATHROOMS: 2½
WIDTH: 54' - 0"
DEPTH: 41' - 6"
FOUNDATION:
BASEMENT, CRAWLSPACE

SEARCH ONLINE @ Eplans.com

plan# HPK0600128

STYLE: TRANSITIONAL
FIRST FLOOR: 1,036 SQ. FT.
SECOND FLOOR: 861 SQ. FT.
TOTAL: 1,897 SQ. FT.
BEDROOMS: 3
BATHROOMS: 2½
WIDTH: 48' - 0"
DEPTH: 38' - 0"
FOUNDATION: BASEMENT

SEARCH ONLINE 𝓁 EPLANS.COM

The refined exterior of this distinctive plan introduces a charming and livable home. Highlights of the floor plan include a furniture alcove in the formal dining room, a high ceiling and French doors topped with arched windows in the great room, a wood rail at the split stairs, a walk-in pantry in the kitchen, and a laundry room that's roomy enough to do a family-size laundry with helpers. The view from the foyer through the great room to the rear yard enhances indoor/outdoor entertaining, while the spacious kitchen and breakfast area encourage relaxed gatherings. The second floor features a window seat at the top of the stairs and a computer desk in the extra-large hallway. The deluxe master suite offers a whirlpool tub, separate vanities, a shower stall, and a spacious walk-in closet.

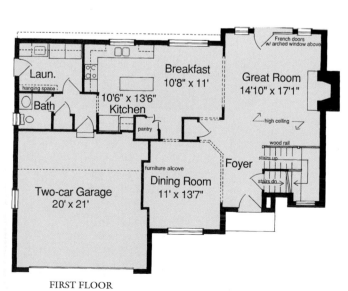

FIRST FLOOR

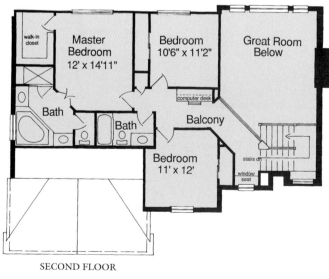

SECOND FLOOR

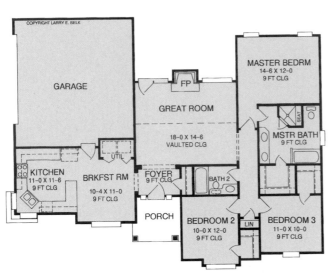

COPYRIGHT LARRY E. BELK

GARAGE

FP

GREAT ROOM
18-0 X 14-6
VAULTED CLG

MASTER BEDRM
14-6 X 12-0
9 FT CLG

MSTR BATH
9 FT CLG

SEAT

UTIL

KITCHEN
11-0 X 11-6
9 FT CLG

BRKFST RM
10-4 X 11-0
9 FT CLG

FOYER
9 FT CLG

BATH 2

PORCH

BEDROOM 2
10-0 X 12-0
9 FT CLG

LIN

BEDROOM 3
11-0 X 10-0
9 FT CLG

plan# HPK0600129

STYLE: FRENCH COUNTRY
SQUARE FOOTAGE: 1,464
BEDROOMS: 3
BATHROOMS: 2
WIDTH: 56' - 2"
DEPTH: 45' - 2"
FOUNDATION:
CRAWLSPACE, SLAB

SEARCH ONLINE @ EPLANS.COM

14'-4" X 11'-0"
4,30 X 3,30

14'-4" X 12'-6"
4,30 X 3,75

SECOND FLOOR

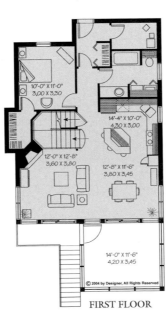

10'-0" X 11'-0"
3,00 X 3,30

14'-4" X 10'-0"
4,30 X 3,00

12'-0" X 12'-8"
3,60 X 3,80

12'-8" X 11'-6"
3,80 X 3,45

© 2004 by Designer, All Rights Reserved

14'-0" X 11'-6"
4,20 X 3,45

FIRST FLOOR

plan# HPK0630003

STYLE: BUNGALOW
FIRST FLOOR: 908 SQ. FT.
SECOND FLOOR: 576 SQ. FT.
TOTAL: 1,484 SQ. FT.
BEDROOMS: 3
BATHROOMS: 2
WIDTH: 26' - 0"
DEPTH: 48' - 0"
FOUNDATION: FINISHED
WALKOUT BASEMENT

SEARCH ONLINE @ EPLANS.COM

plan# HPK0600131

STYLE: TRADITIONAL
FIRST FLOOR: 929 SQ. FT.
SECOND FLOOR: 1,058 SQ. FT.
TOTAL: 1,987 SQ. FT.
BONUS SPACE: 163 SQ. FT.
BEDROOMS: 4
BATHROOMS: 3
WIDTH: 50' - 4"
DEPTH: 47' 4"

SEARCH ONLINE @ EPLANS.COM

Family-style living with a modern layout and a stylish facade—you've got it all with this plan. It all starts with a front covered porch that leads into a spacious foyer. To the left is the huge hearth-warmed great room, which opens into the light-filled island kitchen. Both the kitchen and the great room access the corner flex room—make it a formal dining room, an office, whatever you wish! This room, as well as the eating area opposite the kitchen, opens to the long back porch. A full bath, hidden behind the staircase, completes the first floor. Upstairs, four bedrooms— including a deluxe master suite with a tray ceiling and large bath— share a balcony overlook and 163 square feet of storage space. The two-car garage features kitchen entry and plenty of extra room.

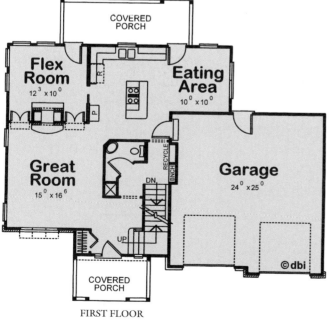

FIRST FLOOR

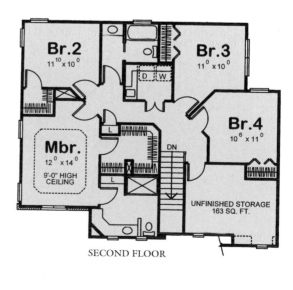

SECOND FLOOR

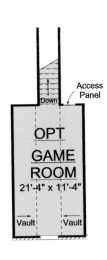

plan# HPK0600132

STYLE: EUROPEAN COTTAGE
SQUARE FOOTAGE: 1,595
BONUS SPACE: 312 SQ. FT.
BEDROOMS: 3
BATHROOMS: 2
WIDTH: 49' - 0"
DEPTH: 60' - 0"

SEARCH ONLINE @ EPLANS.COM

Varying rooflines and strong brick columns leading to the entrance provide bold first impressions to visitors of this home. Come inside to find a practical and inviting floor plan filled with thoughtful touches. Secluded to the far left of the plan are two bedrooms which share a full bath; the master suite is tucked away in the back right corner of the plan with an enormous walk-in closet and master bath. Living spaces are open to each other, with the kitchen easily serving the nook and living room—adorned with a lovely plant ledge—and a dining room nearby. Venture upstairs to the optional game room and finish it at your leisure.

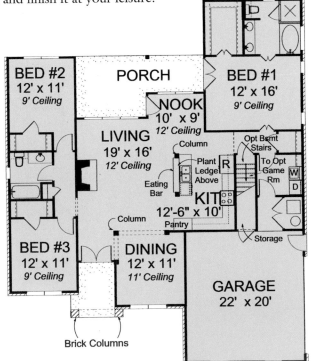

plan # HPK0600133

STYLE: TRADITIONAL
SQUARE FOOTAGE: 1,947
BONUS SPACE: 255 SQ. FT.
BEDROOMS: 3
BATHROOMS: 2½
WIDTH: 59' - 4"
DEPTH: 62' - 2"
FOUNDATION: BASEMENT

SEARCH ONLINE @ EPLANS.COM

Twin columns frame the arched entry to this three-bedroom, single-level home. Three additional columns define the formal dining room to the right of the entry foyer. The large gathering room, with a fireplace and built in bookshelves, opens to the breakfast area, which accesses the rear deck/terrace—a perfect location for a barbecue grill. Two family bedrooms share a full bath to the left of the gathering room. The master suite features a sloped ceiling, an oval garden tub, and His and Hers walk-in closets. Future expansion is possible with a bonus room over the garage.

DECK

BREAKFAST
11'-4" X 8'-6"

BEDROOM NO. 3
11'-6" X 11'-0"

GREAT ROOM
14'-0" X 17'-6"

KITCHEN
11'-4" X 10'-0"

MASTER
BEDROOM
12'-4" X 15'-6"

BATH

DN.

HIS

PWDR.

MASTER
BATH

BEDROOM NO. 2
11'-0" X 14'-8"

FOYER
6'-6" X 6'-6"

DINING ROOM
11'-4" X 10'-6"

LAUNDRY

HERS

TWO-CAR GARAGE
20'-4" X 19'-4"

QUOTE ONE®

plan # HPK0600134

STYLE: TRADITIONAL
SQUARE FOOTAGE: 1,733
BEDROOMS: 3
BATHROOMS: 2½
WIDTH: 55' - 6"
DEPTH: 57' - 6"
FOUNDATION: WALKOUT
BASEMENT

SEARCH ONLINE @ EPLANS.COM

Delightfully different, this brick one-story home has everything for the active family. The foyer opens to a formal dining room, accented with four columns, and a great room with a fireplace and French doors to the rear deck. The efficient kitchen has an attached light-filled breakfast nook. The master bath features a tray ceiling, His and Hers walk-in closets, a double-sink vanity, and a huge garden tub. The two-car garage is accessed through the laundry room.

plan # HPK0600135

STYLE: FRENCH
SQUARE FOOTAGE: 1,828
BEDROOMS: 4
BATHROOMS: 2
WIDTH: 64' - 0"
DEPTH: 62' - 0"
FOUNDATION: CRAWLSPACE,
BASEMENT, SLAB

SEARCH ONLINE @ EPLANS.COM

With hipped roofs and muntin windows, this attractive facade brings curb appeal to this European-style home. The dining room sits just left of the entry, which leads to the living room with a fireplace. The spacious kitchen's angled counter overlooks the breakfast room, which leads to the utility room and the master bedroom. The master suite contains a vast walk-in closet, a vanity with a sink in the dressing room, and a full bath. Three additional bedrooms occupy the right side of the home and share a full bath and a linen closet.

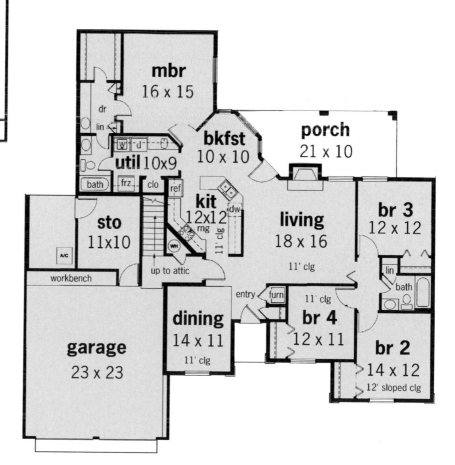

plan# HPK0600136

STYLE: TRADITIONAL
SQUARE FOOTAGE: 1,890
BEDROOMS: 3
BATHROOMS: 2
WIDTH: 65' - 10"
DEPTH: 53' - 5"
FOUNDATION:
CRAWLSPACE, SLAB

SEARCH ONLINE @ EPLANS.COM

This classic home exudes elegance and style and offers sophisticated amenities in a compact size. Ten-foot ceilings throughout the plan lend an aura of spacious hospitality. A generous living room with a sloped ceiling, built-in bookcases, and a centerpiece fireplace offers views as well as access to the rear yard. The nearby breakfast room shares an informal eating counter with the ample kitchen, which serves the coffer-ceilinged dining room through French doors. Three bedrooms include a sumptuous master suite with windowed whirlpool tub and walk-in closet and two family bedrooms that share a full bath.

MASTER BATH
SEAT

MASTER BEDRM
14-4 X 15-6
10 FT CLG
FP

PORCH

BRKFST RM
10-8 X 11-8
10 FT CLG

UTIL
8-0 X 5-8

STORAGE

STORAGE

LIVING ROOM
17-4 X 15-8
10 FT CLG

KITCHEN
10-8 X 13-6
10 FT CLG

GARAGE

BATH 2

LIN

BEDROOM 2
12-6 X 11-6

BEDROOM 3
12-0 X 13-4
10 FT CLG

FOYER
10 FT CLG

DINING ROOM
11-0 X 13-0
10 FT COFFERED CLG

PORCH

plan# HPK0600137

STYLE: TRADITIONAL
SQUARE FOOTAGE: 1,792
BEDROOMS: 3
BATHROOMS: 2
WIDTH: 68' - 0"
DEPTH: 62' - 0"
FOUNDATION: BASEMENT,
CRAWLSPACE, SLAB

SEARCH ONLINE @ EPLANS.COM

Light dazzles through arched transoms, and double columns add a Mediterranean aura to this three-bedroom home. Inside, a corner fireplace warms the living room, and a ribbon of windows views the rear deck and porch. A door between the living and dining rooms opens to a rear porch, a deck, and a patio area. Two family bedrooms share a full bath to the right of the living room. Secluded to the left of the plan, the spacious master suite enjoys a cathedral ceiling, walk-in closet, and luxurious bath. A cozy eating area adjoins the kitchen, which shares a serving bar with the dining room.

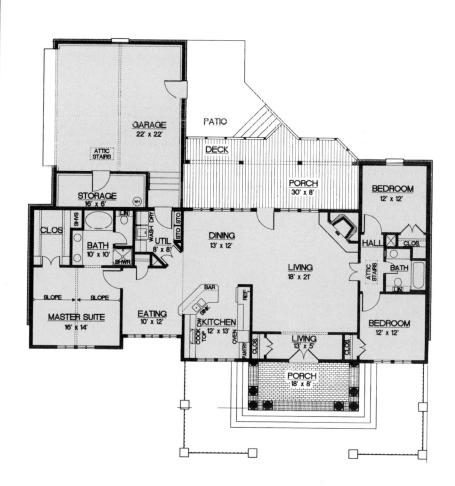

plan# HPK0600138

STYLE: MEDITERRANEAN
SQUARE FOOTAGE: 1,883
BEDROOMS: 3
BATHROOMS: 2
WIDTH: 58' - 10"
DEPTH: 54' - 2"
FOUNDATION: CRAWLSPACE,
SLAB, BASEMENT

SEARCH ONLINE @ EPLANS.COM

With down-home country charisma and a touch of Craftsman detail, this winsome design will certainly be the hallmark of your neighborhood. Come in from the covered porch, where the foyer opens to the dining room, defined by an elegant tray ceiling. The living room enjoys plenty of light and the warmth of a raised-hearth fireplace. A uniquely shaped island enhances the kitchen, which opens to the dinette and hearth room. Two nearby bedrooms, or make one a study, share a full bath. The master suite delights in the luxury of a spa tub and compartmented toilet in the private bath. A two-car garage completes this lovely plan.

Hearth Room 14⁸x12⁰

Bedroom/ Study 11⁰x11⁴

Dinette 10⁰x10⁰

Desk

Transom Above

Study

Book Case

Master Suite 13⁴x14⁸

Living Room 13⁴x16⁰ 10⁰High Ceiling.

Kitchen 11⁸x10⁸

Bedroom 11⁰x11⁰

DN

Dining Room 10⁸x13⁸

Garage 20⁸x20⁸

Covered Porch

plan # HPK0600139

STYLE: FRENCH
SQUARE FOOTAGE: 1,655
BEDROOMS: 3
BATHROOMS: 2
WIDTH: 52' - 0"
DEPTH: 66' - 0"
FOUNDATION:
CRAWLSPACE, SLAB

SEARCH ONLINE @ EPLANS.COM

Elegantly arched doors and windows decorate the exterior of this fine home, which offers an intriguing floor plan. The living room features a soaring 15-foot ceiling and adjoins the octagonal dining room. Both rooms offer views of the skylit rear porch; a skylight also brightens the kitchen. The lavish master suite includes a walk-in closet, access to a small side porch, and a full bath with a corner marble tub. Two additional bedrooms, thoughtfully placed apart from the master suite, share a full bath.

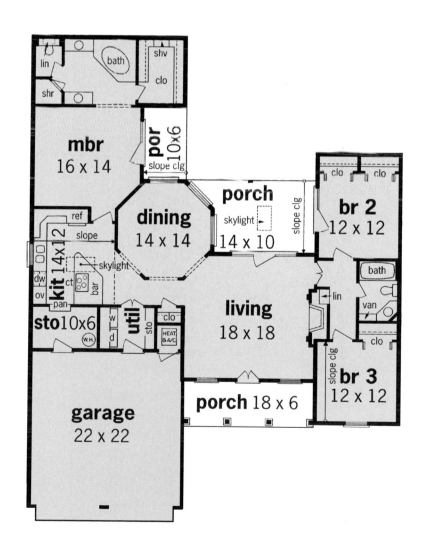

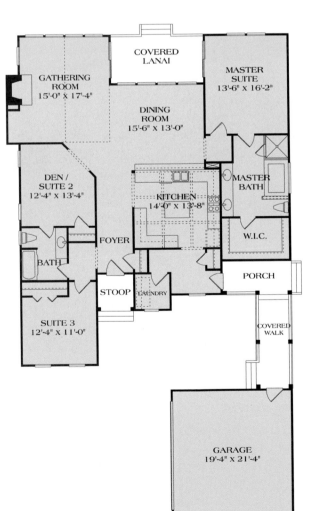

plan# HPK0600140

STYLE: TRANSITIONAL
SQUARE FOOTAGE: 1,911
BEDROOMS: 3
BATHROOMS: 2
WIDTH: 45' - 0"
DEPTH: 78' - 5"
FOUNDATION: CRAWLSPACE

SEARCH ONLINE @ EPLANS.COM

Clean lines and an efficient floor plan make this striking home surprisingly economical to build. Stucco and decorative shutters create a welcoming facade as you enter from the covered stoop. Inside, the island kitchen is created for family get-togethers, with lots of space and an open design that encourages conversation from the naturally lit dining room. The gathering room has a dramatic vaulted ceiling and a warming fireplace. At the rear, the master suite accesses a covered lanai and enjoys a sumptuous bath. Two secondary bedrooms are on the far left, or make one a comfortable den.

plan# HPK0600141

STYLE: EUROPEAN COTTAGE
SQUARE FOOTAGE: 1,810
BEDROOMS: 3
BATHROOMS: 2
WIDTH: 51' - 4"
DEPTH: 51' - 4"
FOUNDATION: CRAWLSPACE,
SLAB, BASEMENT

SEARCH ONLINE @ EPLANS.COM

Bright and airy, this European cottage has a charming street presence and light-filled interior. Upon entry, the dining room is on the left, hosting a large multi-pane window and a cut-out buffet niche. The family room is just beyond, with a cozy fireplace and volume ceiling. The kitchen and bayed dinette are subtly defined by a kitchen island. The master suite is tucked away with a private bath that includes a makeup area and garden tub. On the far right, one bedroom (or make it a study with French doors) shares a bath with a slightly smaller bedroom.

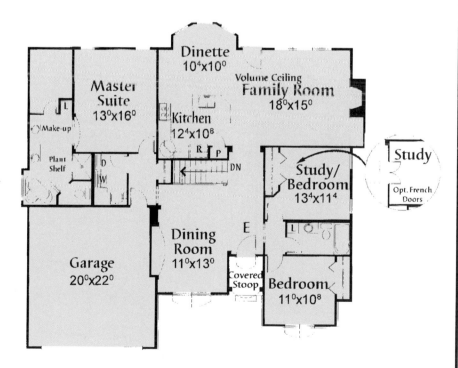

plan# HPK0600142

STYLE: TRADITIONAL
SQUARE FOOTAGE: 1,575
BEDROOMS: 3
BATHROOMS: 2
WIDTH: 52' - 0"
DEPTH: 52' - 6"
FOUNDATION: CRAWLSPACE, SLAB, BASEMENT

SEARCH ONLINE @ EPLANS.COM

A lovely facade opens this one-story home, with gable ends and dormer windows as decorative features. The interior features vaulted family and dining rooms—a fireplace in the family room offers warmth. Defined by columns, the formal dining experience is enhanced. The kitchen attaches to a bayed breakfast nook with a vaulted ceiling. A split floor plan has the family bedrooms on the right side and the master suite on the left. The master bedroom has a tray ceiling, vaulted bath, and walk-in closet.

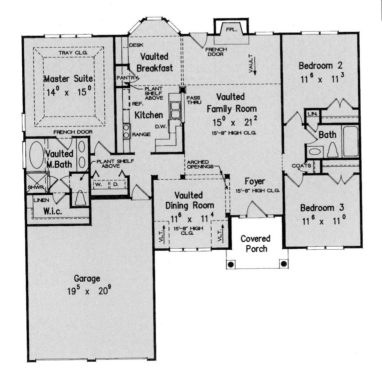

OPTIONAL LAYOUT

plan# HPK0600143

STYLE: CONTEMPORARY
SQUARE FOOTAGE: 1,595
BEDROOMS: 3
BATHROOMS: 2
WIDTH: 52' - 8"
DEPTH: 42' - 8"
FOUNDATION: SLAB,
BASEMENT, CRAWLSPACE

SEARCH ONLINE @ EPLANS.COM

This traditional facade captures
a bit of Southwestern flair in its stucco
detailing. An arched, recessed entry brings
drama to the forefront. Inside, a dining
room with a 10-foot ceiling resides to the
right of the foyer; two bedrooms, one that
could double as a study, share a full bath to
the left. Just ahead lies the great room with
its fireplace and volume ceiling. This space
is expanded by its open flow to the breakfast area, which enjoys a snack bar to the
large kitchen. A comfortable master suite is
secluded at the rear of the home with its
own elegant bath. The two-car garage can
be accessed from the convenient laundry
room off the kitchen.

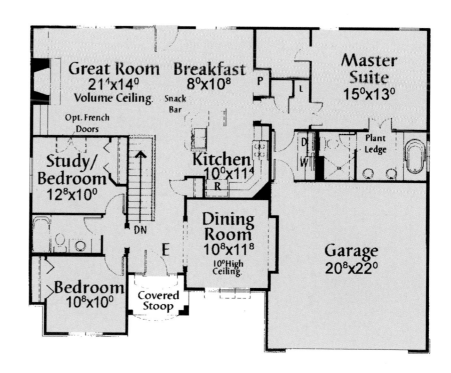

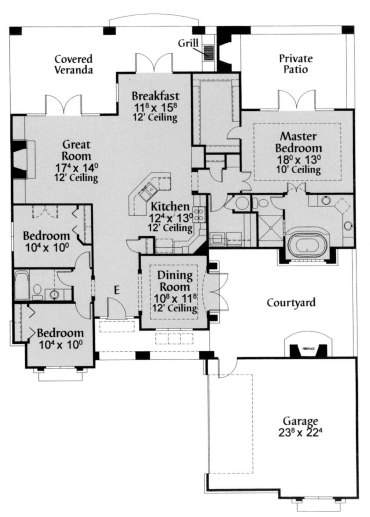

plan# HPK0600144

STYLE: SW CONTEMPORARY
SQUARE FOOTAGE: 1,841
BEDROOMS: 3
BATHROOMS: 2
WIDTH: 55' - 8"
DEPTH: 78' - 0"
FOUNDATION: SLAB

SEARCH ONLINE @ EPLANS.COM

Three fireplaces—one in the courtyard, a second in the great room, and a third on the private master-suite patio—add extra warmth to this new Pueblo-style home. This design also boasts a great indoor/outdoor relationship: the dining room opens to the courtyard, and the great room and breakfast area both feature French doors that open to a covered rear veranda. Other notable features include built-in shelves in the great room, a spa tub in the master bath, and a built-in grill on the veranda.

plan # HPK0600145

STYLE: SW CONTEMPORARY
SQUARE FOOTAGE: 1,950
BEDROOMS: 3
BATHROOMS: 2
WIDTH: 65' - 4"
DEPTH: 60' - 0"
FOUNDATION: SLAB

SEARCH ONLINE @ Eplans.com

Clean lines and plenty of windows add style to this contemporary Pueblo design. A fireplace makes the expansive entry courtyard even more welcoming. Inside, another fireplace, a wet bar, and a curved wall of windows enhance the great room. The kitchen easily serves the formal dining room and the breakfast area, which opens to a covered rear veranda. A split-bedroom plan places the master suite, with its indulgent dual-vanity bath and walk-in closet, to the right of the plan; two family bedrooms sit to the left of the plan.

plan# HPK0600146

STYLE: SANTA FE
SQUARE FOOTAGE: 1,923
BEDROOMS: 3
BATHROOMS: 2
WIDTH: 55' - 8"
DEPTH: 62' - 8"
FOUNDATION: SLAB

SEARCH ONLINE @ EPLANS.COM

Bold rooflines announce the glass-door entrance of this updated Santa Fe design. The foyer opens directly to a gathering room with a 13-foot ceiling and corner fireplace. A nearby wet bar is great for guests. The kitchen easily serves the sunlit dining area, which opens to the rear veranda (with a fireplace!). Family bedrooms reside to the right and include a comfortable master suite with a private bath, and two secondary bedrooms. One bedroom also makes a fine study.

plan # HPK0600147

STYLE: SW CONTEMPORARY
SQUARE FOOTAGE: 1,987
BEDROOMS: 2
BATHROOMS: 2
WIDTH: 49' - 11"
DEPTH: 75' - 4"
FOUNDATION: SLAB

SEARCH ONLINE @ EPLANS.COM

Santa Fe style meets traditional

family home in this updated casita. Inside, 12-foot ceilings crown most of the living areas. The formal dining room and hearth-warmed family room are defined by tray ceilings. The island-cooktop kitchen is open for increased flow. The master suite features a box-vault ceiling, access to the rear veranda, and a lavish bath. A bedroom at the front of the home acts as a quiet study. The secluded home office is brightened by a bayed wall.

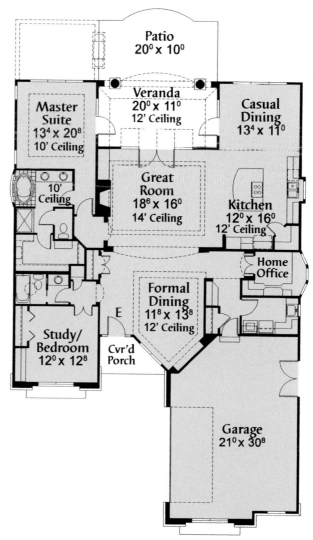

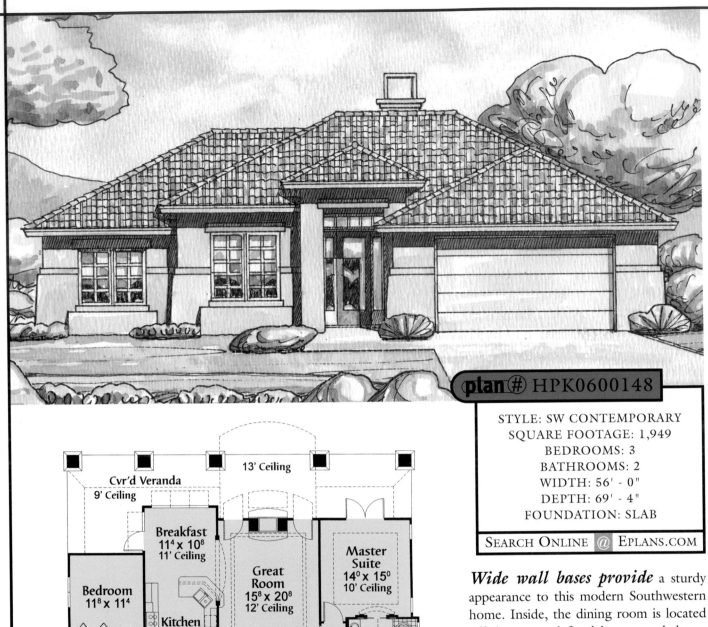

plan# HPK0600148

STYLE: SW CONTEMPORARY
SQUARE FOOTAGE: 1,949
BEDROOMS: 3
BATHROOMS: 2
WIDTH: 56' - 0"
DEPTH: 69' - 4"
FOUNDATION: SLAB

SEARCH ONLINE @ EPLANS.COM

Wide wall bases provide a sturdy appearance to this modern Southwestern home. Inside, the dining room is located off the entry, defined by a rounded tray ceiling. Just ahead, a large, modified-galley kitchen serves the breakfast nook with ease; a serving counter overlooks the great room's striking fireplace. A wet bar is an added benefit, great for entertaining. The nearby master suite enjoys French-door veranda access and a vaulted bath. Two additional bedrooms share a hall bath to the left of the plan.

© 2002 Donald A. Gardner, Inc.

plan# HPK0600149

STYLE: SANTA FE
SQUARE FOOTAGE: 1,895
BEDROOMS: 3
BATHROOMS: 2
WIDTH: 65' - 10"
DEPTH: 59' - 9"

SEARCH ONLINE @ EPLANS.COM

Giddyup! Santa Fe style at its best brings you back to the days of open skies and covered wagons. Rich with history on the outside, this plan's interior has all the up-to-date amenities that today's families require. The arched loggia entry opens to a soaring foyer, flanked on the right by a formal dining room. To the left is a bedroom that could easily become a study. Straight ahead, the hearth-warmed great room enjoys sliding-glass-door access to the rear loggia. Another bedroom is tucked in the back left corner, convenient to a full hall bath. On the other side of the great room, a roomy kitchen opens to a breakfast nook with a curved wall of windows. Secluded to the back is the luxurious master suite, featuring a 10-foot ceiling and spectacular private bath. The two-car garage opens to a utility room with a handy linen closet.

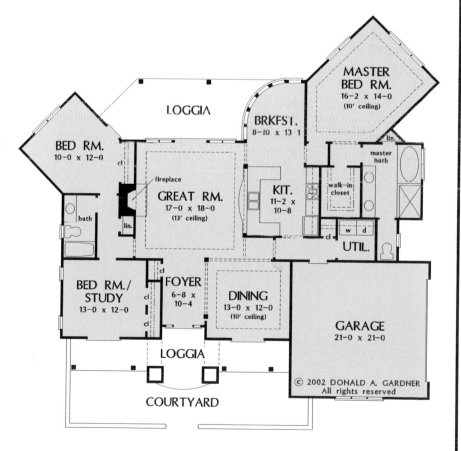

LOGGIA

BED RM.
10-0 x 12-0

fireplace

GREAT RM.
17-0 x 18-0
(13' ceiling)

bath

BRKFST.
8-10 x 13-1

KIT.
11-2 x
10-8

MASTER
BED RM.
16-2 x 14-0
(10' ceiling)

master
bath

walk-in
closet

w d

UTIL.

BED RM./
STUDY
13-0 x 12-0

FOYER
6-8 x
10-4

DINING
13-0 x 12-0
(10' ceiling)

GARAGE
21-0 x 21-0

LOGGIA

COURTYARD

plan# HPK0600150

STYLE: SEASIDE
FIRST FLOOR: 1,122 SQ. FT.
SECOND FLOOR: 528 SQ. FT.
TOTAL: 1,650 SQ. FT.
BEDROOMS: 4
BATHROOMS: 2
WIDTH: 34' - 0"
DEPTH: 52' - 5"
FOUNDATION: PIER

SEARCH ONLINE @ EPLANS.COM

This lovely seaside vacation home is perfect for seasonal family getaways or for the family that lives coastal year round. The spacious front deck is great for private sunbathing or outdoor barbecues, providing breathtaking ocean views. The two-story living room is warmed by a fireplace on breezy beach nights, while the island kitchen overlooks the open dining area nearby. Two first-floor family bedrooms share a hall bath. Upstairs, the master bedroom features a walk-in closet, dressing area with a vanity and access to a whirlpool tub shared with an additional family bedroom.

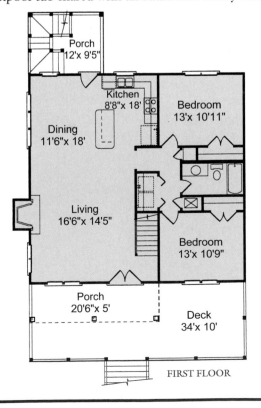

Porch
12'x 9'5"

Kitchen
8'8"x 18'

Dining
11'6"x 18'

Bedroom
13'x 10'11"

Living
16'6"x 14'5"

Bedroom
13'x 10'9"

Porch
20'6"x 5'

Deck
34'x 10'

FIRST FLOOR

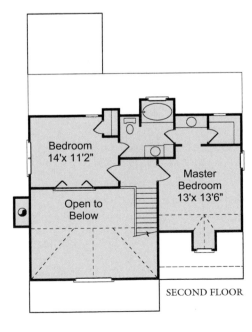

Bedroom
14'x 11'2"

Open to
Below

Master
Bedroom
13'x 13'6"

SECOND FLOOR

plan # HPK0600151

STYLE: SEASIDE
FIRST FLOOR: 731 SQ. FT.
SECOND FLOOR: 935 SQ. FT.
TOTAL: 1,666 SQ. FT.
BEDROOMS: 3
BATHROOMS: 3
WIDTH: 35' - 0"
DEPTH: 38' - 0"
FOUNDATION: PIER

SEARCH ONLINE @ EPLANS.COM

This pier-foundation home has an abundance of amenities to offer, not the least being the loft lookout. Inside, the living room is complete with a corner gas fireplace. The spacious kitchen features a cooktop island, an adjacent breakfast nook and easy access to the dining room. From this room, a set of French doors leads out to a small deck—perfect for dining alfresco. Upstairs, the sleeping zone consists of two family bedrooms sharing a full hall bath, and a deluxe master suite. Amenities in this suite include two walk-in closets and a private bath.

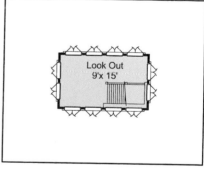

THIRD FLOOR

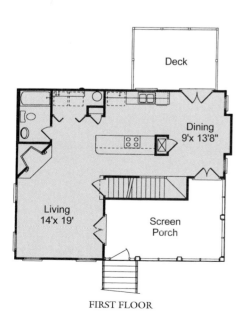

FIRST FLOOR

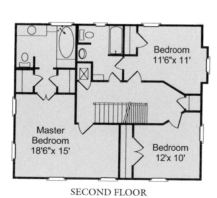

SECOND FLOOR

In contrast to smaller homes, plans within the 2,000 to 3,000 square-foot range—sometimes called "family homes"—devote space toward one or two additional bedrooms, to accommodate a growing family. Formal spaces tend to gain more definition as separate rooms—such as dining rooms or offices—but maintaining flow-through and spaciousness remain important goals. Porches and decks still provide supplemental space for larger gatherings and, as in the example of this stately Charleston-style home, contribute favorably to the exterior architecture.

The concept of the master suite as a privileged and secluded part of the home arrives with family-sized designs.

A gorgeous balance of exterior materials and windows will have visitors admiring the home from every angle.

The plan featured here is no exception: a fully-trimmed master suite resides away from the most highly trafficked parts of the home and the other bedrooms. It comprises a large bedroom facing the rear and side of the plan, a master bath designed for two, and an ample walk-in closet. To preserve the master bath for exclusive use by the homeowners, a half-bath/powder room has been placed near the foyer.

Well-designed homes of this size will find easy access to natural light from exterior windows without needing special accommodations, such as skylights or additional dormers. Homeowners can take advantage of natural lighting situations by replacing an extra bedroom with a study or library. ●

CONCRETE IDEAS

The proper choice of paving materials can free up funds and beautify the landscape even when budgets reach their limits. When considering materials, think of the front walkway as an extension of the home's foyer. Take cues from the existing landscape, the home's architecture, and your personal taste. Also, how will the walkway material will be affected by weather? Crushed gravel, for instance, is a poor choice for wintry areas because it cannot be shoveled.

CONCRETE PAVERS

Appearance: A wide range of surface finishes—smooth to textured. Many available colors, shapes, and laying patterns can complement the architectural style of your home.

Initial Cost & Installation: Moderate—Tightly fitted and uniform units are placed over a sand bed and a compacted aggregated base. Immediately ready for use. Can be installed by homeowner. Factory-made pavers last for decades.

Maintenance: Low—Stained or broken pavers can be easily replaced without patches. Dark-colored pavers can help hide stains. Ants and weeds in joints can be prevented with sealers or herbicides.

COBBLE STONE

Appearance: Gives elegant, permanent, yet informal Old-World feel.

Initial Cost & Installation: Very high—Each unit must be fitted together by hand.

Maintenance: Low—High-quality stone lasts for decades. Wide joints may encourage weeds and ants. Rough surface makes walking and driving difficult.

STAMPED CONCRETE

Appearance: Surface is usually colored. Patterns look good from a distance, but close up, surface looks artificial.

Initial Cost & Installation: High—Difficult for homeowner to install. Requires special equipment to stamp stone or paver patterns into surface. Surface sealer often used.

Maintenance: Moderate—Cracking will likely develop. Difficult to match original color or pattern in repaired areas. Repairs leave unattractive patch.

CLAY PAVERS

Appearance: Mostly shades of red and red-brown. Limited number of shapes available.

Initial Cost & Installation: High—Concrete base often required, which increases cost. Inconsistent dimensions make units slow to install and difficult to maintain straight pattern lines.

Maintenance: Low—Irregularities in surface make them prone to damage, especially edge chipping.

ORDINARY CONCRETE

Appearance: Gray or light brown. Can be colored throughout or on surface only.

Initial Cost & Installation: Moderate—Difficult for homeowner to install. Must wait five to seven days for hardening before use. Surface quality depends on weather at time of pour and expertise of installers.

Maintenance: Moderate—Cracking will likely develop. Repairs and replaced sections leave unsightly patches. Oil stains difficult to remove.

CRUSHED STONE OR GRAVEL

Appearance: Typically a rustic look. Appearance varies with color and shape of stones.

Initial Cost & Installation: Low—Dumped and spread over soil (no base required).

Maintenance: High—Scattered stone must be replaced and revealed regularly. Ruts from tires will likely develop.

ASPHALT

Appearance: Limited color options. Difficult to get neat-looking edges. Cracks will likely develop. Stamped and colored asphalt looks fake.

Initial Cost & Installation: Low—Goes in quickly over compacted aggregated base. Can't be installed by homeowner.

Maintenance: High—Wear and weather will break down surface. Black seal coat required every two to three years. Ruts or pothole repairs make ugly patches. Subject to erosion from oil drippings.

Above: A massive stone fireplace warms
the great room and brings counterbal-
ance to its many windows. Left: This
tastefully furnished dining room enjoys
sweeping views of the front landscape.

Columns and a balcony form elegant interior lines in the foyer.

A splendid covered porch provides the perfect place to relax and enjoy a summer afternoon.

plan# HPK0600152

STYLE: COUNTRY COTTAGE
FIRST FLOOR: 1,804 SQ. FT.
SECOND FLOOR: 1,041 SQ. FT.
TOTAL: 2,845 SQ. FT.
BEDROOMS: 4
BATHROOMS: 3½
WIDTH: 57' - 3"
DEPTH: 71' - 0"
FOUNDATION:
WALKOUT BASEMENT

SEARCH ONLINE @ EPLANS.COM

Two Car Garage
21³ x 21⁰

Porch

Master Suite
14⁶ x 15⁰

Great Room
17⁶ x 17⁶

Breakfast
16⁹ x 11⁰

Kitchen
13⁰ x 11⁶

Master Bath

WIC

Foyer

Dining Room
13⁶ x 14⁹

Porch

Porch

Porch

FIRST FLOOR

Bedroom #2
15⁰ x 10⁹

Bedroom #3
13⁰ x 11⁹

Bedroom #4
13⁶ x 14⁹

SECOND FLOOR

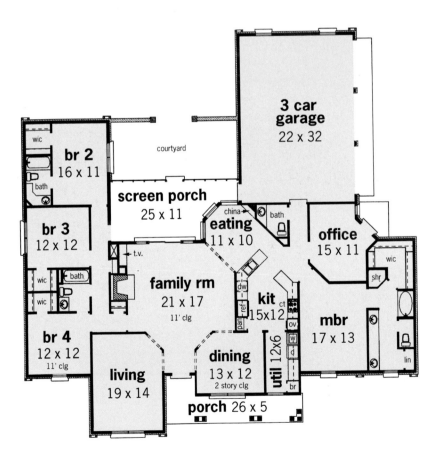

plan # HPK0600154

STYLE: TRADITIONAL
SQUARE FOOTAGE: 2,682
BEDROOMS: 4
BATHROOMS: 3½
WIDTH: 74' - 6"
DEPTH: 75' - 0"
FOUNDATION: SLAB,
CRAWLSPACE

SEARCH ONLINE @ EPLANS.COM

A hipped roof, dormers, and plenty of muntin windows with keystones give this traditional home a welcome invitation. Located in the center of this home, the family room features a built-in entertainment center—note the sliding-door access to the rear screened porch and courtyard. A two-story dining room shows off elegance as it accesses the gourmet kitchen. The lavish master suite includes a private bath and a huge walk-in closet. Completing this plan are three additional family bedrooms, located to the far left of the home, and a full bath. All three family bedrooms include walk-in closets.

Floor plan labels:
- wic
- br 2 16 x 11
- bath
- courtyard
- 3 car garage 22 x 32
- br 3 12 x 12
- screen porch 25 x 11
- china
- eating 11 x 10
- bath
- office 15 x 11
- wic
- wic
- bath
- t.v.
- family rm 21 x 17 11' clg
- shr
- br 4 12 x 12 11' clg
- kit 15x12
- mbr 17 x 13
- living 19 x 14
- dining 13 x 12 2 story clg
- util 12x6
- lin
- porch 26 x 5

plan# HPK0600155

STYLE: FRENCH
SQUARE FOOTAGE: 2,396
BEDROOMS: 4
BATHROOMS: 2
WIDTH: 72' - 0"
DEPTH: 62' - 0"
FOUNDATION: BASEMENT,
CRAWLSPACE, SLAB

SEARCH ONLINE @ EPLANS.COM

Long and low, but sporting a high roofline, this one-story plan offers the best in family livability. The recessed front porch opens to an entry hall that leads to a huge living area with a fireplace. An angled eating area is close by and connects to the galley-style kitchen. The formal dining area also connects to the kitchen, but retains access to the entry hall for convenience. Family bedrooms on the left side of the plan share a full bath. The master suite sits behind the two-car garage and is graced by patio access and a fine bath.

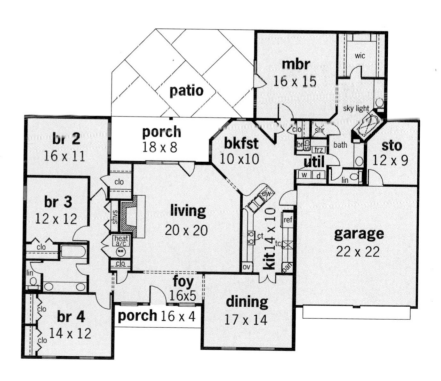

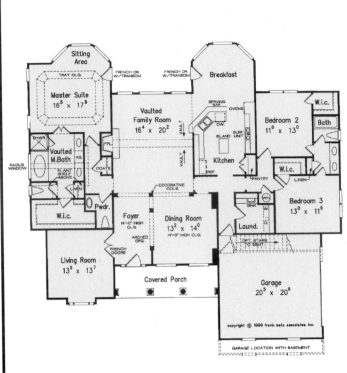

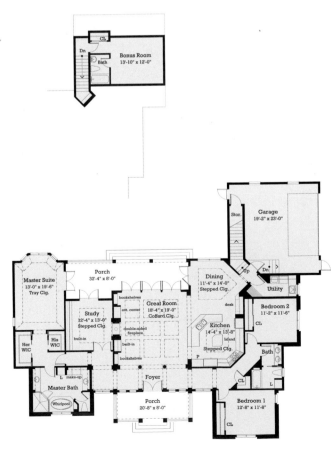

plan# HPK0600156

STYLE: EUROPEAN COTTAGE
SQUARE FOOTAGE: 2,388
BEDROOMS: 3
BATHROOMS: 2½
WIDTH: 63' - 0"
DEPTH: 60' - 0"
FOUNDATION: CRAWLSPACE,
BASEMENT, SLAB

SEARCH ONLINE @ EPLANS.COM

plan# HPK0600157

STYLE: FARMHOUSE
SQUARE FOOTAGE: 2,454
BONUS SPACE: 256 SQ. FT.
BEDROOMS: 3
BATHROOMS: 2
WIDTH: 80' - 6"
DEPTH: 66' - 6"
FOUNDATION: CRAWLSPACE

SEARCH ONLINE @ EPLANS.COM

plan# HPK0600158

STYLE: MEDITERRANEAN
SQUARE FOOTAGE: 2,241
BEDROOMS: 4
BATHROOMS: 2½
WIDTH: 55' - 0"
DEPTH: 61' - 0"
FOUNDATION: SLAB

SEARCH ONLINE @ EPLANS.COM

A stucco facade and corner quoins lend European charm to this traditional design. The floor plan conveniently places sleeping quarters to one side of the plan and living areas to the other. Four bedrooms sit to the right of the plan—one is a large master suite with two walk-in closets and a private bath, and three are secondary bedrooms that share a full hall bath. To the left, columns separate the dining room from the central living room, which features a fireplace and overlooks the rear porch. The kitchen includes wrapping counters and shares a snack bar with the breakfast nook. Just beyond the breakfast nook, a utility room and half-bath complete the plan.

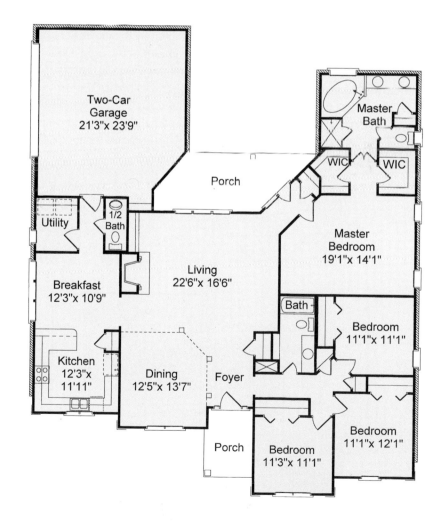

Classic symmetry and four elegant columns make this home a gem in any neighborhood. Inside, luxury is evident by the dimensions of each room. The foyer is flanked by a large, yet cozy library to the right and a gracefully formal living room to the left. It's just a couple of steps up into the formal dining room here, making this area perfect for entertaining. Toward the rear of the home, casual living takes place, with a huge family room connecting to a sunny breakfast room and near an efficient kitchen. The bedrooms are upstairs and include a deluxe master suite with a sumptuous private bath.

plan # HPK0600159

STYLE: INTERNATIONAL
FIRST FLOOR: 1,482 SQ. FT.
SECOND FLOOR: 1,460 SQ. FT.
TOTAL: 2,942 SQ. FT.
BEDROOMS: 4
BATHROOMS: 2½
WIDTH: 48' - 0"
DEPTH: 52' - 0"
FOUNDATION: BASEMENT

SEARCH ONLINE @ EPLANS.COM

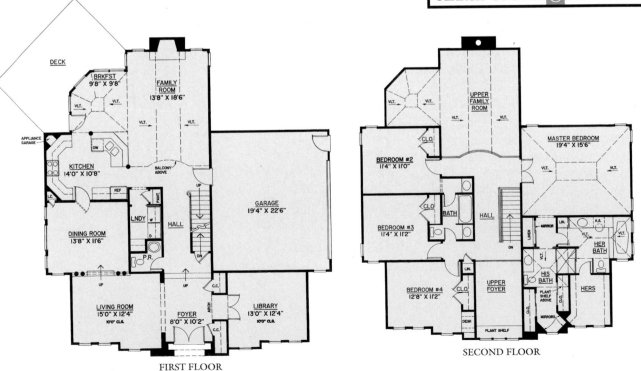

FIRST FLOOR

SECOND FLOOR

plan # HPK0600160 LD

STYLE: NEOCLASSIC
FIRST FLOOR: 2,328 SQ. FT.
SECOND FLOOR: 603 SQ. FT.
TOTAL: 2,931 SQ. FT.
BEDROOMS: 3
BATHROOMS: 2½ + ½
WIDTH: 69' - 4"
DEPTH: 66' - 0"
FOUNDATION: BASEMENT

SEARCH ONLINE @ EPLANS.COM

This home will keep even the most active family from feeling cramped. A broad foyer opens to a living room that measures 24 feet across and features sliding glass doors to a rear terrace and a covered porch. Adjacent to the kitchen is a conversation area with additional access to the covered porch and also includes a snack bar, fireplace, and window bay. A butler's pantry leads to the formal dining room. Placed conveniently on the first floor, the master bedroom features a roomy bath with a huge walk-in closet and dual vanities. A library with plenty of blank wall space for bookcases completes this level. Two large bedrooms are found on the second floor and share a full hall bath.

MOVE-UP HOMES

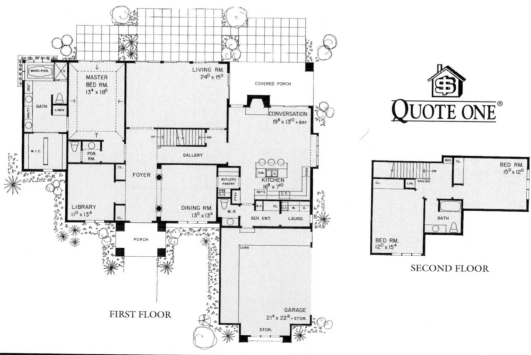

FIRST FLOOR

SECOND FLOOR

Multipane windows, shutters, and shingle accents adorn the stucco facade of this wonderful French Country home. Inside, the foyer introduces the hearth-warmed great room that features French-door access to the rear deck. The dining room, defined from the foyer and great room by columns, enjoys front-yard views. The master bedroom includes two walk-in closets, rear-deck access, and a dual-vanity bath. The informal living areas have an open plan. The box-bayed breakfast nook joins the cooktop-island kitchen and hearth-warmed family room. The second floor holds two bedrooms with walk-in closets, a study, and an unfinished bedroom for future expansion.

plan # HPK0600161

STYLE: EUROPEAN COTTAGE
FIRST FLOOR: 1,840 SQ. FT.
SECOND FLOOR: 840 SQ. FT.
TOTAL: 2,680 SQ. FT.
BONUS SPACE: 295 SQ. FT.
BEDROOMS: 3
BATHROOMS: 2½
WIDTH: 66' - 0"
DEPTH: 65' - 10"
FOUNDATION: CRAWLSPACE

SEARCH ONLINE @ EPLANS.COM

FIRST FLOOR

SECOND FLOOR

plan # HPK0600162

STYLE: FRENCH
FIRST FLOOR: 1,900 SQ. FT.
SECOND FLOOR: 890 SQ. FT.
TOTAL: 2,790 SQ. FT.
BEDROOMS: 4
BATHROOMS: 2½
WIDTH: 63' - 0"
DEPTH: 51' - 0"
FOUNDATION:
WALKOUT BASEMENT

SEARCH ONLINE @ EPLANS.COM

A perfect blend of stucco and stacked stone sets off keystones, transoms, and arches in this French Country facade to inspire an elegant spirit. The foyer is flanked by the spacious dining room and study, which is accented by a vaulted ceiling and a fireplace. A great room with a full wall of glass connects the interior with the outdoors. A first-floor master suite offers both style and intimacy with a coffered ceiling and a secluded bath.

FIRST FLOOR

SECOND FLOOR

QUOTE ONE®

Sitting Area

Master Suite
16⁶ x 14⁰

TRAY CEILING

Vaulted M.Bath

W.i.c.

Pwdr.

Vaulted Family Room
15⁸ x 20²

Kitchen
11'-0" HIGH CLG.

Breakfast
11'-0" HIGH CLG.

Bedroom 2
11⁰ x 13⁰

W.i.c.

Bath

W.i.c.

Bedroom 3
12¹⁰ x 11⁶

Foyer
14'-0" HIGH CLG.

Dining Room
12⁰ x 14⁰
14'-0" HIGH CLG.

Laund.

Living Room
13⁵ x 14⁰

COVERED ENTRY

Garage
20⁵ x 20⁹

GARAGE LOCATION WITH BASEMENT

copyright © 1995 frank betz associates, inc.

SECOND FLOOR

BED RM.
11-4 x 11-4

attic storage

LOFT
9-0 x 9-0

family room below

railing

BONUS RM.
14-9 x 13-0

6-3 x 5-10

bath

attic storage

BED RM.
11-4 x 11-4

foyer below

FIRST FLOOR

PATIO

MASTER BED RM.
13-4 x 16-8

FAMILY RM.
18-0 x 16-6
(cathedral ceiling)
fireplace
balcony above

BRKFST.
11-4 x 10-0

UTILITY
8-4 x 6-0

storage

KIT.
11-4 x 12-0

GARAGE
21-0 x 24-0

walk-in closet

walk-in closet

pd. rm.

master bath

LIVING RM./ STUDY
12-0 x 12-0
shelves

DINING
11-4 x 13-0

FOYER
9-8 x 11-10

storage

PORCH

© 1998 Donald A Gardner, Inc.

plan # HPK0600163

STYLE: COUNTRY COTTAGE
SQUARE FOOTAGE: 2,322
BEDROOMS: 3
BATHROOMS: 2½
WIDTH: 62' - 0"
DEPTH: 61' - 0"
FOUNDATION: CRAWLSPACE,
SLAB, BASEMENT

SEARCH ONLINE @ EPLANS.COM

plan # HPK0600164

STYLE: TRADITIONAL
FIRST FLOOR: 1,701 SQ. FT.
SECOND FLOOR: 534 SQ. FT.
TOTAL: 2,235 SQ. FT.
BONUS SPACE: 274 SQ. FT.
BEDROOMS: 3
BATHROOMS: 2½
WIDTH: 65' - 11"
DEPTH: 43' - 5"

SEARCH ONLINE @ EPLANS.COM

plan # HPK0600165

STYLE: FRENCH
FIRST FLOOR: 1,530 SQ. FT.
SECOND FLOOR: 1,252 SQ. FT.
TOTAL: 2,782 SQ. FT.
BONUS SPACE: 264 SQ. FT.
BEDROOMS: 4
BATHROOMS: 3½
WIDTH: 62' - 0"
DEPTH: 47' - 0"
FOUNDATION: BASEMENT

SEARCH ONLINE @ EPLANS.COM

Chateau style shapes the facade of this alluring European manor. Double doors open into a two-story foyer flanked on either side by a formal dining room with a butler's tray and a parlor. Straight ahead, the living room/den is warmed by a fireplace and features a wet bar. Nearby, the guest bedroom accesses the powder room. The island countertop kitchen provides a walk-in pantry and is open to the breakfast room. The vaulted keeping room is illuminated by dazzling skylights and is warmed by a fireplace. A garage completes the first floor. Upstairs, the lavish master suite provides a private bath and huge walk-in closet. Two additional bedrooms that feature walk-in closets share a bath between them. Down the hall, a bonus room is reserved for future use. The second-floor laundry is made convenient for family use.

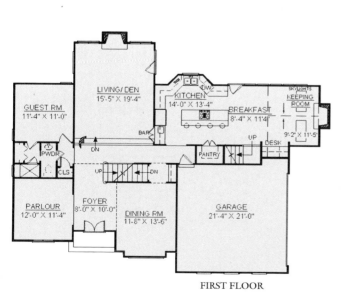

FIRST FLOOR

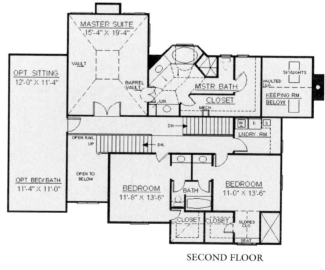

SECOND FLOOR

plan# HPK0600166

STYLE: COUNTRY COTTAGE
FIRST FLOOR: 1,883 SQ. FT.
SECOND FLOOR: 803 SQ. FT.
TOTAL: 2,686 SQ. FT.
BEDROOMS: 4
BATHROOMS: 3½
WIDTH: 58' - 6"
DEPTH: 59' - 4"
FOUNDATION:
CRAWLSPACE, BASEMENT

SEARCH ONLINE @ EPLANS.COM

A grand facade is a perfect introduction to this stately two-story home that's designed for both formal and casual family living. A two-story foyer that leads to the vaulted living room is punctuated by a dramatic arch with a plant shelf above. Formal entertaining areas are nicely balanced with the vaulted family room and the gourmet kitchen and breakfast nook. The first-floor master suite is designed for luxury and privacy. Upstairs are three family bedrooms—each has a walk-in closet and private bath access.

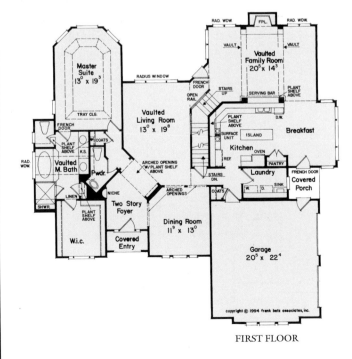

FIRST FLOOR

SECOND FLOOR

plan # HPK0600167

STYLE: EUROPEAN COTTAGE
FIRST FLOOR: 1,763 SQ. FT.
SECOND FLOOR: 947 SQ. FT.
TOTAL: 2,710 SQ. FT.
BEDROOMS: 3
BATHROOMS: 2½
WIDTH: 50' - 0"
DEPTH: 75' - 4"
FOUNDATION:
WALKOUT BASEMENT

SEARCH ONLINE @ EPLANS.COM

A special feature of this classy home is the second-floor media room and adjoining exercise area. Convenient to two upstairs bedrooms and a full bath, the media room is a great place for family computers and a fax machine. On the main level, a gourmet kitchen provides a snack counter and a walk-in pantry. Double doors open to a gallery hall that leads to the formal dining room—an enchanting retreat for chandelier-lit evenings—that provides a breathtaking view of the front yard. A classic great room is warmed by a cozy fireplace and brightened by a wall of windows. The outdoor living area is spacious enough for grand events. The master suite is brightened by sweeping views of the backyard and a romantic fireplace just for two.

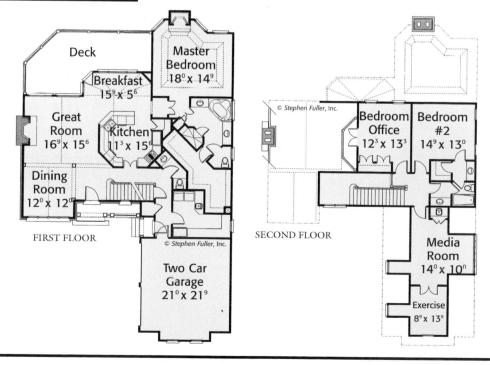

Deck

Master Bedroom
18⁰ x 14⁹

Breakfast
15⁹ x 5⁶

Great Room
16⁹ x 15⁶

Kitchen
11³ x 15⁶

Dining Room
12⁰ x 12⁰

© Stephen Fuller, Inc.

FIRST FLOOR

Two Car Garage
21⁰ x 21⁹

SECOND FLOOR

© Stephen Fuller, Inc.

Bedroom Office
12³ x 13³

Bedroom #2
14⁹ x 13⁰

Media Room
14⁰ x 10⁰

Exercise
8⁹ x 13⁹

SECOND FLOOR

BEDROOM 4
12' X 11'8"
8'CLG.

BEDROOM 3
13'4" X 11'6"
8'CLG.

DN
RAIL

FUTURE
BONUS ROOM
30' X 14'

FIRST FLOOR

BEDROOM 2
12'6" X 11'4"
9'CLG.

LIVING
19'8" X 16'
12'CLG.
SLOPE
9' TO 12'

BOOKS
ARCH
BOOKS

MASTER
BEDROOM
16'6" X 13'4"
SLOPE
9' TO 12'

NOOK
11'8" X 11'8"
9'CLG.
EATING BAR

KITCHEN
13'6" X 13'6"
9'CLG.
ISLAND

DRESSER

BOOKS
STUDY
11' X 11'4"
9'CLG.

11'CLG.

DINING
12' X 11'8"
9'CLG.

PANTRY

W D
LAUNDRY

UP
DN

OPTIONAL BASEMENT
STAIRS

ARCH

GARAGE
29'6" X 20'6"

plan# HPK0600168

STYLE: EUROPEAN COTTAGE
FIRST FLOOR: 2,014 SQ. FT.
SECOND FLOOR: 573 SQ. FT.
TOTAL: 2,587 SQ. FT.
BONUS SPACE: 420 SQ. FT.
BEDROOMS: 4
BATHROOMS: 3
WIDTH: 56' - 0"
DEPTH: 71' - 0"

Covered Patio

SITTING AREA

MstrBed
16x17
PULLMAN CEILING
FROM 8'-0" TO 10'-0"

Brkfst Area
13x10
10'-0" CLG. HT.

Bed#2
12x10
9'-0" CLG. HT.

Bed#3
12x12
9'-0" CLG. HT.

W.I. Closet

MstrBth
VAULTED CLG. FROM
8'-0" TO 11'-6"

Great Room
20x17
11'-6" CLG. HT.

Entertainment
Center

Kitchen
13x12
10'-0" CLG. HT.

Bth
#2

W.I.
Closet

Niche

Bth#3

WALK-IN
CLOSET
9'-0" CLG. HT.

Gallery
11'-0" CLG. HT.

Utl
9'-0" CLG. HT.

Bed#4
11x12
9'-0" CLG. HT.

Coats

Pantry

Closet

Coats Strg

PWDR
Pedestal

Entry
11'-0" CLG. HT.

Formal
Dining
11x13
11'-0" CLG. HT.

Three-Car Garage
8'-4" CLG. HT.

Chest

Study
12x11
9'-0" CLG. HT.

Books

Covered
Porch

plan# HPK0600169

STYLE: FRENCH
SQUARE FOOTAGE: 2,590
BEDROOMS: 4
BATHROOMS: 3½
WIDTH: 73' - 6"
DEPTH: 64' - 10"
FOUNDATION: SLAB

plan # HPK0600170

L

STYLE: FRENCH
FIRST FLOOR: 1,566 SQ. FT.
SECOND FLOOR: 837 SQ. FT.
TOTAL: 2,403 SQ. FT.
BEDROOMS: 4
BATHROOMS: 3½
WIDTH: 116' - 3"
DEPTH: 55' - 1"
FOUNDATION: BASEMENT

SEARCH ONLINE @ EPLANS.COM

Be the owner of your own country estate—this two-story home gives the look and feel of grand-style living without the expense of large square footage. The entry leads to a massive foyer and great hall. There's space enough here for living and dining areas. Two window seats in the great hall overlook the rear veranda. One fireplace warms the living area, another looks through the dining room to the kitchen and breakfast nook. A screened porch offers casual dining space for warm weather. The master suite has another fireplace and a window seat and adjoins a luxurious master bath with a separate tub and shower. The second floor contains three family bedrooms and two full baths. A separate apartment over the garage includes its own living room, kitchen, and bedroom.

FIRST FLOOR

SECOND FLOOR

plan # HPK0600171

The side-loading three-car garage is set back and hidden from view, keeping this home's facade clean and fresh. The family room and entry flank the study where it widens into the gallery. From here you enter the magnificent great room with its fireplace and patio beyond, or turn left to reach the lavish master suite. To the right, find the two family bedrooms with the shared full bath, or the diamond-shaped kitchen with the adjoining breakfast nook. The utility room is tucked behind the staircase that rises to the future bonus room.

STYLE: EUROPEAN COTTAGE
SQUARE FOOTAGE: 2,530
BONUS SPACE: 270 SQ. FT.
BEDROOMS: 3
BATHROOMS: 2½
WIDTH: 83' - 10"
DEPTH: 51' - 10"
FOUNDATION: SLAB

SEARCH ONLINE @ EPLANS.COM

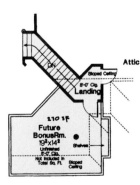

plan # HPK0600172

STYLE: TRANSITIONAL
FIRST FLOOR: 1,915 SQ. FT.
SECOND FLOOR: 823 SQ. FT.
TOTAL: 2,738 SQ. FT.
BEDROOMS: 4
BATHROOMS: 3½
WIDTH: 63' - 4"
DEPTH: 48' - 0"
FOUNDATION: BASEMENT

SEARCH ONLINE @ EPLANS.COM

A European feel is shown on the exterior facade of this exciting two-story home and hints at the exquisite grace of the interior. The sensational view at the foyer includes high windows across the rear wall, a fireplace, open stairs with rich wood trim, and volume ceilings. The formal dining room offers dimension to the entry and is conveniently located for serving from the kitchen. The spacious breakfast room, wraparound bar in the kitchen, and open hearth room offer a cozy gathering place for family members. The deluxe master bedroom suite boasts an 11-foot ceiling, a sitting area, and a garden bath. The second-floor balcony leads to a bedroom suite with a private bath and two additional bedrooms with large closets and private access to a shared bath.

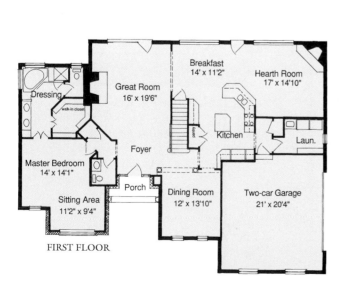

FIRST FLOOR

SECOND FLOOR

SECOND FLOOR

FIRST FLOOR

ptan# HPK0600173

STYLE: COUNTRY COTTAGE
FIRST FLOOR: 1,355 SQ. FT.
SECOND FLOOR: 1,347 SQ. FT.
TOTAL: 2,702 SQ. FT.
BONUS SPACE: 285 SQ. FT.
BEDROOMS: 4
BATHROOMS: 4
WIDTH: 41' - 0"
DEPTH: 66' - 0"
FOUNDATION:
CRAWLSPACE, BASEMENT

SEARCH ONLINE @ EPLANS.COM

SECOND FLOOR

FIRST FLOOR

ptan# HPK0600174

STYLE: NORMAN
FIRST FLOOR: 1,932 SQ. FT.
SECOND FLOOR: 1,052 SQ. FT.
TOTAL: 2,984 SQ. FT.
BEDROOMS: 4
BATHROOMS: 3½
WIDTH: 50' - 0"
DEPTH: 51' - 0"
FOUNDATION:
SLAB, BASEMENT

SEARCH ONLINE @ EPLANS.COM

plan # HPK0600175

STYLE: CAPE COD
FIRST FLOOR: 1,626 SQ. FT.
SECOND FLOOR: 475 SQ. FT.
TOTAL: 2,101 SQ. FT.
BEDROOMS: 3
BATHROOMS: 2½
WIDTH: 59' - 0"
DEPTH: 60' - 8"
FOUNDATION: BASEMENT

SEARCH ONLINE @ EPLANS.COM

An exterior with a rich solid look and an exciting roofline is very important to the discriminating buyer. An octagonal and vaulted master bedroom with a vaulted ceiling and a sunken great room with a balcony above provide this home with all the amenities. The island kitchen is easily accessible to both the breakfast area and the bayed dining area. The tapered staircase leads to two family bedrooms, each with their own access to a full dual-vanity bath. Both bedrooms have a vast closet area with double doors.

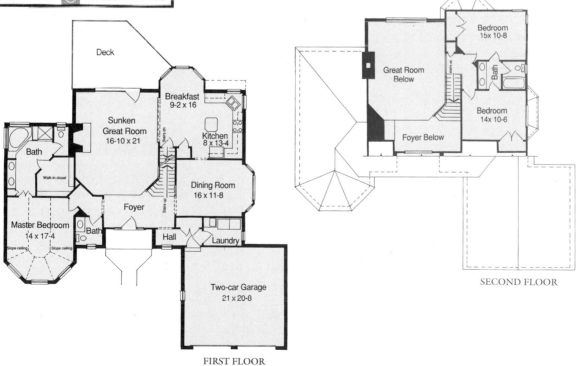

FIRST FLOOR

SECOND FLOOR

SECOND FLOOR

FIRST FLOOR

QUOTE ONE®

plan # HPK0600178

STYLE: TRANSITIONAL
FIRST FLOOR: 1,915 SQ. FT.
SECOND FLOOR: 823 SQ. FT.
TOTAL: 2,738 SQ. FT.
BEDROOMS: 4
BATHROOMS: 3½
WIDTH: 63' - 4"
DEPTH: 48' - 0"
FOUNDATION: BASEMENT

SEARCH ONLINE @ EPLANS.COM

A luxuriously styled exterior with wood and stone trim, a boxed window, and an octagonal tower combine with a functional floor plan to create a home that will excite the most discriminating buyer. The spectacular view offered at the foyer includes high windows across the rear wall, a fireplace, open stairs with rich wood trim, and a volume ceiling. The formal dining room adds dimension to the entry. The spacious breakfast room opens to the hearth room, offering a comfortable gathering place. The first-floor master suite boasts a sitting alcove and a deluxe bath. The second-floor balcony leads to three family bedrooms.

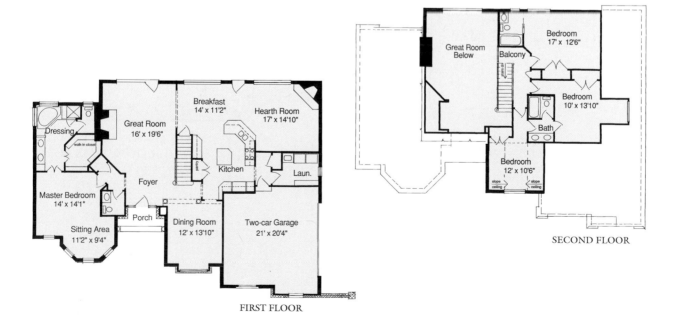

FIRST FLOOR

SECOND FLOOR

QUOTE ONE®

BEDROOM NO. 3
11'-6" X 11'-0"

BATH

BEDROOM NO. 2
11'-4" X 11'-0"

SUN ROOM
12'-0" X 13'-8"

PORCH

MASTER
BATH

W.I.C.

PORCH

BREAKFAST
10'-0" X 9'-0"

MASTER BEDROOM
13'-4" X 15'-6"

FAMILY ROOM
18'-0" X 14'-0"

LAUNDRY

KITCHEN
12'-0" X 13'-2"

BATH

STORAGE

DN

DINING ROOM
11'-4" X 11'-4"

FOYER
6'-8" X 11'-10"

TWO CAR GARAGE
20'-4" X 19'-8"

PORCH

DEN/GUEST
BEDROOM
11'-4" X 14'-0"

plan# HPK0600179

STYLE: COUNTRY COTTAGE
SQUARE FOOTAGE: 2,170
BEDROOMS: 4
BATHROOMS: 3
WIDTH: 62' - 0"
DEPTH: 61' - 6"
FOUNDATION: WALKOUT
BASEMENT

SEARCH ONLINE @ EPLANS.COM

VAULT
PLANT SHELF

Great Room
Below

Bath

LINEN

Bedroom 3
12⁰ x 12⁰

OPEN RAIL   OVERLOOK

Foyer
Below

STAIRS
DN

Bedroom 2
12⁰ x 12³

W.i.c.

W.i.c.

PLANT SHELF

Opt. Bonus
Room
11⁵ x 20¹⁰

SECOND FLOOR

RADIUS
WINDOW

TRANSOM
ABOVE

PPL.

TRANSOM
ABOVE

FRENCH
DOOR

SEAT
SHWR.

Vaulted
M.Bath
12'-0" HIGH
CLG.

Vaulted
Great Room
15⁰ x 19⁰

SERVING
BAR

Breakfast

ISLAND

DW.

Bedroom 4/
Study
11⁶ x 11⁰

PANTRY

PLANT
SHELF
ABOVE

FRENCH
DOOR

His   Hers

LINEN

KS.

PLANT
SHELF
ABOVE

RANGE

REF.

Kitchen

Bath

TRAY CLG.

Master Suite
13⁰ x 15⁰

OPEN RAIL

STAIRS
DN

COATS

SINK
W.   D.

Laund.

Two Story
Foyer

Dining Room
12⁰ x 12³

Covered
Entry

Sitting Area
11⁰ x 6⁵

Garage
19⁵ x 22³

copyright © 1998 frank betz associates, inc.

FIRST FLOOR

plan# HPK0600180

STYLE: COUNTRY COTTAGE
FIRST FLOOR: 1,688 SQ. FT.
SECOND FLOOR: 558 SQ. FT.
TOTAL: 2,246 SQ. FT.
BONUS SPACE: 269 SQ. FT.
BEDROOMS: 4
BATHROOMS: 3
WIDTH: 54' - 0"
DEPTH: 48' - 0"
FOUNDATION: CRAWLSPACE,
SLAB, BASEMENT

SEARCH ONLINE @ EPLANS.COM

plan # HPK0600181

STYLE: TRANSITIONAL
FIRST FLOOR: 1,309 SQ. FT.
SECOND FLOOR: 1,119 SQ. FT.
TOTAL: 2,428 SQ. FT.
BEDROOMS: 4
BATHROOMS: 2½
WIDTH: 54' - 6"
DEPTH: 41' - 10"
FOUNDATION: BASEMENT

SEARCH ONLINE @ EPLANS.COM

This traditional home boasts elegant arched windows and gabled rooflines. From the porch, enter the foyer that is flanked by the formal living room with an arched ceiling and dining room with a bay window. The family room features a spacious layout and enjoys a warming hearth, picture windows that bring in natural light, and access to the rear property. The breakfast room pairs up with the gourmet kitchen and the snack bar to serve the family and handle entertaining needs. Upstairs, three family bedrooms share a full bath that has dual vanities. The master suite is made for luxury with a compartmented toilet, separate bath and shower, His and Hers vanities, and an oversized walk-in closet.

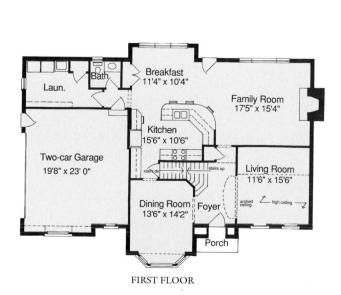

FIRST FLOOR

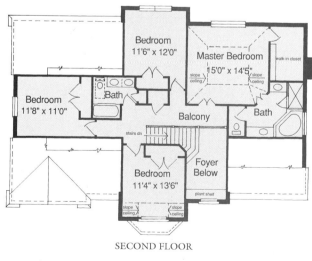

SECOND FLOOR

plan# HPK0600182

STYLE: TRADITIONAL
SQUARE FOOTAGE: 2,172
BEDROOMS: 3
BATHROOMS: 3
WIDTH: 76' - 0"
DEPTH: 46' - 0"

SEARCH ONLINE @ EPLANS.COM

QUOTE ONE®

Pto.
PARTIALLY COVERED

TRANSOMS   TRANSOMS

Gar.
20⁴ x 28⁷

Kit.
9⁰ x 14⁰

Bfst.
10⁰ x 14⁰

Grt. rm.
16⁰ x 20⁰
11'-0" CEILING

Mbr.
13⁰ x 16⁴
10'-0" CEILING

DESK

BOOKS

PANT.

SERVERY

WHIRL-POOL

STORAGE

SKYLIGHT

Br.3
11⁰ x 12⁰
OPTIONAL DEN

Din.
12⁰ x 15⁴
11'-0" CEILING

E.

COVERED STOOP

Liv.
12⁰ x 13⁴
OPT. BEDROOM
11'-0" CEILING

Br.2
11⁰ x 12⁰

DN

This one-story home with grand rooflines enjoys a convenient floor plan. The great room with a fireplace complements a front-facing living room. The formal dining room with a tray ceiling sits just across the hall from the living room and is also easily accessible to the kitchen. An island, pantry, breakfast room, and patio are highlights in the kitchen. A bedroom at this end of the house works fine as an office or guest bedroom. Two additional bedrooms are to the right of the plan: a master suite with a grand bath and an additional family bedroom.

plan # HPK0600183

STYLE: TRADITIONAL
FIRST FLOOR: 1,207 SQ. FT.
SECOND FLOOR: 1,181 SQ. FT.
TOTAL: 2,388 SQ. FT.
BEDROOMS: 4
BATHROOMS: 2½
WIDTH: 59' - 10"
DEPTH: 37' - 4"
FOUNDATION: BASEMENT

SEARCH ONLINE @ Eplans.com

Homeowners are perfectly pampered in this luxurious home. Double gables, an exciting arched entry, wood trim, and sidelights adorn the exterior, while the interior blends formal spaces with casual living areas. The large island kitchen serves both the dining room and the sunny breakfast bay. The cozy family room offers a warming fireplace and access to the rear deck. The master suite and three family bedrooms are located on the second floor.

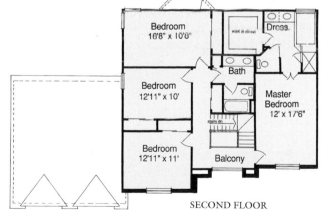

SECOND FLOOR

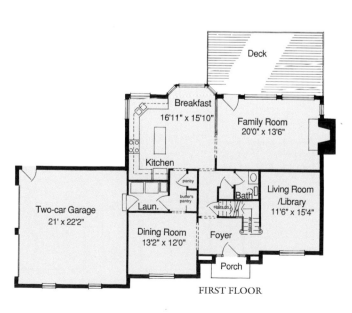

FIRST FLOOR

plan# HPK0600184

Arch-top and multipane window treatments give the elevation of this four-bedroom, two-story home an unmistakable elegance. Inside, the floor plan is equally appealing. Note the bay windows in the formal dining room and living area, visible from the entrance foyer. The large family room has a fireplace and opens to the food-preparation area via an angled breakfast bar. A spacious, sunlit breakfast area adjoins the kitchen which features a nearby walk-in pantry and internal access to the garage. The second-floor master suite is highlighted by a tray ceiling, walk-in closet, and luxurious master bath including a large tub, shower, and dual vanities. A separate bedroom suite and two family bedrooms sharing a full bath complete the second floor with a conveniently placed upstairs laundry.

STYLE: TRADITIONAL
FIRST FLOOR: 1,230 SQ. FT.
SECOND FLOOR: 1,496 SQ. FT.
TOTAL: 2,726 SQ. FT.
BEDROOMS: 4
BATHROOMS: 3½
WIDTH: 60' - 0"
DEPTH: 34' - 6"
FOUNDATION: CRAWLSPACE,
SLAB, BASEMENT

SEARCH ONLINE @ EPLANS.COM

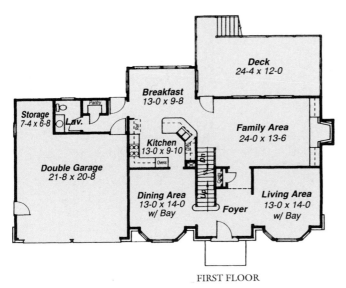

FIRST FLOOR

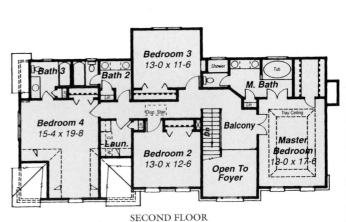

SECOND FLOOR

plan # HPK0600185

STYLE: TRADITIONAL
FIRST FLOOR: 1,583 SQ. FT.
SECOND FLOOR: 1,331 SQ. FT.
TOTAL: 2,914 SQ. FT.
BEDROOMS: 4
BATHROOMS: 3½
WIDTH: 58' - 0"
DEPTH: 59' - 4"

SEARCH ONLINE @ EPLANS.COM

A dramatic elevation with bright windows hints at the luxurious floor plan of this four-bedroom, two-story home. Upon entry, a beautiful staircase and formal living spaces are in sight. To the right, transom windows and a volume ceiling grace the living room. The dining room accommodates a hutch. The large family room includes elegant bowed windows and a showy three-sided fireplace. A bright dinette and snack bar are served by the open island kitchen. Step up a half-flight of stairs to a private den with double doors and a special ceiling treatment. All secondary bedrooms access either a Hollywood bath or a private bath. A tiered ceiling, sumptuous bath, and two closets highlight the master suite.

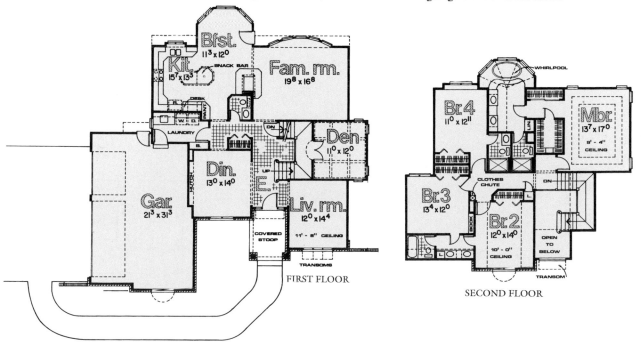

FIRST FLOOR

SECOND FLOOR

plan# HPK0600186

An impressive two-story entrance welcomes you to this stately home. Massive chimneys and pillars and varying rooflines add interest to the stucco exterior. The foyer, lighted by a clerestory window, opens to the formal living and dining rooms. The living room—which could also serve as a study—features a fireplace, as does the family room. Both rooms access the patio. The L-shaped island kitchen opens to a bay-windowed breakfast nook, which is echoed by the sitting area in the master suite. A room next to the kitchen could serve as a bedroom or a home office. The second floor contains two family bedrooms plus a bonus room for future expansion.

STYLE: TRADITIONAL
FIRST FLOOR: 2,249 SQ. FT.
SECOND FLOOR: 620 SQ. FT.
TOTAL: 2,869 SQ. FT.
BONUS SPACE: 308 SQ. FT.
BEDROOMS: 4
BATHROOMS: 3½
WIDTH: 69' - 6"
DEPTH: 52' - 0"

SEARCH ONLINE @ EPLANS.COM

FIRST FLOOR

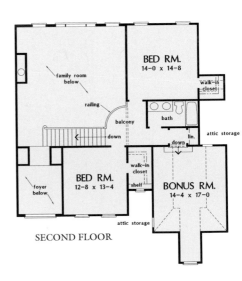

SECOND FLOOR

plan # HPK0600187

STYLE: TRADITIONAL
FIRST FLOOR: 1,860 SQ. FT.
SECOND FLOOR: 848 SQ. FT.
TOTAL: 2,708 SQ. FT.
BEDROOMS: 4
BATHROOMS: 3½
WIDTH: 56' - 0"
DEPTH: 59' - 4"

SEARCH ONLINE @ EPLANS.COM

The gorgeous entry of this traditional home opens to a formal dining room, which offers hutch space, and a volume living room with a see-through fireplace to the spacious family room. Adjacent is the bayed breakfast area and the island kitchen with a wraparound counter and a walk-in pantry. The master suite is highlighted with a formal ceiling in the bedroom and a bath with a two-person whirlpool tub, bayed windows and a double vanity. Upstairs, two bedrooms share private access to a compartmented bath; another bedroom has a private bath.

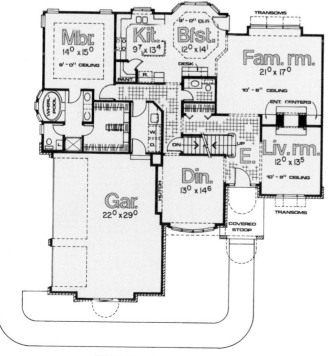

FIRST FLOOR

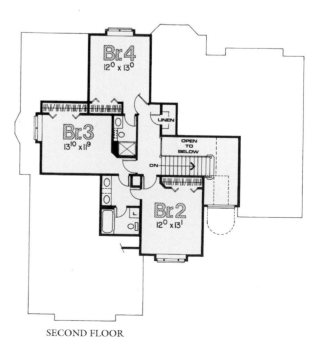

SECOND FLOOR

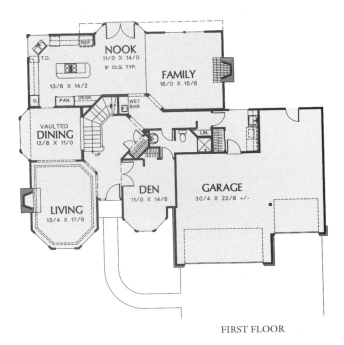

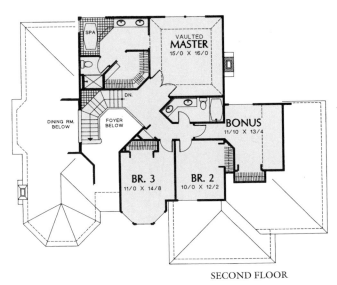

plan # HPK0600188

L

This country home offers a fresh face and plenty of personality, starting with its sunny bay with transom windows and a two-story turret. Inside, the foyer opens to a quiet den—the lower bay of the turret—through French doors. A formal living room with a tray ceiling leads to the vaulted dining room, which is served by a gourmet kitchen. To the rear of the plan, a spacious family area offers its own fireplace with a tiled hearth. Upstairs, a secluded master suite boasts a corner tiled-rim spa tub and an angled walk-in closet. Two family bedrooms share a full bath and a hall that leads to a sizable bonus room.

STYLE: TRADITIONAL
FIRST FLOOR: 1,586 SQ. FT.
SECOND FLOOR: 960 SQ. FT.
TOTAL: 2,546 SQ. FT.
BONUS SPACE: 194 SQ. FT.
BEDROOMS: 3
BATHROOMS: 3
WIDTH: 63' - 0"
DEPTH: 50' - 0"
FOUNDATION: CRAWLSPACE

SEARCH ONLINE @ EPLANS.COM

FIRST FLOOR

SECOND FLOOR

plan# HPK0600189

STYLE: CONTEMPORARY
FIRST FLOOR: 1,481 SQ. FT.
SECOND FLOOR: 1,315 SQ. FT.
TOTAL: 2,796 SQ. FT.
BEDROOMS: 4
BATHROOMS: 2½
WIDTH: 53' - 10"
DEPTH: 41' - 0"
FOUNDATION: BASEMENT,
CRAWLSPACE, SLAB

SEARCH ONLINE @ EPLANS.COM

Striking reverse gable elements with specialty windows set into a broad, encompassing, hipped roof provide this home its distinctive curb appeal. High entry doors capped by a dramatic window lead into a two-story reception foyer with a panoramic view of the house. The living room features a vaulted ceiling and a wraparound front bay. The kitchen includes an expansive wraparound counter, large center island, 10-foot ceiling and bayed breakfast area. The sensational private master suite contains two walk-in closets, a dressing alcove, a fireplace, and a beautiful bath with a vaulted ceiling, whirlpool tub, and specialty window.

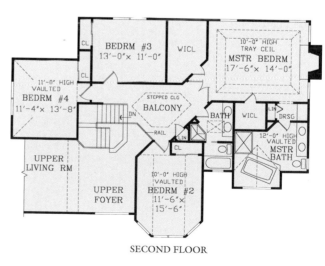

SECOND FLOOR

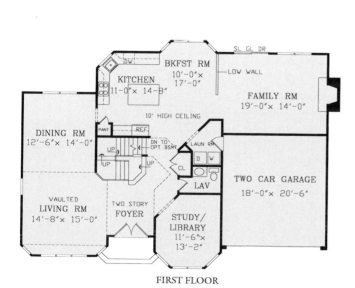

FIRST FLOOR

plan# HPK0600190

STYLE: CONTEMPORARY
FIRST FLOOR: 1,890 SQ. FT.
SECOND FLOOR: 923 SQ. FT.
TOTAL: 2,813 SQ. FT.
BEDROOMS: 4
BATHROOMS: 2½
WIDTH: 84' - 10"
DEPTH: 48' - 0"
FOUNDATION: CRAWLSPACE,
SLAB, BASEMENT

SEARCH ONLINE @ EPLANS.COM

Whether finished in traditional siding or cool stucco, this contemporary home will catch the eye of passersby. Inside, a soaring cathedral ceiling flows from the foyer to the vast living room, defined by an upper-level bridge. On the left, a large dining room serves up elegant meals with the help of a butler's pantry. The breakfast nook is just off the gourmet kitchen and offers sliding glass doors to the rear property. The right wing hosts a den and the magnificent master suite. Upstairs, three family bedrooms share a full bath and a skylit family room. A lovely guest suite with a sitting area also resides on this level. Completing the plan is a three-car garage with mudroom access.

FIRST FLOOR

SECOND FLOOR

plan # HPK0600191

STYLE: CONTEMPORARY
FIRST FLOOR: 1,575 SQ. FT.
SECOND FLOOR: 1,338 SQ. FT.
TOTAL: 2,913 SQ. FT.
BEDROOMS: 4
BATHROOMS: 3
WIDTH: 66' - 0"
DEPTH: 48' - 0"
FOUNDATION: CRAWLSPACE

SEARCH ONLINE @ EPLANS.COM

This two-story home is impressive from the first glance. A two-story bay window graces both the cozy den on the first floor and the deluxe master suite on the second floor. Inside, to the right of the foyer is the formal living room, enhanced by a corner full of windows and by a warming fireplace. This room opens to the rear of the plan into a formal dining room, which is just steps away from a large and efficient island kitchen. Casual living is comfortable in the attached nook, with the nearby family room sporting a second fireplace. Upstairs, three family bedrooms offer plenty of storage and share a hall bath. The master suite is impressive with its tray ceiling, large walk-in closet, twin vanities, and corner spa. A three-car garage easily holds the family fleet.

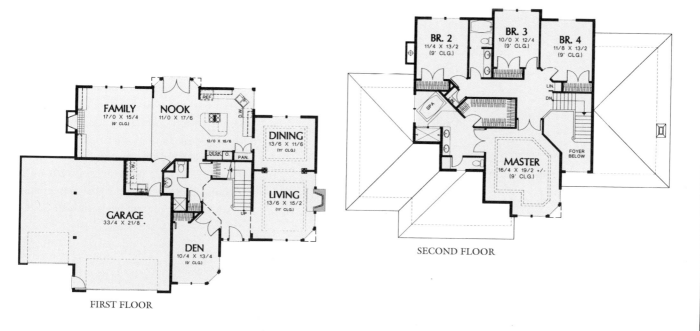

FIRST FLOOR

SECOND FLOOR

plan# HPK0600192

STYLE: INTERNATIONAL
SQUARE FOOTAGE: 2,293
BONUS SPACE: 509 SQ. FT.
BEDROOMS: 3
BATHROOMS: 2
WIDTH: 51' - 0"
DEPTH: 79' - 4"
FOUNDATION: SLAB

SEARCH ONLINE @ EPLANS.COM

Multiple rooflines, shutters, and a charming vaulted entry lend interest and depth to the exterior of this well-designed three-bedroom home. Inside, double doors to the left open to a cozy den. The dining room, open to the family room and foyer, features a stunning ceiling design. A fireplace and patio access and view adorn the family room. Two family bedrooms share a double-sink bathroom to the right, while the master bedroom resides to the left. Note the private patio access, two walk-in closets, and luxurious bath that ensure a restful retreat for the homeowner.

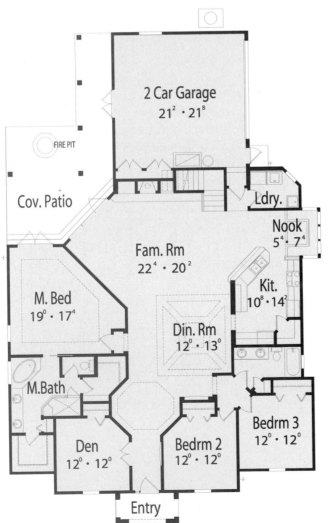

FIRE PIT

2 Car Garage
21² · 21⁸

Cov. Patio

Ldry.

Nook
5⁴ · 7⁴

Fam. Rm
22⁴ · 20²

Kit.
10⁸ · 14²

M. Bed
19⁰ · 17⁴

Din. Rm
12⁰ · 13⁰

M. Bath

Den
12⁰ · 12⁰

Bedrm 2
12⁰ · 12⁰

Bedrm 3
12⁰ · 12⁰

Entry

plan # HPK0600193

L

STYLE: FRENCH
SQUARE FOOTAGE: 2,775
BEDROOMS: 3
BATHROOMS: 2½
WIDTH: 74' - 0"
DEPTH: 59' - 0"
FOUNDATION: CRAWLSPACE

SEARCH ONLINE @ EPLANS.COM

A quaint dining gazebo adds a delightful touch to the facade of this lovely home. It complements the formal living room, with a fireplace, found just to the right of the entry foyer (be sure to notice the elegant guest bath to the left). Family living takes place at the rear of the plan in a large family room with a through-fireplace to the study. A breakfast nook enhances the well-appointed kitchen. The master suite has a vaulted ceiling and boasts a huge walk-in closet and a pampering bath. Two family bedrooms share a full bath.

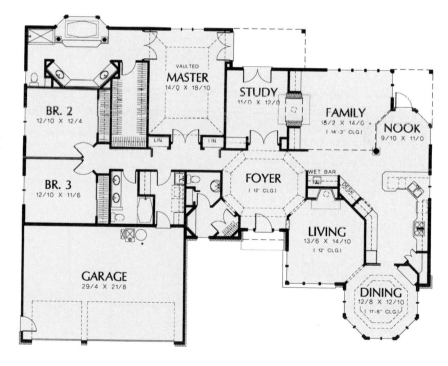

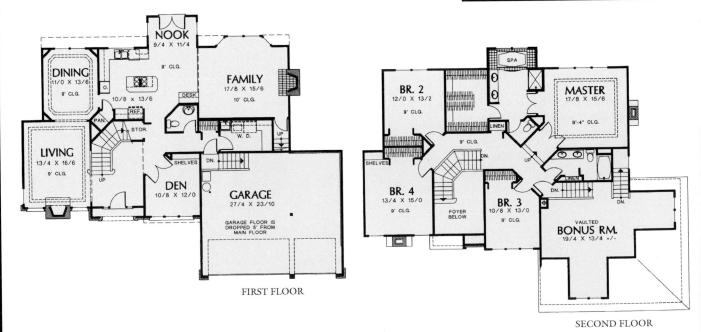

plan# HPK0600194

L

STYLE: TUDOR
FIRST FLOOR: 1,484 SQ. FT.
SECOND FLOOR: 1,402 SQ. FT.
TOTAL: 2,886 SQ. FT.
BONUS SPACE: 430 SQ. FT.
BEDROOMS: 4
BATHROOMS: 2½
WIDTH: 63' - 0"
DEPTH: 51' - 0"
FOUNDATION: CRAWLSPACE

SEARCH ONLINE @ EPLANS.COM

This impressive Tudor is designed for lots that slope up slightly from the street—the garage is five feet below the main level. Just to the right of the entry, the den is arranged to work well as an office. Formal living areas include a living room with a fireplace and an elegant dining room. The family room also offers a fireplace and is close to the bumped-out nook. On the upper level, all the bedrooms are generously sized, and the master suite features a tray ceiling and a huge walk-in closet. A large vaulted bonus room is provided with convenient access from both the family room and the garage. Three family bedrooms and a full bath complete the upper level.

FIRST FLOOR

SECOND FLOOR

plan # HPK0600195 LD

STYLE: COUNTRY COTTAGE
FIRST FLOOR: 1,372 SQ. FT.
SECOND FLOOR: 1,245 SQ. FT.
TOTAL: 2,617 SQ. FT.
BEDROOMS: 4
BATHROOMS: 2½ + ½
WIDTH: 70' - 0"
DEPTH: 38' - 4"
FOUNDATION: BASEMENT

SEARCH ONLINE @ EPLANS.COM

This elegant Tudor house is perfect for the family that wants to move up in living area, style, and luxury. As you enter this home, you will find a living room with a fireplace to the right. The adjacent formal dining room easily leads to the kitchen. The open kitchen/breakfast room accesses the rear terrace. Sunk down a few steps, the spacious family room is highlighted with a fireplace and access to the rear covered porch. Upstairs, the family will enjoy three bedrooms and a full bath, along with a spacious master suite.

QUOTE ONE®

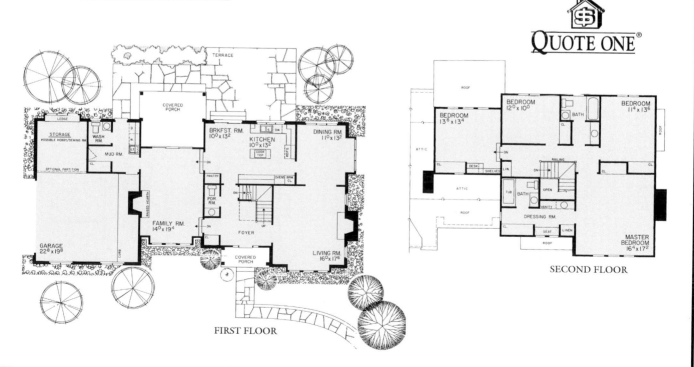

FIRST FLOOR

SECOND FLOOR

plan# HPK0600196

Multipane glass windows, French doors, and an arched pediment with columns create a spectacular exterior with this blue-ribbon European design. A two-story foyer opens to formal areas and, through French doors, to a secluded den with built-in cabinetry and a coat closet. The gourmet kitchen enjoys a morning nook. Second-floor sleeping quarters include a master bedroom with a tile-rimmed spa tub, twin vanities, and a walk-in closet. This plan offers the option of replacing the family room's vaulted ceiling with a fifth bedroom above.

STYLE: TRADITIONAL
FIRST FLOOR: 1,470 SQ. FT.
SECOND FLOOR: 1,269 SQ. FT.
TOTAL: 2,739 SQ. FT.
BEDROOMS: 4
BATHROOMS: 2½
WIDTH: 70' - 0"
DEPTH: 47' - 0"
FOUNDATION: CRAWLSPACE

SEARCH ONLINE @ EPLANS.COM

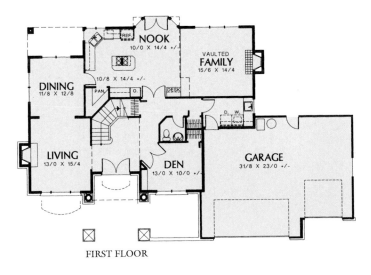

FIRST FLOOR

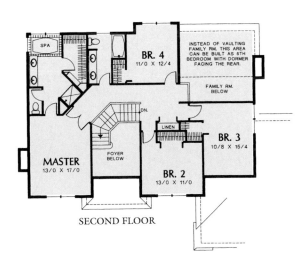

SECOND FLOOR

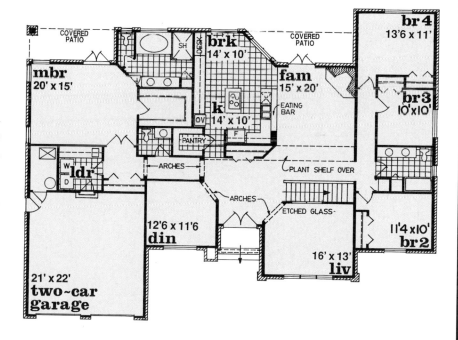

plan# HPK0600197

STYLE: EUROPEAN COTTAGE
SQUARE FOOTAGE: 2,547
BEDROOMS: 4
BATHROOMS: 2½
WIDTH: 74' - 8"
DEPTH: 56' - 8"
FOUNDATION:
CRAWLSPACE, BASEMENT

SEARCH ONLINE @ EPLANS.COM

A brick exterior with traditional arch details and elegant rooflines defines this stately ranch home. Formal dining and living rooms open through arches from the front entry foyer. Chefs can utilize their talents in the spacious kitchen with its center cooktop island, abundant counter space, and light-filled breakfast nook. The family room is separated from the kitchen by a snack counter and features a corner fireplace and double doors to the rear patio. The private master suite, separated from family bedrooms, offers a walk-in closet and a luxurious bath with a whirlpool spa, oversized shower, twin vanities, and compartmented toilet. Three additional bedrooms allow design flexibility—use one as a guest room, den, or home office.

plan# HPK0600198

STYLE: TRADITIONAL
SQUARE FOOTAGE: 2,398
BONUS SPACE: 302 SQ. FT.
BEDROOMS: 3
BATHROOMS: 2½
WIDTH: 69' - 0"
DEPTH: 60' - 4"
FOUNDATION: BASEMENT

SEARCH ONLINE @ EPLANS.COM

A luxurious dual master suite is the highlight of this exquisite brick ranch design. Details including a double-course brick water table, finely crafted window and eve trim, and a stately front porch create a truly elegant facade. For those seeking a classic traditional home offering posh appointments, spacious rooms, and carefully planned livability, this is the perfect home plan. Protected by the lovely front porch, the entry features high ceilings and leads directly to the family room with its 14-foot ceiling and fireplace. Just off the entry, stairs lead to the bonus room. Each of the secondary bedrooms provides direct access to the shared bath. The master suite is truly a luxurious escape, with its study, spacious dual bed areas, fireplace, and sumptuous bath.

plan # HPK0600199

D

STYLE: TRANSITIONAL
FIRST FLOOR: 1,425 SQ. FT.
SECOND FLOOR: 704 SQ. FT.
TOTAL: 2,129 SQ. FT.
BEDROOMS: 3
BATHROOMS: 2
WIDTH: 55' - 4"
DEPTH: 52' - 4"
FOUNDATION: BASEMENT

SEARCH ONLINE @ EPLANS.COM

This charming Tudor adaptation features a complete second-floor master bedroom suite with a balcony overlooking the living room, plus a studio. The first floor contains a convenient kitchen with a pass-through to the breakfast room. There's also a formal dining room just steps away. An adjacent rear living room enjoys its own fireplace. Other features include a rear media room or optional third bedroom. A downstairs bedroom enjoys an excellent front view. The master suite on the second level is complete with two walk-in closets and a luxurious bath.

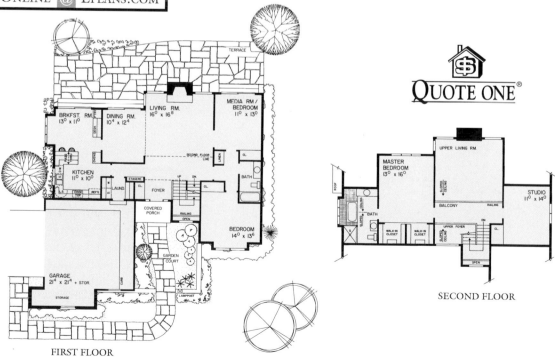

FIRST FLOOR

SECOND FLOOR

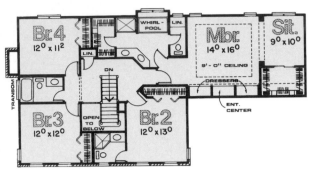

SECOND FLOOR

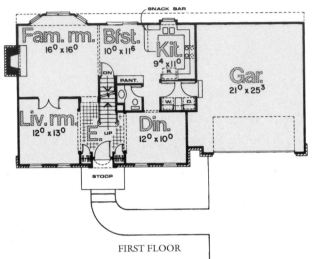

FIRST FLOOR

SECOND FLOOR

FIRST FLOOR

plan # HPK0600202

STYLE: TRADITIONAL
FIRST FLOOR: 1,377 SQ. FT.
SECOND FLOOR: 1,083 SQ. FT.
TOTAL: 2,460 SQ. FT.
BONUS SPACE: 597 SQ. FT.
BEDROOMS: 5
BATHROOMS: 3½
WIDTH: 78' - 8"
DEPTH: 36' - 2"
FOUNDATION: CRAWLSPACE,
SLAB, BASEMENT

SEARCH ONLINE @ EPLANS.COM

This stately home is well-suited for many purposes— delightful entertaining, raising a big family, and putting up a live-in relative or college-aged daughter or son. The living room, warmed by a fireplace and sporting a wet bar, will be the site of many memorable evenings. The front dining area has easy access to the well-equipped kitchen with a huge island snack counter. A family room with its own fireplace and a skylight opens onto the rear deck guaranteeing this will be a favorite pole of attraction for family members. A luxurious master suite with its own sitting room and pampering bath is on the second level, as are three family bedrooms that share a bath. Above the garage and with its own stairway is a suite that includes a bedroom, bath, and a loft living area with a kitchenette.

SECOND FLOOR

FIRST FLOOR

plan # HPK0600203

D

This Early American design offers great livability with an expansive living room accented by a fireplace. Nearby, an efficient island kitchen serves the formal dining room and a cozy breakfast nook. A quiet study with built-in bookshelves sits to the left of the foyer. A convenient powder room rounds out the first floor. Upstairs, the master bedroom includes a walk-in closet and a private bath; two family bedrooms share a full dual-vanity bath just across the hall. The two-car, side-loading garage makes this plan perfect for a corner lot.

STYLE: EUROPEAN COTTAGE
FIRST FLOOR: 1,388 SQ. FT.
SECOND FLOOR: 809 SQ. FT.
TOTAL: 2,197 SQ. FT.
BEDROOMS: 3
BATHROOMS: 2½
WIDTH: 73' - 4"
DEPTH: 32' - 0"
FOUNDATION:
UNFINISHED BASEMENT

SEARCH ONLINE @ EPLANS.COM

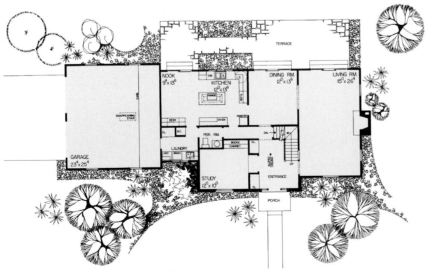

FIRST FLOOR

SECOND FLOOR

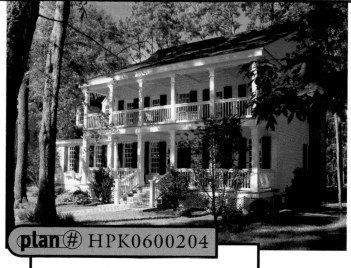

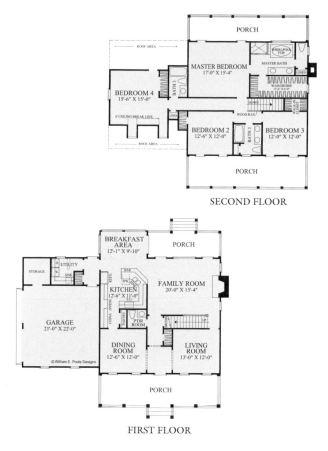

SECOND FLOOR

FIRST FLOOR

plan # HPK0600204

STYLE: SOUTHERN
COLONIAL
FIRST FLOOR: 1,273 SQ. FT.
SECOND FLOOR: 1,358 SQ. FT.
TOTAL: 2,631 SQ. FT.
BEDROOMS: 4
BATHROOMS: 3½
WIDTH: 54' - 10"
DEPTH: 48' - 6"
FOUNDATION: CRAWLSPACE

SEARCH ONLINE @ EPLANS.COM

plan # HPK0600205

STYLE: GREEK REVIVAL
FIRST FLOOR: 1,688 SQ. FT.
SECOND FLOOR: 630 SQ. FT.
TOTAL: 2,318 SQ. FT.
BONUS SPACE: 506 SQ. FT.
BEDROOMS: 3
BATHROOMS: 3½
WIDTH: 44' - 4"
DEPTH: 62' - 4"
FOUNDATION:
CRAWLSPACE, BASEMENT

SEARCH ONLINE @ EPLANS.COM

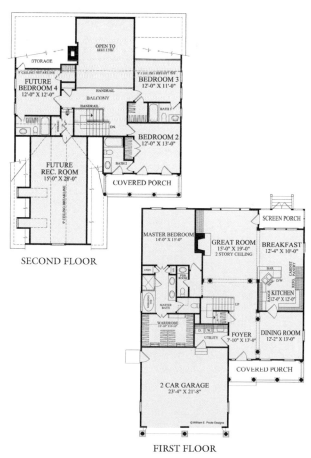

SECOND FLOOR

FIRST FLOOR

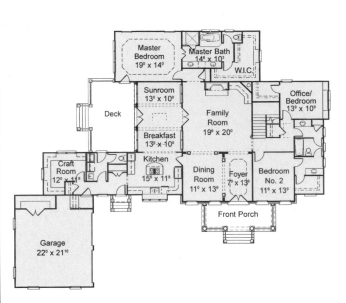

Master
Bedroom
19⁰ x 14⁰

Master Bath
14⁰ x 10³

W.I.C.

Sunroom
13⁰ x 10⁰

Deck

Family
Room
19⁶ x 20⁰

Office/
Bedroom
13⁰ x 10⁰

Breakfast
13⁰ x 10⁰

Kitchen
15⁶ x 11⁸

Craft
Room
12⁰ x 11⁸

Dining
Room
11⁰ x 13⁶

Foyer
7⁸ x 13⁶

Bedroom
No. 2
11⁶ x 13⁹

Front Porch

Garage
22⁰ x 21¹⁰

plan # HPK0600206

STYLE: TRADITIONAL
SQUARE FOOTAGE: 2,752
BEDROOMS: 3
BATHROOMS: 2½
WIDTH: 90' - 0"
DEPTH: 72' - 10"
FOUNDATION: BASEMENT

SEARCH ONLINE @ EPLANS.COM

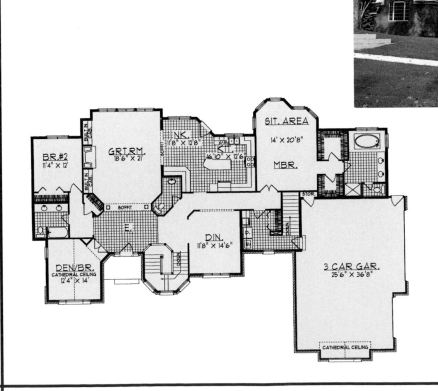

BR.#2
11'4" x 12'

GRT.RM.
18'6" X 21'

NK.
11'8" x 12'8"

SIT. AREA
14' X 20'8"

KIT.
16'10" X 12'6"

MBR.

E.

DIN.
11'8" X 14'6"

DEN/BR.
CATHEDRAL CEILING
12'4" X 14'

3 CAR GAR.
25'6" X 36'8"

CATHEDRAL CEILING

plan # HPK0600207

STYLE: RANCH
SQUARE FOOTAGE: 2,600
BEDROOMS: 3
BATHROOMS: 2½
WIDTH: 87' - 0"
DEPTH: 60' - 0"
FOUNDATION: BASEMENT

SEARCH ONLINE @ EPLANS.COM

plan # HPK0600208

STYLE: TRADITIONAL
FIRST FLOOR: 2,270 SQ. FT.
SECOND FLOOR: 685 SQ. FT.
TOTAL: 2,955 SQ. FT.
BONUS SPACE: 563 SQ. FT.
BEDROOMS: 3
BATHROOMS: 2½
WIDTH: 75' - 1"
DEPTH: 53' 6"

SEARCH ONLINE @ EPLANS.COM

Hipped rooflines, sunburst windows, and French-style shutters are the defining elements of this home's exterior. Inside, the foyer is flanked by the dining room and the study. Further on, the lavish great room can be entered through two stately columns and is complete with a fireplace, built-in shelves, a vaulted ceiling, and views to the rear patio. The island kitchen easily accesses a pantry and a desk and flows into the bayed breakfast area. The first-floor master bedroom enjoys a fireplace, two walk-in closets, and an amenity-filled private bath. Two additional bedrooms reside upstairs, along with a sizable bonus room.

FIRST FLOOR

SECOND FLOOR

This sturdy Southern Colonial home is perfect for a large family that likes to stretch out—and it's great for entertaining, too. Upstairs, four bedrooms, including a ravishing master suite, provide ample sleeping quarters. A laundry is conveniently located on this level. Downstairs, a den that could serve as a guest bedroom enjoys hall access to a full bath. Nearby is a study. The two-story family room opens one way to the formal dining area, and the other way to the casual eating area and kitchen, outfitted with a time-saving island counter.

plan# HPK0600209

STYLE: SOUTHERN COLONIAL
FIRST FLOOR: 1,364 SQ. FT.
SECOND FLOOR: 1,398 SQ. FT.
TOTAL: 2,762 SQ. FT.
BEDROOMS: 5
BATHROOMS: 4
WIDTH: 51' - 0"
DEPTH: 45' - 4"
FOUNDATION: CRAWLSPACE, BASEMENT

SEARCH ONLINE @ EPLANS.COM

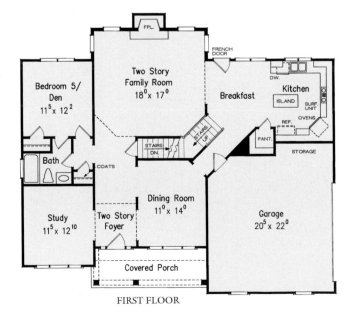

FIRST FLOOR

SECOND FLOOR

plan# HPK0600210

STYLE: FARMHOUSE
FIRST FLOOR: 1,250 SQ. FT.
SECOND FLOOR: 1,166 SQ. FT.
TOTAL: 2,416 SQ. FT.
BEDROOMS: 4
BATHROOMS: 2½
WIDTH: 64' - 0"
DEPTH: 52' - 0"
FOUNDATION. BASEMENT

SEARCH ONLINE @ EPLANS.COM

With its classic features, this home is reminiscent of Main Street, USA. The two-story foyer is flanked by the formal living and dining rooms, and the stairs are tucked back in the center of the house. Columns create a separation from the family room to the breakfast area, keeping that open feeling across the entire rear of the house. Corner windows in the kitchen look into the side yard and rear screened porch. The porch leads to the rear deck, which also ties into the side porch, creating outdoor living on three sides of the house. As you ascend the staircase to the second floor, you will pass a lighted panel of stained glass on the landing, creating the illusion of a window wall. The second floor features four bedrooms and a compartmented hall bath.

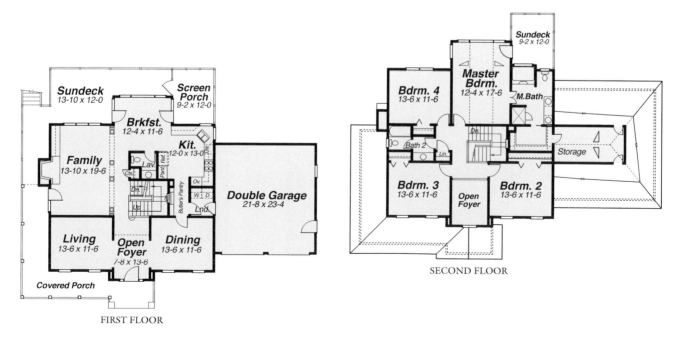

FIRST FLOOR

SECOND FLOOR

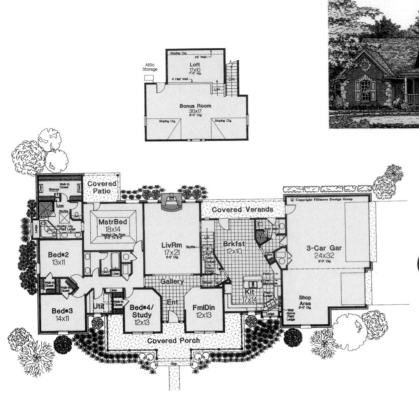

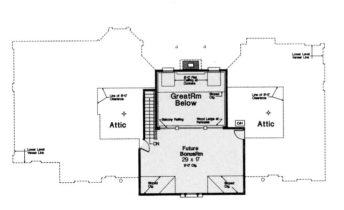

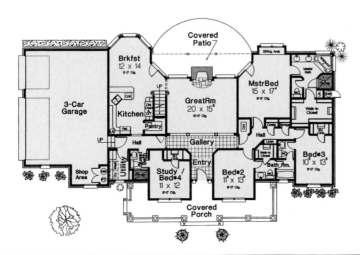

plan # HPK0600213

STYLE: VICTORIAN
FIRST FLOOR: 1,600 SQ. FT.
SECOND FLOOR: 790 SQ. FT.
TOTAL: 2,390 SQ. FT.
BEDROOMS: 4
BATHROOMS: 3½
WIDTH: 45' - 0"
DEPTH: 54' - 0"
FOUNDATION: CRAWLSPACE

SEARCH ONLINE @ EPLANS.COM

Queen Anne houses, with their projecting bays, towers, and wraparound porches, are the apex of the Victorian era. This up-to-date rendition of the beloved style captures a floor plan that is as dramatic on the inside as it is on the outside. The front-facing pediment ornamented with typical gable detailing highlights the front doorway and provides additional welcome to this enchanted abode. The angles and bays that occur in every first-floor room add visual excitement to formal and informal living and dining areas. A well-lit breakfast bay with its soaring ceiling is a spectacular addition to this classic plan. The first-floor master suite features two walk-in closets. Three upstairs bedrooms also have spacious walk-in closets.

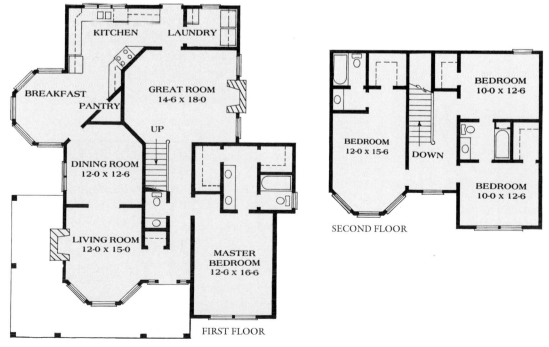

FIRST FLOOR

SECOND FLOOR

SECOND FLOOR

Sleeping Quarters
11² × 10⁰

Sleeping Quarters
11⁰ × 13⁶

Sleeping Quarters
11⁰ × 13⁰
10'-0" Ceiling

Breakfast
10⁰ × 11⁰

Great Room
18⁰ × 16⁰
12'-10" Ceiling

Kitchen
10⁰ × 13³

Hearth Room
14⁰ × 15⁷

Storage

Master Sleeping Quarters
13³ × 17⁰
10'-0" Ceiling

Dining Room
12⁰ × 15²

Garage
19⁴ × 20⁴

FIRST FLOOR

QUOTE ONE®

plan# HPK0600214

STYLE: VICTORIAN
FIRST FLOOR: 1,653 SQ. FT.
SECOND FLOOR: 700 SQ. FT.
TOTAL: 2,353 SQ. FT.
BEDROOMS: 4
BATHROOMS: 2½
WIDTH: 54' - 0"
DEPTH: 50' - 0"

SEARCH ONLINE @ EPLANS.COM

Sleeping Quarters
11⁰ × 10⁰

9'-0" Ceiling

Master Sleeping Quarters
12⁰ × 17⁰

Sleeping Quarters
10⁰ × 11⁰

Sleeping Quarters
11⁰ × 12⁸
11'-6" Ceiling

SECOND FLOOR

DECK

Breakfast
9⁸ × 12⁰

Kitchen
10⁰ × 10⁰

Gathering Room
17³ × 15⁰
8'-8" Ceiling

Dining Room
12⁰ × 12⁰

Storage

Parlor
12⁰ × 16⁴
12'-0" Ceiling

Garage
19⁴ × 22⁰

FIRST FLOOR

QUOTE ONE®

plan# HPK0600215

STYLE: VICTORIAN
FIRST FLOOR: 1,113 SQ. FT.
SECOND FLOOR: 965 SQ. FT.
TOTAL: 2,078 SQ. FT.
BEDROOMS: 4
BATHROOMS: 2½
WIDTH: 46' - 0"
DEPTH: 41' - 5"

SEARCH ONLINE @ EPLANS.COM

plan # HPK0600216

L

STYLE: FARMHOUSE
FIRST FLOOR: 1,375 SQ. FT.
SECOND FLOOR: 1,016 SQ. FT.
TOTAL: 2,391 SQ. FT.
BEDROOMS: 3
BATHROOMS: 2½
WIDTH: 62' - 7"
DEPTH: 54' - 0"
FOUNDATION: BASEMENT

SEARCH ONLINE @ EPLANS.COM

Covered porches, front and back, are a fine preview to the livable nature of this Victorian home. Living areas are defined in a family room with a fireplace, formal living and dining rooms, and a kitchen with a breakfast room. An ample laundry room, a garage with a storage area, and a powder room round out the first floor. Three second-floor bedrooms are joined by a study and two full baths. The master suite on this floor has two closets, including an ample walk-in, as well as a relaxing bath with a tile-rimmed whirlpool tub and a separate shower with a seat.

FIRST FLOOR

SECOND FLOOR

QUOTE ONE®

plan# HPK0600217

STYLE: TRADITIONAL
FIRST FLOOR: 1,499 SQ. FT.
SECOND FLOOR: 956 SQ. FT.
TOTAL: 2,455 SQ. FT.
BEDROOMS: 4
BATHROOMS: 3
WIDTH: 69' - 2"
DEPTH: 47' - 6"
FOUNDATION: BASEMENT,
CRAWLSPACE, SLAB

SEARCH ONLINE @ EPLANS.COM

Victorian country style never looked so good! Turrets and carousel bays adorn the facade and create charming, comfortable living spaces inside, as bright windows flood the home with natural light. Enter from a wraparound covered porch to the two-story foyer. On the right, a wet bar complements the vaulted living room. Continue into the elegant dining room and gourmet kitchen with an island cooktop. The sunken family room is inviting and offers French doors to the rear property. A den at the front of the home makes an ideal guest room. Upstairs, the master suite achieves country glamour with a turret sitting area, lavish bath, and oversized walk-in closet. Two additional bedrooms share a full bath to complete the plan.

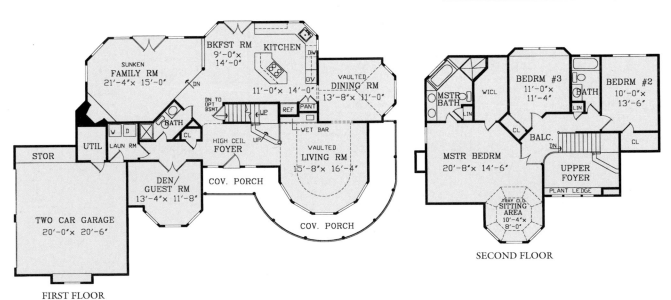

FIRST FLOOR

SECOND FLOOR

plan # HPK0600218

STYLE: VICTORIAN
FIRST FLOOR: 1,960 SQ. FT.
SECOND FLOOR: 736 SQ. FT.
TOTAL: 2,696 SQ. FT.
BEDROOMS: 4
BATHROOMS: 3
WIDTH: 69' - 2"
DEPTH: 50' - 2"
FOUNDATION: SLAB,
CRAWLSPACE, BASEMENT

SEARCH ONLINE @ EPLANS.COM

A circular front room with a wraparound porch, a conical tower, and gingerbread trim all add to the overall attraction of this Victorian home. The porch ends at a broad covered entrance. The dramatic, spacious great room features a vaulted ceiling, semi-circular roof monitor, and diagonally placed corner fireplace. The extraordinary kitchen includes angled counters, a corner sink, center island with space for informal dining, and an airy breakfast nook with French doors to the patio. Entrance to the wonderful first-floor master suite is through angled double doors. A high tray ceiling, large walk-in closet, and dressing alcove are featured. A gorgeous compartmented bath is bathed in sunlight from two glass-block walls, and includes a whirlpool tub and double vanity.

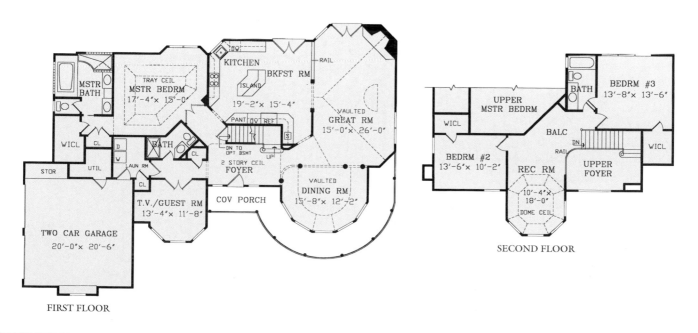

FIRST FLOOR

SECOND FLOOR

plan# HPK0600219

Country Victoriana embellishes this beautiful home.

Perfect for a corner lot, this home begs for porch swings and lemonade. Inside, extra-high ceilings expand the space, as a thoughtful floor plan invites family and friends. The two-story great room enjoys a warming fireplace and wonderful rear views. The country kitchen has a preparation island and easily serves the sunny bayed nook and the formal dining room. To the far left, a bedroom serves as a perfect guest room; to the far right, a turret houses a private den. Upstairs, two bedrooms (one in a turret) share a full bath and ample bonus space. The master suite opens through French doors to reveal a grand bedroom and a sumptuous bath with a bumped-out spa tub.

STYLE: FARMHOUSE
FIRST FLOOR: 1,464 SQ. FT.
SECOND FLOOR: 1,054 SQ. FT.
TOTAL: 2,518 SQ. FT.
BONUS SPACE: 332 SQ. FT.
BEDROOMS: 4
BATHROOMS: 3
WIDTH: 59' - 0"
DEPTH: 51' - 6"
FOUNDATION: CRAWLSPACE

SEARCH ONLINE @ EPLANS.COM

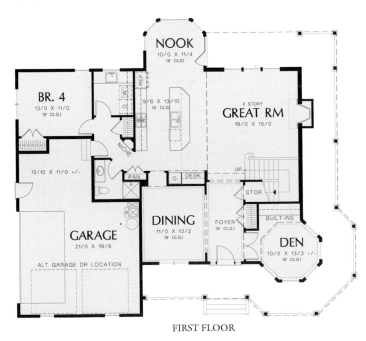

FIRST FLOOR

SECOND FLOOR

ORDER BLUEPRINTS 24 HOURS, 7 DAYS A WEEK, AT 1-800-521-6797

plan # HPK0600220

L

STYLE: VICTORIAN
FIRST FLOOR: 1,269 SQ. FT.
SECOND FLOOR: 1,227 SQ. FT.
TOTAL: 2,496 SQ. FT.
BEDROOMS: 4
BATHROOMS: 2½
WIDTH: 70' - 0"
DEPTH: 44' - 5"
FOUNDATION: BASEMENT

SEARCH ONLINE @ EPLANS.COM

Sunbursts, simple balusters, and a stylish turret set off this Victorian exterior, complete with two finely detailed covered porches. An unrestrained floor plan offers bays and nooks, open spaces, and cozy niches—a proper combination for an active family. Formal living and dining areas invite gatherings, whether large or small, planned or casual—but the heart of the home is the family area. A wide bay window and a fireplace with an extended hearth warm up both the family room and breakfast area; the nearby kitchen offers a snack counter for easy meals. The second floor includes three family bedrooms and a lavish master suite with an oversized whirlpool spa and two walk-in closets.

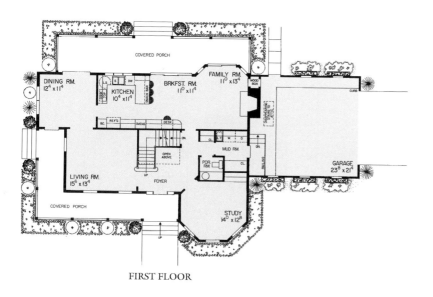

FIRST FLOOR

QUOTE ONE®

SECOND FLOOR

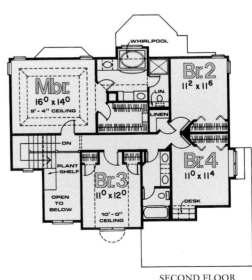

plan# HPK0600221

STYLE: FARMHOUSE
FIRST FLOOR: 1,150 SQ. FT.
SECOND FLOOR: 1,120 SQ. FT.
TOTAL: 2,270 SQ. FT.
BEDROOMS: 4
BATHROOMS: 2½
WIDTH: 46' - 0"
DEPTH: 48' - 0"

SEARCH ONLINE @ EPLANS.COM

Lap siding, special windows, and a covered porch enhance the elevation of this popular-style home. The spacious two-story entry surveys the formal dining room, which includes hutch space. An entertainment center, a through-fireplace, and bayed windows add appeal to the great room. Families will love the spacious kitchen with its breakfast and hearth rooms. Comfortable secondary bedrooms and a sumptuous master bedroom feature privacy by design. Bedroom 3 is highlighted by a half-round window, volume ceiling, and double closets, while Bedroom 4 contains a built-in desk. The master suite possesses a vaulted ceiling, large walk-in closet, His and Hers vanities, and an oval whirlpool tub.

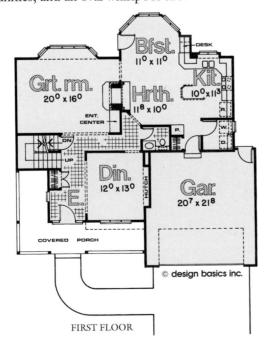

FIRST FLOOR

SECOND FLOOR

plan # HPK0600222

STYLE: TRADITIONAL
FIRST FLOOR: 1,875 SQ. FT.
SECOND FLOOR: 687 SQ. FT.
TOTAL: 2,562 SQ. FT.
BEDROOMS: 4
BATHROOMS: 2½
WIDTH: 60' - 0"
DEPTH: 59' - 4"

SEARCH ONLINE @ EPLANS.COM

Beyond the entry of this attractive two-story home, 15-foot arched openings frame the great room. French doors in the breakfast room open to a versatile office with a sloping 10-foot ceiling. A convenient utility area off the kitchen features access to the garage, a half-bath, and a generous laundry room complete with a folding table. A private entrance into the master suite reveals a pleasing interior. On the second floor, three large secondary bedrooms share a bath with dual sinks.

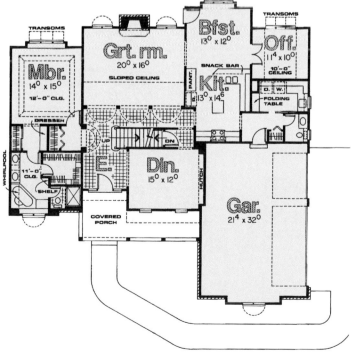

FIRST FLOOR

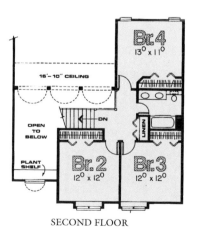

SECOND FLOOR

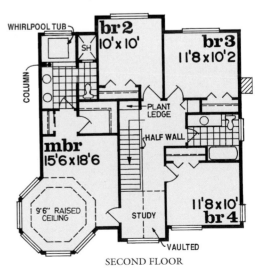

plan# HPK0600223

A turret roof, prominent bay window, and wraparound veranda designate this four-bedroom design as classic Victorian. The plans include two second-level layouts—one with four bedrooms or one with three bedrooms and a vaulted ceiling over the family room. Both include a lavish master suite with an octagonal tray ceiling in the sitting room, a walk-in closet, and a private bath with a columned whirlpool spa and separate shower. The first floor holds a formal living room with windows overlooking the veranda, a formal dining room, and a family room with a fireplace. The U-shaped kitchen has a sunny breakfast bay. A half-bath and a laundry room are found in the service area that also leads to the two-car garage.

STYLE: COUNTRY COTTAGE
FIRST FLOOR: 1,180 SQ. FT.
SECOND FLOOR: 1,121 SQ. FT.
TOTAL: 2,301 SQ. FT.
BEDROOMS: 4
BATHROOMS: 2½
WIDTH: 48' - 0"
DEPTH: 52' - 6"
FOUNDATION: BASEMENT, CRAWLSPACE

SEARCH ONLINE @ EPLANS.COM

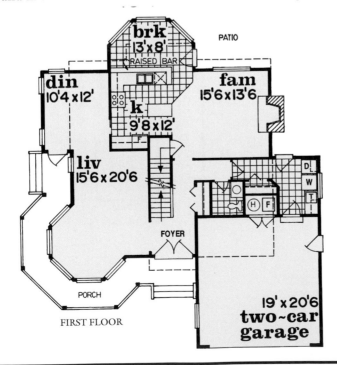

plan # HPK0600224

STYLE: COUNTRY COTTAGE
FIRST FLOOR: 1,291 SQ. FT.
SECOND FLOOR: 1,291 SQ. FT.
TOTAL: 2,582 SQ. FT.
BEDROOMS: 4
BATHROOMS: 3
WIDTH: 64' - 6"
DEPTH: 47' - 0"
FOUNDATION:
CRAWLSPACE, BASEMENT

SEARCH ONLINE @ EPLANS.COM

Traditional with an essence of farmhouse flavor, this four-bedroom home begins with a wraparound covered porch. The floor plan revolves around a central hall, with a formal living room and dining room on the left and private den on the right. The bayed breakfast room is located near the L-shaped kitchen with an island work center. Both the family room and the living room are warmed by hearths. Two rear porches are reached through doors in the family room and the bayed dining room. The master suite on the second level has a bayed sitting room. Note the window seat on the second-floor landing.

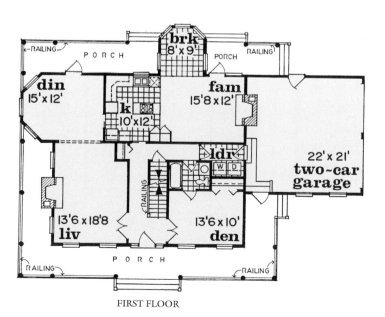

FIRST FLOOR

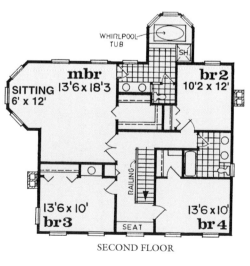

SECOND FLOOR

plan# HPK0600225

STYLE: CRAFTSMAN
SQUARE FOOTAGE: 2,097
BONUS SPACE: 352 SQ. FT.
BEDROOMS: 4
BATHROOMS: 3
WIDTH: 64' - 10"
DEPTH: 59' - 6"

SEARCH ONLINE @ EPLANS.COM

Graceful arches contrast with high gables for a stunning exterior on this Craftsman home. Windows with decorative transoms and several French doors flood the open floor plan with natural light. Tray ceilings in the dining room and master bedroom as well as cathedral ceilings in the bedroom/study, great room, kitchen, and breakfast area create architectural interest and visual space. Built-ins in the great room and additional space in the garage offer convenient storage. A screened porch allows for comfortable outdoor entertaining; a bonus room, near two additional bedrooms, offers flexibility. Positioned for privacy, the master suite features access to the screened porch, dual walk-in closets, and a well-appointed bath, including a private toilet, garden tub, double vanity, and spacious shower.

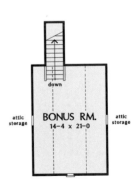

plan # HPK0600226

STYLE: CRAFTSMAN
FIRST FLOOR: 1,371 SQ. FT.
SECOND FLOOR: 916 SQ. FT.
TOTAL: 2,287 SQ. FT.
BEDROOMS: 3
BATHROOMS: 2½
WIDTH: 43' - 0"
DEPTH: 69' - 0"
FOUNDATION: CRAWLSPACE

SEARCH ONLINE @ EPLANS.COM

The decorative pillars and the wraparound porch are just the beginning of this comfortable home. Inside, an angled U-shaped stairway leads to the second-floor sleeping zone. On the first floor, French doors lead to a bay-windowed den that shares a see-through fireplace with the two-story family room. The large island kitchen includes a writing desk, a corner sink, a breakfast nook, and access to the laundry room, the powder room, and the two-car garage. Upstairs, the master suite is a real treat with its French-door access, vaulted ceiling, and luxurious bath. Two other bedrooms and a full bath complete the second floor.

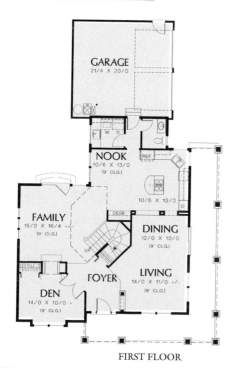

FIRST FLOOR

QUOTE ONE®

SECOND FLOOR

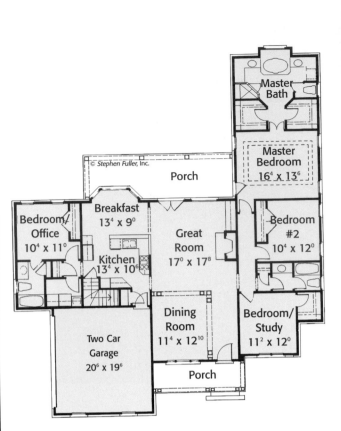

© Stephen Fuller, Inc.

Master Bath

Master Bedroom
16⁴ x 13⁶

Porch

Breakfast
13⁴ x 9⁰

Bedroom/ Office
10⁴ x 11⁰

Great Room
17⁰ x 17⁸

Bedroom #2
10⁴ x 12⁰

Kitchen
13⁴ x 10⁶

Dining Room
11⁴ x 12¹⁰

Bedroom/ Study
11² x 12⁰

Two Car Garage
20⁶ x 19⁶

Porch

plan# HPK0600227

STYLE: COUNTRY COTTAGE
SQUARE FOOTAGE: 2,090
BEDROOMS: 4
BATHROOMS: 3
WIDTH: 61' - 0"
DEPTH: 70' - 6"
FOUNDATION:
WALKOUT BASEMENT

SEARCH ONLINE @ EPLANS.COM

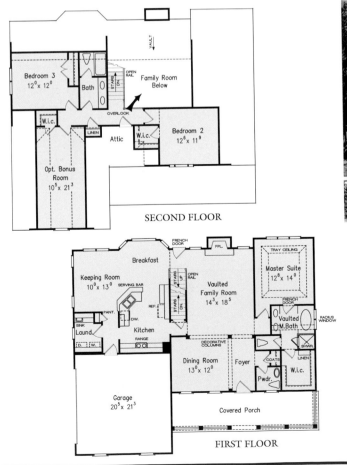

Bedroom 3
12⁰ x 12⁰

Bath

Family Room Below

OVERLOOK

Attic

W.i.c.

Bedroom 2
12⁶ x 11⁹

LINEN

Opt. Bonus Room
10⁵ x 21³

SECOND FLOOR

Keeping Room
10⁰ x 13⁰

Breakfast

SERVING BAR

FPL.

Master Suite
12⁸ x 14⁰

TRAY CEILING

Vaulted Family Room
14³ x 18⁵

PANT.

Kitchen

RANGE

Vaulted M.Bath

RADIUS WINDOW

SINK
Laund.

DECORATIVE COLUMNS

Dining Room
13⁰ x 12⁰

Foyer

COATS

W.i.c.

PWDR.

LINEN

SHWR.

Garage
20⁵ x 21³

Covered Porch

FIRST FLOOR

plan# HPK0600228

STYLE: COUNTRY COTTAGE
FIRST FLOOR: 1,480 SQ. FT.
SECOND FLOOR: 544 SQ. FT.
TOTAL: 2,024 SQ. FT.
BONUS SPACE: 253 SQ. FT.
BEDROOMS: 3
BATHROOMS: 2½
WIDTH: 52' - 0"
DEPTH: 46' - 4"
FOUNDATION: CRAWLSPACE,
BASEMENT, SLAB

SEARCH ONLINE @ EPLANS.COM

plan # HPK0600229

STYLE: TRADITIONAL
FIRST FLOOR: 1,331 SQ. FT.
SECOND FLOOR: 680 SQ. FT.
TOTAL: 2,011 SQ. FT.
BEDROOMS: 3
BATHROOMS: 2½
WIDTH: 42' - 6"
DEPTH: 69' - 0"
FOUNDATION: SLAB

SEARCH ONLINE @ EPLANS.COM

This charming traditional home bears the warming touch of an exterior with muntin windows, a transom, and wood siding. The covered porch welcomes the entrance to this home as it leads to the foyer and into this well-thought-out plan. The elegant dining room awaits near the gourmet kitchen for easy access. The breakfast nook and a snack bar to the opposite end are for more informal gatherings. The utility room is conveniently located to the rear of the home and accesses the two-car carport. The spacious great room is sure to entertain with its cozy fireplace and French doors that access the rear patio. The lavish master bedroom enjoys a huge walk-in closet and a private bath with a pampering garden tub. Upstairs, two additional family bedrooms enjoy a full bath and a study, and a railing overlooks the great room below.

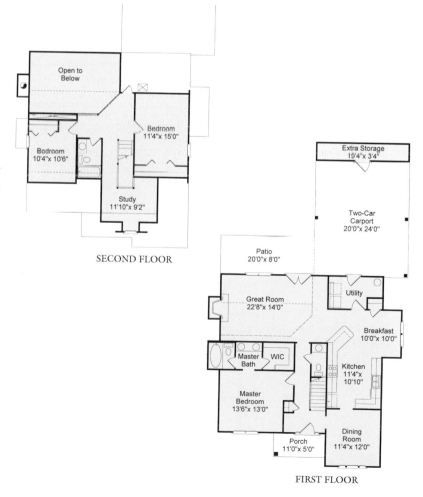

SECOND FLOOR

FIRST FLOOR

plan # HPK0600230

STYLE: TRADITIONAL
FIRST FLOOR: 1,568 SQ. FT.
SECOND FLOOR: 680 SQ. FT.
TOTAL: 2,248 SQ. FT.
BEDROOMS: 4
BATHROOMS: 2½
WIDTH: 50' - 0"
DEPTH: 48' - 0"

SEARCH ONLINE @ EPLANS.COM

Dramatic gables and a vintage frame shape the exterior of this family design. Formal rooms flank the foyer; ahead, the vaulted family room is warmed by a corner fireplace. The kitchen is thoughtfully placed between the dining room and casual breakfast nook. The master suite is a pampering retreat with a walk-in closet and private bath with a whirlpool tub. Upstairs, three additional bedrooms—all with walk-in closets—share a full bath.

FIRST FLOOR

© W. L. Martin Designs

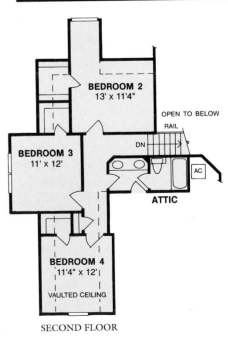

SECOND FLOOR

plan# HPK0600231

STYLE: TRADITIONAL
SQUARE FOOTAGE: 2,663
BONUS SPACE: 653 SQ. FT.
BEDROOMS: 4
BATHROOMS: 2½
WIDTH: 72' - 7"
DEPTH: 71' - 5"

SEARCH ONLINE @ EPLANS.COM

MOVE-UP HOMES

This home's personality is reflected in charming arch-top windows, set off with keystones and decorative shutters. A columned foyer enjoys natural light from a clerestory window and opens to the great room, which boasts a cathedral ceiling and sliding glass doors to the sunroom. An extended-hearth fireplace adds warmth to the living area. Open planning allows the nearby gourmet kitchen to share the glow of the hearth. The breakfast room really lets the sunshine in with a triple window to the rear property. The master suite offers private access to the rear deck with a spa and features a cozy fireplace, a relaxing bath, and a generous walk-in closet. Three family bedrooms—or make one a study—share a full bath and a powder room on the other side of the plan.

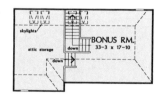

© 1993 Donald A. Gardner Architects, Inc.

SECOND FLOOR

FIRST FLOOR

plan# HPK0600232

STYLE: FARMHOUSE
FIRST FLOOR: 1,188 SQ. FT.
SECOND FLOOR: 1,172 SQ. FT.
TOTAL: 2,360 SQ. FT.
BEDROOMS: 4
BATHROOMS: 2½
WIDTH: 58' - 0"
DEPTH: 40' - 0"

SEARCH ONLINE @ EPLANS.COM

SECOND FLOOR

FIRST FLOOR

plan# HPK0600233

STYLE: COUNTRY COTTAGE
FIRST FLOOR: 1,516 SQ. FT.
SECOND FLOOR: 840 SQ. FT.
TOTAL: 2,356 SQ. FT.
BEDROOMS: 4
BATHROOMS: 2½
WIDTH: 46' - 10"
DEPTH: 73' - 5"
FOUNDATION: SLAB

SEARCH ONLINE @ EPLANS.COM

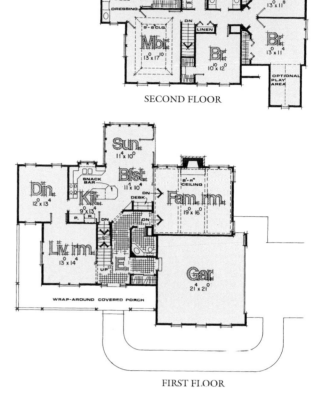

SECOND FLOOR

FIRST FLOOR

plan # HPK0600234

STYLE: FARMHOUSE
FIRST FLOOR: 1,322 SQ. FT.
SECOND FLOOR: 1,272 SQ. FT.
TOTAL: 2,594 SQ. FT.
BEDROOMS: 4
BATHROOMS: 2½
WIDTH: 56' - 0"
DEPTH: 48' - 0"

SEARCH ONLINE @ EPLANS.COM

SECOND FLOOR

plan # HPK0600005 LD

STYLE: FARMHOUSE
FIRST FLOOR: 1,370 SQ. FT.
SECOND FLOOR: 969 SQ. FT.
TOTAL: 2,339 SQ. FT.
BEDROOMS: 4
BATHROOMS: 2½
WIDTH: 59' - 8"
DEPTH: 44' - 0"
FOUNDATION: BASEMENT

SEARCH ONLINE @ EPLANS.COM

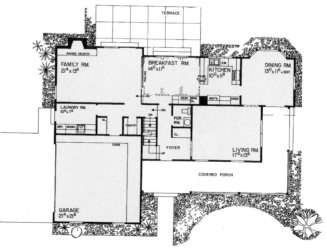

FIRST FLOOR

SECOND FLOOR

FIRST FLOOR

plan # HPK0600235

STYLE: COUNTRY COTTAGE
FIRST FLOOR: 1,569 SQ. FT.
SECOND FLOOR: 682 SQ. FT.
TOTAL: 2,251 SQ. FT.
BONUS SPACE: 332 SQ. FT.
BEDROOMS: 3
BATHROOMS: 2½
WIDTH: 64' - 8"
DEPTH: 43' - 4"

SEARCH ONLINE @ Eplans.com

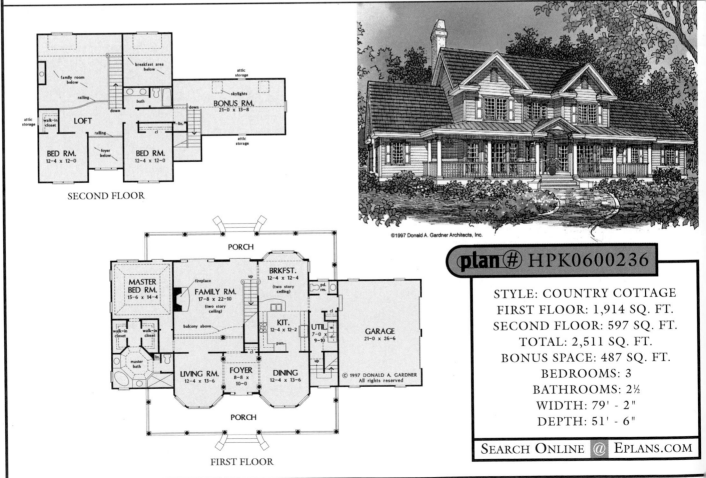

SECOND FLOOR

FIRST FLOOR

plan # HPK0600236

STYLE: COUNTRY COTTAGE
FIRST FLOOR: 1,914 SQ. FT.
SECOND FLOOR: 597 SQ. FT.
TOTAL: 2,511 SQ. FT.
BONUS SPACE: 487 SQ. FT.
BEDROOMS: 3
BATHROOMS: 2½
WIDTH: 79' - 2"
DEPTH: 51' - 6"

SEARCH ONLINE @ Eplans.com

plan(#) HPK0600237

STYLE: COUNTRY COTTAGE
FIRST FLOOR: 1,927 SQ. FT.
SECOND FLOOR: 879 SQ. FT.
TOTAL: 2,806 SQ. FT.
BONUS SPACE: 459 SQ. FT.
BEDROOMS: 4
BATHROOMS: 3½
WIDTH: 71' - 0"
DEPTH: 53' - 0"
FOUNDATION: CRAWLSPACE

SEARCH ONLINE @ EPLANS.COM

This charming Southern plantation home packs quite a punch in 2,800 square feet! The elegant foyer is flanked by the formal dining room and the living room. To the rear, the family room enjoys a fireplace and expansive view of the outdoors. An archway leads to the breakfast area and on to the island kitchen. The luxurious master suite is tucked away for privacy behind the two-car garage. Three additional bedrooms rest on the second floor where they share two full baths. Space above the garage is available for future development.

SECOND FLOOR

FIRST FLOOR

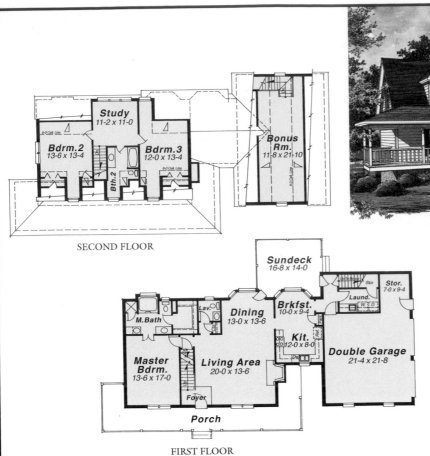

Study
11-2 x 11-0

Bdrm.2
13-6 x 13-4

Bdrm.3
12-0 x 13-4

Bth.2

Bonus Rm.
11-8 x 21-10

SECOND FLOOR

Sundeck
16-8 x 14-0

M.Bath

Lav.

Dining
13-0 x 13-6

Brkfst.
10-0 x 9-4

Laund.

Stor.
7-0 x 9-4

Stor.

Master Bdrm.
13-6 x 17-0

Living Area
20-0 x 13-6

Kit.
12-0 x 8-0

Double Garage
21-4 x 21-8

Foyer

Porch

FIRST FLOOR

plan # HPK0600238

STYLE: COUNTRY COTTAGE
FIRST FLOOR: 1,362 SQ. FT.
SECOND FLOOR: 729 SQ. FT.
TOTAL: 2,091 SQ. FT.
BONUS SPACE: 384 SQ. FT.
BEDROOMS: 3
BATHROOMS: 2½
WIDTH: 72' - 0"
DEPTH: 38' - 0"
FOUNDATION: BASEMENT,
SLAB, CRAWLSPACE

SEARCH ONLINE @ EPLANS.COM

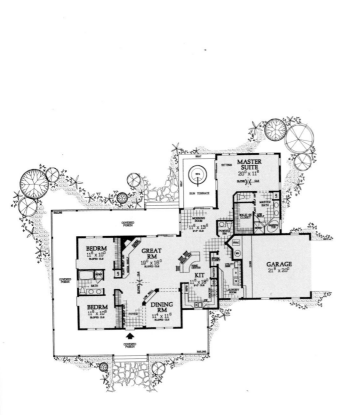

MASTER SUITE
20-0 x 11-8

BEDRM
11-8 x 10-0

GREAT RM
19-0 x 18-0

KIT

GARAGE
21-8 x 20-0

BEDRM
11-8 x 10-0

DINING RM
11-8 x 11-8

plan # HPK0600239

LD

STYLE: FARMHOUSE
SQUARE FOOTAGE: 2,090
BEDROOMS: 3
BATHROOMS: 2½
WIDTH: 84' - 6"
DEPTH: 64' - 0"
FOUNDATION: CRAWLSPACE

SEARCH ONLINE @ EPLANS.COM

plan # HPK0600240

STYLE: COUNTRY COTTAGE
FIRST FLOOR: 1,704 SQ. FT.
SECOND FLOOR: 734 SQ. FT.
TOTAL: 2,438 SQ. FT.
BONUS SPACE: 479 SQ. FT.
BEDROOMS: 3
BATHROOMS: 3½
WIDTH: 50' - 0"
DEPTH: 82' 6"
FOUNDATION: CRAWLSPACE

SEARCH ONLINE @ EPLANS.COM

Elegant country—that's one way to describe this attractive three-bedroom home. Inside, comfort is evidently the theme, with the formal dining room flowing into the U-shaped kitchen and casual dining taking place in the sunny breakfast area. The spacious, vaulted great room offers a fireplace and built-ins. The first-floor master suite is complete with a walk in closet, a whirlpool tub, and a separate shower. Upstairs, the sleeping quarters include two family bedrooms with private baths and walk-in closets.

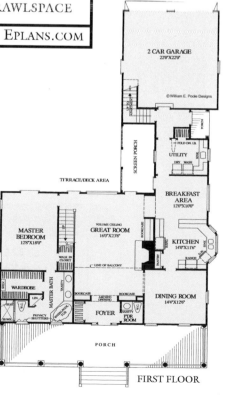

FIRST FLOOR

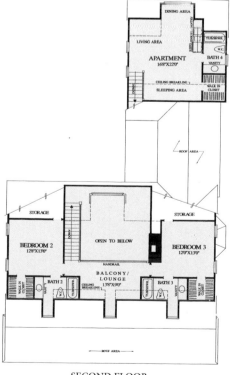

SECOND FLOOR

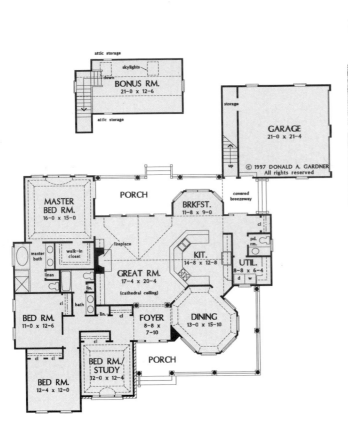

attic storage

BONUS RM.
21-0 x 12-6

skylights
down
attic storage

storage

GARAGE
21-0 x 21-4

up

© 1997 DONALD A. GARDNER
All rights reserved

PORCH

BRKFST.
11-8 x 9-0

covered breezeway

cl

pd. rm.

MASTER BED RM.
16-0 x 15-0

master bath

walk-in closet

fireplace

KIT.
14-8 x 12-8

UTIL.
8-8 x 6-4

d w

linen

GREAT RM.
17-4 x 20-4

(cathedral ceiling)

lin.

bath

cl

BED RM.
11-0 x 12-6

cl

lin. cl

FOYER
8-8 x 7-10

DINING
13-0 x 15-10

cl

BED RM./ STUDY
12-0 x 12-4

PORCH

BED RM.
12-4 x 12-0

B. NATHAN

plan # HPK0600241

STYLE: COUNTRY COTTAGE
SQUARE FOOTAGE: 2,273
BONUS SPACE: 342 SQ. FT.
BEDROOMS: 4
BATHROOMS: 2½
WIDTH: 74' - 8"
DEPTH: 75' - 10"

SEARCH ONLINE @ EPLANS.COM

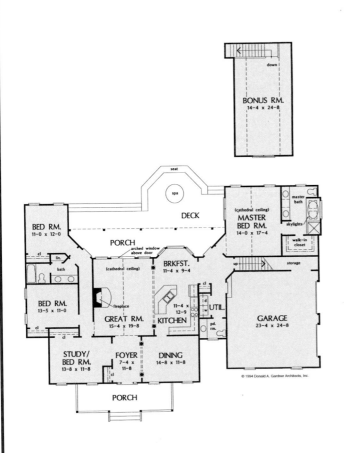

down

BONUS RM.
14-4 x 24-8

seat

spa

DECK

master bath

MASTER BED RM.
14-0 x 17-4

(cathedral ceiling)

skylights

walk-in closet

storage

BED RM.
11-0 x 12-0

cl lin.

bath

PORCH

arched window above door

(cathedral ceiling)

BRKFST.
11-4 x 9-4

up

BED RM.
13-5 x 11-0

fireplace

GREAT RM.
15-4 x 19-8

11-4 x 12-9

KITCHEN

d

UTIL.

pd. rm.

GARAGE
23-4 x 24-8

cl

d

STUDY/ BED RM.
13-8 x 11-8

FOYER
7-4 x 11-8

DINING
14-8 x 11-8

© 1994 Donald A. Gardner Architects, Inc.

PORCH

E. NATHAN

plan # HPK0600242

STYLE: FARMHOUSE
SQUARE FOOTAGE: 2,207
BONUS SPACE: 435 SQ. FT.
BEDROOMS: 4
BATHROOMS: 2½
WIDTH: 76' - 1"
DEPTH: 50' - 0"

SEARCH ONLINE @ EPLANS.COM

plan# HPK0600243

STYLE: TRADITIONAL
FIRST FLOOR: 2,017 SQ. FT.
SECOND FLOOR: 550 SQ. FT.
TOTAL: 2,567 SQ. FT.
STORAGE/BONUS SPACE:
300 SQ. FT.
BEDROOMS: 4
BATHROOMS: 3
WIDTH: 62' - 4"
DEPTH: 52' - 6"
FOUNDATION: CRAWLSPACE,
SLAB, BASEMENT

SEARCH ONLINE @ EPLANS.COM

Elegant country living can be yours in this four-bedroom home. Transoms flash over windows, a porch welcomes guests, and a sunburst over the entry door lights the foyer. Inside, ceiling details highlight many rooms, beginning in the dining room with an octagonal stepped ceiling. A serving counter connects the formal dining room to the kitchen. The kitchen features a hexagonal work island, pantry, and a snack bar adjoining the informal dining area. The great room features a corner fireplace and built-in shelves. An entrancing tray ceiling plays up the master bedroom, joining a bay-windowed sitting area, built-ins, and a sumptuous bathroom as luxurious touches to this suite.

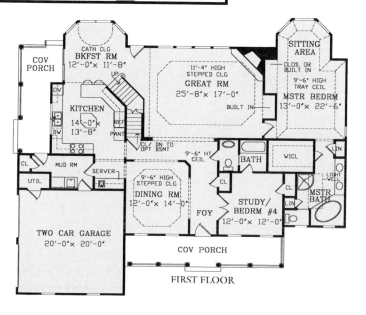

FIRST FLOOR

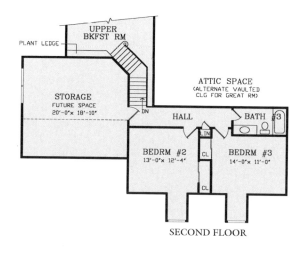

SECOND FLOOR

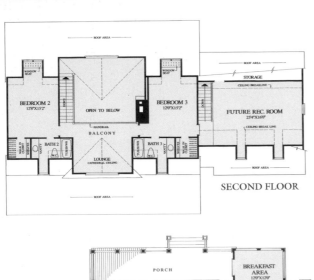

SECOND FLOOR

FIRST FLOOR

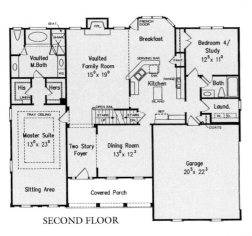

SECOND FLOOR

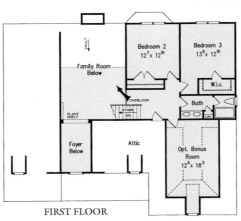

FIRST FLOOR

plan # HPK0600246

STYLE: COUNTRY COTTAGE
FIRST FLOOR: 1,819 SQ. FT.
SECOND FLOOR: 638 SQ. FT.
TOTAL: 2,457 SQ. FT.
BONUS SPACE: 385 SQ. FT.
BEDROOMS: 3
BATHROOMS: 2½
WIDTH: 47' - 4"
DEPTH: 82' - 8"
FOUNDATION:
CRAWLSPACE, BASEMENT

SEARCH ONLINE @ EPLANS.COM

Graceful dormers top a welcoming covered porch that is enhanced by Victorian details on this fine three-bedroom home. Inside, the foyer leads past the formal dining room back to the spacious two-story great room. Here, a fireplace, built-ins, and outdoor access make any gathering special. The nearby kitchen features a work island, a pantry, a serving bar, and an adjacent bayed breakfast area. Located on the first floor for privacy, the master suite is designed to pamper. Upstairs, two family bedrooms share a hall bath. Note the bonus space above the two-car garage.

FIRST FLOOR

SECOND FLOOR

© 1998 Donald A. Gardner, Inc.

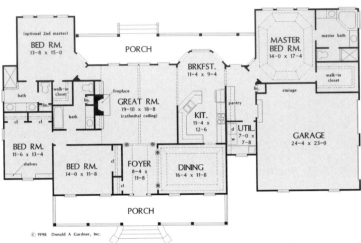

BED RM.
13–8 x 15–0
(optional 2nd master)

PORCH

BRKFST.
11–4 x 9–4

MASTER BED RM.
14–0 x 17–4

master bath

walk-in closet

walk-in closet

bath

lin.

fireplace

GREAT RM.
19–10 x 18–8
(cathedral ceiling)

KIT.
11–4 x 12–6

pantry

storage

BED RM.
11–6 x 13–4

shelves

BED RM.
14–0 x 11–8

cl.

FOYER
8–4 x 11–8

DINING
16–4 x 11–8

d **UTIL.**
7–0 x 7–8

GARAGE
24–4 x 23–0

PORCH

© 1998 Donald A Gardner, Inc.

---

plan # HPK0600247

STYLE: TRADITIONAL
SQUARE FOOTAGE: 2,487
BEDROOMS: 4
BATHROOMS: 3
WIDTH: 86' - 2"
DEPTH: 51' - 8"

clerestory window with arched top

great room below

railing

balcony

BED RM.
12–8 x 12–0

down

bath

BED RM.
12–8 x 12–0

foyer below

clerestory with palladian window

SECOND FLOOR

Quote One

© 1993 Donald A. Gardner Architects, Inc.

seat   seat

spa **DECK**

SCREENED PORCH
15–4 x 10–0

PORCH

MASTER BED RM.
16–8 x 15–6

GREAT RM.
17–4 x 19–4
(sloped ceiling)

fireplace

cabinets

balcony above

BRKFST.
10–8 x 9–0

UTILITY
7–8 x 9–4

KITCHEN
12–8 x 12–8

walk-in closet

lin.

master bath

sto.

cl.

bath

FOYER
11–8 x 7–0

up

DINING
15–0 x 12–4

PORCH

up   storage

GARAGE
22–4 x 25–8

covered breezeway

FIRST FLOOR

---

plan # HPK0600248

STYLE: FARMHOUSE
FIRST FLOOR: 1,618 SQ. FT.
SECOND FLOOR: 570 SQ. FT.
TOTAL: 2,188 SQ. FT.
BONUS SPACE: 495 SQ. FT.
BEDROOMS: 3
BATHROOMS: 2½
WIDTH: 87' - 0"
DEPTH: 57' - 0"

ORDER BLUEPRINTS 24 HOURS, 7 DAYS A WEEK, AT 1-800-521-6797

plan # HPK0600249

STYLE: COLONIAL
SQUARE FOOTAGE: 2,595
BONUS SPACE: 1,480 SQ. FT.
BEDROOMS: 4
BATHROOMS: 2½
WIDTH: 78' - 8"
DEPTH: 67' - 0"
FOUNDATION: BASEMENT

SEARCH ONLINE @ EPLANS.COM

This home has a touch of modernism with all the comforts of country style. The pillared front porch allows for summer evening relaxation. The foyer extends into the bright great room equipped with a fireplace. The large kitchen is stationed between the vaulted dining room and airy breakfast nook. Two walk-in closets, dual vanities, and a spacious bath complement the master suite. Each of the three family bedrooms features closet space. The entire second floor is left for future development, whether it be a guest room, rec room, or study—or all three.

This classic two-story farmhouse offers two porches for outdoor living. Inside, an elegant dining room is accented with twin columns. The expansive kitchen is nestled between the sunny breakfast area and the dining room, with a half-bath and utility room close at hand. The living room delights with a window wall, corner fireplace, and access to the rear porch. The master suite pampers with two walk-in closets, a double-sink vanity, and a separate shower and tub. Three bedrooms on the second floor share a full bath.

plan # HPK0600250

STYLE: COUNTRY COTTAGE
FIRST FLOOR: 1,533 SQ. FT.
SECOND FLOOR: 895 SQ. FT.
TOTAL: 2,428 SQ. FT.
BEDROOMS: 4
BATHROOMS: 2½
WIDTH: 45' - 10 "
DEPTH: 48' - 5 "
FOUNDATION: BASEMENT

SEARCH ONLINE @ EPLANS.COM

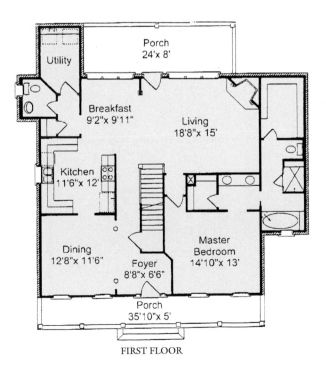

FIRST FLOOR

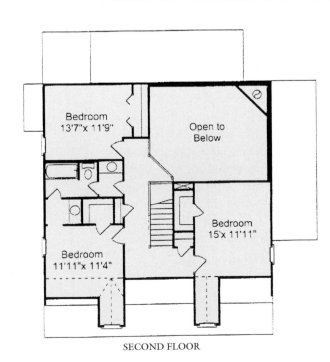

SECOND FLOOR

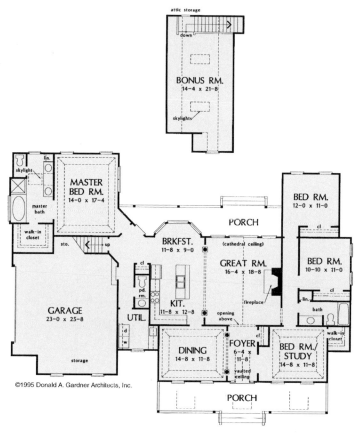

attic storage
down

BONUS RM.
14-4 x 21-8

skylights

MASTER
BED RM.
14-0 x 17-4

skylight

lin.

master
bath

walk-in
closet

sto.

up

BRKFST.
11-8 9-0

cl

pd.
rm.

KIT.
11-8 x 12-8

UTIL.

d
w

GARAGE
23-0 x 25-8

storage

DINING
14-8 x 11-8

PORCH

(cathedral ceiling)

GREAT RM.
16-4 x 18-8

fireplace

opening
above

FOYER
6-4 x
11-8

vaulted
ceiling

BED RM.
12-0 x 11-0

cl

BED RM.
10-10 x 11-0

cl

lin.

bath

walk-in
closet

BED RM./
STUDY
14-8 x 11-8

PORCH

©1995 Donald A. Gardner Architects, Inc.

plan # HPK0600251

STYLE: FARMHOUSE
SQUARE FOOTAGE: 2,192
BONUS SPACE: 390 SQ. FT.
BEDROOMS: 4
BATHROOMS: 2½
WIDTH: 74' - 10"
DEPTH: 55' - 8"

SEARCH ONLINE @ EPLANS.COM

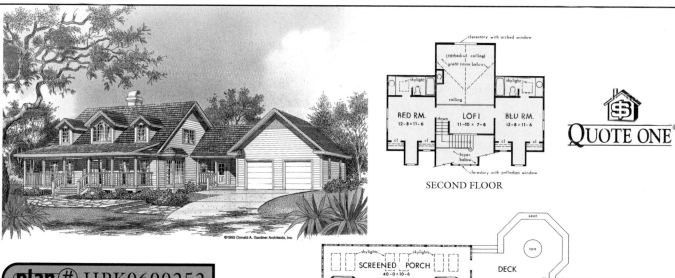

clerestory with arched window

(cathedral ceiling)
great room below

skylight

skylight

BED RM.
12-8 x 11-6

LOFT
11-10 x 7-6

BED RM.
12-8 x 11-6

railing

down

cl

cl

cl

cl

foyer
below

clerestory with palladian window

SECOND FLOOR

QUOTE ONE®

seat

spa

skylights   skylights

SCREENED   PORCH
40-0 x 10-6

DECK

storage   storage

MASTER
BED RM.
12-8 x 17-2

walk-in
closet

master
bath

bath

lin.

GREAT RM.
15-4 x 24-0

fireplace

balcony above

BRKFST.
10-4 x 8-6

KITCHEN
12-8 x 14-6

UTILITY
9-6 x 9-8

cl

covered
breezeway

GARAGE
23-4 x 21-8

BED RM./
STUDY
12-8 x 11-0

cl

up

FOYER
15-4 x 9-8

DINING
14-8 x 12-8

PORCH
40-0 x 8-0

©1992 Donald A. Gardner Architects, Inc.

FIRST FLOOR

plan # HPK0600252

STYLE: FARMHOUSE
FIRST FLOOR: 1,766 SQ. FT.
SECOND FLOOR: 670 SQ. FT.
TOTAL: 2,436 SQ. FT.
BEDROOMS: 4
BATHROOMS: 3½
WIDTH: 59' - 10"
DEPTH: 53' - 4"

SEARCH ONLINE @ EPLANS.COM

Plan 1

- Mbr. 13⁰ x 16⁵
- Grt. rm. 16⁰ x 20⁰ — 10'-0" CEILING
- Bfst. 10⁰ x 11⁴
- Kit. 8¹⁰ x 13⁸
- Gar. 21⁰ x 25⁴
- TRANSOMS
- PANT.
- R.
- D. W.
- DN
- Br. 2 11⁰ x 13⁰ — 9'-0" CEILING
- Br. 3 12⁰ x 11⁴ — 10'-0" CEILING
- E.
- Din. 12⁰ x 15⁴ — 10'-0" CEILING
- Off. 11⁰ x 18⁰ — 9'-0" CEILING
- COVERED PORCH

plan# HPK0600253

STYLE: TRADITIONAL
SQUARE FOOTAGE: 2,151
BEDROOMS: 3
BATHROOMS: 2
WIDTH: 76' - 8"
DEPTH: 40' - 0"

SEARCH ONLINE @ EPLANS.COM

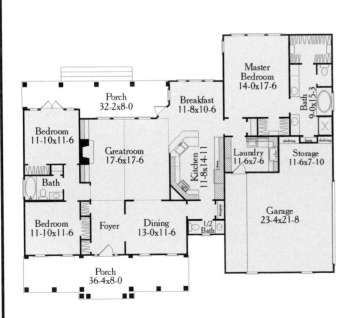

- Porch 32-2x8-0
- Breakfast 11-8x10-6
- Master Bedroom 14-0x17-6
- Bath 9-0x15-3
- Bedroom 11-10x11-6
- Greatroom 17-6x17-6
- Kitchen 11-8x14-11
- Laundry 11-6x7-6
- Storage 11-6x7-10
- Bath
- Bedroom 11-10x11-6
- Foyer
- Dining 13-0x11-6
- 1/2 Bath
- Garage 23-4x21-8
- Porch 36-4x8-0

plan# HPK0600254

STYLE: TRADITIONAL
SQUARE FOOTAGE: 2,046
BEDROOMS: 3
BATHROOMS: 2½
WIDTH: 68' - 2"
DEPTH: 57' - 4"
FOUNDATION: CRAWLSPACE, SLAB, BASEMENT

SEARCH ONLINE @ EPLANS.COM

plan # HPK0600255

STYLE: PLANTATION
SQUARE FOOTAGE: 2,497
BONUS SPACE: 966 SQ. FT.
BEDROOMS: 3
BATHROOMS: 3½
WIDTH: 87' - 0"
DEPTH: 57' - 3"
FOUNDATION: CRAWLSPACE,
SLAB, BASEMENT

SEARCH ONLINE @ EPLANS.COM

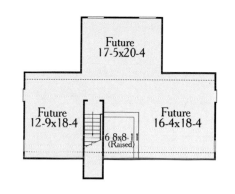

This symmetrical, elegant home features a gabled porch complemented by columns. The breakfast room, adjacent to the kitchen, opens to a rear porch. The spacious great room provides a fireplace and a view of the patio. A lovely bayed window brightens the master suite, which includes a walk-in closet and a bath with a garden tub and a separate shower. Two secondary bedrooms each offer a private bath. A winding staircase leads to second-level future space.

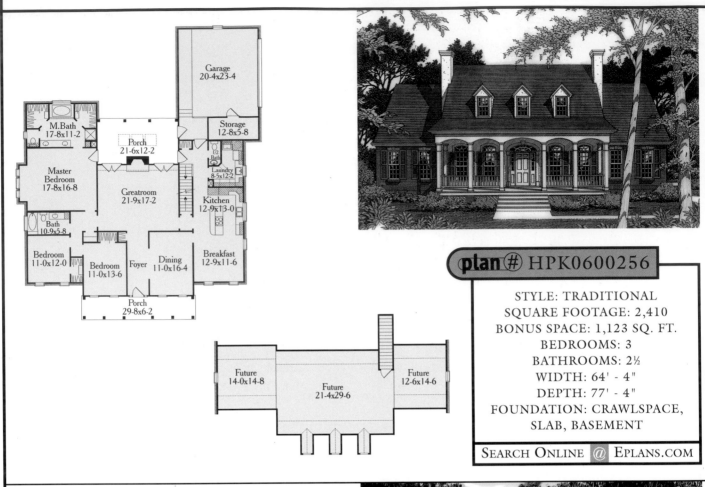

plan # HPK0600256

STYLE: TRADITIONAL
SQUARE FOOTAGE: 2,410
BONUS SPACE: 1,123 SQ. FT.
BEDROOMS: 3
BATHROOMS: 2½
WIDTH: 64' - 4"
DEPTH: 77' - 4"
FOUNDATION: CRAWLSPACE,
SLAB, BASEMENT

SEARCH ONLINE @ EPLANS.com

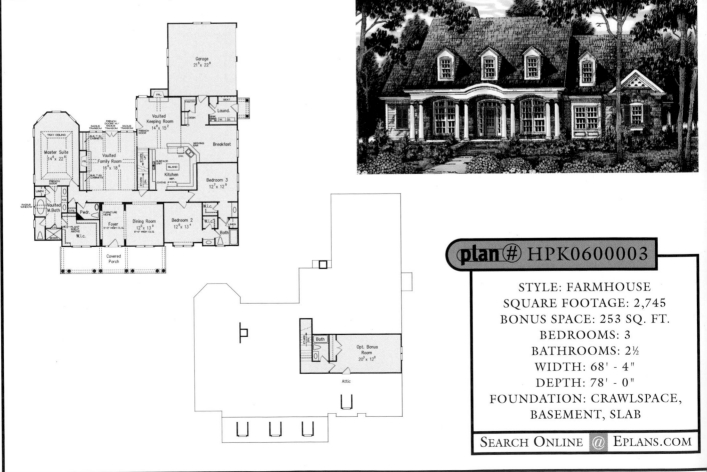

plan # HPK0600003

STYLE: FARMHOUSE
SQUARE FOOTAGE: 2,745
BONUS SPACE: 253 SQ. FT.
BEDROOMS: 3
BATHROOMS: 2½
WIDTH: 68' - 4"
DEPTH: 78' - 0"
FOUNDATION: CRAWLSPACE,
BASEMENT, SLAB

SEARCH ONLINE @ EPLANS.com

plan# HPK0600257

STYLE: COUNTRY COTTAGE
FIRST FLOOR: 1,883 SQ. FT.
SECOND FLOOR: 803 SQ. FT.
TOTAL: 2,686 SQ. FT.
BONUS SPACE: 489 SQ. FT.
BEDROOMS: 3
BATHROOMS: 3½
WIDTH: 63' - 0"
DEPTH: 81' - 10"
FOUNDATION: CRAWLSPACE

SEARCH ONLINE @ EPLANS.COM

Where creeks converge and marsh grasses sway in gentle breezes, this is a classical low country home. Steep rooflines, high ceilings, front and back porches, plus long and low windows are typical details of these charming planters' cottages. The foyer is flanked by the formal dining room and the living room, which opens to the family room. Here, several windows look out to the terrace and a fireplace removes the chill on a winter's night. The sunny breakfast room, which adjoins the kitchen, offers a wonderful space for casual dining. Two bedrooms, the lavish master suite, and the two-car garage complete the floor plan.

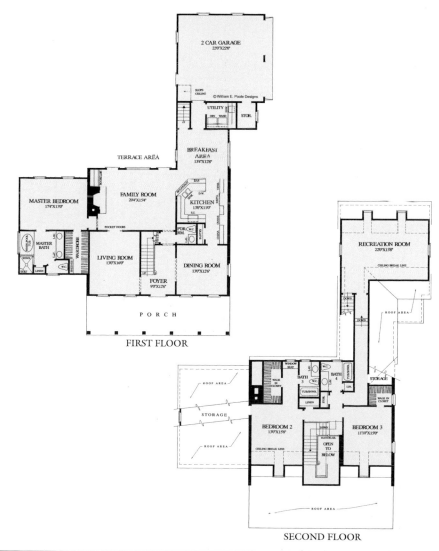

FIRST FLOOR

SECOND FLOOR

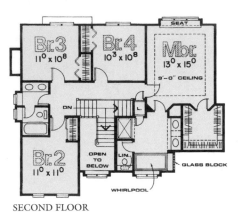

SECOND FLOOR

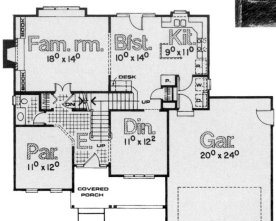

FIRST FLOOR

plan# HPK0600258

STYLE: FARMHOUSE
FIRST FLOOR: 1,082 SQ. FT.
SECOND FLOOR: 1,021 SQ. FT.
TOTAL: 2,103 SQ. FT.
BEDROOMS: 4
BATHROOMS: 2½
WIDTH: 50' - 0"
DEPTH: 40' - 0"

SEARCH ONLINE @ EPLANS.COM

SECOND FLOOR

FIRST FLOOR

plan# HPK0600259

STYLE: FARMHOUSE
FIRST FLOOR: 1,913 SQ. FT.
SECOND FLOOR: 997 SQ. FT.
TOTAL: 2,910 SQ. FT.
BONUS SPACE: 377 SQ. FT.
BEDROOMS: 4
BATHROOMS: 3½
WIDTH: 63' - 0"
DEPTH: 59' - 4"
FOUNDATION:
CRAWLSPACE, BASEMENT

SEARCH ONLINE @ EPLANS.COM

plan # HPK0600260

STYLE: COUNTRY COTTAGE
FIRST FLOOR: 1,098 SQ. FT.
SECOND FLOOR: 996 SQ. FT.
TOTAL: 2,094 SQ. FT.
BEDROOMS: 4
BATHROOMS: 2½
WIDTH: 62' - 6"
DEPTH: 40' - 0"
FOUNDATION:
CRAWLSPACE, BASEMENT

SEARCH ONLINE @ EPLANS.COM

A covered railed veranda and shuttered windows decorate this deluxe farmhouse. Flanking the foyer are a den with a double-door entry and the living room/dining room combination with a fireplace. Enter the L-shaped kitchen from either the central hall or from an entry at the dining room. An island work counter and planning desk add to the kitchen's efficiency. A light filled breakfast room serves casual meals. Sleeping quarters occupy the second floor. The master bedroom presents two separate closets, a sitting area, and a whirlpool tub. Three additional bedrooms have generous closet space and share a full hall bath.

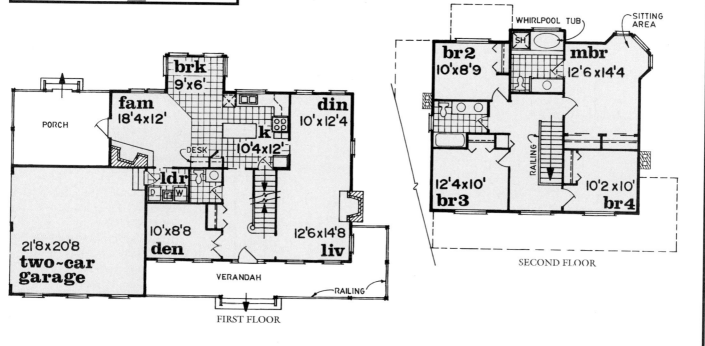

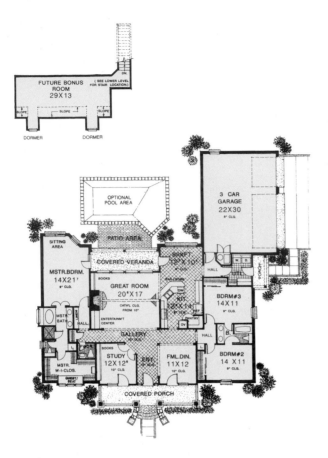

FUTURE BONUS
ROOM
29X13

(SEE LOWER LEVEL
FOR STAIR LOCATION)

DORMER   DORMER

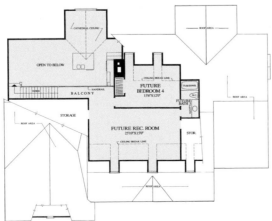

plan # HPK0600263

STYLE: COUNTRY COTTAGE
SQUARE FOOTAGE: 2,151
BONUS SPACE: 814 SQ. FT.
BEDROOMS: 3
BATHROOMS: 2
WIDTH: 61' - 0"
DEPTH: 55' - 8"
FOUNDATION:
CRAWLSPACE, BASEMENT

SEARCH ONLINE @ EPLANS.COM

Country flavor is well established on this fine three-bedroom home. The covered front porch welcomes friends and family alike to the foyer, where the formal dining room opens off to the left. The vaulted ceiling in the great room enhances the warmth of the fireplace and the wall of windows. An efficient kitchen works well with the bayed breakfast area. The secluded master suite offers a walk-in closet and a lavish bath; on the other side of the home, two family bedrooms share a full bath. Upstairs, an optional fourth bedroom is available for guests or in-laws and provides access to a large recreation room.

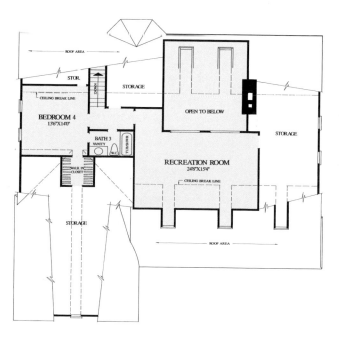

SECOND FLOOR

Bedroom 3
11⁰ x 12⁰

W.i.c.
W.i.c.
Bath
LINEN
Family Room Below
OPEN RAIL STAIRS DN.
Bath
Foyer Below
Bedroom 2
12³ x 12⁹
Bedroom 4
11⁷ x 13⁰
W.i.c.
Opt. Bonus Room
11⁵ x 12⁰

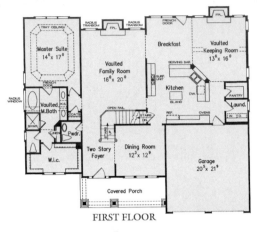

FIRST FLOOR

Master Suite
14⁰ x 17⁰
Vaulted M.Bath
Vaulted Family Room
16⁰ x 20⁰
Breakfast
Vaulted Keeping Room
13⁸ x 16⁰
Kitchen
Two Story Foyer
Dining Room
12³ x 12⁹
Garage
20⁵ x 21⁹
W.i.c.
Covered Porch
Laund.
Pantry

plan# HPK0600264

STYLE: CRAFTSMAN
FIRST FLOOR: 1,909 SQ. FT.
SECOND FLOOR: 835 SQ. FT.
TOTAL: 2,744 SQ. FT.
BEDROOMS: 4
BATHROOMS: 3½
WIDTH: 56' - 0"
DEPTH: 51' - 4"
FOUNDATION:
CRAWLSPACE, BASEMENT

SEARCH ONLINE @ Eplans.com

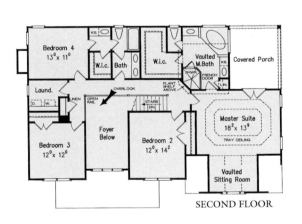

SECOND FLOOR

Bedroom 4
13⁰ x 11⁰
W.i.c.
Bath
W.i.c.
Vaulted M.Bath
Covered Porch
Laund.
OVERLOOK
OPEN RAIL
STAIRS DN.
Foyer Below
Master Suite
18² x 13⁹
TRAY CEILING
Bedroom 3
12⁰ x 12⁰
Bedroom 2
12⁰ x 14²
Vaulted Sitting Room

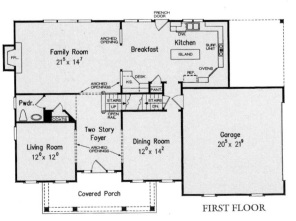

FIRST FLOOR

Family Room
21⁵ x 14⁷
Breakfast
Kitchen
Pwdr.
Living Room
12⁰ x 12⁰
Two Story Foyer
Dining Room
12⁰ x 14²
Garage
20⁵ x 21⁹
Covered Porch

plan# HPK0600265

STYLE: CRAFTSMAN
FIRST FLOOR: 1,249 SQ. FT.
SECOND FLOOR: 1,458 SQ. FT.
TOTAL: 2,707 SQ. FT.
BEDROOMS: 4
BATHROOMS: 2½
WIDTH: 57' - 4"
DEPTH: 39' - 0"
FOUNDATION:
CRAWLSPACE, BASEMENT

SEARCH ONLINE @ Eplans.com

plan # HPK0600266

L

STYLE: TRADITIONAL
FIRST FLOOR: 1,200 SQ. FT.
SECOND FLOOR: 1,339 SQ. FT.
TOTAL: 2,539 SQ. FT.
BEDROOMS: 5
BATHROOMS: 2½
WIDTH: 56' - 0"
DEPTH: 40' - 0"
FOUNDATION: CRAWLSPACE

SEARCH ONLINE @ EPLANS.COM

A covered front porch introduces this home's comfortable living pattern. The two-story foyer opens to a living room with a fireplace and lots of natural light. In the kitchen, an island cooktop, pantry, built-in planning desk, and a nook with double doors to outside livability all aim to please. A spacious family room with another fireplace will accommodate casual living. Upstairs, five bedrooms—or four and a den—make room for all family members and guests. The master bedroom suite exudes elegance with a beautiful ceiling and a pampering spa bath. A full hall bath with a skylight and dual lavatories serves the secondary bedrooms.

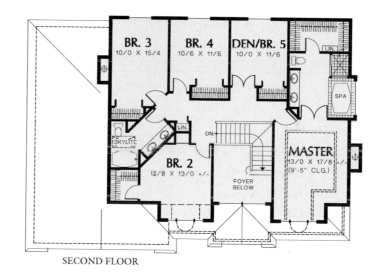

SECOND FLOOR

FIRST FLOOR

Covered Porch

Family
20⁸ · 15⁸
10' Ceiling

Nook

Master
Bedroom
14⁴ · 21⁰
10' Ceiling

Bath

Living
13⁴ · 12²
10' Ceiling

Kitchen

Bedroom 4
13⁸ · 12⁰
10' Ceiling

Bath

W.I.C.   W.I.C.

Bedroom 2
11⁸ · 11⁸
10' Ceiling

Foyer

Dining
11⁸ · 14⁸
10' Ceiling

Utility

Bedroom 3
13⁸ · 12⁰
10' Ceiling

Master
Bath
10' Ceiling

Entry

W.I.C.   Bath   down

Future
Space
22² · 14⁸

3 Car Garage
22² · 31⁸
8' Ceiling

plan # HPK0600267

STYLE: FLORIDIAN
SQUARE FOOTAGE: 2,755
BONUS SPACE: 440 SQ. FT.
BEDROOMS: 4
BATHROOMS: 3
WIDTH: 73' - 0"
DEPTH: 82' - 8"
FOUNDATION: SLAB

SEARCH ONLINE @ Eplans.com

Porch
54'-0" x 12'-0"

Nook
11'-0" x 8'-6"

Desk

Kitchen

Master Bedroom
15'-2" x 15'-6"
Tray Clg.

built-in

Great Room
21'-6" x 15'-6"
Coffered Clg.

glass
hutch

Island

Bedroom 2
13'-2" x 11'-10"

fireplace

built-in

13'-0" x 11'-8"

CL

Her
WIC

His
WIC

art niche

Linen

Bath

M.
Bath

make-up

Study
12'-10" x 14'-10"
Beamed Clg.

built-in

Foyer

Dining
12'-0" x 14'-6"
Stepped Clg.

art niche

Pwdr.

Utility

CL

Bedroom 1
13'-6" x 12'-0"

Porch
36'-6" x 8'-0"

workbench

Storage

Garage
23'-0" x 24'-0"

plan # HPK0600268

STYLE: FARMHOUSE
SQUARE FOOTAGE: 2,555
BEDROOMS: 3
BATHROOMS: 2½
WIDTH: 70' - 6"
DEPTH: 76' - 6"
FOUNDATION: CRAWLSPACE

SEARCH ONLINE @ Eplans.com

plan # HPK0600269

STYLE: COUNTRY COTTAGE
FIRST FLOOR: 1,205 SQ. FT.
SECOND FLOOR: 1,123 SQ. FT.
TOTAL: 2,328 SQ. FT.
BEDROOMS: 4
BATHROOMS: 2½
WIDTH: 57' - 2"
DEPTH: 58' - 7"
FOUNDATION: CRAWLSPACE

SEARCH ONLINE @ EPLANS.COM

A covered porch, multipane windows, and shingle-with-stone siding combine to give this bungalow plenty of curb appeal. Inside, the foyer is flanked by the formal living room and an angled staircase. The formal dining room adjoins the living room, and the kitchen is accessible through double doors. A large family room is graced by a fireplace and opens off a cozy eating nook. The second level presents many attractive angles. The master suite has a spacious walk-in closet and a sumptuous bath complete with a garden tub and separate shower. Three family bedrooms share a full hall bath.

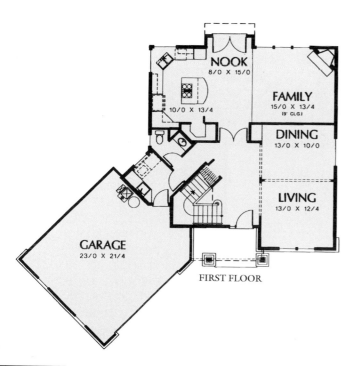

FIRST FLOOR

SECOND FLOOR

SECOND FLOOR

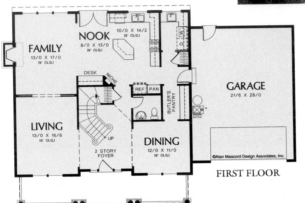

FIRST FLOOR

plan # HPK0600270

STYLE: COUNTRY COTTAGE
FIRST FLOOR: 1,319 SQ. FT.
SECOND FLOOR: 1,181 SQ. FT.
TOTAL: 2,500 SQ. FT.
BONUS SPACE: 371 SQ. FT.
BEDROOMS: 4
BATHROOMS: 2½
WIDTH: 60' - 0"
DEPTH: 42' - 0"
FOUNDATION: CRAWLSPACE

SEARCH ONLINE @ EPLANS.COM

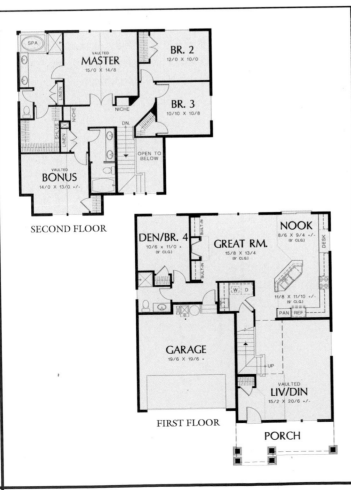

SECOND FLOOR

FIRST FLOOR

PORCH

plan # HPK0600271

STYLE: CRAFTSMAN
FIRST FLOOR: 1,252 SQ. FT.
SECOND FLOOR: 985 SQ. FT.
TOTAL: 2,237 SQ. FT.
BONUS SPACE: 183 SQ. FT.
BEDROOMS: 4
BATHROOMS: 3
WIDTH: 40' - 0"
DEPTH: 51' - 0"
FOUNDATION:
CRAWLSPACE, BASEMENT

SEARCH ONLINE @ EPLANS.COM

plan # HPK0600272

STYLE: COUNTRY COTTAGE
FIRST FLOOR: 1,333 SQ. FT.
SECOND FLOOR: 1,129 SQ. FT.
TOTAL: 2,462 SQ. FT.
BEDROOMS: 4
BATHROOMS: 2½
WIDTH: 69' - 8"
DEPTH: 49' 0"
FOUNDATION:
CRAWLSPACE, BASEMENT

SEARCH ONLINE @ EPLANS.COM

A large wraparound porch graces the exterior of this home and gives it great outdoor livability. The raised foyer spills into a hearth-warmed living room and to the bay-windowed dining room beyond. French doors open from the breakfast and dining rooms to the spacious porch. Built-ins surround another hearth in the family room. The front study is adorned by a beamed ceiling and also features built-ins. Three bedrooms and a master suite are found on the second floor. The master suite features a walk-in closet and a private bath. Don't miss the workshop area in the garage.

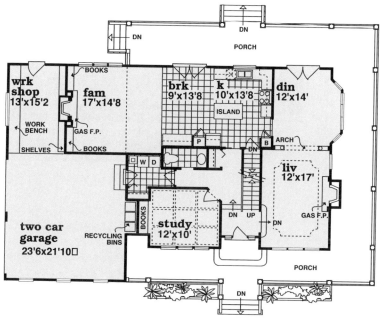

FIRST FLOOR

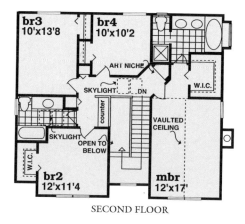

SECOND FLOOR

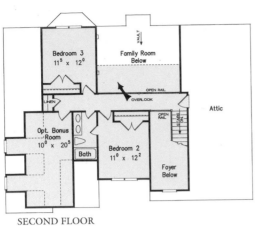

SECOND FLOOR

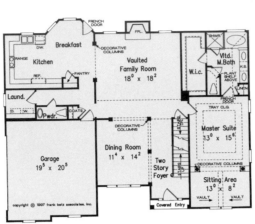

FIRST FLOOR

SECOND FLOOR

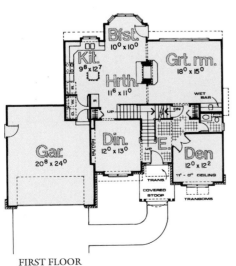

FIRST FLOOR

plan # HPK0600275

STYLE: TRADITIONAL
FIRST FLOOR: 1,733 SQ. FT.
SECOND FLOOR: 672 SQ. FT.
TOTAL: 2,405 SQ. FT.
BEDROOMS: 4
BATHROOMS: 2½
WIDTH: 60' - 0"
DEPTH: 55' - 4"

SEARCH ONLINE @ EPLANS.COM

Split-bedroom floor planning highlights this volume-look home. The owners suite on the first floor is completely private and perfectly pampering with a huge walk-in closet, double vanity, and separate tub and shower. The great room and hearth room share a through-fireplace and are complemented by a breakfast area and island kitchen. Formal entertaining is enhanced by the dining room with hutch space and boxed window. A guest half bath just off the hearth room will be appreciated by visitors. Three family bedrooms upstairs share a full bath that has a double vanity.

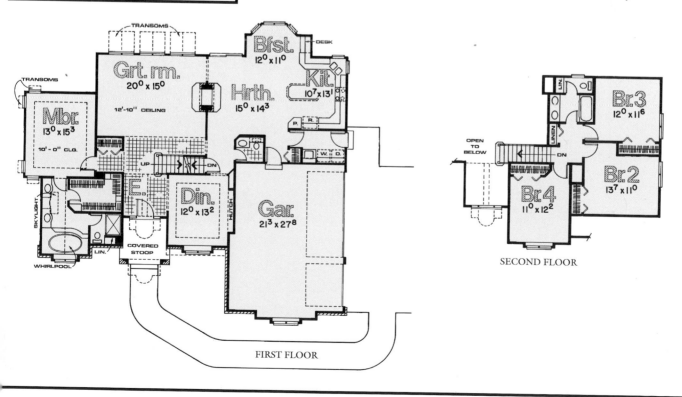

FIRST FLOOR

SECOND FLOOR

FIRST FLOOR

Bath
Dressing
Dining 12'2" x 11'10"
Deck
walk-in closet
Sitting Area 11'10" x 11'10"
Master Bedroom 14'4" x 11'10"
Kitchen 11'7" x 14'6"
Great Room 15' x 16'6"
Bedroom 10'9" x 10'6"
Hall
Bath
Laun. 9'2" x 7'4"
Hall
Raised Foyer
Porch
Bedroom /Library 12'10" x 11'6"
Two-car Garage 21' x 25'9"

BASEMENT

Patio
Rec. Room
Bedroom 11'11" x 13'
Kitchen
Bath
Sauna
Basement Storage
Bath
Exercise Room 11'11" x 15'2"

plan# HPK0600276

STYLE: TRANSITIONAL
SQUARE FOOTAGE: 2,041
BASEMENT: 1,802 SQ. FT.
BEDROOMS: 3
BATHROOMS: 2
WIDTH: 67' - 6"
DEPTH: 63' - 6"
FOUNDATION: BASEMENT

SEARCH ONLINE @ EPLANS.COM

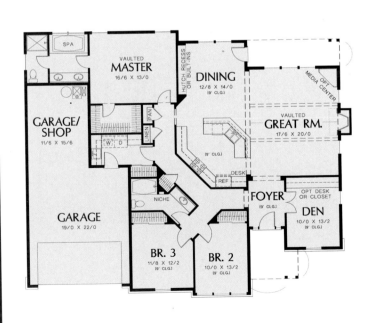

SPA
VAULTED MASTER 16/6 X 13/0
DINING 12/8 X 14/0 (9' CLG.)
OPT. MEDIA CENTER
GARAGE/ SHOP 11/6 X 15/6
LINEN PAN
W D
HUTCH RECESS OR BUILT-INS
VAULTED GREAT RM. 17/6 X 20/0
(9' CLG.)
DESK
REF
GARAGE 19/0 X 22/0
NICHE
FOYER (9' CLG.)
OPT DESK OR CLOSET
DEN 10/0 X 13/2 (9' CLG.)
BR. 3 11/8 X 12/2 (9' CLG.)
BR. 2 10/0 X 13/2 (9' CLG.)

plan# HPK0600277

STYLE: TRADITIONAL
SQUARE FOOTAGE: 2,001
BEDROOMS: 3
BATHROOMS: 2
WIDTH: 60' - 0"
DEPTH: 50' - 0"
FOUNDATION: CRAWLSPACE

SEARCH ONLINE @ EPLANS.COM

plan # HPK0600278

STYLE: TRADITIONAL
FIRST FLOOR: 1,604 SQ. FT.
SECOND FLOOR: 1,230 SQ. FT.
TOTAL: 2,834 SQ. FT.
BONUS SPACE: 284 SQ. FT.
BEDROOMS: 3
BATHROOMS: 2½
WIDTH: 60' - 0"
DEPTH: 52' - 0"
FOUNDATION: CRAWLSPACE

SEARCH ONLINE @ EPLANS.COM

The combination of stone and siding gives the facade of this traditional home an inviting feel. Inside, the first floor is a study in family togetherness. The expansive kitchen invites friends and family to share in the cooking experience, be it by conversing from the adjoining nook or adjacent family room, or actually getting their hands dirty at the convenient island counter. The dining room and nearby living room with a fireplace are perfect for formal entertaining. Completing this level are a den, a half-bath, and the three-car garage. Bedrooms dominate the second level, including a vaulted master suite and pampering master bath, along with bonus space to finish as you please.

FIRST FLOOR

SECOND FLOOR

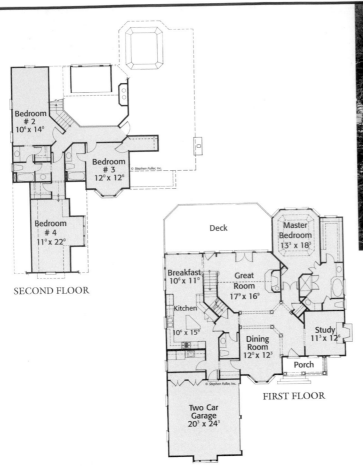

Bedroom
2
10⁶ x 14⁰

Bedroom # 3
12⁰ x 12⁶

© Stephen Fuller, Inc.

Bedroom
4
11⁰ x 22⁰

SECOND FLOOR

Deck

Master
Bedroom
13³ x 18³

Breakfast
10⁶ x 11⁰

Great
Room
17⁹ x 16⁹

Kitchen
10⁶ x 15⁹

Study
11³ x 12⁶

Dining
Room
12⁰ x 12³

Porch

© Stephen Fuller, Inc.

Two Car
Garage
20³ x 24³

FIRST FLOOR

plan # HPK0600279

STYLE: COUNTRY COTTAGE
FIRST FLOOR: 1,944 SQ. FT.
SECOND FLOOR: 1,055 SQ. FT.
TOTAL: 2,999 SQ. FT.
BEDROOMS: 4
BATHROOMS: 3½
WIDTH: 51' - 6"
DEPTH: 72' - 0"
FOUNDATION:
WALKOUT BASEMENT

SEARCH ONLINE @ EPLANS.COM

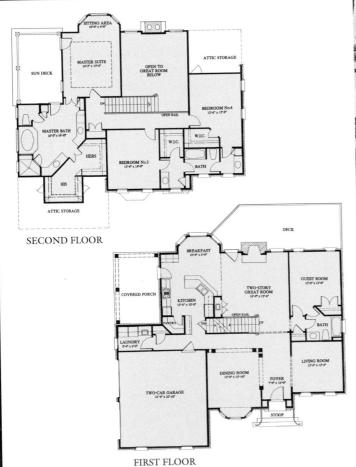

SITTING AREA
10'-0" x 4'-0"

SUN DECK

MASTER SUITE
14'-7" x 15'-0"

OPEN TO
GREAT ROOM
BELOW

ATTIC STORAGE

MASTER BATH
10'-7" x 10'-10"

BEDROOM No.4
12'-6" x 12'-6"

HERS

W.I.C.

W.I.C.

HIS

BEDROOM No.3
12'-6" x 14'-0"

BATH

ATTIC STORAGE

SECOND FLOOR

BREAKFAST
10'-0" x 6'-0"

DECK

COVERED PORCH

KITCHEN
12'-4" x 10'-0"

TWO-STORY
GREAT ROOM
16'-0" x 15'-0"

GUEST ROOM
12'-6" x 13'-0"

PANTRY

LAUNDRY
8'-6" x 6'-6"

BATH

OPEN RAIL

LIVING ROOM
12'-6" x 12'-6"

TWO-CAR GARAGE
21'-6" x 22'-10"

DINING ROOM
12'-4" x 13'-10"

FOYER
7'-0" x 10'-0"

STOOP

FIRST FLOOR

plan # HPK0600280

STYLE: FARMHOUSE
FIRST FLOOR: 1,581 SQ. FT.
SECOND FLOOR: 1,415 SQ. FT.
TOTAL: 2,996 SQ. FT.
BEDROOMS: 4
BATHROOMS: 3
WIDTH: 55' - 0"
DEPTH: 52' - 0"
FOUNDATION:
WALKOUT BASEMENT

SEARCH ONLINE @ EPLANS.COM

plan# HPK0600281

STYLE: FARMHOUSE
FIRST FLOOR: 1,944 SQ. FT.
SECOND FLOOR: 954 SQ. FT.
TOTAL: 2,898 SQ. FT.
BEDROOMS: 4
BATHROOMS: 3½
WIDTH: 51' - 6"
DEPTH: 73' - 0"
FOUNDATION:
WALKOUT BASEMENT

SEARCH ONLINE @ EPLANS.COM

This gracious home combines warm, informal materials with a modern, livable floor plan to create a true Southern classic. The dining room, study, and great room work together to create one large, exciting space. Just beyond the open rail, the breakfast room is lined with windows. Plenty of counter space and storage make the kitchen user-friendly. The master suite, with its tray ceiling and decorative wall niche, is a welcome retreat. Upstairs, two additional bedrooms have their own vanities within a shared bath; the third bedroom or guest room includes its own bath and walk-in closet.

FIRST FLOOR

SECOND FLOOR

QUOTE ONE®

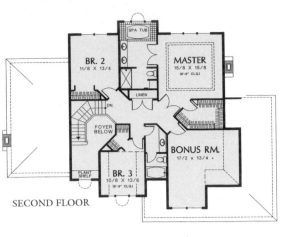

SECOND FLOOR

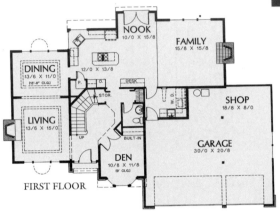

FIRST FLOOR

plan# HPK0600282

L

STYLE: TRADITIONAL
FIRST FLOOR: 1,465 SQ. FT.
SECOND FLOOR: 1,103 SQ. FT.
TOTAL: 2,568 SQ. FT.
BONUS SPACE: 303 SQ. FT.
BEDROOMS: 3
BATHROOMS: 2½
WIDTH: 63' - 0"
DEPTH: 48' - 0"
FOUNDATION: CRAWLSPACE

SEARCH ONLINE @ EPLANS.COM

SECOND FLOOR

FIRST FLOOR

plan# HPK0600283

STYLE: TRADITIONAL
FIRST FLOOR: 1,551 SQ. FT.
SECOND FLOOR: 725 SQ. FT.
TOTAL: 2,276 SQ. FT.
BEDROOMS: 4
BATHROOMS: 2½
WIDTH: 54' - 0"
DEPTH: 50' - 0"

SEARCH ONLINE @ EPLANS.COM

plan# HPK0600284

STYLE: TRADITIONAL
FIRST FLOOR: 1,580 SQ. FT.
SECOND FLOOR: 595 SQ. FT.
TOTAL: 2,175 SQ. FT.
BEDROOMS: 3
BATHROOMS: 2½
WIDTH: 50' - 2"
DEPTH: 70' - 11"
FOUNDATION:
WALKOUT BASEMENT

SEARCH ONLINE @ EPLANS.COM

This home is a true Southern
original. Inside, the spacious foyer leads directly to a large vaulted great room with its handsome fireplace. The dining room, just off the foyer, features a dramatic vaulted ceiling. The spacious kitchen offers both storage and large work areas opening up to the breakfast room. At the rear of the home you will find the master suite with its garden bath, His and Hers vanities, and an oversize closet. The second floor provides two additional bedrooms with a shared bath and a balcony overlook to the foyer below.

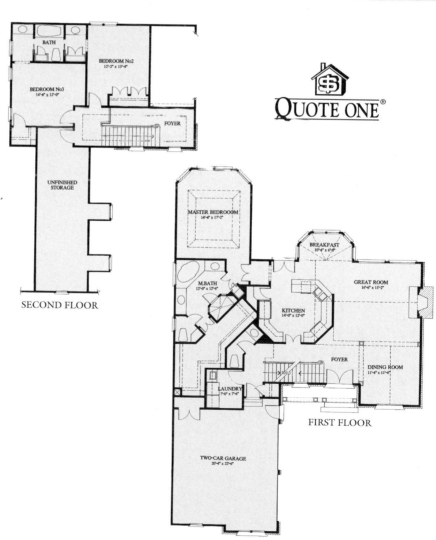

QUOTE ONE®

SECOND FLOOR

FIRST FLOOR

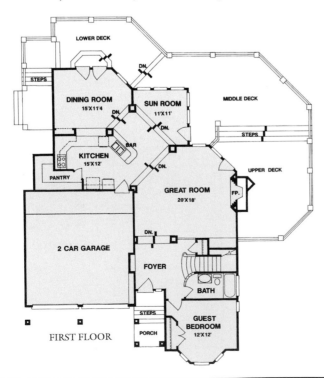

plan# HPK0600285 **L**

STYLE: CONTEMPORARY
FIRST FLOOR: 1,309 SQ. FT.
SECOND FLOOR: 1,343 SQ. FT.
TOTAL: 2,652 SQ. FT.
BEDROOMS: 3
BATHROOMS: 3
WIDTH: 44' - 4"
DEPTH: 58' - 2"
FOUNDATION: CRAWLSPACE

SEARCH ONLINE @ EPLANS.COM

Clean, contemporary lines, a unique floor plan, and a metal roof with a cupola set this farmhouse apart. Remote-control transoms in the cupola open to create an airy and decidedly unique foyer. The great room, sunroom, dining room, and kitchen flow from one to another for casual entertaining with flair. The rear of the home is fashioned with plenty of windows overlooking the multilevel deck. A front bedroom and bath would make a comfortable guest suite. The master bedroom and bath upstairs are bridged by a pipe-rail balcony that also gives access to a rear deck. An additional bedroom, home office, and bath complete this very special plan.

FIRST FLOOR

SECOND FLOOR

plan# HPK0600286

STYLE: SEASIDE
FIRST FLOOR: 1,552 SQ. FT.
SECOND FLOOR: 653 SQ. FT.
TOTAL: 2,205 SQ. FT.
BEDROOMS: 3
BATHROOMS: 2
WIDTH: 60' - 0"
DEPTH: 50' - 0"
FOUNDATION: PIER

SEARCH ONLINE @ EPLANS.COM

A split staircase adds flair to this European-style coastal home, where a fireplace brings warmth on chilly evenings. The foyer opens to the expansive living/dining area and island kitchen. A multitude of windows fills the interior with sunlight and ocean breezes. The wraparound rear deck finds access near the kitchen. The utility room is conveniently tucked between the kitchen and the two first-floor bedrooms. The second-floor master suite offers a private deck and a luxurious bath with a garden tub, shower, and walk-in closet.

MOVE-UP HOMES

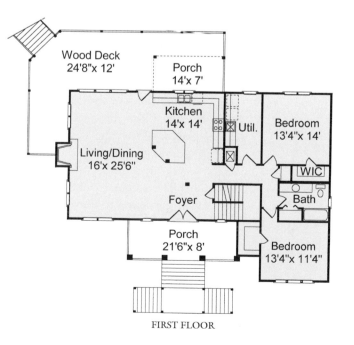

FIRST FLOOR

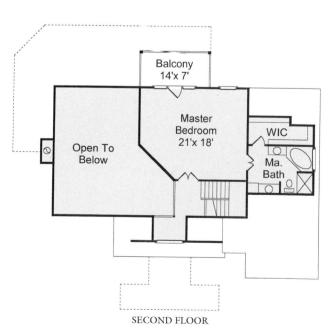

SECOND FLOOR

plan # HPK0600287

STYLE: TIDEWATER
FIRST FLOOR: 2,096 SQ. FT.
SECOND FLOOR: 892 SQ. FT.
TOTAL: 2,988 SQ. FT.
BEDROOMS: 3
BATHROOMS: 3½
WIDTH: 58' - 0"
DEPTH: 54' - 0"
FOUNDATION:
ISLAND BASEMENT

SEARCH ONLINE @ EPLANS.COM

SECOND FLOOR

FIRST FLOOR

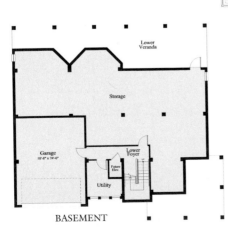

BASEMENT

The variety in the rooflines of this striking waterfront home will certainly make it the envy of the neighborhood. The two-story great room, with its fireplace and built-ins, is a short flight down from the foyer. The three sets of French doors give access to the covered lanai. The huge, well-equipped kitchen will easily serve the gourmet who loves to entertain. The stepped ceiling and bay window in the dining room will add style to every meal. The master suite completes the first level. Two bedrooms and two full baths, along with an expansive loft, constitute the second level. Bedroom 3 has an attached sundeck.

plan# HPK0600288

L

STYLE: FLORIDIAN
FIRST FLOOR: 2,066 SQ. FT.
SECOND FLOOR: 809 SQ. FT.
TOTAL: 2,875 SQ. FT.
BONUS SPACE: 1,260 SQ. FT.
BEDROOMS: 3
BATHROOMS: 3½
WIDTH: 64' - 0"
DEPTH: 45' - 0"
FOUNDATION: PIER

SEARCH ONLINE @ EPLANS.COM

If entertaining is your passion, then this is the design for you. With a large, open floor plan and an array of amenities, every gathering will be a success. The foyer embraces living areas accented by a glass fireplace and a wet bar. The grand room and dining room each access a screened veranda for outside enjoyments. The gourmet kitchen delights with its openness to the rest of the house. A morning nook here also adds a nice touch. Two bedrooms and a study radiate from the first-floor living areas. Upstairs is a masterful master suite. It contains a huge walk-in closet, a whirlpool tub, and a private sundeck with a spa.

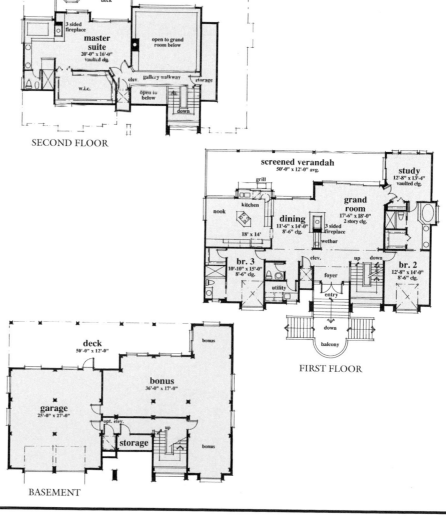

SECOND FLOOR

FIRST FLOOR

BASEMENT

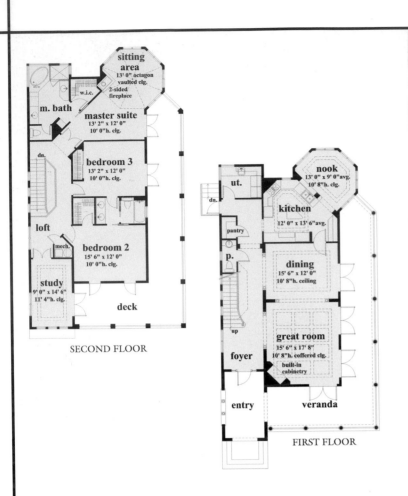

sitting area
13' 0" octagon
vaulted clg.
2-sided
fireplace

w.i.c.

m. bath

master suite
13' 2" x 12' 0"
10' 0"h. clg.

dn.

bedroom 3
13' 2" x 12' 0"
10' 0"h. clg.

loft

mech.

bedroom 2
15' 6" x 12' 0"
10' 0"h. clg.

study
9' 0" x 14' 6"
11' 4"h. clg.

deck

SECOND FLOOR

ut.

dn.

nook
13' 0" x 9' 0"avg.
10' 8"h. clg.

pantry

kitchen
12' 0" x 13' 6"avg.

p.

dining
15' 6" x 12' 0"
10' 8"h. ceiling

up

great room
15' 6" x 17' 8"
10' 8"h. coffered clg.

foyer

built-in
cabinetry

entry

veranda

FIRST FLOOR

plan # HPK0600289

STYLE: ITALIANATE
FIRST FLOOR: 1,266 SQ. FT.
SECOND FLOOR: 1,324 SQ. FT.
TOTAL: 2,590 SQ. FT.
BEDROOMS: 3
BATHROOMS: 2½
WIDTH: 34' - 0"
DEPTH: 63' - 2"
FOUNDATION: SLAB

SEARCH ONLINE @ EPLANS.COM

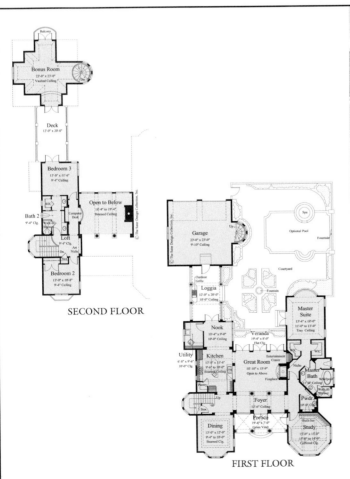

Balcony

Bonus Room
23'-0" x 23'-0"
Vaulted Ceiling

Deck
17'-0" x 20'-0"

Bedroom 3
17'-0" x 11'-6"
9'-4" Ceiling

Bath 2
9'-4" Ceiling

W.I.C.

Computer Desk

Walk-In Shower

Open to Below
10'-4" to 19'-4"
Beamed Ceiling

Loft
9'-4" Ceiling

Art Niche

Bedroom 2
17'-0" x 10'-8"
9'-4" Ceiling

SECOND FLOOR

Garage
23'-0" x 23'-0"
9'-0" Ceiling

Up

Spa

Optional Pool

Fountain

Courtyard

Outdoor Grille

Loggia
12'-0" x 20'-0"
10'-0" Ceiling

Fountain

Nook
10'-4" x 9'-0"
10'-0" Ceiling

Veranda
19'-4" x 6'-0"
Flat Clg.

Master Suite
17'-4" x 16'-0"
11'-0" to 13'-0"
Tray Ceiling

Utility
6'-8" x 9'-6"
10'-0" Clg.

Kitchen
17'-0" x
9'-0" to 10'-0"
Beamed Ceiling

Pantry

Entertainment Center

Great Room
17'-10" x 19'-0"
Open to Above
Fireplace

Niche

Master Bath
13'-0" Ceiling

Walk-In

W.I.C.

Foyer
17'-6" Ceiling

Up

Pwdr.

Dn.

Dining
17'-0" x 15'-0"
9'-4" to 10'-0"
Beamed Ceiling

Portico
19'-4" x 7'-0"
Groin Vault

Study
17'-4" x 15'-0"
9'-4" to 14'-0"
Coffered Clg.

FIRST FLOOR

© The Sater Design Collection, Inc.

plan # HPK0600290

STYLE: MEDITERRANEAN
FIRST FLOOR: 2,084 SQ. FT.
SECOND FLOOR: 652 SQ. FT.
TOTAL: 2,736 SQ. FT.
BONUS SPACE: 375 SQ. FT.
BEDROOMS: 3
BATHROOMS: 2½
WIDTH: 60' - 6"
DEPTH: 94' - 0"
FOUNDATION: SLAB

SEARCH ONLINE @ EPLANS.COM

plan # HPK0600291

STYLE: ITALIANATE
SQUARE FOOTAGE: 2,385
BEDROOMS: 3
BATHROOMS: 3
WIDTH: 60' - 0"
DEPTH: 52' - 0"
FOUNDATION: SLAB

SEARCH ONLINE @ EPLANS.COM

This enticing European villa boasts an Italian charm and a distinct Mediterranean feel. The foyer steps lead up to the formal living areas. To the left, a study is expanded by a vaulted ceiling and double doors that open to the front balcony. The island kitchen is conveniently open to a breakfast nook. The guest quarters reside on the right side of the plan—one suite boasts a private bath; the other uses a full hall bath. The secluded master suite features two walk-in closets and a pampering whirlpool master bath. The home is completed by a basement-level garage.

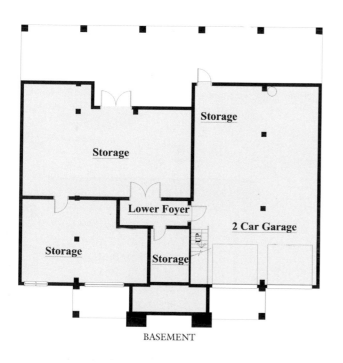

BASEMENT

FIRST FLOOR

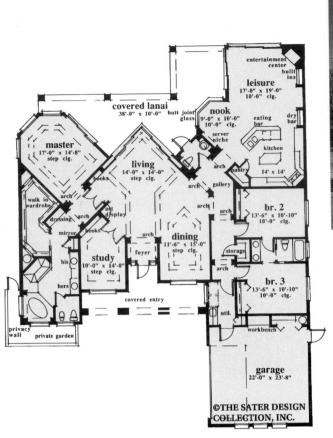

covered lanai
38'-0" x 10'-0" butt joint glass

leisure
17'-0" x 19'-0"
10'-0" clg.

entertainment center
built ins

nook
9'-0" x 10'-0"
10'-0" clg.

eating bar

dry bar

master
17'-0" x 14'-8"
step clg.

living
14'-0" x 14'-0"
step clg.

server niche

kitchen
14' x 14'

pantry

walk in wardrobe

arch

arch

gallery

books

arch

art display

br. 2
13'-6" x 10'-10"
10'-0" clg.

dressing

arch

books

arch

arch

mirror

study
10'-0" x 14'-0"
step clg.

arch

dining
11'-6" x 15'-0"
step clg.

foyer

his

storage

hers

arch

br. 3
13'-6" x 10'-10"
10'-0" clg.

covered entry

util.

privacy wall

private garden

workbench

garage
22'-0" x 23'-8"

©THE SATER DESIGN COLLECTION, INC.

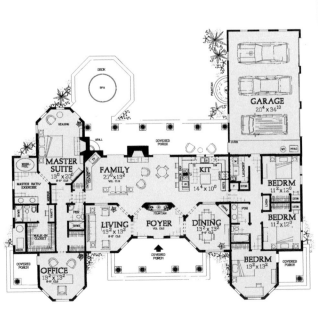

MASTER SUITE
13'0 x 20'0

FAMILY
27'0 x 13'2

KIT
14'4 x 10'0

GARAGE
20'4 x 34'10

BEDRM
11'2 x 12'0

MASTER BATH/EXERCISE

LAUNDRY

WALK-IN CLOSET

LIVING
13'2 x 13'2

FOYER

DINING
13'2 x 13'2

BEDRM
11'2 x 12'0

OFFICE
19'2 x 19'2

COVERED PORCH

BEDRM
13'2 x 13'2

COVERED PORCH

plan # HPK0600294

L

STYLE: FLORIDIAN
SQUARE FOOTAGE: 2,794
BEDROOMS: 3
BATHROOMS: 3
WIDTH: 70' - 0"
DEPTH: 98' - 0"
FOUNDATION: SLAB

SEARCH ONLINE @ EPLANS.COM

Classic columns, circle-head windows, and a bay-windowed study give this stucco home a wonderful street presence. The foyer leads to the formal living and dining areas. An arched buffet server separates these rooms and contributes an open feeling. The kitchen, nook, and leisure room are grouped for informal living. A desk/message center in the island kitchen, art niches in the nook, and a fireplace with an entertainment center and shelves add custom touches. Two secondary suites have guest baths and offer full privacy from the master wing. The master suite hosts a private garden area; the bath features a walk-in shower that overlooks the garden and a water closet room with space for books or a television. Large His and Hers walk-in closets complete these private quarters.

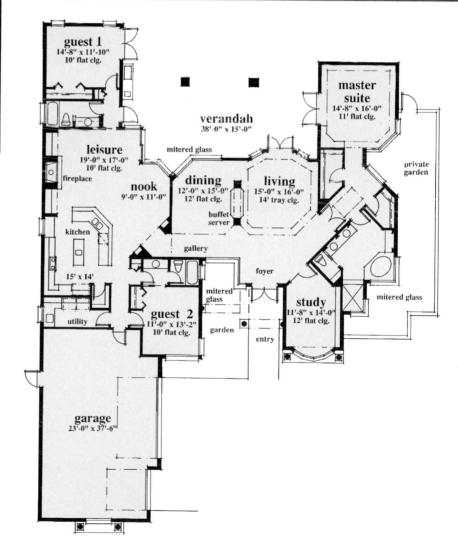

A mix of stone and brick materials, plus matching pavers for the walkway, bring about a stately feel in this modern home.

Plans for homes larger than 3,000 square feet will appeal to homeowners who are looking to do more than just comfortably shelter their family—to find a design that brings distinction and excitement to their new home. Such a home may trade off economy of space or strict functionality in layout for highly specialized rooms and architectural details that express a unique vision of home living.

This feature home exemplifies the guiding spirit of plans in this category. The contrasting use of brick and stone materials and the expressive facade delivers visual interest to the exterior. We also start to see high-end design elements, such as arches and porticos. Inside, the layout is less committed to right angles and square rooms; for instance, the great room is rhomboid in shape, defined loosely by columns and a central fireplace. The island kitchen holds breakfast-bar style seating that extends at a diagonal angle from the walls of the room. Downstairs, the media room takes a diagonal orientation, lining up with the wet bar at the top right of the plan.

The concept of the pampering master suite, introduced by the family-sized home, really takes wing in the move-up home. The home featured here devotes nearly one-third of the main floor to the master suite, including an impressive bath that features a corner whirlpool tub, compartmented toilet, separate vanities, and an oversized stall shower. Two rooms adjoin the bath: a spacious walk-in closet and a second area designated as an exercise room. Other options for the space include a dressing room or simply a second walk-in. The master bedroom enjoys a private fireplace.

Move-up homes are a good fit for empty nesters looking to treat themselves to a new, larger home, or those who want to care for elderly parents or family members with special-needs. In the latter cases, a guest suite can serve as a second master suite—an attractive option in this home, which provides the guest bedroom with private access to the rear porch. Additional bedrooms on the lower level can accommodate visiting children or relatives. ●

Left: The right amount of landscaping supports the home's unassuming exterior. Below: In the dining room, columns set off a gorgeous tray ceiling, with soft rounded forms found throughout the home.

THE OUTDOOR ROOM

Don't let valuable real estate like deck and patio space become an afterthought to home design. Choose the options and materials that complement the architecture of the home and invite year-round use for the family.

PRETTY PORCH

With nine styles of urethane balustrade systems (below) you have a virtually maintenance-free way to create a porch that dresses up your home's exterior. Style Solutions.

DESIGNER DECK

Creating designer decks that mix colors and textures is now possible with Accents wood-grain boards (above). These decks offer the rich look of natural wood without the stain and sealing requirements. The Accents line's tool and bracket assembly system makes installation quick and easy. Trex.

VERSATILE BRICK

Almost every home style—from Colonial to Mediterranean—can benefit from the versatility and beauty of brick (above). The right material for a driveway or a walkway, properly installed hard-fired brick offers enduring beauty without the problems of insect damage or water infiltration. Acme Brick.

Above: Rich cabinetry and a multi-use island will please every gourmet and keep family close for everyday meals. Opposite bottom: Built-in shelves and a matching mantel bring function and elegance to the great room. The floor plan preserves open spaces throughout the heart of the home but still establishes a sense of separation between rooms.

The fireplace and niche match the des... of the built-in shelvin... right. The result is a v... inviting common a...

LONG-LASTING

Composite Decking and Railing cuts, drills, and fastens like wood, but the product contains no knots and it never rots, splinters, or splits (left). Pairing the beauty of wood with the performance characteristics of polymer resin gives you a long-lasting deck with a 10-year limited warranty. WeatherBest.

SPLASH HIT

Patio Stone limestone (left) helps to beautify landscape areas and pool surrounds while providing a cool walking surface. Patio Stone comes in either smooth or shell limestone and is shipped in 3-by-4-foot slabs that can be cut for random patterns. Texas Quarries

DECKED OUT

Great for new and replacement decks, ChoiceDek (right) is an ultra-modern engineered decking product made from recycled polyethelene plastic and wood fibers. The result? An attractive, durable, low-maintenance deck that's great for walkways or pool decks. Weyerhaeuser.

NATURAL BEAUTY

A redwood deck (right) helps you create an "outdoor room" for large gatherings. Offering stunning beauty, redwood heartwood's durability is organic and gives you a natural alternative to chemically treated woods and petroleum-based products. California Redwood Association.

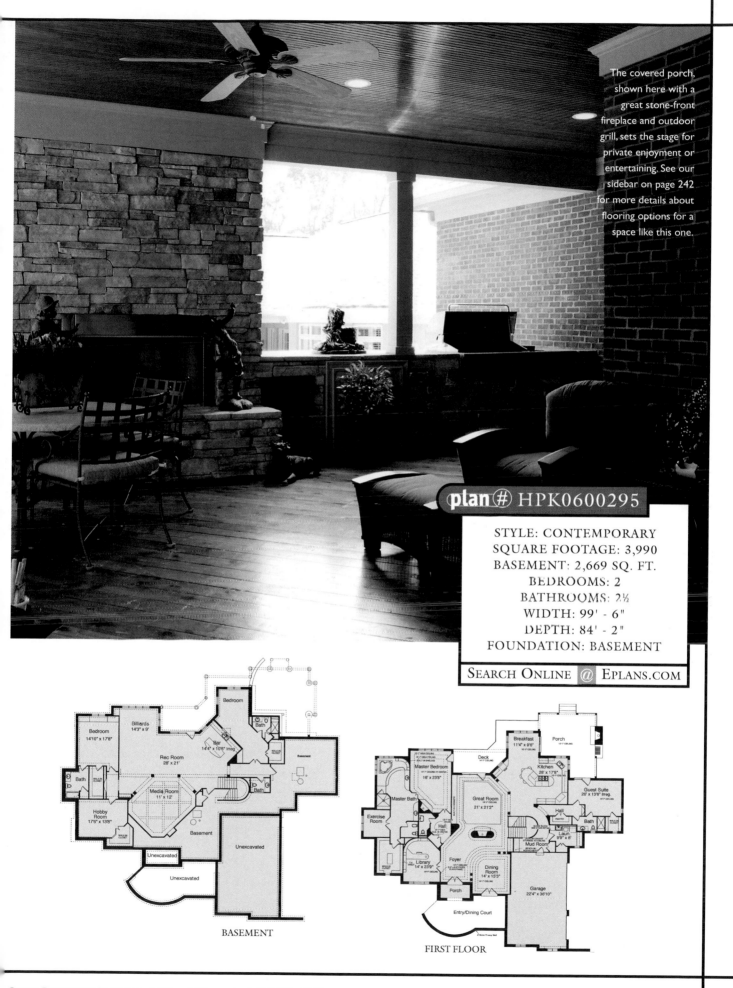

The covered porch, shown here with a great stone-front fireplace and outdoor grill, sets the stage for private enjoyment or entertaining. See our sidebar on page 242 for more details about flooring options for a space like this one.

plan **#** HPK0600295

STYLE: CONTEMPORARY
SQUARE FOOTAGE: 3,990
BASEMENT: 2,669 SQ. FT.
BEDROOMS: 2
BATHROOMS: 2½
WIDTH: 99' - 6"
DEPTH: 84' - 2"
FOUNDATION: BASEMENT

SEARCH ONLINE @ EPLANS.COM

BASEMENT

FIRST FLOOR

SECOND FLOOR

Bedroom 5
13⁰ x 12⁴

Breakfast

Vaulted
Family Room
19⁸ x 15⁸

Master Suite
14³ x 18⁰

Bath

Laund.

Kitchen

Pantry

M.Bath

His

Three Car
Garage
20⁰ x 32⁸

Dining Room
13⁰ x 16⁰

Two Story
Foyer

Pwdr.

Living Room
13⁰ x 15⁴
9'-6" HIGH CLG.

Hers

Covered Entry

FIRST FLOOR

plan# HPK0600297

STYLE: FRENCH
FIRST FLOOR: 2,384 SQ. FT.
SECOND FLOOR: 1,234 SQ. FT.
TOTAL: 3,618 SQ. FT.
BONUS SPACE: 344 SQ. FT.
BEDROOMS: 5
BATHROOMS: 4½
WIDTH: 64' - 6"
DEPTH: 57' - 10"
FOUNDATION: CRAWLSPACE,
SLAB, BASEMENT

SEARCH ONLINE @ EPLANS.COM

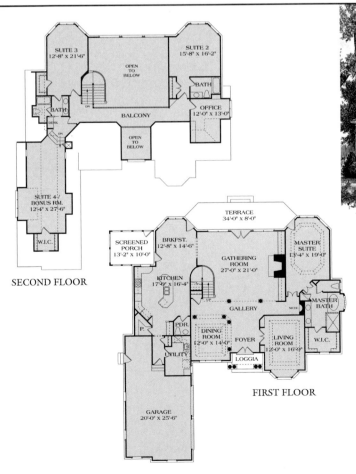

SUITE 3
12'-8" x 21'-6"

OPEN TO BELOW

SUITE 2
15'-8" x 16'-2"

BATH

BATH

BALCONY

OFFICE
12'-0" x 13'-0"

OPEN TO BELOW

SUITE 4 /
BONUS RM.
12'-4" x 27'-6"

W.I.C.

SECOND FLOOR

TERRACE
34'-0" x 8'-0"

SCREENED
PORCH
13'-2" x 10'-0"

BRKFST.
12'-8" x 14'-6"

GATHERING
ROOM
27'-0" x 21'-0"

MASTER
SUITE
13'-4" x 19'-4"

KITCHEN
17'-0" x 16'-4"

GALLERY

MASTER
BATH

PDR.

DINING
ROOM
12'-0" x 14'-0"

FOYER

LIVING
ROOM
12'-0" x 16'-9"

W.I.C.

UTILITY

LOGGIA

GARAGE
20'-0" x 25'-6"

FIRST FLOOR

plan# HPK0600298

STYLE: TRADITIONAL
FIRST FLOOR: 2,534 SQ. FT.
SECOND FLOOR: 1,230 SQ. FT.
TOTAL: 3,764 SQ. FT.
BONUS SPACE: 454 SQ. FT.
BEDROOMS: 3
BATHROOMS: 3½
WIDTH: 67' - 8"
DEPTH: 77' - 4"
FOUNDATION: CRAWLSPACE

SEARCH ONLINE @ EPLANS.COM

plan # HPK0600299

STYLE: TRANSITIONAL
FIRST FLOOR: 2,144 SQ. FT.
SECOND FLOOR: 1,253 SQ. FT.
TOTAL: 3,397 SQ. FT.
BEDROOMS: 3
BATHROOMS: 3½
WIDTH: 64' - 11"
DEPTH: 76' - 7"

SEARCH ONLINE @ EPLANS.COM

This two-story beauty is rich in luxurious style. A dramatic entrance welcomes you to the foyer, where a stunning curved staircase greets you. A turret-style dining room is flooded with light from the bayed windows. Across the gallery, the living room features a through-fireplace to the family room. The island kitchen is open to the breakfast room, which accesses the rear porch and the family room equipped with built-ins. The first-floor master bedroom offers a bath with a whirlpool tub, two walk-in closets, and a dressing room. Two additional bedrooms, a study, and a game room with sundeck access all reside on the second floor.

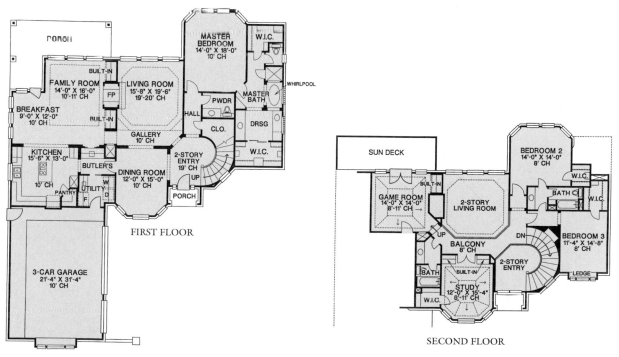

FIRST FLOOR

SECOND FLOOR

plan # HPK0600300

European flair abounds in this two-story design with a gabled, hipped roof and beautiful Palladian windows. The grand staircase creates an elegant first impression in the foyer. To the right is the formal dining room with the expansive kitchen and breakfast nook discretely tucked away behind a privacy door. To the left, the living room offers a fireplace flanked by windows. Four bedrooms reside on the second floor, including a magnificent master suite complete with a bayed sitting area. As an extra treat, a billiard room is located above the two-car garage.

STYLE: EUROPEAN COTTAGE
FIRST FLOOR: 1,262 SQ. FT.
SECOND FLOOR: 1,816 SQ. FT.
TOTAL: 3,078 SQ. FT.
BEDROOMS: 4
BATHROOMS: 2½
WIDTH: 62' - 0"
DEPTH: 48' - 4"
FOUNDATION: BASEMENT

SEARCH ONLINE @ EPLANS.COM

FIRST FLOOR

SECOND FLOOR

plan # HPK0600301

STYLE: EUROPEAN
FIRST FLOOR: 1,896 SQ. FT.
SECOND FLOOR: 1,500 SQ. FT.
TOTAL: 3,396 SQ. FT.
BEDROOMS: 4
BATHROOMS: 3
WIDTH: 66' - 6"
DEPTH: 52' - 3"
FOUNDATION:
WALKOUT BASEMENT

SEARCH ONLINE @ EPLANS.COM

This magnificent home reflects architectural elegance at its finest, executed in stucco and stone. Perhaps its most distinctive feature is the octagonal living room, which forms the focal point. Its attached dining room is bathed in natural light from a bay window. The island kitchen is nearby and has an attached octagonal breakfast room. The family room contains two sets of French doors and a fireplace. An optional room may be used for a guest room, music room, or study. The second floor holds two family bedrooms and a master suite with a sitting room. Additional storage space is located over the garage.

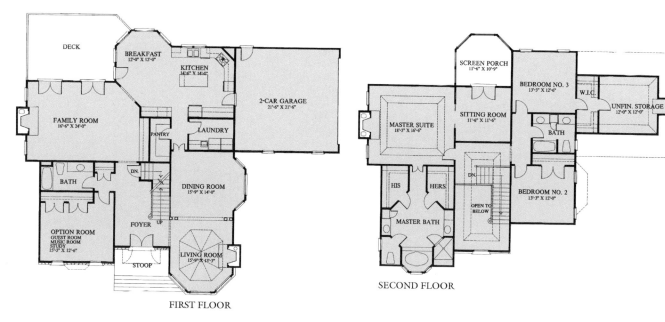

FIRST FLOOR

SECOND FLOOR

Lovely stucco columns and a copper standing-seam roof highlight this stone-and-brick facade. An elegant New World interior starts with a sensational winding staircase, a carved handrail, and honey-hued hardwood floor. An open, two-story formal dining room enjoys front-property views and leads to the gourmet kitchen through the butler's pantry, announced by an archway. Beyond the foyer, tall windows brighten the two-story family room and bring in a sense of the outdoors; a fireplace makes the space cozy and warm. The center food-prep island counter overlooks a breakfast niche that offers wide views through walls of windows and access to the rear porch.

plan# HPK0600302

STYLE: EUROPEAN COTTAGE
FIRST FLOOR: 2,612 SQ. FT.
SECOND FLOOR: 1,300 SQ. FT.
TOTAL: 3,912 SQ. FT.
BONUS SPACE: 330 SQ. FT.
BEDROOMS: 4
BATHROOMS: 3½
WIDTH: 95' - 6"
DEPTH: 64' - 0"
FOUNDATION: BASEMENT

SEARCH ONLINE @ EPLANS.COM

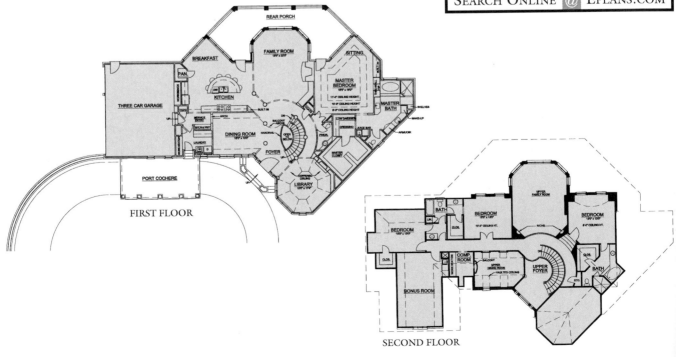

FIRST FLOOR

SECOND FLOOR

plan# HPK0600303

STYLE: MEDITERRANEAN
FIRST FLOOR: 2,215 SQ. FT.
SECOND FLOOR: 1,123 SQ. FT.
TOTAL: 3,338 SQ. FT.
BEDROOMS: 4
BATHROOMS: 3½
WIDTH: 100' - 0"
DEPTH: 54' - 8"
FOUNDATION: BASEMENT

SEARCH ONLINE @ EPLANS.COM

Ample square footage and a luxurious design make this Mediterranean home feel like a palace. Homeowners will relish in the entire left wing of the first floor; this is where the master bedroom and bath reside in privacy and comfort. Nearby, find the study and family room. On the right side of the plan sit an island kitchen with convenient breakfast area, and a formal dining room. Three family bedrooms are upstairs, along with two full baths, an office area, and views of the two-story grand room below.

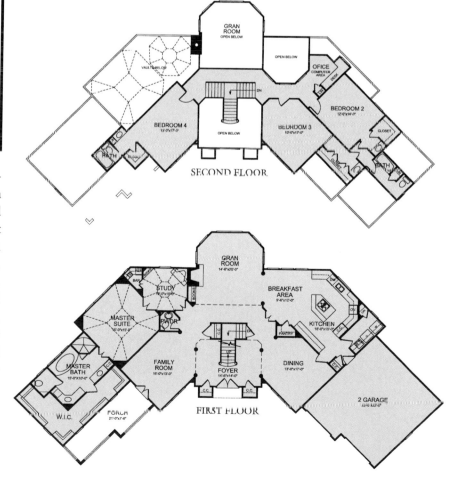

SECOND FLOOR

FIRST FLOOR

SECOND FLOOR

plan# HPK0600304

STYLE: COUNTRY COTTAGE
FIRST FLOOR: 2,438 SQ. FT.
SECOND FLOOR: 882 SQ. FT.
TOTAL: 3,320 SQ. FT.
BONUS SPACE: 230 SQ. FT.
BEDROOMS: 4
BATHROOMS: 4½
WIDTH: 70' - 0"
DEPTH: 63' - 2"
FOUNDATION:
SLAB, BASEMENT

SEARCH ONLINE @ EPLANS.COM

FIRST FLOOR

SECOND FLOOR

plan# HPK0600305

STYLE: EUROPEAN COTTAGE
FIRST FLOOR: 2,237 SQ. FT.
SECOND FLOOR: 931 SQ. FT.
TOTAL: 3,168 SQ. FT.
BONUS SPACE: 304 SQ. FT.
BEDROOMS: 4
BATHROOMS: 3½
WIDTH: 68' - 0"
DEPTH: 55' - 6"
FOUNDATION: SLAB

SEARCH ONLINE @ EPLANS.COM

FIRST FLOOR

plan # HPK0600306

STYLE: FRENCH
FIRST FLOOR: 2,479 SQ. FT.
SECOND FLOOR: 956 SQ. FT.
TOTAL: 3,435 SQ. FT.
BEDROOMS: 4
BATHROOMS: 3½
WIDTH: 67' - 6"
DEPTH: 75' - 6"
FOUNDATION: BASEMENT

SEARCH ONLINE @ EPLANS.COM

Rich with Old World elements, this English country manor steps sweetly into the future with great rooms and splendid outdoor spaces. Varied window treatments define this elegant facade, enhanced by a massive stone turret. A leaded-glass paneled door with sidelights leads to a gallery-style foyer. Grand interior vistas are provided by a soaring triple window capped with an arch-top transom. The living area leads to the breakfast bay and gourmet kitchen. This culinary paradise features a food-preparation island and a peninsula snack counter. Double doors open to a quiet library with a turret style bay window. The master retreat boasts views of the secluded side property.

FIRST FLOOR

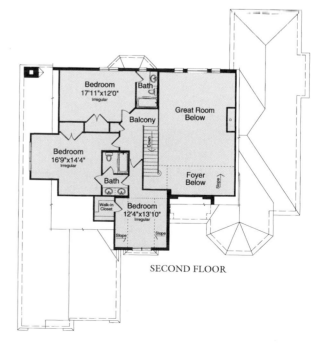

SECOND FLOOR

FAMILY HOMES

SECOND FLOOR

FIRST FLOOR

plan# HPK0600307

STYLE: TRADITIONAL
FIRST FLOOR: 2,658 SQ. FT.
SECOND FLOOR: 854 SQ. FT.
TOTAL: 3,512 SQ. FT.
BONUS SPACE: 150 SQ. FT.
BEDROOMS: 4
BATHROOMS: 3½
WIDTH: 86' - 0"
DEPTH: 58' - 1"
FOUNDATION: BASEMENT,
CRAWLSPACE, SLAB

SEARCH ONLINE @ EPLANS.COM

SECOND FLOOR

FIRST FLOOR

plan# HPK0600308

STYLE: EUROPEAN COTTAGE
FIRST FLOOR: 2,700 SQ. FT.
SECOND FLOOR: 990 SQ. FT.
TOTAL: 3,690 SQ. FT.
BONUS SPACE: 365 SQ. FT.
BEDROOMS: 4
BATHROOMS: 3½
WIDTH: 76' - 0"
DEPTH: 74' - 1"
FOUNDATION: SLAB,
BASEMENT, CRAWLSPACE

SEARCH ONLINE @ EPLANS.COM

plan # HPK0600309

STYLE: TRANSITIONAL
FIRST FLOOR: 2,452 SQ. FT.
SECOND FLOOR: 715 SQ. FT.
TOTAL: 3,167 SQ. FT.
BONUS SPACE: 379 SQ. FT.
BEDROOMS: 4
BATHROOMS: 3½
WIDTH: 73' - 6"
DEPTH: 69' - 11"
FOUNDATION: CRAWLSPACE

SEARCH ONLINE @ EPLANS.COM

Take one look at this grand European manor from one of our top designers, and you'll see why it is quickly becoming a best seller. The elegant foyer opens to the great room, impressive with a two-story tray ceiling, extended-hearth fireplace, and defining columns. Sliding glass doors here and in the formal dining room provide sweeping views and patio access. The kitchen, with a cooktop island, flows into the breakfast area. The slope-ceilinged sun room is a charming spot to settle down with a good book. In the right wing, a study/guest suite has French doors and a private bath. The master suite has vintage tones, with a sloped ceiling, bumped-out garden tub, and column accents. Two upper-level bedrooms enjoy private vanities, a shared bath, and bonus space.

FIRST FLOOR

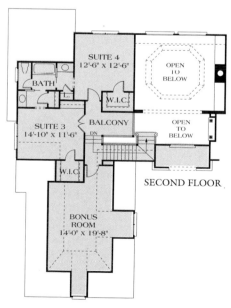

SECOND FLOOR

FAMILY HOMES

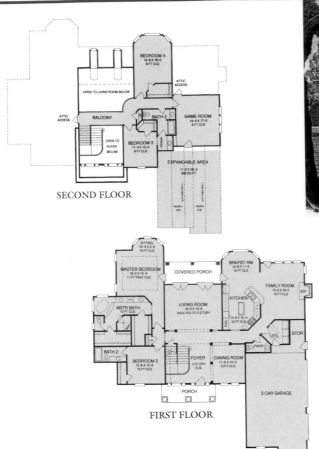

SECOND FLOOR

FIRST FLOOR

plan# HPK0600310

STYLE: EUROPEAN COTTAGE
FIRST FLOOR: 2,657 SQ. FT.
SECOND FLOOR: 1,026 SQ. FT.
TOTAL: 3,683 SQ. FT.
BONUS SPACE: 308 SQ. FT.
BEDROOMS: 4
BATHROOMS: 3½
WIDTH: 75' - 8"
DEPTH: 74' - 2"
FOUNDATION: BASEMENT,
CRAWLSPACE, SLAB

SEARCH ONLINE @ EPLANS.COM

SECOND FLOOR

FIRST FLOOR

plan# HPK0600311

STYLE: FRENCH
FIRST FLOOR: 2,384 SQ. FT.
SECOND FLOOR: 1,050 SQ. FT.
TOTAL: 3,434 SQ. FT.
BONUS SPACE: 228 SQ. FT.
BEDROOMS: 4
BATHROOMS: 3½
WIDTH: 63' - 4"
DEPTH: 57' - 0"
FOUNDATION:
CRAWLSPACE, BASEMENT

SEARCH ONLINE @ EPLANS.COM

plan# HPK0600312

STYLE: FRENCH COUNTRY
FIRST FLOOR: 2,497 SQ. FT.
SECOND FLOOR: 1,167 SQ. FT.
TOTAL: 3,664 SQ. FT.
BEDROOMS: 4
BATHROOMS: 2½
WIDTH: 72' - 4"
DEPTH: 65' - 0"
FOUNDATION: BASEMENT

SEARCH ONLINE @ EPLANS.COM

Lovely peaked rooflines adorn the face of this plan and give prelude to a fine floor plan. A library and formal dining room lie to either side of the entry foyer, which is defined by decorative columns. The great room connects directly to an informal dining space with a pub. The island kitchen is just beyond. The master suite dominates the right side of the first floor and contains a bedroom with a tray ceiling and a bath with a separate tub and shower and two sinks. Three family bedrooms on the second floor revolve around a balcony hall and share a full bath.

FIRST FLOOR

SECOND FLOOR

plan# HPK0600313

From outside to inside, the decorative details on this stucco two-story make it very special. Ceiling adornments are particularly interesting: the two-story foyer and the master bedroom have tray ceilings. The dining room and living room are separated by columns; another column graces the two-story family room. A den is reached through double doors just to the left of the foyer. Use it for an additional bedroom if needed—it has a private bath. There are four upstairs bedrooms in this plan. The master suite includes a fireplace in the vaulted sitting room.

STYLE: EUROPEAN COTTAGE
FIRST FLOOR: 1,583 SQ. FT.
SECOND FLOOR: 1,632 SQ. FT.
TOTAL: 3,215 SQ. FT.
BEDROOMS: 5
BATHROOMS: 4½
WIDTH: 58' - 4"
DEPTH: 50' - 0"
FOUNDATION:
CRAWLSPACE, BASEMENT

SEARCH ONLINE @ EPLANS.COM

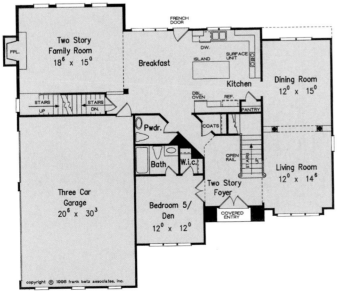

FIRST FLOOR

SECOND FLOOR

plan# HPK0600314

STYLE: FRENCH COUNTRY
FIRST FLOOR: 1,738 SQ. FT.
SECOND FLOOR: 1,326 SQ. FT.
TOTAL: 3,064 SQ. FT.
BONUS SPACE: 120 SQ. FT.
BEDROOMS: 4
BATHROOMS: 3½
WIDTH: 51' - 10"
DEPTH: 67' - 5"
FOUNDATION:
SLAB, CRAWLSPACE

SEARCH ONLINE @ EPLANS.COM

The steeply pitched roof, center dormer with gable, front bay with arched windows, plus brick and masonry construction lend plenty of excitement to the exterior of this roomy, two-story French home. Inside, the foyer swings left past the kitchen and offset breakfast nook to a large two-story living room, with a corner fireplace and double doors to the covered porch. The master bedroom has double walk-in closets, access to the covered porch, and a corner tub in the bath. Upstairs, along an open balcony, three bedrooms with lots of comfy nooks make use of two full baths.

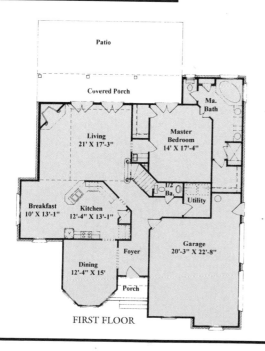

FIRST FLOOR

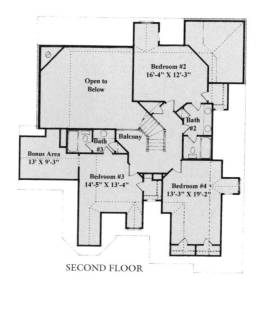

SECOND FLOOR

plan# HPK0600315

STYLE: COUNTRY COTTAGE
FIRST FLOOR: 2,575 SQ. FT.
SECOND FLOOR: 1,075 SQ. FT.
TOTAL: 3,650 SQ. FT.
BEDROOMS: 4
BATHROOMS: 3½
WIDTH: 85' - 0"
DEPTH: 53' - 4"
FOUNDATION: BASEMENT

SEARCH ONLINE @ EPLANS.COM

With multiple rooflines accenting the textured look of European-styled stonework, this lavish home starts off on the right foot. Inside, the two-story foyer is flanked by a cozy den to the right and a formal dining room to the left. The den is topped off by a vaulted ceiling and features useful built-in cabinets, while the dining room is topped by a tray ceiling. Directly ahead is the great room, complete with a fireplace and a bayed sitting area. The kitchen is sure to please with a cooktop island and an adjacent nook area for casual meals. A deluxe master bedroom suite on this level assures privacy. Its amenities include two walk-in closets and a sumptuous bath with a bumped-out bayed tub and a cathedral ceiling. An efficient laundry room completes the first floor. Upstairs, two family bedrooms share a full bath while a third bedroom offers its own bath, making it perfect for a guest suite. A four-car garage will easily shelter the family fleet.

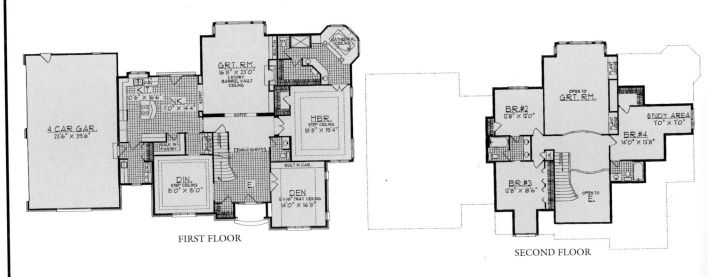

FIRST FLOOR

SECOND FLOOR

plan# HPK0600316

STYLE: EUROPEAN COTTAGE
FIRST FLOOR: 2,854 SQ. FT.
SECOND FLOOR: 484 SQ. FT.
TOTAL: 3,338 SQ. FT.
BEDROOMS: 4
BATHROOMS: 3½
WIDTH: 77' - 4"
DEPTH: 94' - 0"
FOUNDATION: SLAB

SEARCH ONLINE @ EPLANS.COM

This courtyard design allows for intimate poolside gatherings in complete privacy. Varied ceiling designs create more excitement as you enter through mahogany doors, passing the paved courtyard, which is lavishly appointed with tropical flowers and a pool with a waterfall and spa. The generous master suite features sculptured ceilings, and the master bath is sumptuously appointed with grand arches over the spa tub. Two bedrooms upstairs access a private balcony terrace. A privately accessed guest suite/home office rounds out this award-winning design. Note the large summer kitchen near the garage, as well as the intimate sunken powder room tucked under the staircase.

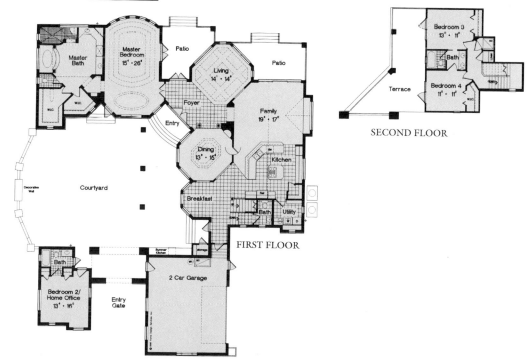

SECOND FLOOR

FIRST FLOOR

SECOND FLOOR

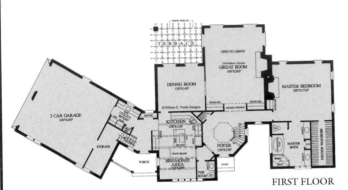

FIRST FLOOR

plan# HPK0600317

STYLE: FRENCH
FIRST FLOOR: 2,272 SQ. FT.
SECOND FLOOR: 1,154 SQ. FT.
TOTAL: 3,426 SQ. FT.
BONUS SPACE: 513 SQ. FT.
BEDROOMS: 4
BATHROOMS: 3½
WIDTH: 102' - 8"
DEPTH: 49' - 6"
FOUNDATION:
BASEMENT, CRAWLSPACE

SEARCH ONLINE @ EPLANS.COM

SECOND FLOOR

plan# HPK0600318

FIRST FLOOR

STYLE: FRENCH
FIRST FLOOR: 2,216 SQ. FT.
SECOND FLOOR: 1,192 SQ. FT.
TOTAL: 3,408 SQ. FT.
BONUS SPACE: 458 SQ. FT.
BEDROOMS: 4
BATHROOMS: 3½
WIDTH: 67' - 10"
DEPTH: 56' - 10"
FOUNDATION: CRAWLSPACE

SEARCH ONLINE @ EPLANS.COM

plan# HPK0600319

STYLE: TRADITIONAL
FIRST FLOOR: 2,345 SQ. FT.
SECOND FLOOR: 1,336 SQ. FT.
TOTAL: 3,681 SQ. FT.
BEDROOMS: 4
BATHROOMS: 3½
WIDTH: 65' - 0"
DEPTH: 66' - 0"
FOUNDATION: CRAWLSPACE

SEARCH ONLINE @ EPLANS.COM

An eye-catching roofline and a gently arched entry draw attention to this home's exterior; the interior contains a wide variety of amenity-packed rooms. On the first floor, the central grand room overlooks both the rear screened porch and a side deck; a wet bar sits just outside the nearby dining room. The gourmet kitchen offers a walk-in pantry and adjoins a cozy "good morning" room, suitable for quiet family meals and open to a small dining deck. A library and gathering room round out the first-floor living space, and a luxurious master suite with a private lounge comprises the sleeping space. Three more family bedrooms— one with a private bath and deck—are found upstairs.

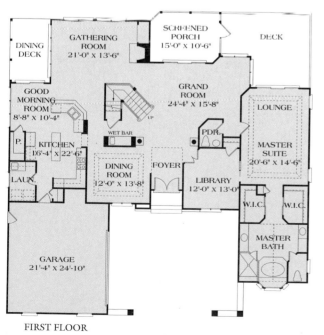

FIRST FLOOR

SECOND FLOOR

European grandeur presents a chateau-style manor with all the exterior details you would expect from French Country and from the interior touches that define a family home. From the portico, the two-story foyer leads through a columned arch to the family room, warmed by a fireplace and flooded with natural light. A country kitchen is open and welcoming with an island cooktop. To the right, a morning room is beautiful as a breakfast area or a sun room. The master suite envelopes the left wing, decadent with bay-window light and an opulent bath. Upstairs, three suites share two baths, one with dual compartmented toilets. The lower level includes a fifth suite and full bath, a recreation room with a corner fireplace, and a living room with screened porch access.

plan# HPK0600320

STYLE: EUROPEAN COTTAGE
FIRST FLOOR: 2,138 SQ. FT.
SECOND FLOOR: 1,252 SQ. FT.
TOTAL: 3,390 SQ. FT.
BASEMENT: 1,332 SQ. FT.
BEDROOMS: 5
BATHROOMS: 4½
WIDTH: 72' - 10"
DEPTH: 49' - 1"
FOUNDATION: BASEMENT

SEARCH ONLINE @ EPLANS.COM

FIRST FLOOR

SECOND FLOOR

BASEMENT

plan# HPK0600321

STYLE: FRENCH COUNTRY
FIRST FLOOR: 2,390 SQ. FT.
SECOND FLOOR: 765 SQ. FT.
TOTAL: 3,155 SQ. FT.
BONUS SPACE: 433 SQ. FT.
BEDROOMS: 4
BATHROOMS: 3½
WIDTH: 87' - 11"
DEPTH: 75' - 2"
FOUNDATION: CRAWLSPACE

SEARCH ONLINE @ EPLANS.COM

The grand exterior of this Normandy country design features a steeply pitched gable roofline. Arched dormers repeat the window accents. Inside, the promise of space is fulfilled with a large gathering room that fills the center of the house and opens to a long trellised veranda. The den or guest suite with a fireplace, the adjacent powder room, and the master suite with a vaulted ceiling and access to the veranda reside in the right wing. Two additional bedrooms with two baths and a loft overlooking the gathering room are upstairs. A large bonus room is found over the garage and can be developed later as office or hobby space.

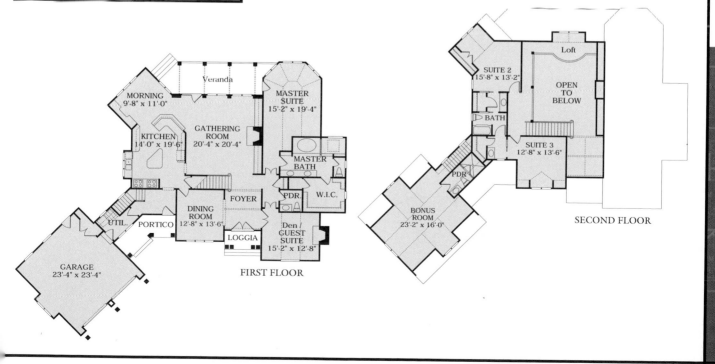

FIRST FLOOR

SECOND FLOOR

FAMILY HOMES

plan# HPK0600322

This lovely Tudor home displays a formal flair, yet reflects the charm and comfort of an English Country house. A dramatic entry with a graceful curved staircase is a fitting introduction to the formal dining and living rooms. Here, the mood is set with a detailed tray ceiling, a fireplace, and spectacular transom windows. The large island kitchen serves the formal and informal dining areas with equal ease. A second fireplace adds charm to the family room, which is further accented with built-in bookcases and a media center. The master suite is fashioned for luxurious relaxation with a vaulted ceiling and an expanded bath. Three additional bedrooms and two full baths complete the second floor, in addition to a large bonus room over the garage.

STYLE: TUDOR
FIRST FLOOR: 2,190 SQ. FT.
SECOND FLOOR: 1,680 SQ. FT.
TOTAL: 3,870 SQ. FT.
BONUS SPACE: 697 SQ. FT.
BEDROOMS: 4
BATHROOMS: 4
WIDTH: 70' - 0"
DEPTH: 76' - 8"
FOUNDATION: CRAWLSPACE

SEARCH ONLINE @ EPLANS.COM

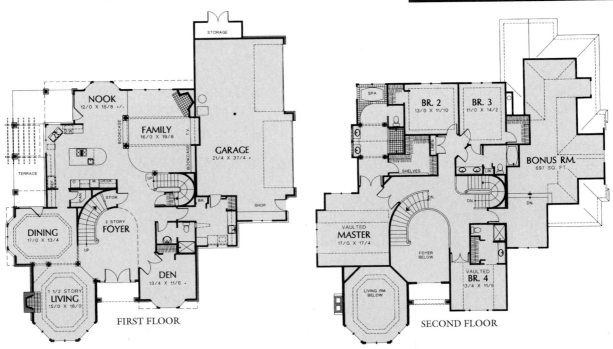

FIRST FLOOR

SECOND FLOOR

plan # **HPK0600323**

LD

STYLE: EUROPEAN COTTAGE
FIRST FLOOR: 1,969 SQ. FT.
SECOND FLOOR: 1,702 SQ. FT.
TOTAL: 3,671 SQ. FT.
BEDROOMS: 5
BATHROOMS: 3½
WIDTH: 79' - 10"
DEPTH: 53' - 6"
FOUNDATION: CRAWLSPACE

SEARCH ONLINE @ EPLANS.COM

Here is truly an exquisite Tudor adaptation. The exterior, with its interesting roof lines, window treatment, stately chimney, and its appealing use of brick and stucco, could hardly be more dramatic. Inside, the delightfully large receiving hall has a two-story ceiling and controls the flexible traffic patterns. The living and dining rooms, with the library nearby, will cater to formal living pursuits. The guest room offers another haven for the enjoyment of peace and quiet. Observe the adjacent full bath. For the family's informal activities there are the interactions of the family room, covered porch, nook, and kitchen zone. Notice the raised-hearth fireplace, the wood boxes, the sliding glass doors, built-in bar, and the kitchen pass-through. Adding to the charm of the family room is its high ceiling. The second floor offers three family bedrooms, a lounge, and a deluxe master suite.

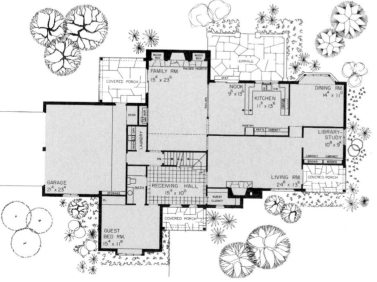

FIRST FLOOR

SECOND FLOOR

plan # HPK0600324

This gigantic country farmhouse is accented by exterior features that really stand out—a steep roof gable, shuttered muntin windows, stone siding, and the double-columned, covered front porch. Inside, the entry is flanked by the study/Bedroom 2 and the dining room. Across the tiled gallery, the great room provides an impressive fireplace and overlooks the rear veranda. The island kitchen opens to a bayed breakfast room. The right side of the home includes a utility room and a three-car garage, and two family bedrooms that share a bath. The master wing of the home enjoys a bayed sitting area, a sumptuous bath, and an enormous walk-in closet. The second-floor bonus room is cooled by a ceiling fan and is perfect for a guest suite.

STYLE: FARMHOUSE
SQUARE FOOTAGE: 3,439
BONUS SPACE: 514 SQ. FT.
BEDROOMS: 4
BATHROOMS: 3½
WIDTH: 100' - 0"
DEPTH: 67' - 11"
FOUNDATION: CRAWLSPACE, SLAB, BASEMENT

SEARCH ONLINE @ EPLANS.COM

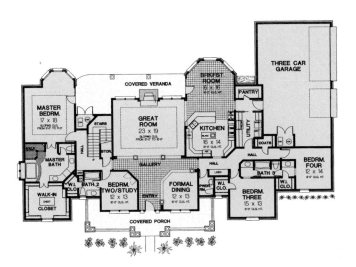

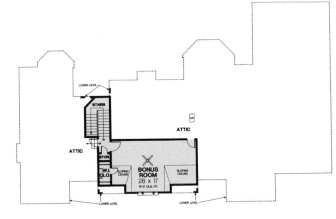

plan# HPK0600325

STYLE: VICTORIAN
FIRST FLOOR: 2,041 SQ. FT.
SECOND FLOOR: 1,098 SQ. FT.
TOTAL: 3,139 SQ. FT.
BONUS SPACE: 385 SQ. FT.
BEDROOMS: 4
BATHROOMS: 3½
WIDTH: 76' - 6"
DEPTH: 62' - 2"
FOUNDATION: SLAB

SEARCH ONLINE @ EPLANS.COM

The turret and the circular covered porch of this Victorian home make a great impression. The foyer carries you past a library and dining room to the hearth-warmed family room. A spacious kitchen with an island acts as a passageway to the nook and dining area. The master bedroom is located on the first floor and offers its own French doors to the rear covered porch. The master bath is designed to cater to both His and Her needs with two walk-in closets, separate vanities, a garden tub, and separate shower. The second-floor balcony looks to the family room below.

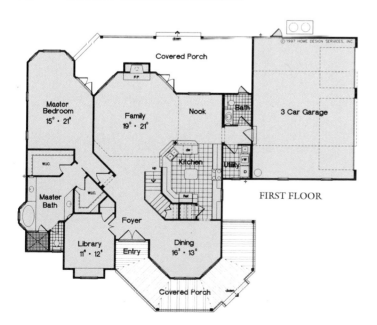

FIRST FLOOR

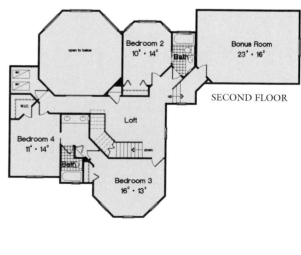

SECOND FLOOR

FAMILY HOMES

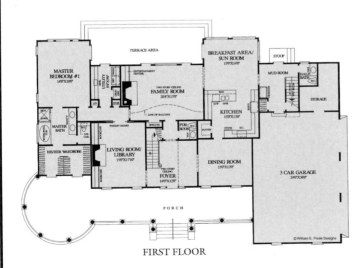

plan# HPK0600326

STYLE: FARMHOUSE
FIRST FLOOR: 2,442 SQ. FT.
SECOND FLOOR: 1,286 SQ. FT.
TOTAL: 3,728 SQ. FT.
BONUS SPACE: 681 SQ. FT.
BEDROOMS: 4
BATHROOMS: 3½ + ½
WIDTH: 84' - 8"
DEPTH: 60' - 0"
FOUNDATION: CRAWLSPACE

SEARCH ONLINE @ EPLANS.COM

With a gazebo-style covered porch and careful exterior
details, you can't help but imagine tea parties, porch swings, and lazy summer evenings. Inside, a living room/library will comfort with its fireplace and built-ins. The family room is graced with a fireplace and a curved, two-story ceiling with an overlook above. The master bedroom is a private retreat with a lovely bath, twin walk-in closets, and rear-porch access. Upstairs, three bedrooms with sizable closets—one bedroom would make an excellent guest suite or alternate master suite—share access to expandable space.

FIRST FLOOR

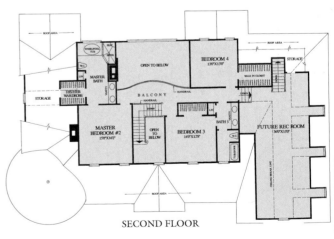

SECOND FLOOR

plan# HPK0600327

STYLE: VICTORIAN
FIRST FLOOR: 1,474 SQ. FT.
SECOND FLOOR: 1,554 SQ. FT.
TOTAL: 3,028 SQ. FT.
BEDROOMS: 4
BATHROOMS: 3½
WIDTH: 76' - 8"
DEPTH: 52' - 8"
FOUNDATION: SLAB

SEARCH ONLINE @ EPLANS.COM

The exterior of this home is sure to get attention with a Victorian turret and its ribbon of windows. Inside the kitchen, a cooktop island and plenty of counter space provide room for meal preparation. In the family room—located near the entrance to the office—a built-in media center and an optional fireplace provide a focal point. Four bedrooms, three full baths, and a vaulted family room occupy the second floor. French doors open to the master bedroom where a fireplace and private balcony satisfy a high standard of living.

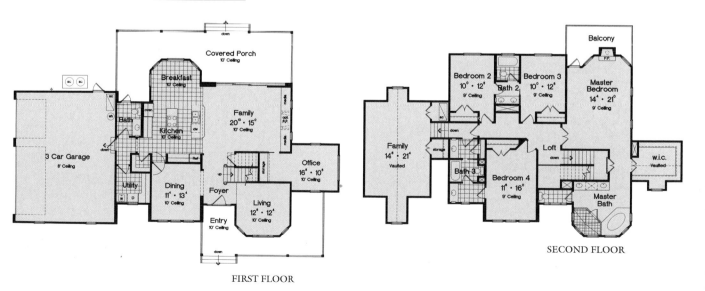

FIRST FLOOR

SECOND FLOOR

FAMILY HOMES

plan# HPK0600328

STYLE: TRADITIONAL
FIRST FLOOR: 2,160 SQ. FT.
SECOND FLOOR: 951 SQ. FT.
TOTAL: 3,111 SQ. FT.
BONUS SPACE: 491 SQ. FT.
BEDROOMS: 4
BATHROOMS: 3½
WIDTH: 61' - 11"
DEPTH: 63' - 11"

SEARCH ONLINE @ EPLANS.COM

Stately and sophisticated, this home showcases drama in the entryway with bold columns and a barrel-vault arch that leads to the double front door. Elliptical transoms and a bonneted roof over the upper foyer soften the facade, contrasting with the hipped roof and gables. Upon entrance, the study and dining room flank a grand staircase. A see-through fireplace, bay window, and walk-in pantry add elegance and convenience. With the kitchen as the heart of the home, a center island allows room for two cooks. All bedrooms feature cathedral ceilings and Palladian windows. The master suite includes twin walk-in closets and a spacious master bath with lush amenities. Note the additional bonus room and garage storage.

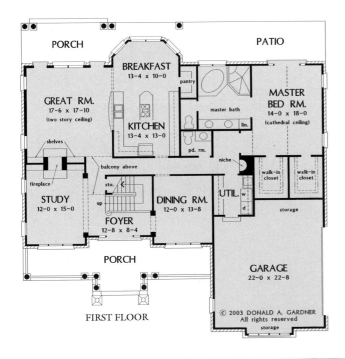

FIRST FLOOR

SECOND FLOOR

plan# HPK0600329

STYLE: TRADITIONAL
FIRST FLOOR: 2,470 SQ. FT.
SECOND FLOOR: 1,000 SQ. FT.
TOTAL: 3,470 SQ. FT.
BEDROOMS: 4
BATHROOMS: 3½ + ½
WIDTH: 79' - 0"
DEPTH: 58' - 0"
FOUNDATION: BASEMENT

SEARCH ONLINE @ EPLANS.COM

Double columns flank the elegant entry to this four-bedroom home. Inside, the two-story foyer leads to a cozy study on the right and a formal dining room on the left. The kitchen features a cooktop island, snack bar into the nook, and access to the nearby sunroom. The first-floor master bedroom is full of amenities: a bayed sitting area, a walk-in closet, and a cathedral ceiling in the lavish bath. Upstairs, a balcony overlooks the family room and the foyer and leads to three secondary bedrooms—each with walk-in closets. The four-car garage will easily shelter the family fleet and also features plenty of storage space.

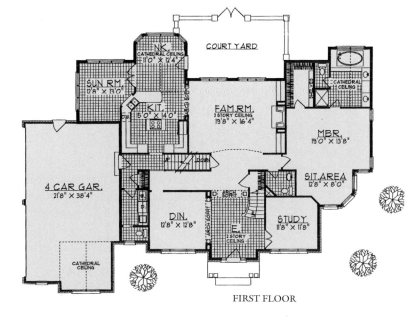

FIRST FLOOR

SECOND FLOOR

FAMILY HOMES

SECOND FLOOR

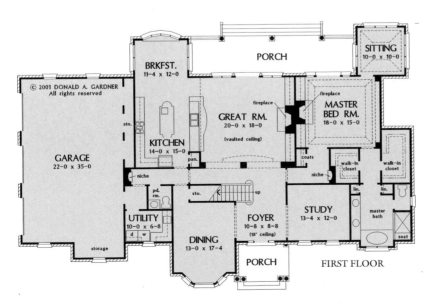

FIRST FLOOR

plan # **HPK0600330**

STYLE: TRADITIONAL
FIRST FLOOR: 2,511 SQ. FT.
SECOND FLOOR: 1,062 SQ. FT.
TOTAL: 3,573 SQ. FT.
BONUS SPACE: 465 SQ. FT.
BEDROOMS: 4
BATHROOMS: 3½
WIDTH: 84' - 11"
DEPTH: 55' - 11"

SEARCH ONLINE @ EPLANS.COM

An abundance of windows and an attractive brick facade enhance the exterior of this traditional two-story home. Inside, a study and formal dining room flank either side of the two-story foyer. Fireplaces warm both the great room and first-floor master suite. The suite also provides a separate sitting room, two walk-in closets, and a private bath. The island kitchen extends into the breakfast room. The second floor features three additional family bedrooms, two baths, and a bonus room fit for a home office.

plan# HPK0600331

STYLE: GEORGIAN
FIRST FLOOR: 2,253 SQ. FT.
SECOND FLOOR: 890 SQ. FT.
TOTAL: 3,143 SQ. FT.
BEDROOMS: 4
BATHROOMS: 3½
WIDTH: 61' - 6"
DEPTH: 64' - 0"
FOUNDATION: BASEMENT

SEARCH ONLINE @ EPLANS.COM

This grand Georgian home begins with a double-door entry topped by a beautiful arched window. Inside, the foyer opens to the two-story living room, which has a wide bow window overlooking the rear property. Double doors open to a study warmed by a fireplace. The kitchen features a walk-in pantry and serves both the formal dining room and the breakfast area, which adjoins the bright keeping room. The master suite, secluded on the first floor, is large and opulent. Three more bedrooms and two baths are upstairs for family and friends.

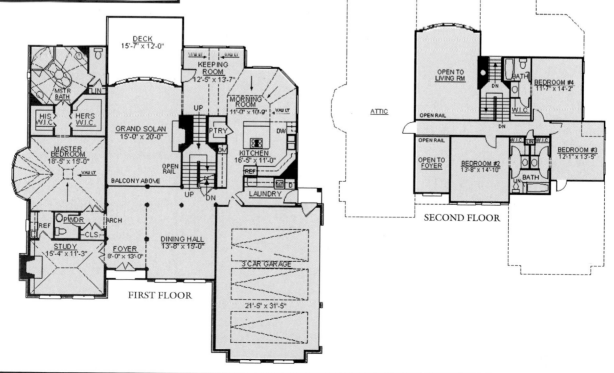

FIRST FLOOR

SECOND FLOOR

FAMILY HOMES

plan# HPK0600332

STYLE: GEORGIAN
SQUARE FOOTAGE: 3,136
BEDROOMS: 4
BATHROOMS: 3½
WIDTH: 80' - 6"
DEPTH: 72' - 4"
FOUNDATION: CRAWLSPACE

SEARCH ONLINE @ EPLANS.COM

SECOND FLOOR

FIRST FLOOR

plan# HPK0600333

STYLE: GEORGIAN
FIRST FLOOR: 2,767 SQ. FT.
SECOND FLOOR: 1,179 SQ. FT.
TOTAL: 3,946 SQ. FT.
BONUS SPACE: 591 SQ. FT.
BEDROOMS: 4
BATHROOMS: 3½ + ½
WIDTH: 79' - 11"
DEPTH: 80' - 6"
FOUNDATION: CRAWLSPACE

SEARCH ONLINE @ EPLANS.COM

plan # HPK0600334

STYLE: GEORGIAN
FIRST FLOOR: 1,455 SQ. FT.
SECOND FLOOR: 1,649 SQ. FT.
TOTAL: 3,104 SQ. FT.
BEDROOMS: 4
BATHROOMS: 3½
WIDTH: 54' - 4"
DEPTH: 46' - 0"
FOUNDATION:
WALKOUT BASEMENT

SEARCH ONLINE @ EPLANS.COM

The double wings, twin chimneys, and center portico of this home work in concert to create a classic architectural statement. The two-story foyer is flanked by the spacious dining room and formal living room, each containing their own fireplaces. A large family room with a full wall of glass opens conveniently to the kitchen and breakfast room. The master suite features a tray ceiling and French doors that open to a covered porch. A grand master bath completes the master suite. Two family bedrooms share a bath, and another has a private bath. Bedroom 4 features a nook for sitting or reading.

QUOTE ONE®

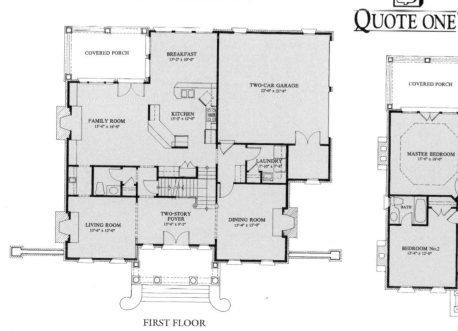

FIRST FLOOR

SECOND FLOOR

FAMILY HOMES

plan# HPK0600335

STYLE: COLONIAL
FIRST FLOOR: 2,086 SQ. FT.
SECOND FLOOR: 1,094 SQ. FT.
TOTAL: 3,180 SQ. FT.
BONUS SPACE: 372 SQ. FT.
BEDROOMS: 4
BATHROOMS: 4½
WIDTH: 64' - 4"
DEPTH: 61' - 10"
FOUNDATION:
CRAWLSPACE, BASEMENT

SEARCH ONLINE @ EPLANS.COM

Take one look at this Colonial haven and you will call it home. A columned front porch and an upstairs deck were built for lazy summer days; the extended-hearth fireplace will warm your heart on chilly winter nights. The living room—with fireplace—and formal dining room are perfect for entertaining. In the bumped-out kitchen and bayed breakfast area, natural light will be the order of the day. The first-floor master suite includes an enormous walk-in closet and a private bath. Upstairs, three generous bedrooms, three baths, and space for expansion will please everyone.

FIRST FLOOR

SECOND FLOOR

plan # HPK0600336

STYLE: GEORGIAN
FIRST FLOOR: 2,081 SQ. FT.
SECOND FLOOR: 940 SQ. FT.
TOTAL: 3,021 SQ. FT.
BEDROOMS: 4
BATHROOMS: 3½
WIDTH: 69' - 9"
DEPTH: 65' - 0"
FOUNDATION:
WALKOUT BASEMENT

SEARCH ONLINE @ EPLANS.COM

This Georgian country-style home displays an impressive appearance. The front porch and columns frame the elegant elliptical entrance. Georgian symmetry balances the living room and dining room off the foyer. The first floor continues into the two-story great room, which offers built-in cabinetry, a fireplace, and a large bay window that overlooks the rear deck. A dramatic tray ceiling, a wall of glass, and access to the rear deck complete the master bedroom. To the left of the great room, a large kitchen opens to a breakfast area with walls of windows. Upstairs, each of three family bedrooms features ample closet space as well as direct access to a bathroom.

FIRST FLOOR

SECOND FLOOR

SECOND FLOOR

MASTER SUITE
21'-8" x 14'-2"

BONUS ROOM
14'-2" x 21'-6"

MASTER BATH

HERS

HIS

BATH

LAUNDRY

W.I.C.

SUITE 2
15'-4" x 13'-4"

SUITE 3
13'-10" x 13'-4"

BATH

DECK

GARAGE
23'-6" x 21'-2"

GATHERING ROOM
21'-6" x 15'-8"

OPT. BAR

BREAKFAST
13'-6" x 9'-8"

GUEST SUITE / HOME OFFICE
14'-10" x 12'-6"

BATH

PANT.

KITCHEN
18'-3" x 12'-10"

LIVING / STUDY
14'-10" x 13'-4"

FOYER

DINING ROOM
14'-10" x 13'-4"

PORTICO

FIRST FLOOR

plan # HPK0600337

STYLE: GEORGIAN
FIRST FLOOR: 1,930 SQ. FT.
SECOND FLOOR: 1,807 SQ. FT.
TOTAL: 3,737 SQ. FT.
BONUS SPACE: 372 SQ. FT.
BEDROOMS: 3
BATHROOMS: 4
WIDTH: 55' - 2"
DEPTH: 60' - 2"
FOUNDATION: CRAWLSPACE

SEARCH ONLINE @ EPLANS.com

FUTURE REC. ROOM
16'9"x23'6"

MASTER BATH 2

HER WARDROBE

BEDROOM 4
14'4"x17'0"

MASTER BEDROOM 2
14'9"x20'0"

OPEN TO BELOW

BEDROOM 3
15'9"x20'0"

BATH

ATTIC STORAGE

SECOND FLOOR

2 CAR GARAGE

WASHING TUB

HER WARDROBE

MASTER BATH

PORCH

UTILITY

MUD ROOM

STORAGE

MASTER BEDROOM
16'0"x17'0"

FAMILY ROOM
19'0"x20'0"

KITCHEN

LIVING ROOM/ LIBRARY
16'0"x20'0"

FOYER

DINING ROOM
15'0"x14'0"

SUNPORCH/BREAKFAST AREA
17'0"x10'0"

PORCH

FIRST FLOOR

plan # HPK0600338

STYLE: GREEK REVIVAL
FIRST FLOOR: 2,473 SQ. FT.
SECOND FLOOR: 1,447 SQ. FT.
TOTAL: 3,920 SQ. FT.
BONUS SPACE: 428 SQ. FT.
BEDROOMS: 4
BATHROOMS: 3½
WIDTH: 68' - 8"
DEPTH: 80' - 0"
FOUNDATION:
CRAWLSPACE, BASEMENT

SEARCH ONLINE @ EPLANS.com

plan # HPK0600339

STYLE: GREEK REVIVAL
FIRST FLOOR: 2,033 SQ. FT.
SECOND FLOOR: 1,447 SQ. FT.
TOTAL: 3,480 SQ. FT.
BONUS SPACE: 411 SQ. FT.
BEDROOMS: 3
BATHROOMS: 3½
WIDTH: 67' - 10"
DEPTH: 64' - 4"
FOUNDATION:
CRAWLSPACE, BASEMENT

SEARCH ONLINE @ EPLANS.COM

Southern grandeur is evident in this wonderful two-story design with its magnificent second-floor balcony. The formal living spaces—dining room and living room—flank the impressive foyer with its stunning staircase. The family room resides in the rear, opening to the terrace. The sunny breakfast bay adjoins the island kitchen for efficient planning. The right wing holds the two-car garage, utility room, a secondary staircase, and a study that can easily be converted to a guest suite with a private bath. The master suite and Bedrooms 2 and 3 are placed on the second floor.

FIRST FLOOR

SECOND FLOOR

plan# HPK0600340

STYLE: GREEK REVIVAL
FIRST FLOOR: 2,746 SQ. FT.
SECOND FLOOR: 992 SQ. FT.
TOTAL: 3,738 SQ. FT.
BONUS SPACE: 453 SQ. FT.
BEDROOMS: 4
BATHROOMS: 3½
WIDTH: 80' - 0"
DEPTH: 58' - 6"
FOUNDATION: CRAWLSPACE

SEARCH ONLINE @ EPLANS.COM

The columned entry of this Colonial home speaks for itself, but the inside actually seals the deal. The cooktop-island kitchen flows easily into the breakfast area and great room. The vaulted-ceiling sunroom accesses a rear covered porch perfect for outdoor entertaining. The master suite enjoys a private entrance to the rear porch, central His and Hers wardrobes, and a spacious bath. Upstairs, three family bedrooms share two full baths. Expansion space makes a future rec room an option. Extra storage space is the garage is an added convenience.

FIRST FLOOR

SECOND FLOOR

plan # HPK0600341

LD

STYLE: CAPE COD
FIRST FLOOR: 2,563 SQ. FT.
SECOND FLOOR: 552 SQ. FT.
TOTAL: 3,115 SQ. FT.
BEDROOMS: 4
BATHROOMS: 2½ + ½
WIDTH: 87' - 8"
DEPTH: 68' - 8"
FOUNDATION: BASEMENT

SEARCH ONLINE @ EPLANS.COM

This fine example of a rambling Cape Cod house illustrates how delightful this style of home can be. This plan delivers exceptional country-estate livability. Both formal and informal living are covered with a large living room with a fireplace and even larger family room with another fireplace, a wet bar, and beamed ceiling. The kitchen and dining room are accented by a charming solarium, which also lights the master bedroom. A secondary bedroom or study opens off the foyer. Upstairs, two additional bedrooms share a full bath. The two car garage connects to the main house via a convenient laundry room.

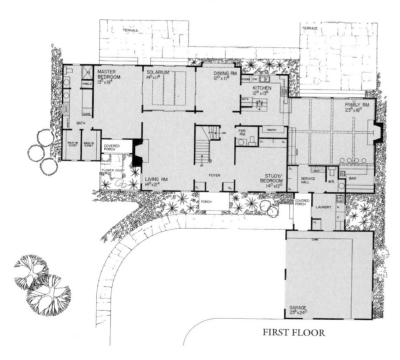

FIRST FLOOR

SECOND FLOOR

QUOTE ONE®

FAMILY HOMES

plan# HPK0600342

STYLE: COUNTRY COTTAGE
FIRST FLOOR: 2,676 SQ. FT.
SECOND FLOOR: 1,023 SQ. FT.
TOTAL: 3,699 SQ. FT.
BONUS SPACE: 487 SQ. FT.
BEDROOMS: 4
BATHROOMS: 3½
WIDTH: 87' - 8"
DEPTH: 63' - 0"

SEARCH ONLINE @ EPLANS.COM

Brimming with luxury and style, this gracious country estate features spacious rooms, volume ceilings, and four porches for extended outdoor living. Fireplaces in the living and family rooms grant warmth and character to these spacious gathering areas; columns add definition to the open living and dining rooms. Built-in bookshelves in the living room are both attractive and functional, as is the built-in desk adjacent to the open U-shaped staircase. The master suite is a haven with a tray ceiling, a sitting alcove, dual walk-in closets, and a luxurious bath. The upstairs balcony overlooks both the foyer and living room and serves as an open, central hallway for the home's three family bedrooms and bonus room.

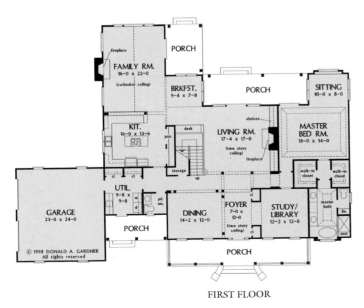

FIRST FLOOR

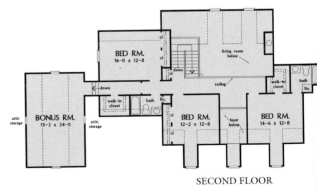

SECOND FLOOR

plan(#) HPK0600343

STYLE: COUNTRY COTTAGE
FIRST FLOOR: 2,142 SQ. FT.
SECOND FLOOR: 960 SQ. FT.
TOTAL: 3,102 SQ. FT.
BONUS SPACE: 327 SQ. FT.
BEDROOMS: 4
BATHROOMS: 3½
WIDTH: 75' - 8"
DEPTH: 53' - 0"
FOUNDATION: CRAWLSPACE

SEARCH ONLINE @ EPLANS.COM

Imagine driving up to this cottage beauty at the end of a long week. The long wraparound porch, hipped rooflines, and shuttered windows will transport you. Inside, the foyer is flanked by a living room on the left and a formal dining room on the right. Across the gallery hall, the hearth-warmed family room will surely become the hub of the home. To the right, the spacious kitchen boasts a worktop island counter, ample pantry space, and a breakfast area. A short hallway opens to the utility room and the two-car garage. The master suite takes up the entire left wing of the home, enjoying an elegant private bath and a walk-in closet that goes on and on. Upstairs, three more bedrooms reside, sharing two full baths. Expandable future space awaits on the right.

FIRST FLOOR

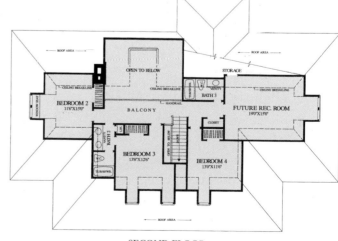

SECOND FLOOR

FAMILY HOMES

plan # HPK0600344

STYLE: FARMHOUSE
FIRST FLOOR: 2,191 SQ. FT.
SECOND FLOOR: 1,220 SQ. FT.
TOTAL: 3,411 SQ. FT.
BONUS SPACE: 280 SQ. FT.
BEDROOMS: 4
BATHROOMS: 3½
WIDTH: 75' - 8"
DEPTH: 54' - 4"
FOUNDATION:
CRAWLSPACE, BASEMENT

SEARCH ONLINE @ EPLANS.COM

This Colonial farmhouse will be the showpiece of your neighborhood. Come in from the wide front porch through French doors topped by a sunburst window. Continue past the formal dining and living rooms to a columned gallery and a large family room with a focal fireplace. The kitchen astounds with a unique layout, an island, and abundant counter and cabinet space. The master bath balances luxury with efficiency. Three upstairs bedrooms enjoy amenities such as dormer windows or walk-in closets. Bonus space is ready for expansion as your needs change.

FIRST FLOOR

SECOND FLOOR

plan # HPK0600345

STYLE: TRADITIONAL
FIRST FLOOR: 2,196 SQ. FT.
SECOND FLOOR: 1,008 SQ. FT.
TOTAL: 3,204 SQ. FT.
BEDROOMS: 4
BATHROOMS: 4
WIDTH: 62' - 4"
DEPTH: 65' - 10"
FOUNDATION: CRAWLSPACE,
SLAB, BASEMENT

SEARCH ONLINE @ EPLANS.COM

This country favorite rambles over 3,000 square feet, yet retains a sense of cozy comfort. Inside, the foyer opens on the left to a formal dining room and on the right to a home office or guest suite. A vaulted great room beckons just ahead; the vault continues to the sunny breakfast room. Equipped for professional chefs, the kitchen pleases with an island cooktop and walk-in pantry. Situated for privacy, the master suite features a bumped-out sitting area and lavish bath with a corner whirlpool tub. Generous upper-level bedrooms share a full bath and loft area.

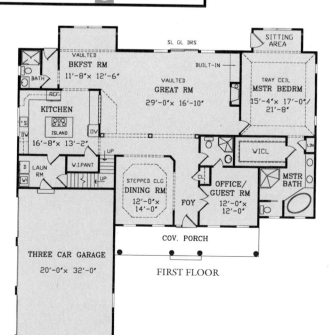

FIRST FLOOR

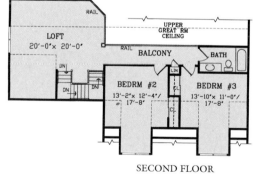

SECOND FLOOR

FAMILY HOMES

plan # HPK0600346

STYLE: FARMHOUSE
FIRST FLOOR: 1,700 SQ. FT.
SECOND FLOOR: 1,585 SQ. FT.
TOTAL: 3,285 SQ. FT.
BONUS SPACE: 176 SQ. FT.
BEDROOMS: 5
BATHROOMS: 4
WIDTH: 60' - 0"
DEPTH: 47' - 6"
FOUNDATION:
WALKOUT BASEMENT

SEARCH ONLINE @ EPLANS.COM

The covered front stoop of this two-story traditionally styled home gives way to the foyer and formal areas inside. A cozy living room with a fireplace sits on the right, and an elongated dining room is on the left. For fine family living, a great room and a kitchen/breakfast area account for the rear of the first-floor plan. A guest room with a nearby full bath finishes off the accommodations. Upstairs, four bedrooms include a master suite fit for royalty. A bonus room rests near Bedroom 3 and would make a great office or additional bedroom.

FIRST FLOOR

SECOND FLOOR

© 1996 Donald A. Gardner Architects, Inc.

plan# HPK0600347

STYLE: TRADITIONAL
FIRST FLOOR: 2,920 SQ. FT.
SECOND FLOOR: 853 SQ. FT.
TOTAL: 3,773 SQ. FT.
BONUS SPACE: 458 SQ. FT.
BEDROOMS: 4
BATHROOMS: 3½
WIDTH: 78' - 7"
DEPTH: 75' - 7"

SEARCH ONLINE @ EPLANS.COM

SECOND FLOOR

attic storage
BONUS RM.
26-8 x 15-4
down
attic storage

BED RM.
13-0 x 12-8

balcony

BED RM.
13-0 x 12-8

GARAGE
22-8 x 22-4

© 1996 Donald A. Gardner Architects, Inc.

PORCH

master bath (vaulted ceiling)

walk-in closet

MASTER BED RM.
16-0 x 17-0

GREAT RM.
29-8 x 17-2
(cathedral ceiling)

fireplace

balcony above

BRKFST.
17-6 x 11-6

PORCH

KITCHEN
16-0 x 14-6

BED RM.
12-0 x 13-10

STUDY/
LIVING RM.
13-0 x 12-8

FOYER
7-0 x 12-8

DINING
13-0 x 15-0

UTILITY

PORCH

FIRST FLOOR

plan# HPK0600348 [L]

STYLE: FARMHOUSE
FIRST FLOOR: 2,347 SQ. FT.
SECOND FLOOR: 1,087 SQ. FT.
TOTAL: 3,434 SQ. FT.
BEDROOMS: 4
BATHROOMS: 2½
WIDTH: 93' - 6"
DEPTH: 61' - 0"
FOUNDATION: BASEMENT

SEARCH ONLINE @ EPLANS.COM

BEDRM
12² x 11⁶

BEDRM
16⁸ x 10⁰

LOFT
14⁸ x 11⁹

BEDRM
15⁸ x 11⁰

SECOND FLOOR

QUOTE ONE®

MASTER SUITE
12⁸ x 16⁸

GREAT RM
24⁸ x 20⁸

NOOK
14⁸ x 10⁰

GARAGE
21⁸ x 29⁰

STUDY/
GUEST
11⁸ x 13⁰

FOYER

KIT

DINING
RM
13⁸ x 12⁶

FIRST FLOOR

SECOND FLOOR

FIRST FLOOR

plan # HPK0600349

STYLE: COUNTRY COTTAGE
FIRST FLOOR: 1,630 SQ. FT.
SECOND FLOOR: 1,763 SQ. FT.
TOTAL: 3,393 SQ. FT.
BONUS SPACE: 598 SQ. FT.
BEDROOMS: 4
BATHROOMS: 2½
WIDTH: 47' - 10"
DEPTH: 52' - 10"
FOUNDATION: CRAWLSPACE

SEARCH ONLINE @ EPLANS.com

SECOND FLOOR

FIRST FLOOR

plan # HPK0600350

STYLE: COLONIAL
FIRST FLOOR: 2,200 SQ. FT.
SECOND FLOOR: 1,001 SQ. FT.
TOTAL: 3,201 SQ. FT.
BONUS SPACE: 674 SQ. FT.
BEDROOMS: 4
BATHROOMS: 3½
WIDTH: 70' - 4"
DEPTH: 74' - 4"
FOUNDATION: CRAWLSPACE

SEARCH ONLINE @ EPLANS.com

plan # HPK0600351

STYLE: PLANTATION
FIRST FLOOR: 2,092 SQ. FT.
SECOND FLOOR: 1,027 SQ. FT.
TOTAL: 3,119 SQ. FT.
BEDROOMS: 4
BATHROOMS: 3½
WIDTH: 66' - 0"
DEPTH: 80' - 0"
FOUNDATION: CRAWLSPACE

SEARCH ONLINE @ EPLANS.COM

This Southern plantation home, featuring traditional accents such as front-facing dormers, a covered front porch, and a stucco-and-brick facade, will be the delight of any fine neighborhood. Inside, a study and formal dining room flank the foyer. The family room shares a two-sided fireplace with the refreshing sunroom, which overlooks the rear deck. The kitchen shares space with an eating area overlooking the front yard. The first-floor master suite features a large closet and a private bath. Three additional bedrooms and two baths are located upstairs.

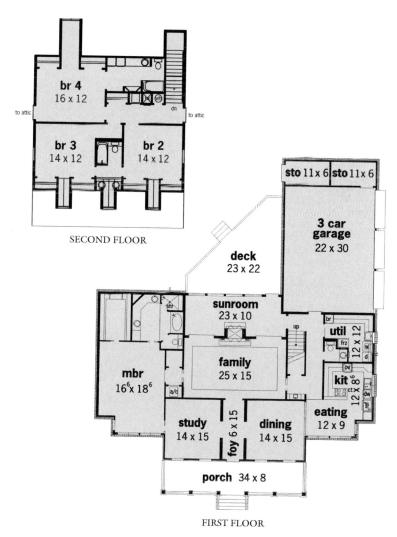

SECOND FLOOR

FIRST FLOOR

FAMILY HOMES

plan# HPK0600352

STYLE: FARMHOUSE
FIRST FLOOR: 2,648 SQ. FT.
SECOND FLOOR: 1,253 SQ. FT.
TOTAL: 3,901 SQ. FT.
BONUS SPACE: 540 SQ. FT.
BEDROOMS: 4
BATHROOMS: 3½
WIDTH: 82' - 0"
DEPTH: 60' - 4"
FOUNDATION: CRAWLSPACE

SEARCH ONLINE @ EPLANS.COM

This delightful home packs quite a punch. The grand staircase in the elegant foyer makes a dazzling first impression. To the left is the living room and on the right is the library, which opens to the sunroom overlooking the deck. The angled, island kitchen is situated conveniently between the breakfast area and the dining room. The master suite finds privacy on the far right. Here the private bath pampers with spaciousness and twin wardrobes. Four additional bedrooms are found on the second floor, along with three full baths.

SECOND FLOOR

FIRST FLOOR

© William E. Poole Designs

plan # HPK0600353

STYLE: TRANSITIONAL
FIRST FLOOR: 2,202 SQ. FT.
SECOND FLOOR: 810 SQ. FT.
TOTAL: 3,012 SQ. FT.
BONUS SPACE: 336 SQ. FT.
BEDROOMS: 4
BATHROOMS: 3½
WIDTH: 62' 0"
DEPTH: 86' - 0"
FOUNDATION: CRAWLSPACE,
SLAB, BASEMENT

SEARCH ONLINE @ EPLANS.COM

Three classic dormers welcome you home. A covered porch and gabled roof offer country comfort. A formal dining room and informal eating area are located only steps away from the fully appointed kitchen. A spacious family room features a fireplace and a built-in entertainment center. The utility room is large enough to handle standard needs; there is even room for a hobby space. For those needing a home office, the bonus space with stairs accessed by an outside entrance is perfect for clients or customers. If it is to be used for a game room, noise will not be a factor because of its isolated location over the garage. The master suite boasts a large sitting area complete with a built-in entertainment center. Three large bedrooms and two full baths are located on the upper level.

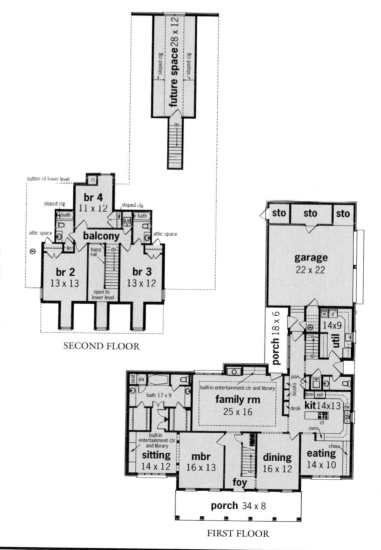

SECOND FLOOR

FIRST FLOOR

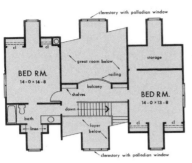

SECOND FLOOR

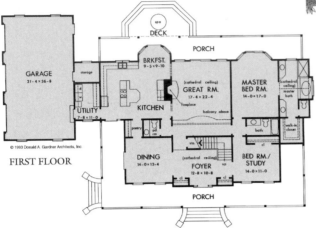

FIRST FLOOR

© 1993 Donald A. Gardner Architects, Inc.

plan # HPK0600354

STYLE: FARMHOUSE
FIRST FLOOR: 2,238 SQ. FT.
SECOND FLOOR: 768 SQ. FT.
TOTAL: 3,006 SQ. FT.
BEDROOMS: 4
BATHROOMS: 3½
WIDTH: 94' - 1"
DEPTH: 59' - 10"

SEARCH ONLINE @ EPLANS.COM

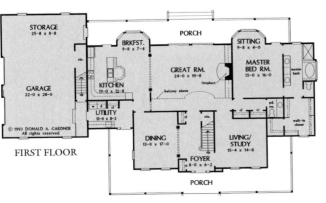

SECOND FLOOR

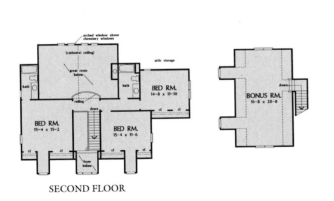

FIRST FLOOR

© 1993 Donald A. Gardner
All rights reserved

plan # HPK0600355

STYLE: COUNTRY COTTAGE
FIRST FLOOR: 2,357 SQ. FT.
SECOND FLOOR: 995 SQ. FT.
TOTAL: 3,352 SQ. FT.
BONUS SPACE: 545 SQ. FT.
BEDROOMS: 4
BATHROOMS: 3½
WIDTH: 95' - 4"
DEPTH: 54' - 10"

SEARCH ONLINE @ EPLANS.COM

plan # HPK0600356

STYLE: FARMHOUSE
FIRST FLOOR: 2,316 SQ. FT.
SECOND FLOOR: 721 SQ. FT.
TOTAL: 3,037 SQ. FT.
BONUS SPACE: 545 SQ. FT.
BEDROOMS: 4
BATHROOMS: 3½
WIDTH: 95' - 4"
DEPTH: 54' - 10"

SEARCH ONLINE @ EPLANS.COM

Three dormers top a very welcoming covered wraparound porch on this attractive country home. The entrance enjoys a Palladian clerestory window, lending an abundance of natural light to the foyer. The great room furthers this feeling of airiness with a balcony above and two sets of sliding glass doors leading to the back porch. For privacy, the master suite occupies the right side of the first floor. With a sitting bay and all the amenities of a modern master bath, this lavish retreat will be a welcome haven for the homeowner. Two family bedrooms reside upstairs, sharing a balcony overlook into the great room.

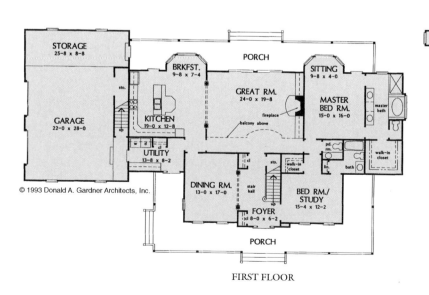

© 1993 Donald A. Gardner Architects, Inc.

FIRST FLOOR

SECOND FLOOR

FAMILY HOMES

plan# HPK0600357

One covered front porch, twin chimneys, and a triplet of dormers add up to create the gorgeous facade of this country cottage. Through the impressive entry and into the foyer, look left to find a convenient powder room, straight ahead to see the friendly family room, and to the right to locate the living room (or library). The kitchen/breakfast area is convenient to the dining room and also provides access to the utility room near a double garage. To the far right of the first level sits the master suite and master bath, complete with a lavish tub and an enormous walk-in closet. The second level includes three bedrooms, two full baths, and a future rec room.

STYLE: COUNTRY COTTAGE
FIRST FLOOR: 2,653 SQ. FT.
SECOND FLOOR: 1,286 SQ. FT.
TOTAL: 3,939 SQ. FT.
BONUS SPACE: 583 SQ. FT.
BEDROOMS: 4
BATHROOMS: 3½
WIDTH: 77' - 8"
DEPTH: 81' - 6"
FOUNDATION: CRAWLSPACE

SEARCH ONLINE @ EPLANS.COM

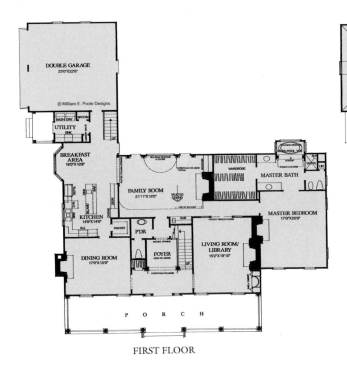

FIRST FLOOR

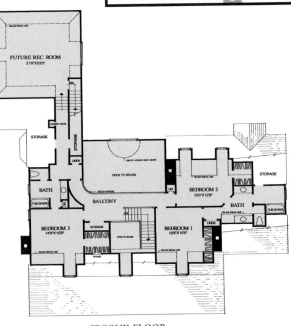

SECOND FLOOR

plan# HPK0600358

STYLE: COUNTRY COTTAGE
FIRST FLOOR: 2,129 SQ. FT.
SECOND FLOOR: 1,206 SQ. FT.
TOTAL: 3,335 SQ. FT.
BONUS SPACE: 422 SQ. FT.
BEDROOMS: 4
BATHROOMS: 4
WIDTH: 59' - 4"
DEPTH: 64' - 0"
FOUNDATION: BASEMENT

SEARCH ONLINE @ EPLANS.COM

French style embellishes this dormered country home. Stepping through French doors to the foyer, the dining area is immediately to the left. To the right is a set of double doors leading to a study or secondary bedroom. A lavish master bedroom provides privacy and plenty of storage space. The living room sports three doors to the rear porch and a lovely fireplace with built-ins. A secluded breakfast nook adjoins an efficient kitchen. Upstairs, two of the three family bedrooms boast dormer windows. Plans include a basement-level garage that adjoins a game room and two handy storage areas.

BASEMENT

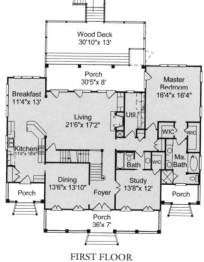

FIRST FLOOR

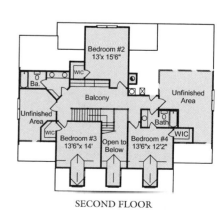

SECOND FLOOR

FAMILY HOMES

SECOND FLOOR

FIRST FLOOR

plan# HPK0600359

STYLE: PLANTATION
FIRST FLOOR: 1,742 SQ. FT.
SECOND FLOOR: 1,624 SQ. FT.
TOTAL: 3,366 SQ. FT.
BEDROOMS: 4
BATHROOMS: 3
WIDTH: 42' - 10"
DEPTH: 77' - 6"
FOUNDATION: PIER

SEARCH ONLINE @ EPLANS.com

SECOND FLOOR

FIRST FLOOR

plan# HPK0600360

STYLE: FARMHOUSE
FIRST FLOOR: 1,995 SQ. FT.
SECOND FLOOR: 1,062 SQ. FT.
TOTAL: 3,057 SQ. FT.
BONUS SPACE: 459 SQ. FT.
BEDROOMS: 4
BATHROOMS: 3½
WIDTH: 71' - 0"
DEPTH: 57' - 4"
FOUNDATION: BASEMENT

SEARCH ONLINE @ EPLANS.com

plan# HPK0600361

STYLE: COUNTRY COTTAGE
FIRST FLOOR: 2,036 SQ. FT.
SECOND FLOOR: 1,230 SQ. FT.
TOTAL: 3,266 SQ. FT.
BEDROOMS: 5
BATHROOMS: 3½
WIDTII: 57' - 4"
DEPTH: 59' - 0"
FOUNDATION: PIER

SEARCH ONLINE @ EPLANS.COM

The standing-seam metal roof adds character to this four- (or five-) bedroom home. The covered front porch, screened porch, and rear deck add outdoor living spaces for nature enthusiasts. A flexible room is found to the left of the foyer and the dining room is to the right. The galley kitchen is accessed through an archway with a sunny breakfast nook adjoining at the back. The lavish master suite is on the left with a private bath that includes access to the laundry room. The second floor holds three bedrooms and a multimedia room whcrc thc family can spcnd quality time in a casual atmosphere.

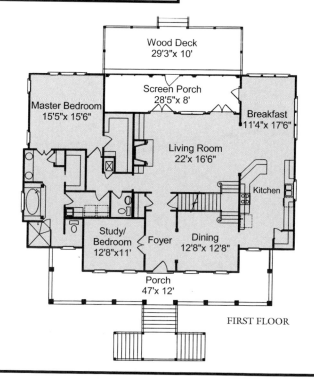

FIRST FLOOR

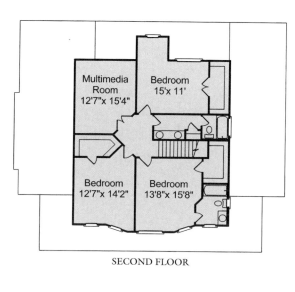

SECOND FLOOR

plan # HPK0600362

This elegant design brings back the sophistication and elegance of days gone by, yet its modern layout creates a natural traffic flow to enhance easy living. Columns partition space without enclosing it, while built-ins in the great room and counter space in the utility/mud room add convenience. The family-efficient floor plan can be witnessed in the kitchen's handy pass-through, and the kitchen has porch access to the rear porch for outdoor entertaining. Cathedral ceilings highlight the master bedroom and bedroom/study, while vaulted ceilings top the breakfast area and loft/study. The bonus room can be used as a home theatre, playroom, or gym, and its position allows it to keep recreational noise away from the house proper.

STYLE: COUNTRY
FIRST FLOOR: 2,477 SQ. FT.
SECOND FLOOR: 742 SQ. FT.
TOTAL: 3,219 SQ. FT.
BONUS SPACE: 419 SQ. FT.
BEDROOMS: 4
BATHROOMS: 4
WIDTH: 99' - 10"
DEPTH: 66' - 2"

SEARCH ONLINE @ EPLANS.COM

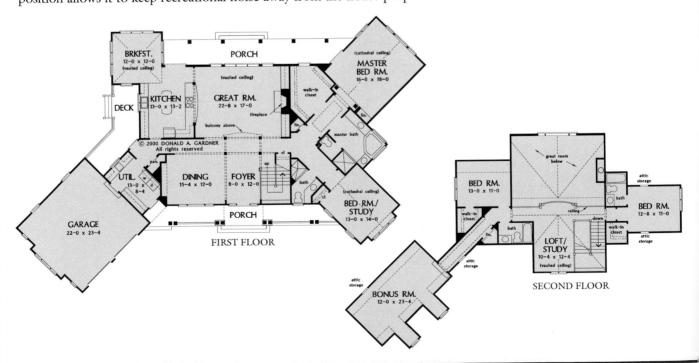

plan # HPK0600363

STYLE: COUNTRY COTTAGE
FIRST FLOOR: 2,086 SQ. FT.
SECOND FLOOR: 1,077 SQ. FT.
TOTAL: 3,163 SQ. FT.
BONUS SPACE: 403 SQ. FT.
BEDROOMS: 4
BATHROOMS: 3½
WIDTH: 81' - 10"
DEPTH: 51' - 8"

SEARCH ONLINE @ EPLANS.COM

This beautiful farmhouse, with its prominent twin gables
and bays, adds just the right amount of country style. The master suite is quietly tucked away downstairs with no rooms directly above. The family cook will love the spacious U-shaped kitchen and adjoining bayed breakfast nook. A bonus room awaits expansion on the second floor, where three large bedrooms share two full baths. Storage space abounds with walk-ins, half-shelves, and linen closets. A curved balcony borders a versatile loft/study, which overlooks the stunning two-story family room.

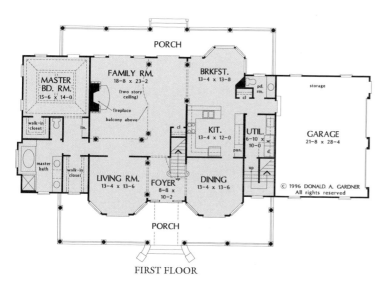

FIRST FLOOR

SECOND FLOOR

FAMILY HOMES

A prominent center gable with an arched window accents the facade of this custom Craftsman home, which features an exterior of cedar shakes, siding, and stone. An open floor plan with generously proportioned rooms contributes to the spacious and relaxed atmosphere. The vaulted great room boasts a rear wall of windows, a fireplace bordered by built-in cabinets, and convenient access to the kitchen. A second-floor loft overlooks the great room for added drama. The master suite is completely secluded and enjoys a cathedral ceiling, back-porch access, a large walk-in closet, and a luxurious bath. The home includes three additional bedrooms and baths as well as a vaulted loft/study and a bonus room.

plan# HPK0600364

STYLE: CRAFTSMAN
FIRST FLOOR: 2,477 SQ. FT.
SECOND FLOOR: 742 SQ. FT.
TOTAL: 3,219 SQ. FT.
BONUS SPACE: 419 SQ. FT.
BEDROOMS: 4
BATHROOMS: 4
WIDTH: 100' - 0"
DEPTH: 66' - 2"

SEARCH ONLINE @ EPLANS.COM

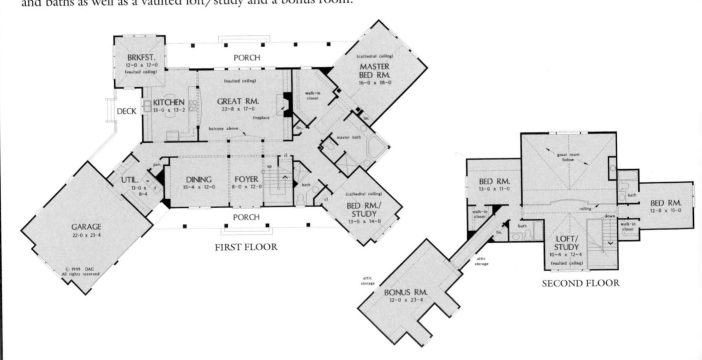

STYLE: FRENCH
SQUARE FOOTAGE: 3,723
BONUS SPACE: 390 SQ. FT.
BEDROOMS: 5
BATHROOMS: 4
WIDTH: 82' - 4"
DEPTH: 89' - 0"
FOUNDATION: SLAB

SEARCH ONLINE @ EPLANS.COM

The warmth of brick facade treatments, intricate molding detailing, and classic Palladian windows set this home apart from the rest. The wood detailing continues inside this magnificent home. The floor plan is a play on octagonal shapes, which create angular vistas throughout the home. Columns and pediments greet you in the formal living and dining rooms, bathed in natural light. The master suite enjoys all the latest amenities, including a sitting room, trayed ceilings, His and Hers bath appointments, doorless shower, and huge closets. The family side of this home enjoys tile-lined traffic areas, large bedrooms, an island kitchen, and a bonus room, which can overlook the golf course or lake, with balcony. Details like a window in the laundry room and direct access to the three car garage make this the perfect house.

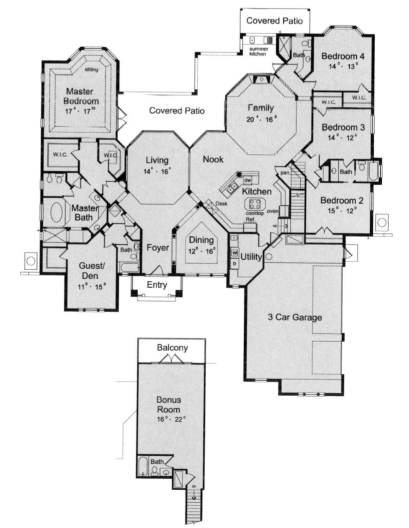

SECOND FLOOR

LIBRARY
9-10 x 9-8

storage
linen
bath
down

living room
below

railing

foyer
below

walk-in
closet
bath

BED RM.
12-0 x 13-0

BED RM.
12-0 x 13-0

walk-in
closet

attic storage

BONUS RM.
13-0 x 23-0

attic storage

©1998 Donald A. Gardner, Inc.

FIRST FLOOR

PORCH

FAMILY RM.
16-0 x 22-0
(cathedral ceiling)

shelves

fireplace

KIT.
16-0 x 15-4

pantry

pd.
rm.

UTIL.
8-0 x
8-4

GARAGE
22-0 x 23-0

storage

BRKFST.
9-4 x 9-0

PATIO

PORCH

SITTING
9-0 x 9-0

MASTER
BED RM.
18-0 x 14-0
(cathedral ceiling)

fireplace

LIVING RM.
18-0 x 15-10
(cathedral ceiling)

shelves

walk-in
closet

shelves

cl.

lin.

master
bath

DINING
12-0 x 14-0

FOYER
10-8 x 8-0
(two story
ceiling)

shelves

STUDY
12-0 x 14-4

walk-in
closet

PORCH

© 1998 Donald A Gardner, Inc.

FIRST FLOOR

plan# HPK0600366

STYLE: BUNGALOW
FIRST FLOOR: 2,755 SQ. FT.
SECOND FLOOR: 735 SQ. FT.
TOTAL: 3,490 SQ. FT.
BONUS SPACE: 481 SQ. FT.
BEDROOMS: 3
BATHROOMS: 3½
WIDTH: 92' - 6"
DEPTH: 69' - 10"

SEARCH ONLINE @ EPLANS.COM

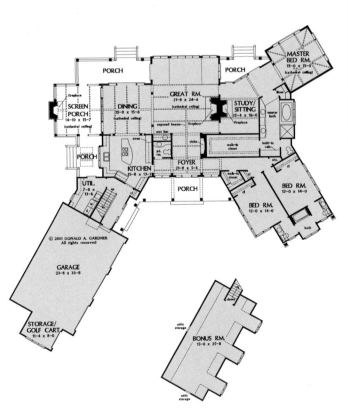

© 2001 Donald A. Gardner, Inc.

PORCH

SCREEN
PORCH
14-10 x 15-7
(cathedral ceiling)

fireplace

DINING
15-8 x 15-4
(cathedral ceiling)

GREAT RM.
21-8 x 24-4
(cathedral ceiling)

exposed beams
fireplace

STUDY/
SITTING
12-4 x 16-0

fireplace

MASTER
BED RM.
15-0 x 15-0
(cathedral ceiling)

linen

master
bath

PORCH

oven

wet bar

walk-in
closet

niche

walk-in
closet

built-in
cab.

KITCHEN
15-8 x 13-2

PORCH

FOYER
21-8 x 5-6

BED RM.
12-0 x 14-0

UTIL.
7-8 x
13-6

walk-in
closet

cl

PORCH

BED RM.
12-0 x 14-0

bath

© 2001 DONALD A. GARDNER
All rights reserved

GARAGE
23-8 x 35-8

STORAGE/
GOLF CART
11-4 x 8-0

attic
storage

BONUS RM.
15 x 35-8

down

attic
storage

plan# HPK0600367

STYLE: CRAFTSMAN
SQUARE FOOTAGE: 3,188
BONUS SPACE: 615 SQ. FT.
BEDROOMS: 3
BATHROOMS: 2½
WIDTH: 106' - 4"
DEPTH: 104' - 1"

SEARCH ONLINE @ EPLANS.COM

plan # HPK0600368

STYLE: CRAFTSMAN
FIRST FLOOR: 2,782 SQ. FT.
SECOND FLOOR: 1,027 SQ. FT.
TOTAL: 3,809 SQ. FT.
BONUS SPACE: 1,316 SQ. FT.
BEDROOMS: 4
BATHROOMS: 4½
WIDTH: 78' - 2"
DEPTH: 74' - 6"
FOUNDATION: BASEMENT

SEARCH ONLINE @ EPLANS.COM

Filled with specialty rooms and abundant amenities, this countryside house is the perfect dream home. Double doors open into an angled foyer, flanked by a music room and a formal great room warmed by a fireplace. The music room leads to the master wing of the home, which includes a spacious bath with a dressing area and double walk-in closet. The great room is the heart of the home—its central position allows access to the island kitchen, formal dining room, and library. Stairs behind the kitchen lead upstairs to a balcony accessing three family bedrooms. The lower level features a billiard room, hobby room, media room, and future possibilities.

BASEMENT

FIRST FLOOR

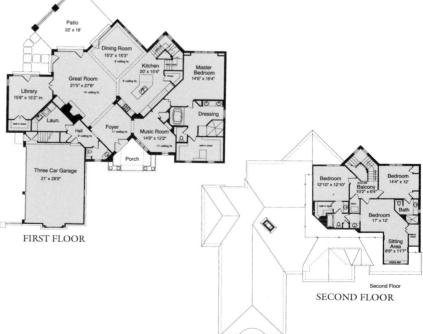

SECOND FLOOR

plan# HPK0600369

If you and your family enjoy doing most of your living on one level, this country cottage is the home for you. Enjoy the large family room, complete with a fireplace and built-in media center, for informal gatherings. It's right next to the C-shaped kitchen with attached breakfast area, which makes serving your gathering a breeze. Front-facing living and dining rooms are included on the first level, along with three of the four bedrooms. To the left, two bedrooms share a full bath; to the right sits the expansive master suite with a bathroom and walk-in closet to die for. Another bedroom and full bath shares space with a future rec room on the second floor, and is made less secluded by the balcony overlooking the first level.

STYLE: COUNTRY COTTAGE
FIRST FLOOR: 2,818 SQ. FT.
SECOND FLOOR: 533 SQ. FT.
TOTAL: 3,351 SQ. FT.
BONUS SPACE: 323 SQ. FT.
BEDROOMS: 4
BATHROOMS: 3½
WIDTH: 69' - 0"
DEPTH: 70' - 11"
FOUNDATION: CRAWLSPACE

SEARCH ONLINE @ EPLANS.COM

FIRST FLOOR

SECOND FLOOR

plan # HPK0600370

STYLE: EUROPEAN COTTAGE
FIRST FLOOR: 2,698 SQ. FT.
SECOND FLOOR: 819 SQ. FT.
TOTAL: 3,517 SQ. FT.
BONUS SPACE: 370 SQ. FT.
BEDROOMS: 3
BATHROOMS: 3½
WIDTH: 90' - 6"
DEPTH: 84' - 0"
FOUNDATION: CRAWLSPACE

SEARCH ONLINE @ EPLANS.COM

If you've ever traveled the European countryside, past rolling hills that range in hue from apple-green to deep, rich emerald, you may have come upon a home much like this one. Stone accents combined with stucco, and shutters that frame multipane windows add a touch of charm that introduces the marvelous floor plan found inside. The foyer opens onto a great room that offers a panoramic view of the veranda and beyond. To the left, you'll find a formal dining room; to the right, a quiet den. Just steps away resides the sitting room that introduces the grand master suite. A kitchen with a nook, laundry room, and large shop area complete the first floor. The second floor contains two family bedrooms, two full baths, and a bonus room.

FIRST FLOOR

SECOND FLOOR

FIRST FLOOR

SECOND FLOOR

plan# HPK0600371

STYLE: FARMHOUSE
FIRST FLOOR: 2,837 SQ. FT.
SECOND FLOOR: 609 SQ. FT.
TOTAL: 3,446 SQ. FT.
BEDROOMS: 4
BATHROOMS: 4
WIDTH: 68' - 0"
DEPTH: 83' - 4"
FOUNDATION: SLAB

SEARCH ONLINE @ Eplans.com

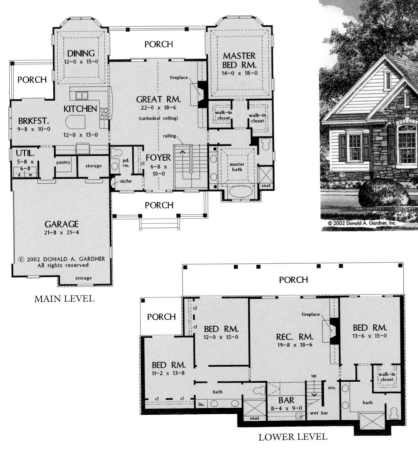

MAIN LEVEL

© 2002 DONALD A. GARDNER
All rights reserved

© 2002 Donald A. Gardner, Inc.

LOWER LEVEL

plan# HPK0600372

STYLE: CRAFTSMAN
MAIN LEVEL: 1,600 SQ. FT.
LOWER LEVEL: 1,720 SQ. FT.
TOTAL: 3,320 SQ. FT.
BEDROOMS: 4
BATHROOMS: 3½
WIDTH: 59' - 0"
DEPTH: 59' - 4"

SEARCH ONLINE @ Eplans.com

plan # HPK0600373

STYLE: CRAFTSMAN
MAIN LEVEL: 2,172 SQ. FT.
LOWER LEVEL: 1,813 SQ. FT.
TOTAL: 3,985 SQ. FT.
BEDROOMS: 4
BATHROOMS: 3½
WIDTH: 75' - 0"
DEPTH: 49' - 0"
FOUNDATION: BASEMENT

SEARCH ONLINE @ EPLANS.COM

With the Craftsman stylings of a mountain lodge, this rustic four-bedroom home is full of surprises. The foyer opens to the right to the great room, warmed by a stone hearth. A corner media center is convenient for entertaining. The dining room, with a furniture alcove, opens to the side terrace, inviting meals alfresco. An angled kitchen provides lots of room to move. The master suite is expansive, with French doors, a private bath, and spa tub. On the lower level, two bedrooms share a bath; a third enjoys a private suite. The games room includes a fireplace, media center, wet bar, and wine cellar. Don't miss the storage capacity and work area in the garage.

LOWER LEVEL

MAIN LEVEL

FAMILY HOMES

© 2001 Donald A. Gardner, Inc.

STYLE: TRADITIONAL
FIRST FLOOR: 2,194 SQ. FT.
SECOND FLOOR: 973 SQ. FT.
TOTAL: 3,167 SQ. FT.
BONUS SPACE: 281 SQ. FT.
BEDROOMS: 4
BATHROOMS: 3½
WIDTH: 71' - 11"
DEPTH: 54' - 4"

SEARCH ONLINE @ EPLANS.COM

This updated farmhouse has been given additional custom-styled features. Twin gables, sidelights, and an arched entryway accent the facade, and decorative ceiling treatments, bay windows, and French doors adorn the interior. From an abundance of counter space and large walk-in pantry to the built-ins and storage areas, this design makes the most of space. Supported by columns, a curved balcony overlooks the stunning two-story great room. The powder room is easily accessible from the common rooms, and angled corners soften the dining room.

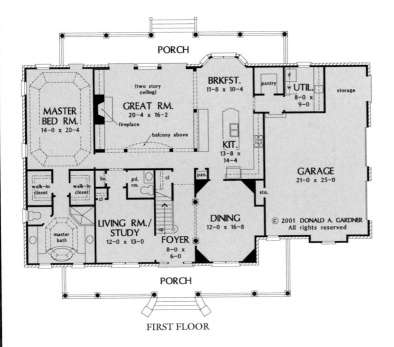

FIRST FLOOR

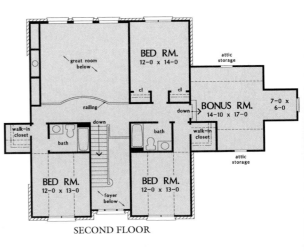

SECOND FLOOR

plan # HPK0600375

STYLE: FRENCH
FIRST FLOOR: 2,346 SQ. FT.
SECOND FLOOR: 1,260 SQ. FT.
TOTAL: 3,606 SQ. FT.
BEDROOMS: 4
BATHROOMS: 3½
WIDTH: 68' - 11"
DEPTH: 58' - 9"
FOUNDATION:
WALKOUT BASEMENT

SEARCH ONLINE @ EPLANS.COM

The European character of this home is enhanced through the use of stucco and stone on the exterior, giving this French Country estate home its charm and beauty. The foyer leads to the dining room and study/living room. The two-story family room is positioned for convenient access to the back staircase, kitchen, wet bar, and deck area. The master bedroom is privately located on the right side of the home with an optional entry to the study and a large garden bath. Upstairs are three additional large bedrooms; two have a shared bath and private vanities and one has a full private bath. All bedrooms conveniently access the back staircase and have open-rail views to the family room below.

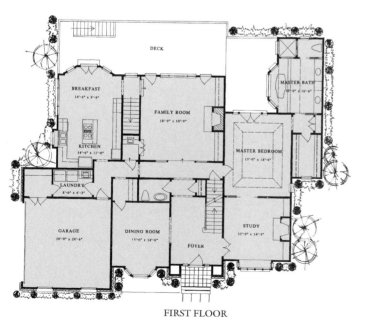

FIRST FLOOR

SECOND FLOOR

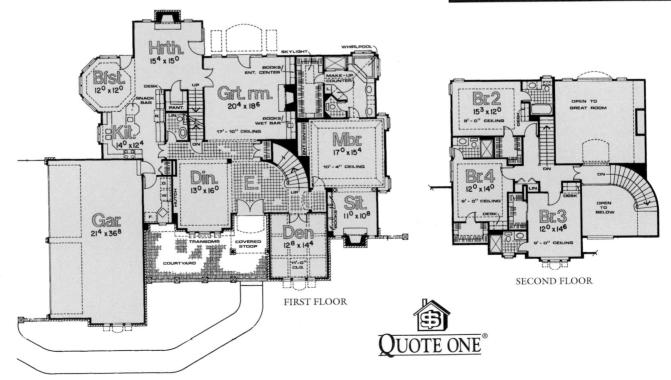

Perhaps the most notable characteristic of this traditional house is its masterful use of space. The glorious great room, open dining room, and handsome den serve as the heart of the home. A cozy hearth room with a fireplace rounds out the kitchen and breakfast area. The master bedroom opens up to a private sitting room with a fireplace. Three family bedrooms occupy the second floor, each with private baths. Other special features include a four-car garage, a corner whirlpool tub in the master bath, a walk-in pantry and snack bar in the kitchen, and transom windows in the dining room.

STYLE: TRADITIONAL
FIRST FLOOR: 2,603 SQ. FT.
SECOND FLOOR: 1,020 SQ. FT.
TOTAL: 3,623 SQ. FT.
BEDROOMS: 4
BATHROOMS: 4½
WIDTH: 76' - 8"
DEPTH: 68' - 0"

SEARCH ONLINE @ EPLANS.COM

FIRST FLOOR

SECOND FLOOR

QUOTE ONE®

plan# HPK0600377

STYLE: FARMHOUSE
FIRST FLOOR: 2,642 SQ. FT.
SECOND FLOOR: 603 SQ. FT.
TOTAL: 3,245 SQ. FT.
BONUS SPACE: 255 SQ. FT.
BEDROOMS: 4
BATHROOMS: 3½
WIDTH: 80' - 0"
DEPTH: 61' - 0"
FOUNDATION: CRAWLSPACE

SEARCH ONLINE @ EPLANS.COM

In this four-bedroom design, the casual areas are free-flowing, open, and soaring, and the formal areas are secluded and well defined. The two-story foyer with a clerestory window leads to a quiet parlor with a vaulted ceiling and a Palladian window. The formal dining room opens from the foyer through decorative columns and is served by a spacious gourmet kitchen. The family room, defined by columns, has an angled corner hearth and is open to the kitchen and breakfast nook. The master suite is full of interesting angles, from the triangular bedroom and multi angled walk-in closet to the corner tub in the sumptuous master bath. A nearby den has its own bathroom and could serve as a guest room. Upstairs, two additional bedrooms share a full bath and a balcony hall.

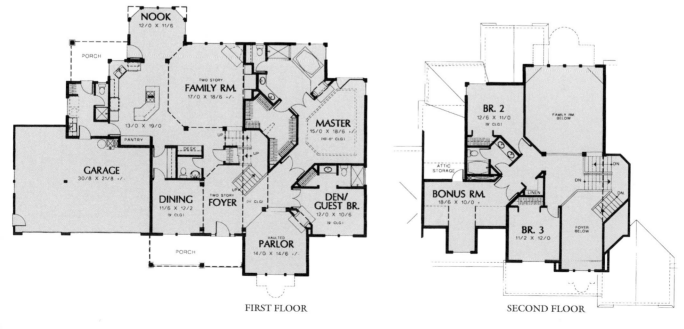

FIRST FLOOR

SECOND FLOOR

FAMILY HOMES

plan# HPK0600378

L

STYLE: TRADITIONAL
FIRST FLOOR: 1,940 SQ. FT.
SECOND FLOOR: 1,578 SQ. FT.
TOTAL: 3,518 SQ. FT.
BONUS SPACE: 292 SQ. FT.
BEDROOMS: 4
BATHROOMS: 3½
WIDTH: 70' - 6"
DEPTH: 59' - 6"
FOUNDATION: CRAWLSPACE

SEARCH ONLINE @ EPLANS.COM

A dramatic entry beckons visitors and family to this elegant brick traditional. The entry contains a curved staircase to the upper floor and leads on the first floor to a formal living room with a fireplace and bay window and to a den with built-in bookshelves. The dining room also has a bay window. It connects to the island kitchen and the breakfast nook, which overlook the family room with its corner fireplace. A rear staircase leads to the second-floor sleeping area with four bedrooms. The master suite is especially appealing with a spa tub, a bay window, and a huge walk-in closet. One of the secondary bedrooms has its own bath; the other two feature window seats.

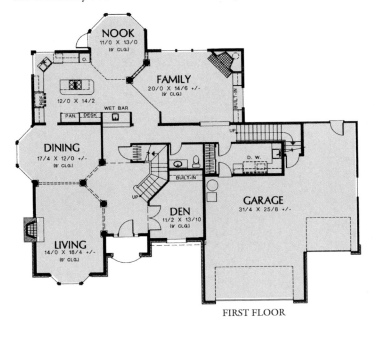

FIRST FLOOR

SECOND FLOOR

plan # HPK0600379

STYLE: EUROPEAN COTTAGE
FIRST FLOOR: 1,664 SQ. FT.
SECOND FLOOR: 1,404 SQ. FT.
TOTAL: 3,068 SQ. FT.
BEDROOMS: 4
BATHROOMS: 2½
WIDTH: 42' - 4"
DEPTH: 50' - 4"
FOUNDATION: BASEMENT

SEARCH ONLINE @ EPLANS.COM

This spacious four-bedroom design offers plenty of extras. Open living and dining areas boast distinctive styling, including the lovely archways from the foyer. Among the extras in the dining area are a serving bar and built-in space for a buffet. The large kitchen offers ample counter space and opens to the breakfast area with a telephone desk, pantry, and double French doors to the patio. The family room features a TV alcove over the gas fireplace. The study, accessed from the front foyer, overlooks the front yard. The luxurious master bedroom boasts its own separate sitting room with a vaulted ceiling.

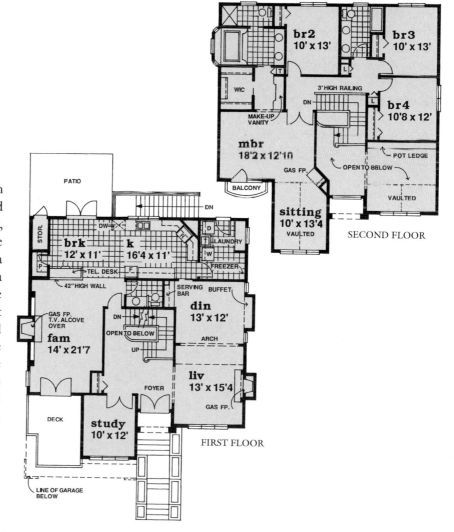

SECOND FLOOR

FIRST FLOOR

plan# HPK0600380

STYLE: TRADITIONAL
FIRST FLOOR: 2,198 SQ. FT.
SECOND FLOOR: 1,028 SQ. FT.
TOTAL: 3,226 SQ. FT.
BONUS SPACE: 466 SQ. FT.
BEDROOMS: 4
BATHROOMS: 3½
WIDTH: 72' - 8"
DEPTH: 56' - 6"
FOUNDATION: CRAWLSPACE

SEARCH ONLINE @ EPLANS.COM

Designed for active lifestyles, this home caters to homeowners who enjoy dinner guests, privacy, luxurious surroundings, and open spaces. The foyer, parlor, and dining hall are defined by four sets of columns and share a gallery hall that runs through the center of the plan. The grand room opens to the deck/terrace, which is also accessed from the sitting area and morning room. The right wing of the plan contains the well-appointed kitchen. The left wing is dominated by the master suite with its sitting bay, fireplace, two walk-in closets, and compartmented bath.

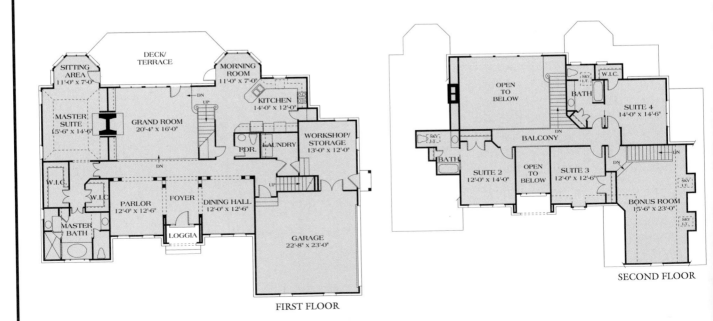

FIRST FLOOR

SECOND FLOOR

plan # HPK0600381

STYLE: TRADITIONAL
FIRST FLOOR: 1,733 SQ. FT.
SECOND FLOOR: 1,586 SQ. FT.
TOTAL: 3,319 SQ. FT.
BEDROOMS: 4
BATHROOMS: 3½
WIDTH: 68' - 0"
DEPTH: 48' - 0"

SEARCH ONLINE @ EPLANS.COM

The creator of this gracious plan seems to have thought of everything. The two-story entry opens to the formal dining room with a detailed ceiling, and into the living room. Double doors lead from the living room to the beam-ceilinged family room, complete with a fireplace and built-in bookshelves. One step down is a cheery sun room with a wet bar and pass-through to the kitchen. The kitchen's work area is well planned with an island work center, built-ins and a pantry. The sunny bayed windows in the breakfast area overlook the rear yard. The spacious second floor features three secondary bedrooms and an enormous master suite, which includes a hearth-warmed sitting area, a walk-in closet and a whirlpool bath.

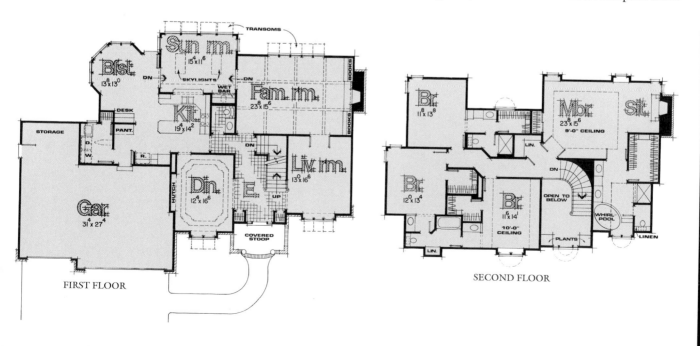

FIRST FLOOR

SECOND FLOOR

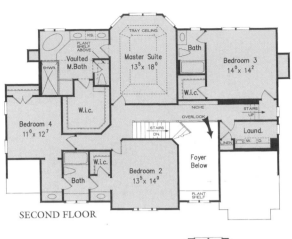

SECOND FLOOR

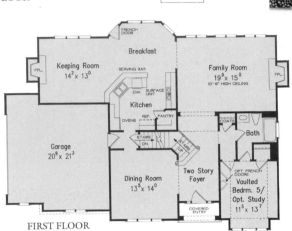

FIRST FLOOR

plan # HPK0600382

STYLE: COUNTRY COTTAGE
FIRST FLOOR: 1,471 SQ. FT.
SECOND FLOOR: 1,580 SQ. FT.
TOTAL: 3,051 SQ. FT.
BEDROOMS: 5
BATHROOMS: 4
WIDTH: 57' - 4"
DEPTH: 42' - 0"
FOUNDATION:
CRAWLSPACE, BASEMENT

SEARCH ONLINE @ EPLANS.COM

SECOND FLOOR

FIRST FLOOR

plan # HPK0600383

STYLE: TRANSITIONAL
FIRST FLOOR: 2,605 SQ. FT.
SECOND FLOOR: 976 SQ. FT.
TOTAL: 3,581 SQ. FT.
BEDROOMS: 4
BATHROOMS: 3½
WIDTH: 75' - 0"
DEPTH: 62' - 8"
FOUNDATION: BASEMENT

SEARCH ONLINE @ EPLANS.COM

STYLE: EUROPEAN COTTAGE
FIRST FLOOR: 2,198 SQ. FT.
SECOND FLOOR: 1,256 SQ. FT.
TOTAL: 3,454 SQ. FT.
BONUS SPACE: 376 SQ. FT.
BEDROOMS: 4
BATHROOMS: 3½
WIDTH: 57' - 6"
DEPTH: 73' - 0"
FOUNDATION: CRAWLSPACE

SEARCH ONLINE @ EPLANS.COM

Stately brick blends with shingles and multipane windows for a handsome European cottage with country flair. A grand foyer opens to the right through French doors into the sloped-ceiling study. To the left, the dining room is punctuated by columns. An upstairs balcony overlooks the great room, thoughtful with a fireplace, built-ins, and terrace access. A uniquely shaped kitchen makes the most of country space, extending to a serving bar that looks out to the bayed breakfast nook. The master suite is a lavish retreat; set in a bay, it offers a walk-in closet built for two and a decadent bath with a spa tub. Upstairs, one bedroom suite has a private bath and two others (one with a sloped ceiling) share a semi-private bath. A sitting area and a bonus room complete the plan.

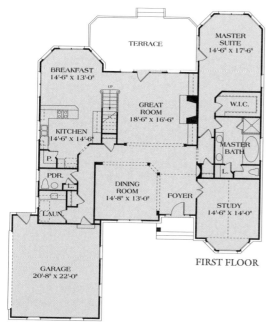

FIRST FLOOR

SECOND FLOOR

FAMILY HOMES

plan# HPK0600385

STYLE: TRADITIONAL
FIRST FLOOR: 2,450 SQ. FT.
SECOND FLOOR: 787 SQ. FT.
TOTAL: 3,237 SQ. FT.
BEDROOMS: 4
BATHROOMS: 3½
WIDTH: 68' - 10"
DEPTH: 64' - 7"
FOUNDATION: BASEMENT

SEARCH ONLINE @ EPLANS.COM

Striking gable rooflines and intriguing multipane windows of diverse shapes and sizes emphatically announce that this is an enchanting place to call "home." The mammoth country kitchen opens to a keeping room with a vault ceiling and fireplace and a cozy breakfast alcove with windows on five sides. The congenial formal dining room is easily served by the kitchen and opens conveniently to the dazzling and aptly named grand room. The front study, a quiet retreat, also enjoys a vault ceiling. An especially attractive feature of the first-floor master suite is a sitting room that opens to the rear yard. A bedroom with a private bath and sitting room shares the second level with two family bedrooms. Unfinished space on this floor can be used as you want. A three-car garage will ably protect the family's vehicles.

FIRST FLOOR

©2001, 02, 03, 04 By Designer

SECOND FLOOR

plan # HPK0600386

STYLE: TRADITIONAL
FIRST FLOOR: 2,297 SQ. FT.
SECOND FLOOR: 830 SQ. FT.
TOTAL: 3,127 SQ. FT.
BEDROOMS: 4
BATHROOMS: 2½
WIDTH: 74' - 8"
DEPTH: 53' - 0"
FOUNDATION: BASEMENT

SEARCH ONLINE @ EPLANS.COM

The splendor of this exciting two-story home begins with the solid brick exterior, multiple gables, and soft wood trim. High ceilings in the foyer and great room showcase the wall of windows across the rear. The dining room is topped with a tray ceiling, and an alcove provides added space to display formal furniture. An expansive gourmet kitchen, island with seating, large breakfast area, and cozy hearth room provide for today's active family lifestyles. From the garage, a hallway offers an orderly and quiet entry. Built-ins for a home computer and bookshelves are shown in the library. Relax and enjoy the master bedroom suite with its many luxurious amenities, including an exciting ceiling treatment and an expansive use of windows. The balcony of the second floor provides a dramatic view to the great room and leads to three additional bedrooms, creating a spectacular family-size home.

FIRST FLOOR

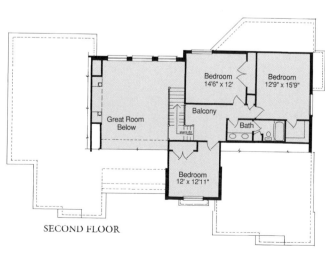

SECOND FLOOR

plan# HPK0600387

STYLE: COUNTRY COTTAGE
FIRST FLOOR: 2,293 SQ. FT.
SECOND FLOOR: 992 SQ. FT.
TOTAL: 3,285 SQ. FT.
BONUS SPACE: 131 SQ. FT.
BEDROOMS: 4
BATHROOMS: 3½
WIDTH: 71' - 0"
DEPTH: 62' - 0"
FOUNDATION:
CRAWLSPACE, BASEMENT

SEARCH ONLINE @ EPLANS.COM

A combination of stone, siding, and multiple rooflines creates a cottage feel to this large home. Inside, the grand room and keeping room feature fireplaces and vaulted ceilings—the grand room adds built-in cabinets and windows with transoms. A sumptuous master suite enjoys a sitting room, a tray ceiling, and a lavish private bath featuring a shower with a built-in seat. The gourmet kitchen enjoys an island countertop, a serving bar, and a walk-in pantry, which accesses the three-car garage. Three additional bedrooms are found upstairs with two full baths—Bedrooms 3 and 4 each include large walk-in closets.

FIRST FLOOR

SECOND FLOOR

plan # HPK0600388

STYLE: TRADITIONAL
FIRST FLOOR: 1,376 SQ. FT.
SECOND FLOOR: 1,639 SQ. FT.
TOTAL: 3,015 SQ. FT.
BASEMENT: 824 SQ. FT.
BEDROOMS: 4
BATHROOMS: 3½
WIDTH: 67' - 8"
DEPTH: 45' - 6"
FOUNDATION: BASEMENT

SEARCH ONLINE @ EPLANS.COM

A handsome brick facade and elegant window treatments introduce this lavish Colonial estate. From the foyer, the study opens to the left through French doors, and a formal dining room to the right is embellished with columns. In the family room, a cozy fireplace and deck access are sure to make this room a favorite. The gourmet kitchen will delight with a cooktop island. The upper-level master suite is romantic with a tray ceiling and a lush bath with a unique garden tub. Three family suites share two full baths. An optional loft and the finished basement allow room to grow.

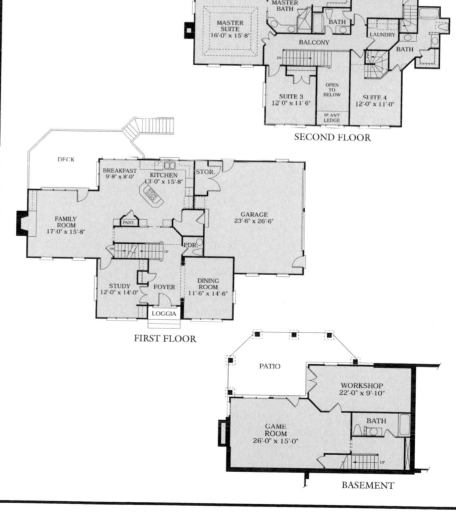

SECOND FLOOR

FIRST FLOOR

BASEMENT

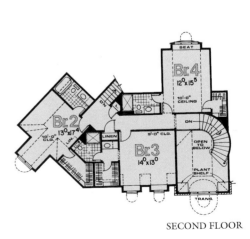

plan# HPK0600389

STYLE: TRADITIONAL
FIRST FLOOR: 2,617 SQ. FT.
SECOND FLOOR: 1,072 SQ. FT.
TOTAL: 3,689 SQ. FT.
BEDROOMS: 4
BATHROOMS: 4½
WIDTH: 83' - 5"
DEPTH: 73' - 4"

SEARCH ONLINE @ EPLANS.COM

A spectacular volume entry with a curving staircase opens through columns to the formal areas of this home. The sunken living room contains a fireplace, a wet bar, and a bowed window; the front-facing dining room offers a built-in hutch. The family room, with bookcases surrounding a fireplace, is open to a bayed breakfast nook, and both are easily served from the nearby kitchen. Placed away from the living area of the home, the den provides a quiet retreat. The master suite on the first floor contains an elegant bath and a huge walk-in closet. Second-floor bedrooms also include walk-in closets and private baths.

FIRST FLOOR

SECOND FLOOR

© 1990 design basics inc.

STYLE: TRADITIONAL
FIRST FLOOR: 2,355 SQ. FT.
SECOND FLOOR: 1,135 SQ. FT.
TOTAL: 3,490 SQ. FT.
BEDROOMS: 4
BATHROOMS: 3½
WIDTH: 64' - 8"
DEPTH: 65' - 4"

SEARCH ONLINE @ EPLANS.COM

Brick, stone quoins, a hipped roof, and unusual window
treatments lend a European air to this striking home. A two-story entry, flanked by a formal dining room with a tray ceiling and a den with a fireplace, leads to the enormous great room, which features a columned doorway. The fantastic kitchen provides room for the hard-working gourmet and an octagonal breakfast bay surrounded by windows. The master suite features a huge walk-in closet, access to the den, and a large bath with a dressing area and a whirlpool tub. Upstairs are three spacious bedrooms, each with walk-in closets and one with a private bath.

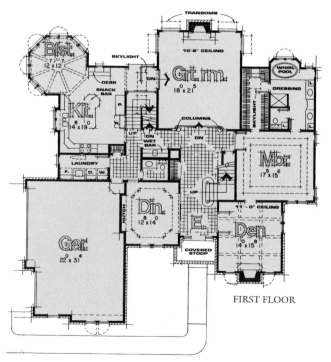

FIRST FLOOR

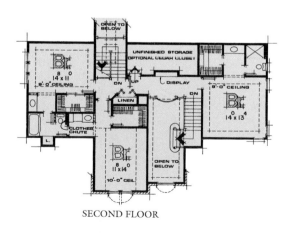

SECOND FLOOR

FAMILY HOMES

Your future dream home awaits in this Early American

Georgian design. Once inside, you are immediately enveloped by a sense of spaciousness. The open layout of the dining room and parlor follows the trend of informality in living areas. A guest room to the left enjoys a private entrance to a full bath. A fireplace in the living room warms the adjacent breakfast nook and island-cooktop kitchen. Upstairs, the master bedroom's intricate design, enhanced by tray ceilings, features a sitting area, a roomy bath, and a large walk-in closet with two entrances. Three additional family bedrooms and two full baths complete the second floor.

plan# HPK0600391

STYLE: GEORGIAN
FIRST FLOOR: 1,813 SQ. FT.
SECOND FLOOR: 1,441 SQ. FT.
TOTAL: 3,254 SQ. FT.
BEDROOMS: 5
BATHROOMS: 4
WIDTH: 49' - 0"
DEPTH: 59' - 0"
FOUNDATION: BASEMENT

SEARCH ONLINE @ EPLANS.COM

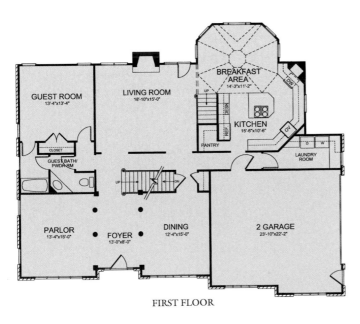

FIRST FLOOR

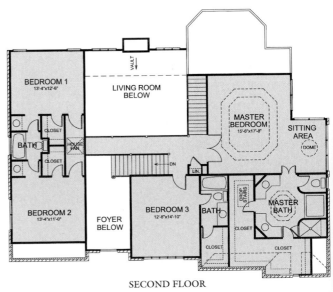

SECOND FLOOR

plan # HPK0600392

STYLE: TRADITIONAL
FIRST FLOOR: 2,813 SQ. FT.
SECOND FLOOR: 1,091 SQ. FT.
TOTAL: 3,904 SQ. FT.
BEDROOMS: 4
BATHROOMS: 3½
WIDTH: 85' - 5"
DEPTH: 74' - 8"

SEARCH ONLINE @ EPLANS.COM

Keystone lintels and an arched transom over the entry spell classic design for this four-bedroom home. The tiled foyer offers entry to any room you choose, whether it's the secluded den with its built-in bookshelves, the formal dining room, the formal living room with its fireplace, or the spacious rear family room and kitchen area with a sunny breakfast nook. The first-floor master suite features a sitting room with bookshelves, two walk-in closets, and a private bath with a corner whirlpool tub. Upstairs, two family bedrooms share a bath and enjoy separate vanities. A third family bedroom features its own full bath and a built-in window seat in a box bay window.

FIRST FLOOR

SECOND FLOOR

FAMILY HOMES

plan# HPK0600393

STYLE: TRADITIONAL
FIRST FLOOR: 2,161 SQ. FT.
SECOND FLOOR: 991 SQ. FT.
TOTAL: 3,152 SQ. FT.
BEDROOMS: 4
BATHROOMS: 3½
WIDTH: 67' - 6"
DEPTH: 53' - 6"
FOUNDATION: BASEMENT

SEARCH ONLINE @ EPLANS.COM

Wonderful multipane windows and double doors grace the exterior of this home and allow natural light to enter the interior. Flanking the central foyer are a parlor and a formal dining room defined by decorative columns. The living room also features columns, along with a fireplace and built-ins. A U-shaped kitchen is joined by a light-filled breakfast area behind the two-car garage. Bedrooms include a grand master suite on the first floor and three family bedrooms on the second floor. Bedroom 1 has a private bath.

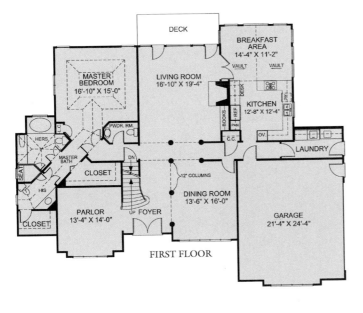

FIRST FLOOR

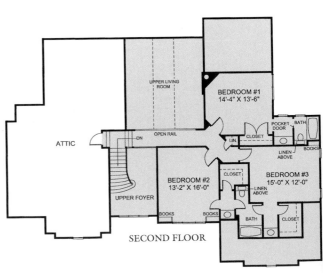

SECOND FLOOR

plan# HPK0600394

STYLE: TRANSITIONAL
FIRST FLOOR: 2,035 SQ. FT.
SECOND FLOOR: 1,028 SQ. FT.
TOTAL: 3,063 SQ. FT.
BEDROOMS: 4
BATHROOMS: 3½
WIDTH: 55' - 8"
DEPTH: 62' - 0"
FOUNDATION: BASEMENT

SEARCH ONLINE @ EPLANS.COM

This narrow-lot design would be ideal for a golf course or lakeside lot. Inside the arched entry, the formal dining room is separated from the foyer and the massive grand room by decorative pillars. At the end of the day, the family will enjoy gathering in the cozy keeping room with its fireplace and easy access to the large island kitchen and the sunny gazebo-style breakfast room. The master suite, located on the first floor for privacy, features a uniquely designed bedroom and a luxurious bath with His and Hers walk-in closets. Your family portraits and favorite art treasures can be displayed along the upstairs gallery, which shares space with three family bedrooms and two full baths.

FIRST FLOOR

SECOND FLOOR

FAMILY HOMES

SECOND FLOOR

FIRST FLOOR

plan # HPK0600395

STYLE: MEDITERRANEAN
FIRST FLOOR: 1,900 SQ. FT.
SECOND FLOOR: 1,676 SQ. FT.
TOTAL: 3,576 SQ. FT.
BEDROOMS: 3
BATHROOMS: 3½
WIDTH: 67' - 0"
DEPTH: 82' - 6"
FOUNDATION: CRAWLSPACE

SEARCH ONLINE @ EPLANS.com

plan # HPK0600396

STYLE: CONTEMPORARY
SQUARE FOOTAGE: 3,883
BEDROOMS: 3
BATHROOMS: 3½
WIDTH: 101' - 4"
DEPTH: 106' - 0"
FOUNDATION: SLAB

SEARCH ONLINE @ EPLANS.com

plan # HPK0600397

STYLE: CONTEMPORARY
FIRST FLOOR: 3,097 SQ. FT.
SECOND FLOOR: 873 SQ. FT.
TOTAL: 3,970 SQ. FT.
BEDROOMS: 3
BATHROOMS: 4
WIDTH: 78' - 0"
DEPTH: 75' - 4"
FOUNDATION: SLAB

SEARCH ONLINE @ EPLANS.COM

Dentils accent the hipped roof, while white double columns outline the entry of this lovely three-bedroom home. Formal entertaining will be enjoyed at the front of the plan, in either the dining room or den. Tucked out of sight from the living room, yet close to the dining area, the island kitchen features acres of counter space and a convenient utility room. The breakfast nook sits open to the family room, sharing the spacious views and warming fireplace of this relaxing informal zone. A wonderful master suite fills the right side of the plan with luxury elements, such as a sitting room, large walk-in closet and soaking tub. Two family bedrooms to the left of the plan share a full bath.

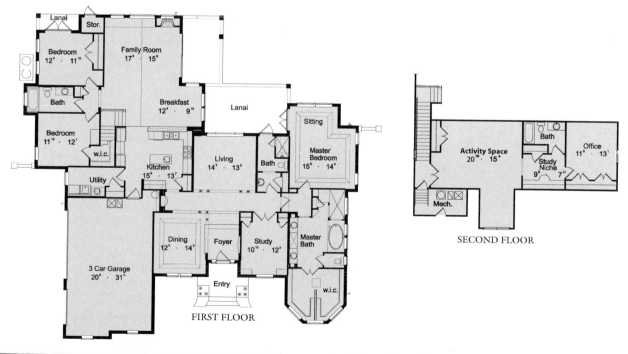

FIRST FLOOR

SECOND FLOOR

FAMILY HOMES

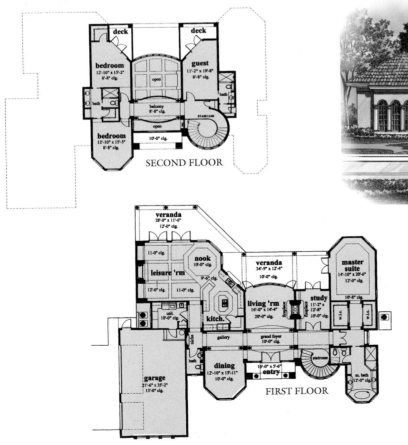

plan# HPK0600398

STYLE: CONTEMPORARY
SQUARE FOOTAGE: 3,556
BEDROOMS: 4
BATHROOMS: 3½
WIDTH: 85' - 0"
DEPTH: 85' - 0"
FOUNDATION: SLAB

SEARCH ONLINE @ EPLANS.COM

plan# HPK0600399

STYLE: ITALIANATE
FIRST FLOOR: 2,841 SQ. FT.
SECOND FLOOR: 1,052 SQ. FT.
TOTAL: 3,893 SQ. FT.
BEDROOMS: 4
BATHROOMS: 3½
WIDTH: 85' - 0"
DEPTH: 76' - 8"
FOUNDATION:
SLAB, BASEMENT

SEARCH ONLINE @ EPLANS.COM

plan# HPK0600400

L

STYLE: FLORIDIAN
FIRST FLOOR: 2,853 SQ. FT.
SECOND FLOOR: 627 SQ. FT.
TOTAL: 3,480 SQ. FT.
BEDROOMS: 3
BATHROOMS: 2½
WIDTH: 80' - 0"
DEPTH: 96' - 0"
FOUNDATION: SLAB

SEARCH ONLINE @ EPLANS.COM

A unique courtyard provides a happy medium for indoor/outdoor living in this design. Inside, the foyer opens to a grand salon with a wall of glass, providing unobstructed views of the backyard. Informal areas include a leisure room with an entertainment center and glass doors that open to a covered poolside lanai. An outdoor fireplace enhances casual gatherings. The master suite is filled with amenities that include a bayed sitting area, access to the rear lanai, His and Hers closets, and a soaking tub. Upstairs, two family bedrooms—both with private decks—share a full bath. A detached guest house has a cabana bath and an outdoor grill area.

FIRST FLOOR

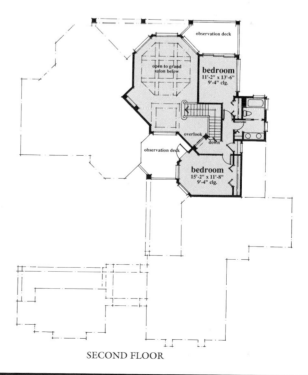

SECOND FLOOR

FAMILY HOMES

plan # HPK0600401

L

This refined hillside home is designed for lots that fall off toward the rear and works especially well with a view out the back. The kitchen and eating nook wrap around the vaulted family room where arched transom windows flank the fireplace. Formal living is graciously centered in the living room that's directly off the foyer and the adjoining dining room. A grand master suite is located on the main level for convenience and privacy. Downstairs, three family bedrooms share a compartmented hall bath.

STYLE: NW CONTEMPORARY
MAIN LEVEL: 2,196 SQ. FT.
LOWER LEVEL: 1,542 SQ. FT.
TOTAL: 3,738 SQ. FT.
BEDROOMS: 4
BATHROOMS: 2½
WIDTH: 72' - 0"
DEPTH: 56' - 0"
FOUNDATION:
CRAWLSPACE, BASEMENT

SEARCH ONLINE @ EPLANS.COM

LOWER LEVEL

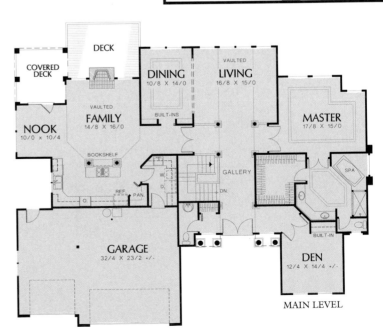

MAIN LEVEL

plan# HPK0600402

STYLE: MEDITERRANEAN
FIRST FLOOR: 2,894 SQ. FT.
SECOND FLOOR: 568 SQ. FT.
TOTAL: 3,462 SQ. FT.
BEDROOMS: 3
BATHROOMS: 3½
WIDTH: 67' - 0"
DEPTH: 102' - 0"
FOUNDATION: SLAB

SEARCH ONLINE @ EPLANS.COM

Two guest suites—one on each floor—enhance the interior of this magnificent stucco home. A grand entrance provides passage to a foyer that opens to the study on the left, the formal dining room on the right, and the formal living room straight ahead. The casual living area combines a kitchen with an island cooktop, a sun-filled breakfast nook, and a spacious leisure room. Arched openings lead into the master bedroom and a lavish bath that enjoys a private garden. The second-floor guest suite includes a loft and a large observation deck.

FIRST FLOOR

SECOND FLOOR

FAMILY HOMES

plan # HPK0600403

STYLE: SW CONTEMPORARY
FIRST FLOOR: 2,132 SQ. FT.
SECOND FLOOR: 1,295 SQ. FT.
TOTAL: 3,427 SQ. FT.
BEDROOMS: 3
BATHROOMS: 3
WIDTH: 91' - 6"
DEPTH: 75' - 6"
FOUNDATION:
CRAWLSPACE, BASEMENT

SEARCH ONLINE @ EPLANS.COM

Sand-finished stucco, distinctive columns, and oversized circle-top windows grace this luxurious three-bedroom home. A sunken living room features a two-sided gas fireplace that it shares with the formal dining room. The den is warmed by a fireplace and features double doors to the front porch. The family room is also sunken and shares a two-sided fireplace with an indoor spa and a glazed roof overhead. Two secondary bedrooms and a master suite are on the second floor. The master suite enjoys a through-fireplace between the bath and the bedroom.

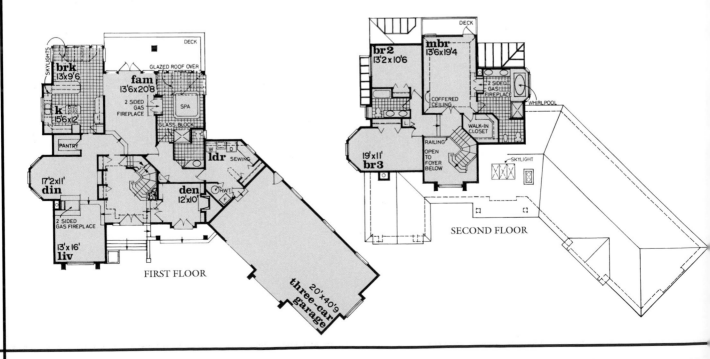

FIRST FLOOR

SECOND FLOOR

plan# HPK0600404

STYLE: MEDITERRANEAN
FIRST FLOOR: 2,260 SQ. FT.
SECOND FLOOR: 1,020 SQ. FT.
TOTAL: 3,280 SQ. FT.
BEDROOMS: 4
BATHROOMS: 2½
WIDTH: 69' - 6"
DEPTH: 88' - 2"
FOUNDATION: BASEMENT

SEARCH ONLINE @ EPLANS.COM

Designed for gracious entertaining, this contemporary Southwest home features all the amenities that will make you a memorable host. From the grand entry, follow the 13-foot ceiling to the great room, where a fireplace warms and French doors expand the space. The central kitchen has a unique inset pantry and an island that overlooks the hearth room's fireplace. Two dining areas, a columned dining room and casual cafe, accommodate any occasion. In the master suite, a tray ceiling traces the shape of the bedroom and sitting room; a private patio and plush bath complete the retreat. Upstairs, three bedrooms share two baths and a home office—a formal study is located near the master suite.

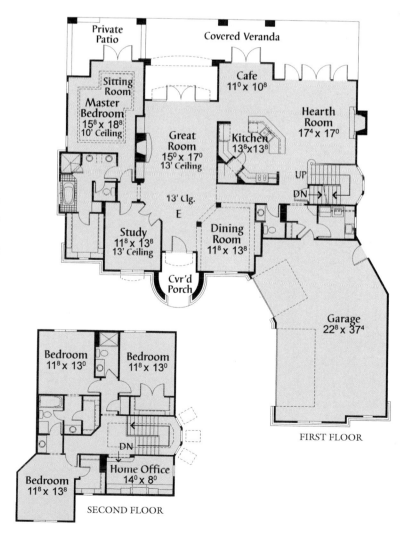

FIRST FLOOR

SECOND FLOOR

FAMILY HOMES

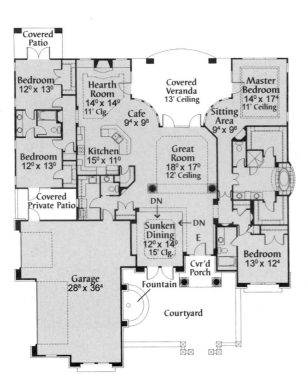

Covered Patio

Bedroom
12⁰ x 13⁰

Hearth Room
14⁰ x 14⁰
11' Clg.

Cafe
9⁴ x 9⁸

Covered Veranda
13' Ceiling

Master Bedroom
14⁰ x 17⁴
11' Ceiling

Sitting Area
9⁴ x 9⁸

Bedroom
12⁰ x 13⁰

Kitchen
15⁰ x 11⁰

Great Room
18⁰ x 17⁰
12' Ceiling

Covered Private Patio

DN

Sunken Dining
12⁰ x 14⁰
15' Clg.

DN E

Bedroom
13⁰ x 12⁴

Garage
28⁸ x 36⁴

Fountain

Cvr'd Porch

Courtyard

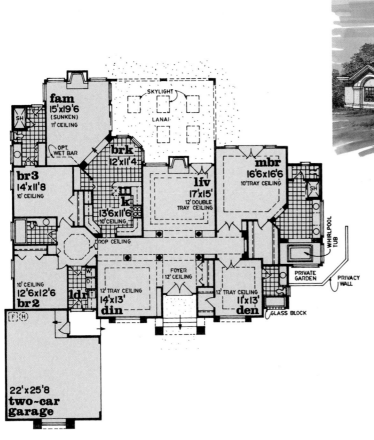

fam
15'x19'6
(SUNKEN)
11' CEILING

SKYLIGHT

LANAI

OPT. WET BAR

brk
12'x11'4

br3
14'x11'8
10' CEILING

k
13'6x11'6
10'CEILING

liv
17'x15'
12' DOUBLE TRAY CEILING

mbr
16'6x16'6
10' TRAY CEILING

WHIRLPOOL TUB

DROP CEILING

10' CEILING
12'6x12'6
br2

ldn

FOYER
12' CEILING

PRIVATE GARDEN

PRIVACY WALL

12' TRAY CEILING
14'x13'
din

12' TRAY CEILING
11'x13'
den

GLASS BLOCK

22'x25'8
two-car garage

STYLE: SW CONTEMPORARY
SQUARE FOOTAGE: 3,505
BEDROOMS: 3
BATHROOMS: 2½
WIDTH: 110' - 7"
DEPTH: 66' - 11"
FOUNDATION: SLAB

SEARCH ONLINE @ EPLANS.COM

Loaded with custom features, this plan is designed to delight the imagination. The foyer enters directly into the commanding sunken gathering room. Framed by an elegant railing, this centerpiece for entertaining is open to both the study and the formal dining room, and offers sliding glass doors to the terrace. A full bar further extends the entertaining possibilities of this room. The country-style kitchen contains an efficient work area, as well as a morning room and sitting area—ideal for family gatherings around the cozy fireplace. The grand master suite has a private terrace, fireplace alcove with built-in seats, and a huge spa-style bath. Two nicely sized bedrooms and a hall bath round out the plan.

QUOTE ONE®

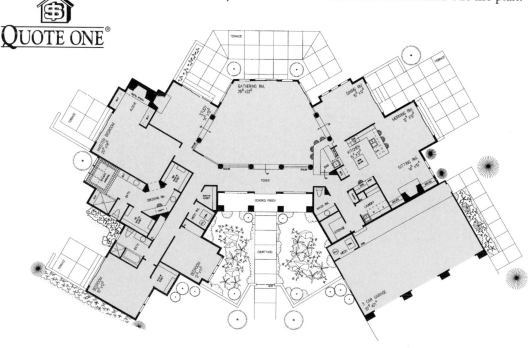

FAMILY HOMES

plan # HPK0600408

This villa-style Southwestern home invokes the use of arches and slightly slanted roofs to balance a squared-off stucco facade. Enter the main level to a living room/dining room on the left. Ahead, an open island kitchen views the gathering room's focal fireplace. The sunny breakfast nook opens on either end to a rear veranda. A guest suite near the kitchen offers a private courtyard. Upstairs, outdoor spaces include a veranda, master patio, and hearth-warmed patio. The master suite is a decadent retreat with a vaulted spa bath and huge walk-in closet. Two more bedrooms access the upper-level family room, or turn it into a splendid bedroom.

STYLE: SW CONTEMPORARY
FIRST FLOOR: 1,527 SQ. FT.
SECOND FLOOR: 1,611 SQ. FT.
TOTAL: 3,138 SQ. FT.
BEDROOMS: 5
BATHROOMS: 4½
WIDTH: 54' - 0"
DEPTH: 67' - 0"
FOUNDATION: SLAB

SEARCH ONLINE @ EPLANS.COM

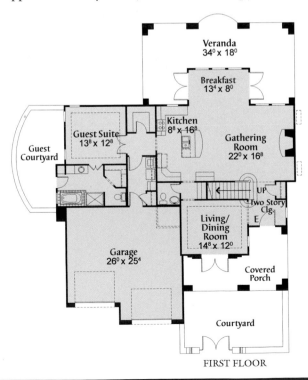

FIRST FLOOR

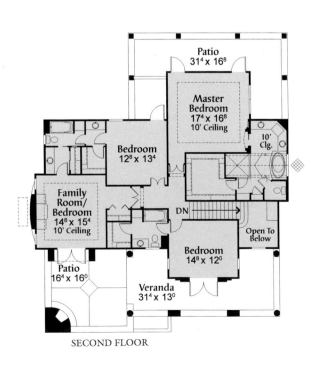

SECOND FLOOR

plan # HPK0600409

STYLE: MEDITERRANEAN
SQUARE FOOTAGE: 3,424
BONUS SPACE: 507 SQ. FT.
BEDROOMS: 5
BATHROOMS: 4
WIDTH: 82' - 4"
DEPTH: 83' - 8"
FOUNDATION: SLAB

SEARCH ONLINE @ EPLANS.COM

This lovely five-bedroom home exudes the beauty and warmth of a Mediterranean villa. The foyer views explode in all directions with the dominant use of octagonal shapes throughout. Double doors lead to the master wing, which abounds with niches. The sitting area of the master bedroom has a commanding view of the rear gardens. A bedroom just off the master suite is perfect for a guest room or office. The formal living and dining rooms share expansive glass walls and marble or tile pathways. The mitered glass wall of the breakfast nook can be viewed from the huge island kitchen. Two secondary bedrooms share the convenience of a Pullman-style bath. An additional rear bedroom completes this design.

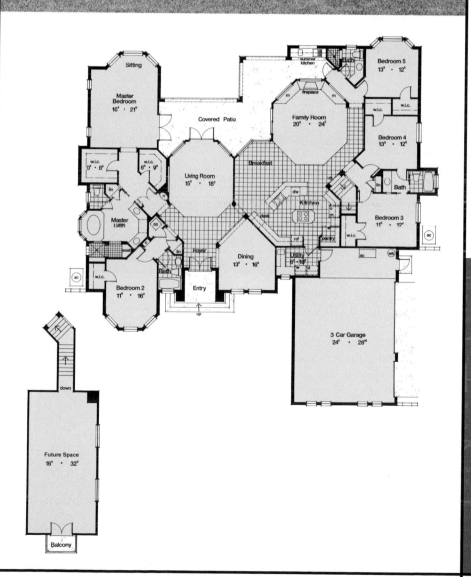

A wealth of elegant details, including decorative chimney tops and balustrades, distinguish this grand Mediterranean-style home.

Luxury homes are for those looking to spare no expense when it comes to style and comfort. Not only impressive for their size, these homes feature the best in materials, available upgrades, and design. The remarkable two-story entry of the plan featured here—rope columns, balustrades, arches, tile roof, side and top door lights—shows the degree of attention designers have given to the homes in this section. Decorative ceilings are also *de rigueur*, as seen in the family room (p. 344) of the featured plan.

These plans also showcase the industry's best solutions for integrating indoor and outdoor living. Luxury homes—particularly in the Mediterranean styles—offer elaborate covered courtyards called lanais, which often include landscaping, water features, wet bars, cabana-like half baths, and outdoor kitchens. Owners will find that a well-conceived lanai allows the home to open up the center and rear of the plan in spectacular ways without sacrificing privacy or security. The same strategy is used in the master suites of some homes to hide a bayed soaking tub from the outside—with a walled privacy garden placed just outside the window. Consider placing a similarly scaled garden outside the kitchen window. An enclosed herb or edible garden can help alleviate site-specific flaws or less-than-picturesque views from this side of the home, besides bringing a quaint, rustic touch to your home.

The cost-cutting method of building interior walls at right angles with as few corners as possible is abandoned for layouts that favor eye-catching forms and decorative trims. As in this great room, fireplaces, art niches, and built-in shelves are standard amenities. Window walls and pocket doors allow the entire rear of the plan to feel and function

Fine furnishing and judicious use of animal-skin patterns bring flair to the often-neglected study.

Left: Rustic treatments for the hood and backsplash invoke a French-country spirit in the kitchen. Below: The spacious family room opens luxuriously into the lanai. Opposite: For such a large design, the plan still harbors intimate spaces for casual gatherings.

FINAL TOUCH

Keep in mind that estate-size homes must make sensitive use of its square footage or risk feeling cavernous and neglected. Novel use of familiar materials can bring accent and warmth to a home in innovative ways.

MAKE AN ENTRANCE. Create an unforgettable passageway with the Adornador door trim system (top, left). Balmer Architectural Mouldings. **FLOOR TO CEILING.** Wood-Haven laminate (top right) adds dimension and character to the "fifth wall" of a room, the ceiling. Armstrong. **HARD TO TOP.** Achieve a traditional look—and avoid the tedious, challenging chore of having to repaint the ceiling every few years—with Prestplate metal plates (center, left). AA-Abbingdon Affiliates. **STEP RIGHT UP.** Reminiscent of an Old-World mansion, the Woodlawn stair bracket will bring grandeur to your home (center, right). Focal Point. **FIND YOUR NICHE.** Make room for elegance with the Prestige line of premium moldings, including the art niche shown (bottom, left). Louisiana-Pacific Moulding. **DENTIL WORK.** Crafted from polyurethane and fiberglass, Century moldings are designed to imitate the look of timeless classics (bottom, right). Century Architectural Specialties. **TOP PLACE FINISH.** Used alone or to accent lighting and ceiling fans, a ceiling medallion is an eye-catching accessory (inset). Style Solutions.

as if they are even larger. Door trims and rows of columns bring definition to spaces without establishing unwanted separations. The result is a layering of spaces and entryways that when seen from the right vantage point establish surprisingly complex interior vistas. The effect is downright breathtaking when walls and spaces are enhanced by a skilled lighting designer.

With the luxury plan the master suite attains the highest comforts of the modern home. The bedrooms often include sitting areas and private porches that take full advantage of the suite's orientation (assuming that the home has been situated on the site with this in mind). The baths are spacious and exquisitely detailed, providing discrete amounts of square footage or physical separation between the tub, shower, toilet, and vanities. Exercise rooms or dressing rooms may complement already comprehensive walk-in closets. In short, the homes collected in this section demonstrate the very best that our designers have to offer. ●

The idea of the central courtyard in Mediterranean homes has inspired this solution (here and at left), which brings light and space to the interior room of a large plan.

Bold colors and Old-World designs are perfectly appropriate in this bath.

plan # HPK0600410

STYLE: MEDITERRANEAN
FIRST FLOOR: 3,633 SQ. FT.
SECOND FLOOR: 695 SQ. FT.
TOTAL: 4,328 SQ. FT.
BEDROOMS: 5
BATHROOMS: 5½
WIDTH: 115' - 7"
DEPTH: 109' - 8"
FOUNDATION: SLAB

SEARCH ONLINE @ EPLANS.COM

SECOND FLOOR

FIRST FLOOR

plan# HPK0600412

STYLE: COLONIAL
FIRST FLOOR: 2,988 SQ. FT.
SECOND FLOOR: 1,216 SQ. FT.
TOTAL: 4,204 SQ. FT.
BONUS SPACE: 485 SQ. FT.
BEDROOMS: 4
BATHROOMS: 4½ + ½
WIDTH: 83' - 0"
DEPTH: 70' - 4"
FOUNDATION:
CRAWLSPACE, BASEMENT

SEARCH ONLINE @ EPLANS.COM

Palladian windows, fluted pilasters, and a pedimented entry give this home a distinctly Colonial flavor. Inside, the two-story foyer is flanked by the formal dining and living rooms. The spacious, two-story family room features a fireplace, built-ins, and backyard access. A large country kitchen provides a work island, walk-in pantry, planning desk, and breakfast area. The lavish master suite offers a tremendous amount of closet space, as well as a pampering bath. A nearby study could also serve as a nursery. Upstairs, three bedrooms, each with a private bath, have access to the future recreation room over the garage.

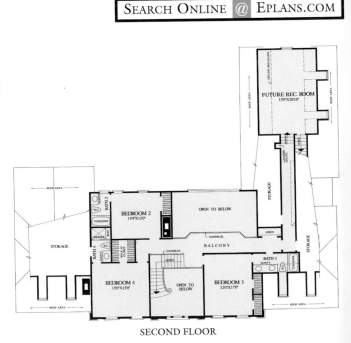

FIRST FLOOR

SECOND FLOOR

plan # HPK0600413

STYLE: FRENCH
FIRST FLOOR: 3,703 SQ. FT.
SECOND FLOOR: 1,427 SQ. FT.
TOTAL: 5,130 SQ. FT.
BONUS SPACE: 1,399 SQ. FT.
BEDROOMS: 4
BATHROOMS: 3½ + ½
WIDTH: 125' - 2"
DEPTH: 58' - 10"
FOUNDATION·
WALKOUT BASEMENT

SEARCH ONLINE @ EPLANS.COM

This magnificent estate is detailed with exterior charm: a porte cochere connecting the detached garage to the house, a covered terrace, and oval windows. The first floor consists of a lavish master suite, a cozy library with a fireplace, a grand room/solarium combination, and an elegant formal dining room with another fireplace. Three bedrooms dominate the second floor—each features a walk-in closet. For the kids, there is a playroom, and, up another flight of stairs, is a room for future expansion into a deluxe studio with a fireplace. Over the three-car garage, there is space for a future mother-in-law or maid's suite.

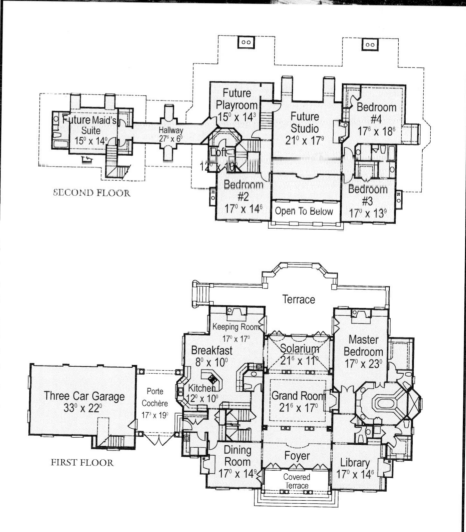

plan # HPK0600414

STYLE: GEORGIAN
FIRST FLOOR: 2,175 SQ. FT.
SECOND FLOOR: 1,927 SQ. FT.
TOTAL: 4,102 SQ. FT.
BASEMENT: 1,927 SQ. FT.
BEDROOMS: 4
BATHROOMS: 3½
WIDTH: 74' - 0"
DEPTH: 82' - 0"
FOUNDATION: BASEMENT

SEARCH ONLINE @ EPLANS.COM

Simply elegant, with dignified details, this beautiful home is reminiscent of English estate homes. Two double garages flank a columned front door and are attached to the main floor by galleries leading to the entry foyer. Here, a double staircase leads upstairs and encourages a view beyond the morning room, grand salon, and rear portico. The gourmet kitchen has a uniquely styled island counter with a cooktop. For formal meals, the dining hall is nearby. The elaborate master bedroom and three staterooms reside on the second level. The master bedroom features a circular shape and enjoys access to a private lanai, a through-fireplace to the master bath, and numerous alcoves and built-in amenities.

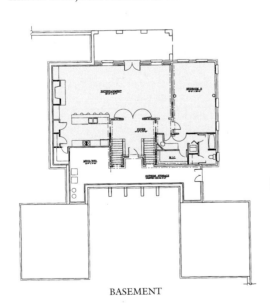

BASEMENT

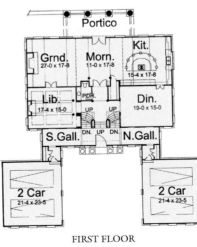

FIRST FLOOR

SECOND FLOOR

plan # HPK0600415

STYLE: TRADITIONAL
FIRST FLOOR: 2,538 SQ. FT.
SECOND FLOOR: 1,581 SQ. FT.
TOTAL: 4,119 SQ. FT.
BASEMENT: 1,773 SQ. FT.
BEDROOMS: 4
BATHROOMS: 3½
WIDTH: 67' - 7"
DEPTH: 84' - 5"
FOUNDATION: BASEMENT

Double columns flank the grand portico of this fine two-story home. Inside, the foyer presents a formal living room. This room welcomes all with a beam ceiling and a wall of windows to the rear veranda. The C-shaped kitchen offers a work-surface island, a walk-in pantry, and easy access to the spacious gathering room. Located on the first floor for privacy, the master suite is lavish with its luxuries. Upstairs, two family suites—each with a walk-in closet—share a full bath, and the large guest suite features another walk-in closet as well as a private bath.

BASEMENT

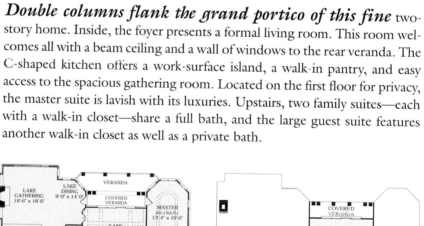

FIRST FLOOR

SECOND FLOOR

plan# HPK0600416

STYLE: FRENCH
FIRST FLOOR: 3,168 SQ. FT.
SECOND FLOOR: 998 SQ. FT.
TOTAL: 4,166 SQ. FT.
BONUS SPACE: 210 SQ. FT.
BEDROOMS: 4
BATHROOMS: 3½
WIDTH: 90' - 0"
DEPTH: 63' - 5"
FOUNDATION: SLAB,
BASEMENT, CRAWLSPACE

SEARCH ONLINE @ EPLANS.COM

Stucco corner quoins, multiple gables, and graceful columns all combine to give this European manor plenty of appeal. Inside, a gallery entry presents a formal dining room on the right, defined by elegant columns, while the formal living room awaits just ahead. The highly efficient kitchen features a worktop island, pantry, and a serving bar to the nearby octagonal breakfast area. The family room offers a built-in entertainment center, a fireplace, and its own covered patio. The left side of the first floor is dedicated to the master suite. Here, the homeowner is pampered with an octagonal study, huge walk-in closet, lavish bath, and a very convenient nursery. The second floor contains two family bedrooms, each with a walk-in closet, and a media area with built-in bookshelves.

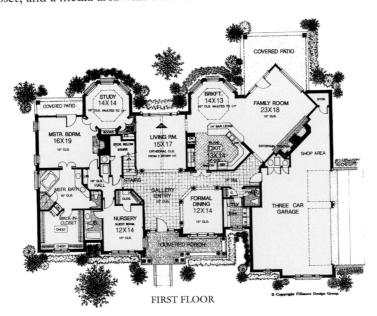

FIRST FLOOR

SECOND FLOOR

plan # HPK0600417

STYLE: COLONIAL
FIRST FLOOR: 4,107 SQ. FT.
SECOND FLOOR: 1,175 SQ. FT.
TOTAL: 5,282 SQ. FT.
BONUS SPACE: 745 SQ. FT.
BEDROOMS: 4
BATHROOMS: 4½
WIDTH: 90' - 0"
DEPTH: 63' - 0"
FOUNDATION: BASEMENT

SEARCH ONLINE @ EPLANS.COM

A sweeping central staircase is just one of the impressive features of this lovely estate home. Four fireplaces—in the library, family room, grand room, and master-suite sitting room—add a warm glow to the interior; the master suite, grand room, and family room all open to outdoor terrace space. There's plenty of room for family and guests—a guest suite sits to the front of the plan, joining the master suite and two more family bedrooms. Upstairs, a large bonus area—possibly a mother-in-law suite— offers a petite kitchen and walk-in closet; a full bath is nearby.

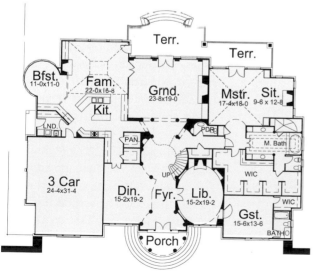

FIRST FLOOR

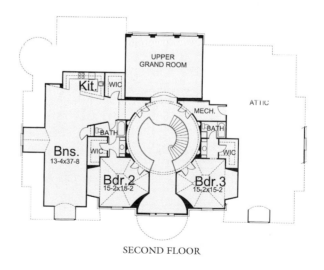

SECOND FLOOR

plan# HPK0600418

LD

STYLE: GEORGIAN
FIRST FLOOR: 2,126 SQ. FT.
SECOND FLOOR: 1,882 SQ. FT.
TOTAL: 4,008 SQ. FT.
BEDROOMS: 4
BATHROOMS: 2½
WIDTH: 92' - 0"
DEPTH: 64' - 4"
FOUNDATION: BASEMENT

SEARCH ONLINE @ EPLANS.COM

SECOND FLOOR

QUOTE ONE®

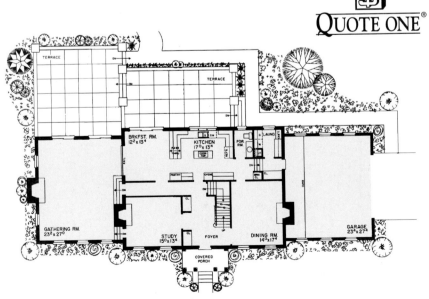

FIRST FLOOR

This historical Georgian home has its roots in the 18th Century. The full two-story center section is delightfully complemented by the one-and-a-half-story wings. An elegant gathering room, three steps down from the rest of the house, provides ample space for entertaining on a grand scale. The study and the formal dining room flank the foyer. Each of these rooms has a fireplace as its highlight. The breakfast room, kitchen, powder room, and laundry room are arranged for maximum efficiency. The second floor houses the family bedrooms. Take special note of the spacious master suite.

plan # HPK0600419

STYLE: GEORGIAN
FIRST FLOOR: 3,599 SQ. FT.
SECOND FLOOR: 1,621 SQ. FT.
TOTAL: 5,220 SQ. FT.
BONUS SPACE: 537 SQ. FT.
BEDROOMS: 4
BATHROOMS: 5½
WIDTH: 108' - 10"
DEPTH: 53' - 10"
FOUNDATION:
SLAB, BASEMENT

SEARCH ONLINE @ EPLANS.COM

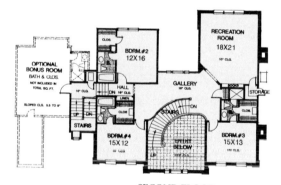

SECOND FLOOR

A grand facade detailed with brick corner quoins, stucco flourishes, arched windows, and an elegant entrance presents this home. A spacious foyer is accented by curving stairs and flanked by a formal living room and a formal dining room. For cozy times, a through-fireplace is located between a large family room and a quiet study. The master bedroom is designed to pamper, with two walk-in closets, a two-sided fireplace, a bayed sitting area, and a lavish private bath. Upstairs, three secondary bedrooms each have a private bath and a walk-in closet. Also on this level is a spacious recreation room, perfect for a game room or children's playroom.

FIRST FLOOR

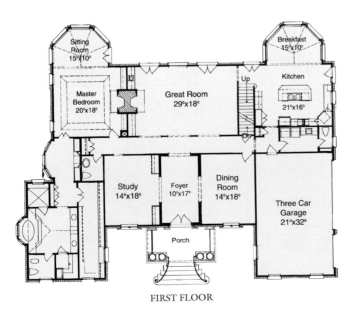

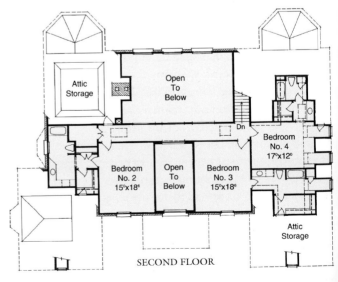

plan # HPK0600420

Classic symmetry sets off this graceful exterior, with two sets of double columns framed by tall windows and topped with a detailed pediment. Just off the foyer, the study and dining room present an elegant impression. The gourmet kitchen offers a food-preparation island and a lovely breakfast bay. The central gallery hall connects casual living areas with the master wing. A delightful dressing area with a split vanity and a bay window indulge the lavish master bath. The master bedroom features a bumped-out glass sitting area, a tray ceiling, and a romantic fireplace. Upstairs, three bedroom suites are pampered with private baths.

STYLE: GREEK REVIVAL
FIRST FLOOR: 3,509 SQ. FT.
SECOND FLOOR: 1,564 SQ. FT.
TOTAL: 5,073 SQ. FT.
BEDROOMS: 4
BATHROOMS: 4½ + ½
WIDTH: 86' - 6"
DEPTH: 67' - 3"
FOUNDATION:
WALKOUT BASEMENT

SEARCH ONLINE @ EPLANS.COM

plan # HPK0600421

STYLE: PLANTATION
FIRST FLOOR: 4,011 SQ. FT.
SECOND FLOOR: 2,198 SQ. FT.
TOTAL: 6,209 SQ. FT.
BASEMENT: 3,071 SQ. FT.
BEDROOMS: 4
BATHROOMS: 3½ + ½
WIDTH: 136' - 0"
DEPTH: 69' - 2"
FOUNDATION: BASEMENT

SEARCH ONLINE @ EPLANS.COM

This magnificent Southern-style mansion offers all the features needed for graceful entertaining and refined living. From the stately columns that welcome visitors at the entry to the splendid spiral stairway winding up to the second level, this home is stunning. An octagonal library towards the front guarantees private quietude. An expansive deck with a covered porch at one end and a pampering hot tub at the other will bring hours of enjoyment. Fantastic meals can be prepared in the spacious country kitchen. A resplendent master suite on the main floor enjoys a roomy dressing area; upstairs, three more bedrooms, one of them a posh guest suite, offer delightful sleeping accommodations. In addition to the formal dining area and impressive hearth room, the first floor also enjoys a music room and a convenient mudroom.

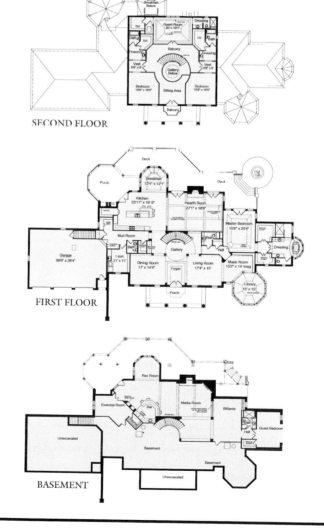

SECOND FLOOR

FIRST FLOOR

BASEMENT

plan# HPK0600422

Although the exterior of this classic estate is pure Colonial, the floor plan is anything but old fashioned. The grand foyer opens up to the sunken two-story living room, detailed with columns, a fireplace, and access to the rear property. To the left, a sunny bayed eating area joins a unique kitchen (with a butler's pantry) and the formal dining room for casual or formal meals. The veranda includes an outdoor grill and bar, perfect for dining alfresco. The right wing is devoted to sumptuous living: enter the master bedroom through a private sitting room with a two-sided fireplace. The sunken sleeping area flows into a pampering bath. Upstairs, dual central staircases present two generous bedrooms, each with a private bath and study area, and a balcony designed to accommodate a library.

STYLE: SOUTHERN
COLONIAL
FIRST FLOOR: 3,439 SQ. FT.
SECOND FLOOR: 803 SQ. FT.
TOTAL: 4,242 SQ. FT.
BEDROOMS: 4
BATHROOMS: 4 + 3 HALF
BATHS
WIDTH: 95' - 0"
DEPTH: 90' - 0"
FOUNDATION: SLAB

SEARCH ONLINE @ EPLANS.COM

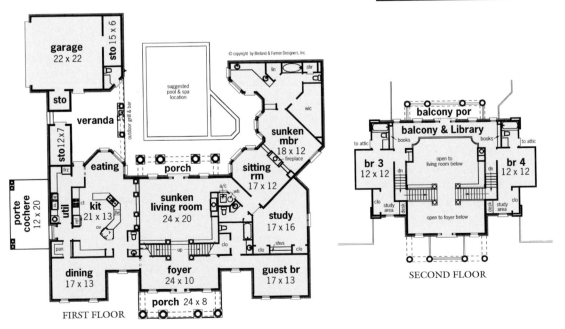

FIRST FLOOR

SECOND FLOOR

plan # HPK0600423

STYLE: EUROPEAN COTTAGE
FIRST FLOOR: 3,170 SQ. FT.
SECOND FLOOR: 1,515 SQ. FT.
TOTAL: 4,685 SQ. FT.
BONUS SPACE: 486 SQ. FT.
BEDROOMS: 4
BATHROOMS: 3½
WIDTH: 76' - 0"
DEPTH: 75' - 8"
FOUNDATION: SLAB

SEARCH ONLINE @ EPLANS.COM

This modern Colonial home exhibits bold style and striking good looks. Historic details inside and out set the tone for a carefully designed plan with today's family in mind. Formal rooms at the front of the home welcome guests; to the rear, the family room basks in the sunlight of wide, tall windows. The well-planned kitchen is equipped with an island and walk-in pantry, and extends into a breakfast bay that is surrounded with natural light. The master wing includes a bayed sunroom and lavish bath with a corner whirlpool tub. Three generous bedrooms, a craft room, and a future game room inhabit the second floor.

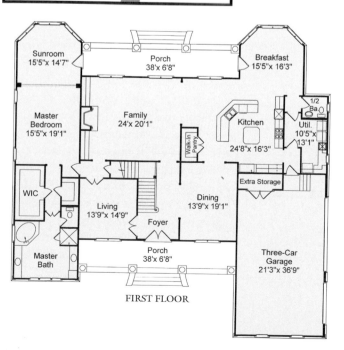

FIRST FLOOR

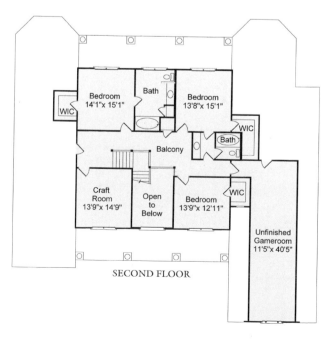

SECOND FLOOR

SECOND FLOOR

FIRST FLOOR

© William E. Poole Designs

plan # HPK0600424

STYLE: COLONIAL
FIRST FLOOR: 2,993 SQ. FT.
SECOND FLOOR: 1,452 SQ. FT.
TOTAL: 4,445 SQ. FT.
BONUS SPACE: 611 SQ. FT.
BEDROOMS: 4
BATHROOMS: 5
WIDTH: 113' - 0"
DEPTH: 65' - 4"
FOUNDATION: CRAWLSPACE

SEARCH ONLINE @ EPLANS.COM

A rear terrace and porch extend the living area and provide ample opportunity for outdoor dining and socializing. Inside, a sunroom offers natural light and a great place to relax any time of day. A first-floor master is a private retreat for the homeowners, conveniently located next to the study. The upgraded laundry room boasts a washer/dryer, deep freezer, built-in ironing board, central table for folding clothes, and a drying closet. A full bath adjacent to the laundry room completes this level. Upstairs houses three additional family bedrooms, three full baths, and a future rec room.

ORDER BLUEPRINTS 24 HOURS, 7 DAYS A WEEK, AT 1-800-521-6797

plan # HPK0600425

STYLE: SOUTHERN
COLONIAL
FIRST FLOOR: 3,170 SQ. FT.
SECOND FLOOR: 1,914 SQ. FT.
TOTAL: 5,084 SQ. FT.
BONUS SPACE: 445 SQ. FT.
BEDROOMS: 4
BATHROOMS: 3½
WIDTH: 100' - 10"
DEPTH: 65' - 5"
FOUNDATION: CRAWLSPACE

SEARCH ONLINE @ EPLANS.COM

This elegantly appointed home is a beauty inside and out. A centerpiece stair rises gracefully from the two-story grand foyer. The kitchen, breakfast room, and family room provide open space for the gathering of family and friends. The beam-ceilinged study and the dining room flank the grand foyer, and each includes a fireplace. The master bedroom features a cozy sitting area and a luxury master bath with His and Hers vanities and walk-in closets. Three large bedrooms and a game room complete the second floor. A large expandable area is available at the top of the rear stair.

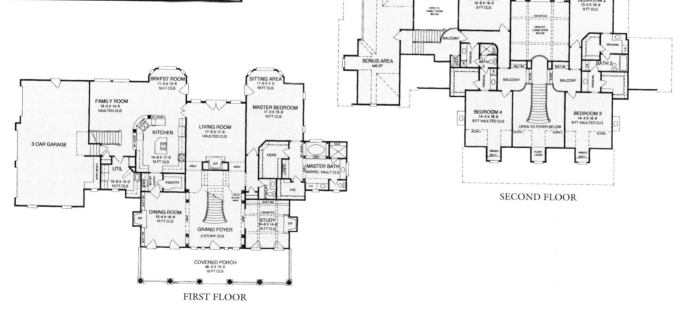

FIRST FLOOR

SECOND FLOOR

plan# HPK0600426

This Southern coastal cottage radiates charm and elegance. Step inside from the covered porch and discover a floor plan with practicality and architectural interest. The foyer has a raised ceiling and is partially open to above. The library and great room offer fireplaces and built-in shelves; the great room also provides rear-porch access. The kitchen, featuring an island with a separate sink, is adjacent to the breakfast room and a study with a built-in desk. On the far right, the master bedroom will amaze, with a sumptuous bath and enormous walk-in closet. Three upstairs bedrooms share a loft and recreation room. Convenient storage opportunities make organization easy.

STYLE: COUNTRY COTTAGE
FIRST FLOOR: 2,891 SQ. FT.
SECOND FLOOR: 1,336 SQ. FT.
TOTAL: 4,227 SQ. FT.
BONUS SPACE: 380 SQ. FT.
BEDROOMS: 4
BATHROOMS: 3½ + ½
WIDTH: 90' - 8"
DEPTH: 56' - 4"
FOUNDATION:
CRAWLSPACE, BASEMENT

SEARCH ONLINE @ EPLANS.COM

FIRST FLOOR

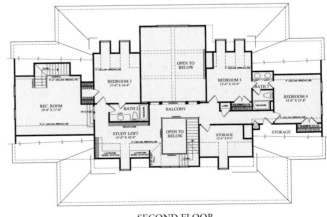

SECOND FLOOR

plan # HPK0600427

STYLE: TRADITIONAL
FIRST FLOOR: 3,414 SQ. FT.
SECOND FLOOR: 1,238 SQ. FT.
TOTAL: 4,652 SQ. FT.
BEDROOMS: 4
BATHROOMS: 3½
WIDTH: 90' - 6"
DEPTH: 78' - 9"
FOUNDATION: BASEMENT

SEARCH ONLINE @ EPLANS.COM

Country meets traditional in this splendid design. A covered front porch offers a place to enjoy the sunrise or place a porch swing. With the formal areas flanking the foyer, an open flow is established between the column-accented dining room and the library with its distinguished beam ceiling. The two-story great room features a wall of windows looking out to the rear grounds. On the left, the gourmet kitchen serves up casual and formal meals to the breakfast and hearth rooms with the dining room just steps away. The master bedroom enjoys a sitting area with an array of view-catching windows, a spacious dressing area, and an accommodating walk-in closet. Three family bedrooms—one with a private bath—complete the second level.

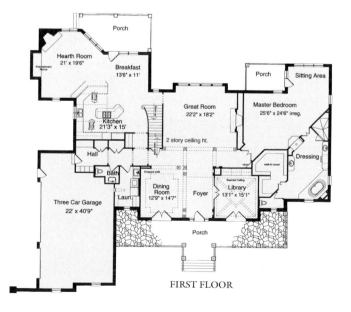

FIRST FLOOR

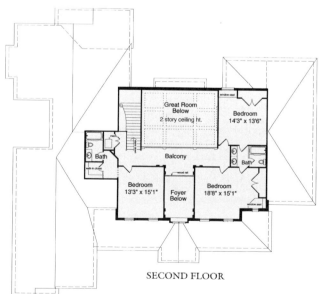

SECOND FLOOR

Early American style abounds in this brick-and-stone home. From the covered front porch, enter to find a library on the right and a columned dining room on the left. In the kitchen, a corner sink and workstation with an arched pass-through allow the chef to prepare meals while keeping an eye on family or guests in the grand room. A sliding glass door off the breakfast nook invites outdoor meals on the optional screened porch and grilling deck. The master suite includes an island walk-in closet and a private bath. A finished walkout basement accommodates two bedrooms and tons of bonus space.

plan# HPK0600428

STYLE: CAPE COD
MAIN LEVEL: 2,298 SQ. FT.
LOWER LEVEL: 1,718 SQ. FT.
TOTAL: 4,016 SQ. FT.
BEDROOMS: 3
BATHROOMS: 2½ + ½
WIDTH: 60' - 0"
DEPTH: 71' - 0"
FOUNDATION: BASEMENT

SEARCH ONLINE @ EPLANS.COM

plan # HPK0600429

STYLE: CRAFTSMAN
FIRST FLOOR: 2,572 SQ. FT.
SECOND FLOOR: 1,578 SQ. FT.
TOTAL: 4,150 SQ. FT.
BONUS SPACE: 315 SQ. FT.
BEDROOMS: 4
BATHROOMS: 4½
WIDTH: 78' - 2"
DEPTH: 68' - 0"
FOUNDATION: CRAWLSPACE

SEARCH ONLINE @ EPLANS.COM

Craftsman detailing and a hint of French flair make this home a standout in any neighborhood. An impressive foyer opens to the left to the great room, with a coffered ceiling, warming fireplace, and a charming alcove set in a turret. The kitchen is designed for entertaining, with an island that doubles as a snack bar and plenty of room to move. An adjacent porch invites dining alfresco. The bayed study is peaceful and quiet. A nearby guest room enjoys a private bath. Upstairs, the master suite is awe-inspiring. A romantic fireplace sets the mood and natural light pours in. A sumptuous spa bath leaves homeowners pampered and relaxed. Two bedroom suites share a vaulted bonus room, perfect as a home gym.

FIRST FLOOR

SECOND FLOOR

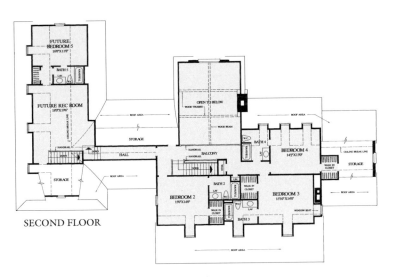

SECOND FLOOR

FIRST FLOOR

plan# HPK0600430

STYLE: COLONIAL
FIRST FLOOR: 3,016 SQ. FT.
SECOND FLOOR: 1,283 SQ. FT.
TOTAL: 4,299 SQ. FT.
BONUS SPACE: 757 SQ. FT.
BEDROOMS: 4
BATHROOMS: 4½ + ½
WIDTH: 105' - 0"
DEPTH: 69' - 0"
FOUNDATION: CRAWLSPACE

SEARCH ONLINE @ EPLANS.COM

With 10-foot wood-beam ceilings on the first floor and nine-foot ceilings upstairs, this Dutch Colonial offers plenty of aesthetic appeal. Enter the foyer to a dining room with an arched entrance on the left, and to the right, a living room/library with transom pocket doors and a fireplace. The kitchen is full of modern amenities, including an island with a vegetable sink and a snack bar. The master wing provides peace and quiet—and a few surprises! Details like a window seat, whirlpool tub, and storage space make it a welcome retreat. Upstairs, three bedroom suites, each with private baths, offer room for family and guests. Future space is available for expansion.

plan# HPK0600431

STYLE: SOUTHERN COLONIAL
FIRST FLOOR: 2,998 SQ. FT.
SECOND FLOOR: 1,556 SQ. FT.
TOTAL: 4,554 SQ. FT.
BONUS SPACE: 741 SQ. FT.
BEDROOMS: 4
BATHROOMS: 4½
WIDTH: 75' - 6"
DEPTH: 91' - 2"
FOUNDATION: CRAWLSPACE

SEARCH ONLINE @ EPLANS.COM

The paired double-end chimneys, reminiscent of the Georgian style of architecture, set this design apart from the rest. The covered entry opens to the columned foyer with the dining room on the left and the living room on the right, each enjoying the warmth and charm of a fireplace. Beyond the grand staircase, the family room delights with a third fireplace and a window wall that opens to the terrace. The expansive kitchen and breakfast area sit on the far left; the master suite is secluded on the the right with its pampering private bath. The second floor holds three additional bedrooms (including a second master bedroom), three full baths, a computer room, and the future recreation room.

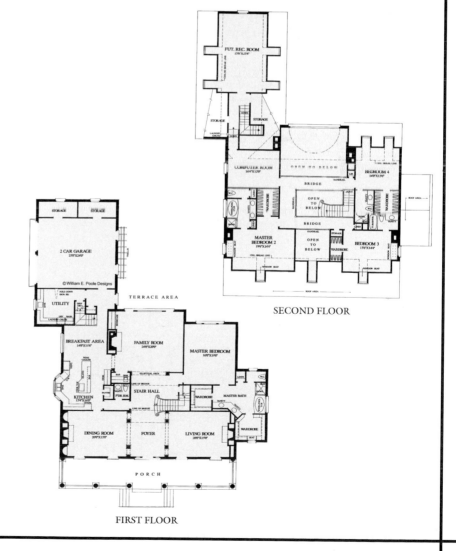

SECOND FLOOR

FIRST FLOOR

With five bedrooms and a wonderful stone-and-siding exterior, this country home will satisfy every need. Two sets of French doors provide access to the dining room and foyer. The great room enjoys a warming fireplace and deck access. The kitchen, breakfast bay, and keeping room feature an open floor plan. A charming sitting area in a bay window sets off the master bedroom. The master bath features a large walk-in closet, two-sink vanity, separate tub and shower, and compartmented toilet. Four bedrooms, an office, and two full baths complete the upper level.

plan# HPK0600432

STYLE: COLONIAL
FARMHOUSE
FIRST FLOOR: 2,628 SQ. FT.
SECOND FLOOR: 1,775 SQ. FT.
TOTAL: 4,403 SQ. FT.
BEDROOMS: 5
BATHROOMS: 3½
WIDTH: 79' - 6"
DEPTH: 65' - 1"
FOUNDATION: UNFINISHED
WALKOUT BASEMENT

SEARCH ONLINE @ EPLANS.COM

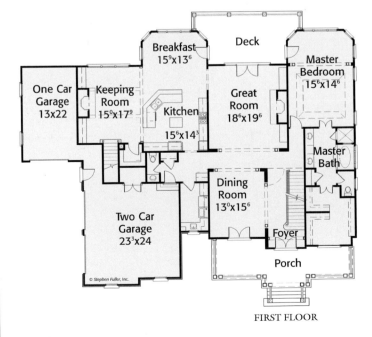

FIRST FLOOR

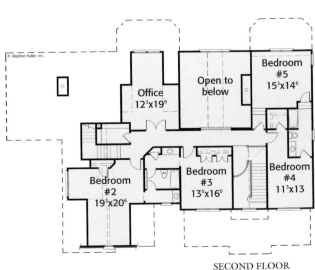

SECOND FLOOR

plan # HPK0600433

STYLE: TRADITIONAL
FIRST FLOOR: 3,218 SQ. FT.
SECOND FLOOR: 1,240 SQ. FT.
TOTAL: 4,458 SQ. FT.
BONUS SPACE: 656 SQ. FT.
BEDROOMS: 4
BATHROOMS: 3½
WIDTH: 76' - 0"
DEPTH: 73' - 10"
FOUNDATION: BASEMENT

SEARCH ONLINE @ EPLANS.COM

This design features a breathtaking facade with an upper rear balcony, four covered porches, and an inconspicuous side garage. The foyer is flanked by the dining room and the two-story library, which includes a fireplace and built-in bookcases. The elegant master bath provides dual vanities, a bright radius window, and a separate leaded-glass shower. A unique double decker walk-in closet provides plenty of storage. Nearby, a home office offers stunning views of the backyard. Upstairs, two family bedrooms share a compartmented bath and a covered porch; a third offers a private bath. A bonus room is included for future expansion.

FIRST FLOOR

SECOND FLOOR

plan # HPK0600434

STYLE: FARMHOUSE
FIRST FLOOR: 3,520 SQ. FT.
SECOND FLOOR: 1,638 SQ. FT.
TOTAL: 5,158 SQ. FT.
BONUS SPACE: 411 SQ. FT.
BEDROOMS: 5
BATHROOMS: 4½
WIDTH: 96' - 6"
DEPTH: 58' - 8"

SEARCH ONLINE @ EPLANS.COM

This custom-designed estate home elegantly combines stone and stucco, arched windows, and stunning exterior details under its formidable hipped roof. The two-story foyer is impressive with its grand staircase, tray ceiling, and overlooking balcony. Equally remarkable is the generous living room with a fireplace and a coffered two-story ceiling. The kitchen, breakfast bay, and family room with a fireplace are all open to one another for a comfortable, casual atmosphere. The first-floor master suite indulges with numerous closets, a dressing room, and a fabulous bath. Upstairs, four more bedrooms are topped by tray ceilings—three have walk-in closets and two have private baths. The three-car garage boasts additional storage and a bonus room above.

FIRST FLOOR

SECOND FLOOR

plan # HPK0600435

STYLE: VICTORIAN
FIRST FLOOR: 2,506 SQ. FT.
SECOND FLOOR: 2,315 SQ. FT.
TOTAL: 4,821 SQ. FT.
BONUS SPACE: 278 SQ. FT.
BEDROOMS: 5
BATHROOMS: 4
WIDTH: 60' - 0"
DEPTH: 97' - 0"
FOUNDATION: CRAWLSPACE

SEARCH ONLINE @ EPLANS.COM

The lacy veranda that embraces the exterior of this Queen Anne home offers outdoor living space under its shady recesses. Inside, the great room features a fireplace, built-in shelves, and a wet bar. The kitchen boasts a walk-in pantry, an island countertop, a breakfast nook with a bayed window, and access to the keeping room and the rear covered porch. The second floor contains three family bedrooms and the master suite. The elegant master suite features a sitting area located within a turret, a spacious walk-in closet, an enormous bath with a step-up tub and dual vanities, and access to its own private exercise room. This home is designed with a two-car garage.

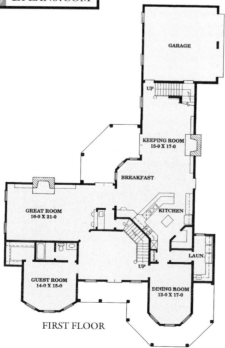

FIRST FLOOR

SECOND FLOOR

plan# HPK0600436

STYLE: CRAFTSMAN
FIRST FLOOR: 2,597 SQ. FT.
SECOND FLOOR: 2,171 SQ. FT.
TOTAL: 4,768 SQ. FT.
BEDROOMS: 4
BATHROOMS: 4½
WIDTH: 76' - 6"
DEPTH: 68' - 6"
FOUNDATION: CRAWLSPACE

SEARCH ONLINE @ EPLANS.COM

This splendid Craftsman home will look good in any neighborhood. Inside, the foyer offers a beautiful wooden bench to the right, flanked by built-in curio cabinets. On the left, double French doors lead to a cozy study. The formal dining room is complete with beamed ceilings, a built-in hutch, and cabinets. The large L-shaped kitchen includes a work island/snack bar, plenty of storage, and an adjacent sunny nook. The two-story great room surely lives up to its name, with a massive stone fireplace and a two-story wall of windows. Upstairs, two family bedrooms share a full bath, while the guest suite features its own bath. The lavish master bedroom suite pampers the homeowner with two walk-in closets, a fireplace, and a private deck.

FIRST FLOOR

SECOND FLOOR

plan ⊕ HPK0600437

STYLE: TRADITIONAL
FIRST FLOOR: 4,205 SQ. FT.
SECOND FLOOR: 1,618 SQ. FT.
TOTAL: 5,823 SQ. FT.
BONUS SPACE: 504 SQ. FT.
BEDROOMS: 4
BATHROOMS: 5½
WIDTH: 104' - 0"
DEPTH: 97' - 0"
FOUNDATION: CRAWLSPACE

SEARCH ONLINE @ EPLANS.COM

A sunlit two-story foyer offers access to every room of this exciting Mediterranean manor. Each main room is provided the added luxury of a coffered ceiling. The bayed formal dining room leads to the gourmet island kitchen through a butler's pantry. A wet bar connects the kitchen to the large family room with its built-in media center and corner fireplace. A breakfast nook offers French-door access to the side yard. The private first-floor master wing includes a quiet den and a large master bedroom with a lavish master bath that features two walk-in closets, a dressing area, and a spa tub. Three upper-level family bedrooms are graced with private baths. A large media room with a built-in media center and a bonus room complete this impressive design.

FIRST FLOOR

SECOND FLOOR

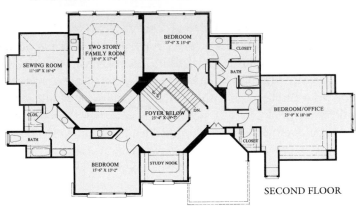

SEWING ROOM
11'-10" X 16'-6"

TWO STORY
FAMILY ROOM
18'-0" X 17'-4"

BEDROOM
15'-6" X 15'-8"

CLOSET

BATH

CLOS.

FOYER BELOW
23'-4" X 19'-2"

DN.

BEDROOM/OFFICE
23'-0" X 18'-10"

BATH

BEDROOM
15'-6" X 13'-2"

STUDY NOOK

CLOSET

SECOND FLOOR

plan # HPK0600438

STYLE: TRADITIONAL
FIRST FLOOR: 3,065 SQ. FT.
SECOND FLOOR: 1,969 SQ. FT.
TOTAL: 5,034 SQ. FT.
BEDROOMS: 4
BATHROOMS: 3½
WIDTH: 88' - 6"
DEPTH: 45' - 0"
FOUNDATION:
WALKOUT BASEMENT

SEARCH ONLINE @ EPLANS.COM

Elegance and luxury define this stately brick-and-stucco home. Creative design continues inside with a dramatic foyer that leads to the formal living and dining rooms and the casual two-story family room. A butler's pantry links the dining room to the grand kitchen. Casual gatherings will be enjoyed in the family room that joins with the breakfast room and kitchen. Here, a solarium and porch invite outdoor living. The exquisite master suite features a lush bath and sunny sitting area. Upstairs, two family bedrooms with private baths, a home office, and a hobby room round out the plan.

QUOTE ONE®

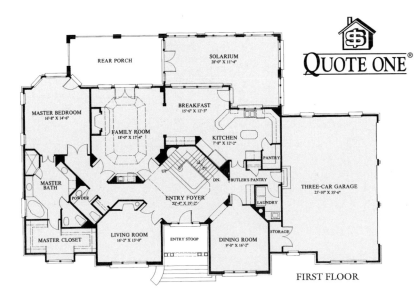

REAR PORCH

SOLARIUM
20'-0" X 11'-4"

MASTER BEDROOM
16'-8" X 14'-6"

BREAKFAST
15'-6" X 12'-3"

FAMILY ROOM
18'-0" X 17'-4"

KITCHEN
7'-8" X 12'-2"

PANTRY

MASTER
BATH

UP

DN.

BUTLER'S PANTRY

THREE-CAR GARAGE
23'-10" X 35'-6"

POWDER

ENTRY FOYER
32'-4" X 19'-2"

LAUNDRY

MASTER CLOSET

LIVING ROOM
16'-2" X 13'-0"

ENTRY STOOP

DINING ROOM
9'-0" X 16'-2"

STORAGE

FIRST FLOOR

plan# HPK0600439

STYLE: FRENCH
FIRST FLOOR: 2,764 SQ. FT.
SECOND FLOOR: 1,598 SQ. FT.
TOTAL: 4,362 SQ. FT.
BEDROOMS: 4
BATHROOMS: 3½
WIDTH: 74' - 6"
DEPTH: 65' - 10"
FOUNDATION:
CRAWLSPACE, UNFINISHED
WALKOUT BASEMENT

SEARCH ONLINE @ EPLANS.COM

The heart of this magnificent design is the two-story living room with its fireplace and built-in bookshelves. To the right rear of the plan lie the more casual rooms—the vaulted family room, island kitchen with pantry, and the breakfast nook. A formal dining room awaits elegant meals at the front of the plan. The private master wing features a secluded study, bayed sitting area, and deluxe vaulted bath. Upstairs, three bedrooms, each with ample closet space, share two full baths, a loft, and a gallery that overlook the first floor.

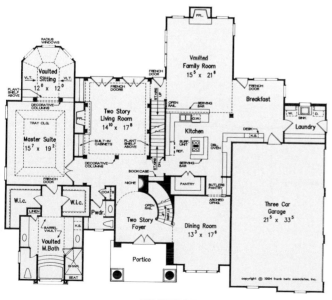

FIRST FLOOR

SECOND FLOOR

plan # HPK0600440

The stone and brick exterior with multiple gables and a side-entry garage create a design that brags great curb appeal. The gourmet kitchen with an island and snack bar combine with the spacious breakfast room and hearth room to create a warm and friendly atmosphere for family living. The luxurious master bedroom with a sitting area and fireplace is complemented by a deluxe dressing room and walk-in closet. The basement level contains an office, media room, billiards room, exercise area, and plenty of storage.

STYLE: TRADITIONAL
MAIN LEVEL: 3,570 SQ. FT.
LOWER LEVEL: 2,367 SQ. FT.
TOTAL: 5,937 SQ. FT.
BEDROOMS: 4
BATHROOMS: 4½
WIDTH: 84' - 6"
DEPTH: 69' - 4"
FOUNDATION: BASEMENT

SEARCH ONLINE @ EPLANS.COM

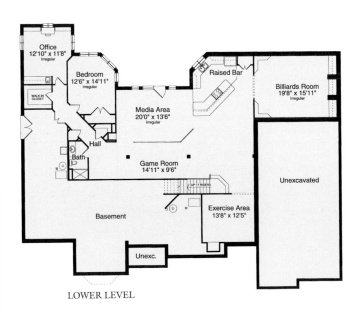

LOWER LEVEL

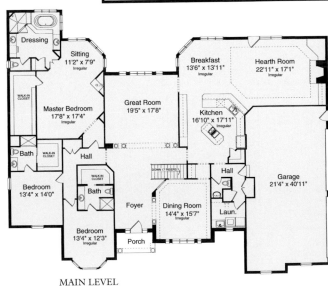

MAIN LEVEL

plan # **HPK0600441**

STYLE: EUROPEAN COTTAGE
FIRST FLOOR: 2,451 SQ. FT.
SECOND FLOOR: 1,762 SQ. FT.
TOTAL: 4,213 SQ. FT.
BONUS SPACE: 353 SQ. FT.
BEDROOMS: 4
BATHROOMS: 3½
WIDTH: 92' - 6"
DEPTH: 46' - 0"
FOUNDATION: CRAWLSPACE

SEARCH ONLINE @ EPLANS.COM

Shingles, stone, and shutters all combine to give this attractive manor a warm and welcoming feel. The two-story foyer presents the formal living room on the right—complete with a fireplace. The spacious family room also features a fireplace, along with a built-in media center, a wall of windows, and a 10-foot ceiling. Open to the family room, the efficient kitchen provides plenty of cabinet and counter space, as well as a nearby bayed nook. A study is available, with built-in bookshelves. Upstairs, the master suite is sure to please. It includes a large walk-in closet, a pampering bath with dual vanities and a tub set in a bay, a 10 foot ceiling, and a corner fireplace. Bedrooms 3 and 4 share a bath, while Bedroom 2 offers privacy. A bonus room is available for future expansion.

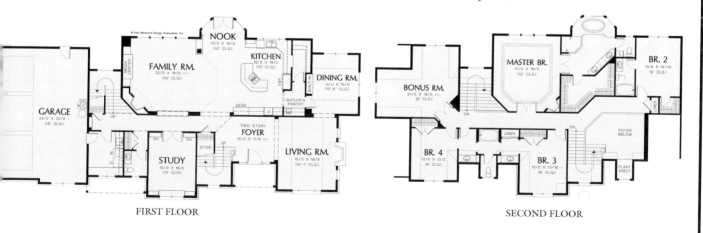

FIRST FLOOR

SECOND FLOOR

plan# HPK0600442

STYLE: PLANTATION
FIRST FLOOR: 2,113 SQ. FT.
SECOND FLOOR: 2,098 SQ. FT.
TOTAL: 4,211 SQ. FT.
BEDROOMS: 5
BATHROOMS: 4½
WIDTH: 68' - 6"
DEPTH: 53' - 0"
FOUNDATION:
SLAB, CRAWLSPACE

SEARCH ONLINE @ EPLANS.COM

This two-story farmhouse has much to offer, with the most exciting feature being the opulent master suite, which takes up almost the entire width of the upper level. French doors access the large master bedroom with its coffered ceiling. Steps lead to a separate sitting room with a fireplace and sun-filled bay window. His and Hers walk-in closets lead the way to a vaulted private bath with separate vanities and a lavish whirlpool tub. On the first floor, an island kitchen and a bayed breakfast room flow into a two-story family room with a raised-hearth fireplace, built-in shelves, and French-door access to the rear yard.

FIRST FLOOR

SECOND FLOOR

plan # HPK0600443

STYLE: COUNTRY COTTAGE
FIRST FLOOR: 3,607 SQ. FT.
SECOND FLOOR: 2,238 SQ. FT.
TOTAL: 5,845 SQ. FT.
BONUS SPACE: 329 SQ. FT.
BEDROOMS: 4
BATHROOMS: 3½
WIDTH: 83' - 6"
DEPTH: 88' - 4"
FOUNDATION: BASEMENT

SEARCH ONLINE @ EPLANS.COM

Gables, varied rooflines, arched windows, and a columned entry—the detailing on this stone manor is exquisite. A two-story foyer opens to the formal dining room, an elegant stair hall, and the grand room, with its fireplace and vaulted ceiling. A short hallway leads to the master suite, tucked quietly to the right of the curved stairwell. The comforting family room offers a fireplace that easily warms the adjoining breakfast area and marvelous, gourmet kitchen. Three additional family bedrooms and an optional bonus/bedroom are housed upstairs along with two full baths.

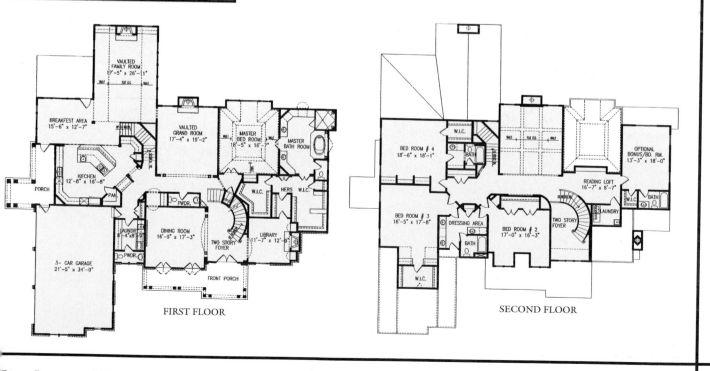

FIRST FLOOR

SECOND FLOOR

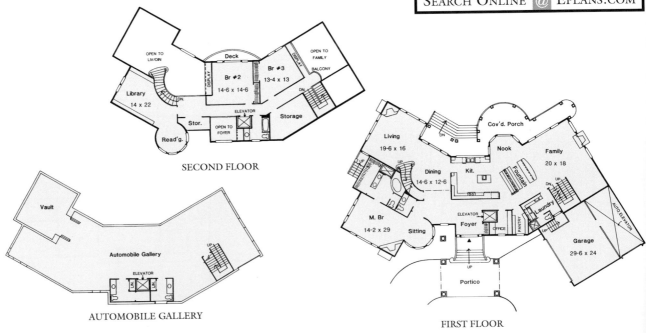

plan# HPK0600444

STYLE: NW CONTEMPORARY
FIRST FLOOR: 3,162 SQ. FT.
SECOND FLOOR: 1,595 SQ. FT.
TOTAL: 4,757 SQ. FT.
AUTO GALLERY: 2,651 SQ. FT.
BEDROOMS: 3
BATHROOMS: 3 + 3 HALF BATHS
WIDTH: 110' - 2"
DEPTH: 68' - 11"
FOUNDATION:
BASEMENT, SLAB

SEARCH ONLINE @ EPLANS.COM

Victorian and Craftsman styles blend and create an inviting and detailed home. A two-story turret houses a second-floor reading room and first-floor master sitting bay. The dining and living areas are open and convenient to the rear porch and gourmet kitchen. An interior fountain divides the breakfast area and the spacious family room. The first-floor master suite features a corner fireplace and private bath. Family quarters, including two bedrooms and a large library, can be found on the second floor. Storage for holiday items and large keepsakes is also provided. On the lower level, a magnificent auto gallery, complete with a special car elevator, is perfect for the auto enthusiast in the family.

SECOND FLOOR

AUTOMOBILE GALLERY

FIRST FLOOR

ORDER BLUEPRINTS 24 HOURS, 7 DAYS A WEEK, AT 1-800-521-6797

plan # HPK0600445

STYLE: CRAFTSMAN
MAIN LEVEL: 3,040 SQ. FT.
LOWER LEVEL: 1,736 SQ. FT.
TOTAL: 4,776 SQ. FT.
BEDROOMS: 5
BATHROOMS: 4½ + ½
WIDTH: 106' - 5"
DEPTH: 104' - 2"

SEARCH ONLINE @ EPLANS.COM

Looking a bit like a mountain resort, this fine rustic-style home is sure to be the envy of your neighborhood. Entering through the elegant front door, one finds an open staircase to the right and a spacious great room directly ahead. Here, a fireplace and a wall of windows give a cozy welcome. A lavish master suite begins with a sitting room complete with a fireplace and continues to a private porch, large walk-in closet, and sumptuous bedroom area. The gourmet kitchen adjoins a sunny dining room that offers access to a screened porch.

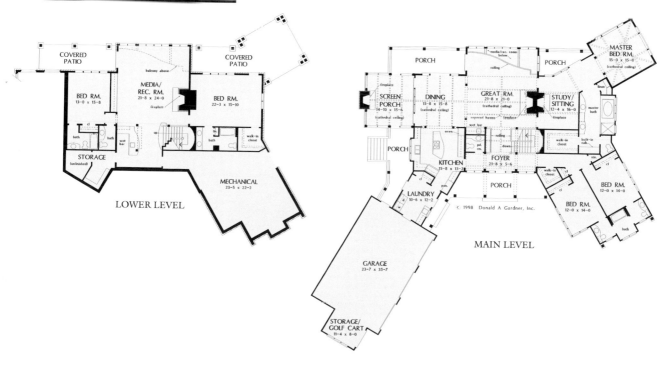

plan# HPK0600446

STYLE: CRAFTSMAN
FIRST FLOOR: 3,203 SQ. FT.
SECOND FLOOR: 1,689 SQ. FT.
TOTAL: 4,892 SQ. FT.
BONUS/BASEMENT:
274/2,135 SQ. FT.
BEDROOMS: 5
BATHROOMS: 5½ + ½
WIDTH: 96' - 9"
DEPTH: 91' - 10"
FOUNDATION: BASEMENT

SEARCH ONLINE @ EPLANS.COM

This magnificent five-bedroom home offers a rustic shingled exterior that is reminiscent of Old World Europe. The elegant foyer opens to the gallery and formal dining room. The living room, to the rear, enjoys a majestic fireplace accented by built-in book shelves. The spacious kitchen to the left adjoins the breakfast nook that boasts a curved window wall. The cozy and informal gathering room sits on the far left. The lavish master suite occupies the right side of the plan with a fireplace and private bath. Three additional bedrooms reside on the second floor; each has a private bath.

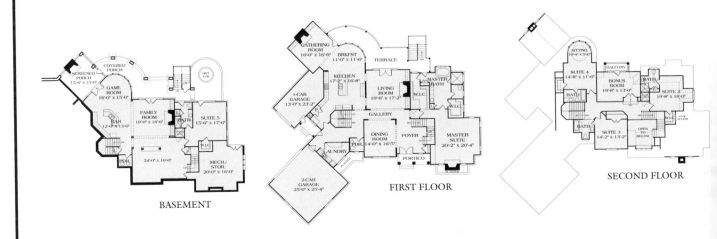

BASEMENT

FIRST FLOOR

SECOND FLOOR

plan # HPK0600447

L

STYLE: TRADITIONAL
FIRST FLOOR: 3,722 SQ. FT.
SECOND FLOOR: 1,859 SQ. FT.
TOTAL: 5,581 SQ. FT.
BEDROOMS: 5
BATHROOMS: 4½
WIDTH: 127' - 10"
DEPTH: 83' - 9"
FOUNDATION: SLAB

SEARCH ONLINE @ EPLANS.COM

A richly detailed entrance sets the elegant tone of this luxurious design. Rising gracefully from the two-story foyer, the staircase is a fine prelude to the great room beyond, where a fantastic span of windows on the back wall overlooks the rear grounds. The dining room is located off the entry and has a lovely coffered ceiling. The kitchen, breakfast room, and sunroom are conveniently grouped for casual entertaining. The elaborate master suite enjoys a coffered ceiling, private sitting room, and spa-style bath. The second level consists of four bedrooms with private baths and a large game room featuring a rear stair.

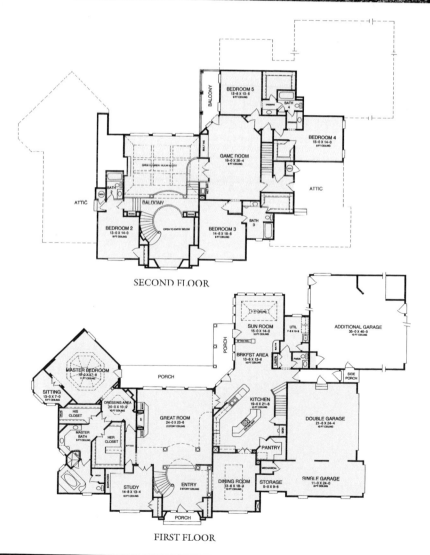

SECOND FLOOR

FIRST FLOOR

Double columns flank a raised loggia that leads to a beautiful two-story foyer. Flanking this elegance to the right is a formal dining room. Straight ahead, under a balcony and defined by yet more pillars, is the spacious grand room. A bow-windowed morning room and a gathering room feature a full view of the rear lanai and beyond. The master bedroom suite is lavish with its amenities, which include a bayed sitting area, direct access to the rear terrace, a walk-in closet, and a sumptuous bath.

plan # HPK0600448

STYLE: TRANSITIONAL
FIRST FLOOR: 2,547 SQ. FT.
SECOND FLOOR: 1,637 SQ. FT.
TOTAL: 4,184 SQ. FT.
BONUS SPACE: 802 SQ. FT.
BEDROOMS: 4
BATHROOMS: 3½
WIDTH: 74' - 0"
DEPTH: 95' - 6"
FOUNDATION: CRAWLSPACE

SEARCH ONLINE @ EPLANS.COM

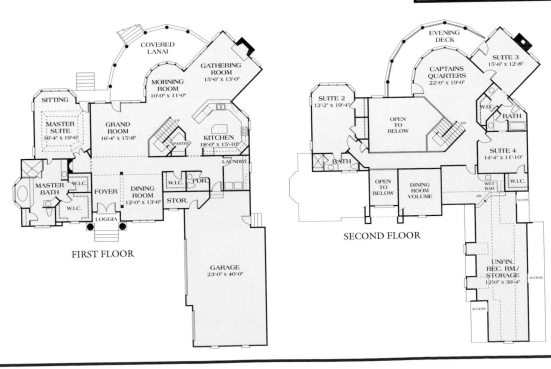

FIRST FLOOR

SECOND FLOOR

plan # HPK0600449

STYLE: EUROPEAN COTTAGE
MAIN LEVEL: 2,582 SQ. FT.
LOWER LEVEL: 1,746 SQ. FT.
TOTAL: 4,328 SQ. FT.
BEDROOMS: 3
BATHROOMS: 3½
WIDTH: 70' - 8"
DEPTH: 64' - 0"
FOUNDATION: BASEMENT

SEARCH ONLINE @ EPLANS.COM

Stone accents provide warmth and character to the exterior of this home. An arched entry leads to the interior, where elegant window styles and dramatic ceiling treatments create an impressive showplace. The gourmet kitchen and breakfast room offer a spacious area for chores and family gatherings, and provide a striking view through the great room to the fireplace. An extravagant master suite and a library with built-in shelves round out the main level. On the lower level, two additional bedrooms, a media room, a billiards room, and an exercise room complete the home.

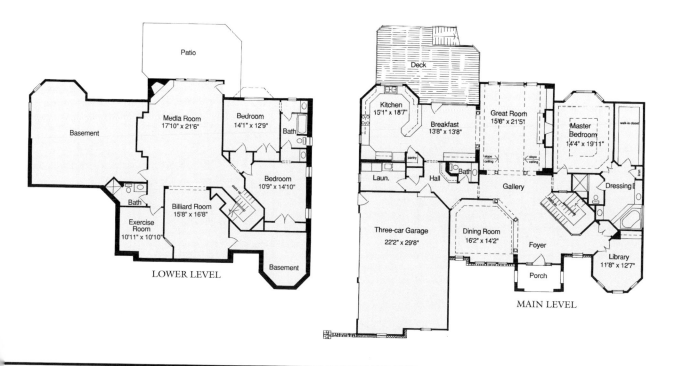

plan # HPK0600450

STYLE: TRADITIONAL
FIRST FLOOR: 2,095 SQ. FT.
SECOND FLOOR: 1,954 SQ. FT.
TOTAL: 4,049 SQ. FT.
BEDROOMS: 5
BATHROOMS: 4½
WIDTH: 56' - 0"
DEPTH: 63' - 0"
FOUNDATION:
CRAWLSPACE, BASEMENT

SEARCH ONLINE @ EPLANS.COM

The French Country facade of this lovely design hints at the enchanting amenities found within. A two-story foyer welcomes you inside. To the right, a bayed living room is separated from the formal dining room by graceful columns. A butler's pantry leads to the gourmet island kitchen. The breakfast room accesses a rear covered porch and shares a casual area with the two-story family room. Here, a fireplace flanked by built-ins adds to the relaxing atmosphere. Bedroom 5 with a private bath converts to an optional study. Upstairs, the master suite offers palatial elegance. Here, the sitting room is warmed by a fireplace flanked by built-ins, and the suite accesses a private second-floor porch. A dressing room leads to the vaulted master bath and enormous His and Hers walk-in closets. Three additional bedrooms are available on the second floor.

FIRST FLOOR

SECOND FLOOR

plan # **HPK0600451**

STYLE: TRANSITIONAL
MAIN LEVEL: 2,562 SQ. FT.
LOWER LEVEL: 1,955 SQ. FT.
TOTAL: 4,517 SQ. FT.
BEDROOMS: 3
BATHROOMS: 2½ + ½
WIDTH: 75' - 8"
DEPTH: 70' - 6"
FOUNDATION: BASEMENT

SEARCH ONLINE @ EPLANS.COM

A brick and stone exterior with a tower and recessed entry creates a strong, solid look to this enchanting home. The large foyer introduces the great room with beamed ceiling and tall windows for a rear view. The dining room is defined by columns and topped with a coffered ceiling. Complementing the kitchen is a convenient walk-in pantry and center island with seating. An extra-large hearth room with gas fireplace and access to the rear deck provides a comfortable family gathering place. The master bedroom with sloped ceiling and a spacious dressing area offers a relaxing retreat. Split stairs located for family convenience introduces the spectacular lower level with a wine room, exercise room, wet bar, and two additional bedrooms.

LOWER LEVEL

MAIN LEVEL

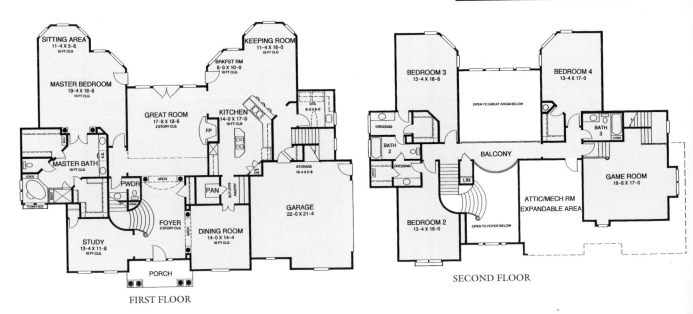

plan# HPK0600452

L

STYLE: NORMAN
FIRST FLOOR: 2,639 SQ. FT.
SECOND FLOOR: 1,625 SQ. FT.
TOTAL: 4,264 SQ. FT.
BEDROOMS: 4
BATHROOMS: 3½
WIDTH: 73' - 8"
DEPTH: 58' - 6"
FOUNDATION: SLAB,
CRAWLSPACE, BASEMENT

SEARCH ONLINE @ EPLANS.COM

This home offers both luxury and practicality. A study and dining room flank the foyer, and the great room offers a warming fireplace and double French-door access to the rear yard. A butler's pantry acts as a helpful buffer between the kitchen and the columned dining room. Double bays at the rear of the home form the keeping room and the breakfast room on one side and the master bedroom on the other. Three family bedrooms and two baths grace the second floor. A game room is perfect for casual family time.

FIRST FLOOR

SECOND FLOOR

ORDER BLUEPRINTS 24 HOURS, 7 DAYS A WEEK, AT 1-800-521-6797

plan # HPK0600453

STYLE: MEDITERRANEAN
FIRST FLOOR: 3,264 SQ. FT.
SECOND FLOOR: 1,671 SQ. FT.
TOTAL: 4,935 SQ. FT.
BEDROOMS: 4
BATHROOMS: 3½
WIDTH: 96' - 10"
DEPTH: 65' - 1"
FOUNDATION:
SLAB, CRAWLSPACE

SEARCH ONLINE @ EPLANS.COM

A very efficient plan that minimizes the use of enclosed hallways creates a very open feeling of space and orderliness. As you enter the foyer you have a clear view through the spacious living room to the covered patio beyond. The formal dining area is to the right and the master wing is to the left. The master bedroom boasts a sitting area, access to the patio, His and Hers walk-in closets, dual vanities, a walk-in shower, and a compartmented toilet. A large island kitchen overlooks the nook and family room, which has a built-in media/fireplace wall. Three additional bedrooms and two full baths complete the plan.

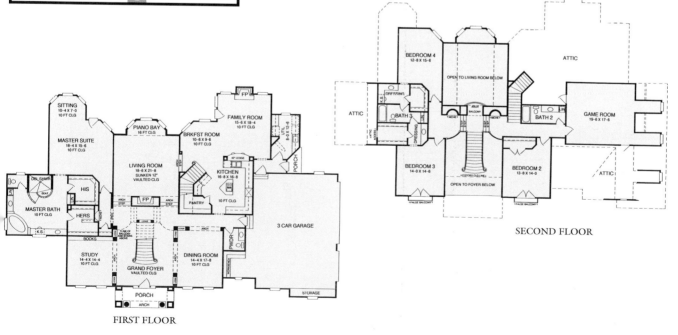

FIRST FLOOR

SECOND FLOOR

plan# HPK0600454

This rustic Craftsman home combines an earthy stone and siding facade with a luxurious floor plan for a wonderful home that will please everyone. The great room greets family and friends with a stone hearth and French doors to the rear deck. With an enormous walk-in pantry and a butler's pantry with a wine niche off the dining room, the vaulted kitchen is ready for entertaining. In the master bedroom, a vaulted ceiling and French doors add simple elegance; the bath pampers with a spa tub and block-glass encased shower. Downstairs—or take the elevator—the games room is the center of attention with a wine cellar, wet bar, fireplace, and media center. Three bedroom suites complete this level.

STYLE: EUROPEAN COTTAGE
MAIN LEVEL: 2,602 SQ. FT.
LOWER LEVEL: 2,440 SQ. FT.
TOTAL: 5,042 SQ. FT.
BEDROOMS: 4
BATHROOMS: 4½ + ½
WIDTH: 88' - 0"
DEPTH: 50' - 0"
FOUNDATION: BASEMENT

SEARCH ONLINE @ EPLANS.COM

LOWER LEVEL

MAIN LEVEL

plan # HPK0600455

STYLE: EUROPEAN COTTAGE
MAIN LEVEL: 2,792 SQ. FT.
LOWER LEVEL: 2,016 SQ. FT.
TOTAL: 4,808 SQ. FT.
BEDROOMS: 4
BATHROOMS: 4½
WIDTH: 81' - 0"
DEPTH: 66' - 0"
FOUNDATION: BASEMENT

SEARCH ONLINE @ EPLANS.COM

This grand manor boasts an open interior packed with fabulous amenities. The spacious foyer opens to the formal dining room, which leads to a well-organized gourmet kitchen through a butler's pantry. Mitered glass allows wide views in the dining room, and French doors open the great room to a wraparound deck. A corner fireplace warms the living space and shares its glow with the central interior. Double doors lead to a secluded den—a room so convenient to the foyer that it would easily convert to a home office. To the rear of the plan, a rambling master suite offers its own access to the rear deck.

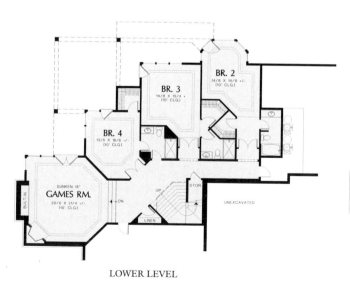

LOWER LEVEL

MAIN LEVEL

plan# HPK0600456

STYLE: FRENCH COUNTRY
FIRST FLOOR: 3,229 SQ. FT.
SECOND FLOOR: 2,219 SQ. FT.
TOTAL: 5,448 SQ. FT.
BONUS SPACE: 603 SQ. FT.
BEDROOMS: 5
BATHROOMS: 5½ + ½
WIDTH: 72' - 11"
DEPTH: 99' - 6"
FOUNDATION: CRAWLSPACE

SEARCH ONLINE @ EPLANS.COM

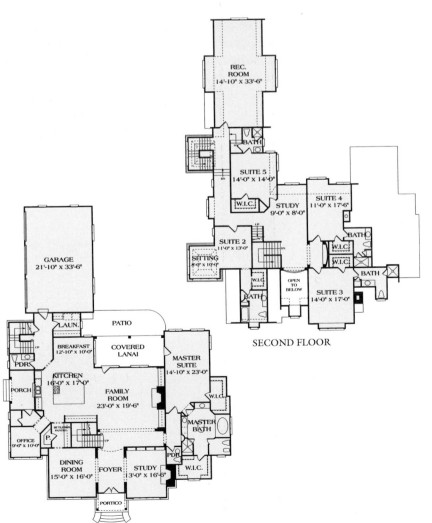

SECOND FLOOR

FIRST FLOOR

Stone and stucco topped by varying roof lines and adorning a plan to be envied—this home is magnificent. Through the elegant portico and into the foyer, let your eye wander to the study on the right or the formal dining room on the left. Ahead you'll find a spacious family room joining with an open island kitchen and breakfast nook. The family room provides acess to the covered lanai, which leads to a rear patio. The master suite and bath, two powder rooms, an office, and a laundry room complete this level—and there's another floor! Find four family bedrooms and private baths, a study, and space for a rec room upstairs.

plan # HPK0600457

STYLE: FRENCH COUNTRY
MAIN LEVEL: 2,981 SQ. FT.
UPPER LEVEL: 1,017 SQ. FT.
LOWER LEVEL: 1,471 SQ. FT.
TOTAL: 5,469 SQ. FT.
BEDROOMS: 4
BATHROOMS: 4½ + ½
WIDTH: 79' - 4"
DEPTH: 91' - 0"
FOUNDATION: BASEMENT

SEARCH ONLINE @ EPLANS.COM

Majestic through and through, this stately home enjoys a stone exterior inspired by classical French architecture. In the center of the main floor, the conservatory and elegant formal dining room reign. The massive country kitchen flows easily into the family room and the casual eating area. It also enjoys a butler's pantry leading to the dining room and a walk-in pantry. An exercise room and resplendent bath are found in the master suite, also on this level. Two more suites with private baths share a sitting room upstairs. The finished basement includes another bedroom suite, a recreation room, office, storage, and a book niche. Additional room is available for setting up a workshop.

LOWER LEVEL

MAIN LEVEL

UPPER LEVEL

plan# HPK0600458

STYLE: COUNTRY COTTAGE
FIRST FLOOR: 3,248 SQ. FT.
SECOND FLOOR: 1,426 SQ. FT.
TOTAL: 4,674 SQ. FT.
BEDROOMS: 5
BATHROOMS: 5½ + ½
WIDTH: 99' - 10"
DEPTH: 74' - 10"
FOUNDATION: BASEMENT

SEARCH ONLINE @ EPLANS.COM

Multiple rooflines; a stone, brick, and siding facade; and an absolutely grand entrance combine to give this home the look of luxury. A striking family room showcases a beautiful fireplace framed with built-ins. The nearby breakfast room streams with light and accesses the rear patio. The kitchen features an island workstation, walk-in pantry, and plenty of counter space. A guest suite is available on the first floor, perfect for when family members visit. The first-floor master suite enjoys easy access to a large study, bayed sitting room, and luxurious bath. Private baths are also included for each of the upstairs bedrooms.

FIRST FLOOR

SECOND FLOOR

plan # HPK0600459

STYLE: FRENCH COUNTRY
FIRST FLOOR: 2,734 SQ. FT.
SECOND FLOOR: 1,605 SQ. FT.
TOTAL: 4,339 SQ. FT.
BONUS/BASEMENT:
391/1,701 SQ. FT.
BEDROOMS: 4
BATHROOMS: 4½
WIDTH: 88' - 0"
DEPTH: 92' - 8"
FOUNDATION: BASEMENT

SEARCH ONLINE @ EPLANS.COM

Attractive stone, curved dormers, and varied rooflines give this fine European manor a graceful dose of class. Inside, the foyer introduces a formal dining room defined by columns and a spacious gathering room with a fireplace. The nearby kitchen features a walk-in pantry, beam ceiling, adjacent breakfast nook, and a screened porch. The first-floor master suite features two walk-in closets, a lavish bath, a corner fireplace, and a sitting room with access to the rear veranda. Upstairs, three suites offer walk-in closets and surround a study loft. On the lower level, a huge recreation room awaits to entertain with a bar, a fireplace, and outdoor access. A secluded office provides a private entrance—perfect for a home business.

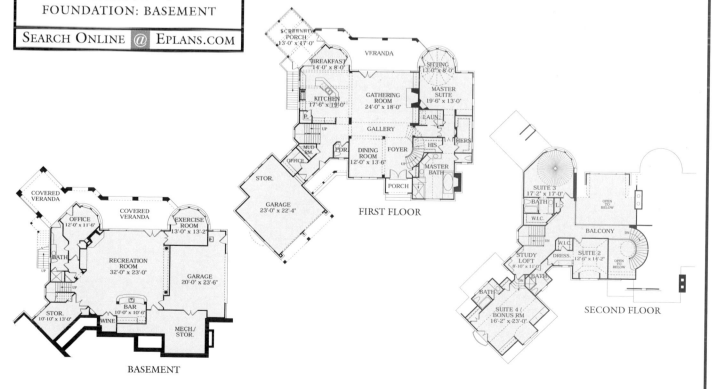

FIRST FLOOR

SECOND FLOOR

BASEMENT

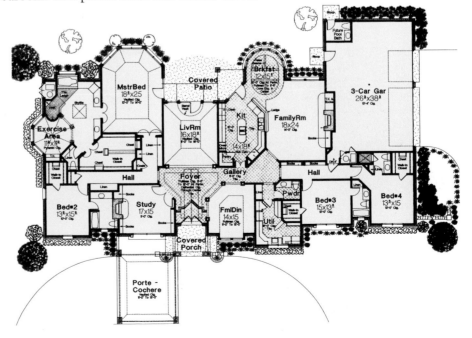

The hipped-roof, French Country exterior, and porte-cochere entrance are just the beginning of this unique and impressive design. An unusual Pullman ceiling graces the foyer as it leads to the formal dining room on the right, to the study with a fireplace on the left, and straight ahead to the formal living room with its covered patio access. A gallery directs you to the island kitchen with its abundant counter space and adjacent sun-filled breakfast bay. On the left side of the home, a spectacular master suite will become your favorite haven and the envy of your guests. The master bedroom includes a coffered ceiling, a bayed sitting area, and patio access. The master bath features a large, doorless shower, a separate exercise room, and a huge walk-in closet with built-in chests. All of the family bedrooms offer private baths and walk-in closets.

plan # HPK0600460

STYLE: COUNTRY COTTAGE
SQUARE FOOTAGE: 4,615
BEDROOMS: 4
BATHROOMS: 4½
WIDTH: 109' - 10"
DEPTH: 89' - 4"
FOUNDATION: SLAB

SEARCH ONLINE @ EPLANS.COM

ORDER BLUEPRINTS 24 HOURS, 7 DAYS A WEEK, AT 1-800-521-6797

plan# HPK0600461

STYLE: FRENCH COUNTRY
FIRST FLOOR: 5,394 SQ. FT.
SECOND FLOOR: 1,305 SQ. FT.
TOTAL: 6,699 SQ. FT.
BONUS SPACE: 414 SQ. FT.
BEDROOMS: 5
BATHROOMS: 3½ + ½
WIDTH: 124' - 10"
DEPTH: 83' - 2"
FOUNDATION: CRAWLSPACE

SEARCH ONLINE @ EPLANS.COM

This elegant French Country estate features a plush world of luxury within. A beautiful curved staircase cascades into the welcoming foyer, which is flanked by a formal living room and the dining room with a fireplace. A butler's pantry leads to the island kitchen, which is efficiently enhanced by a walk-in storage pantry. The kitchen easily serves the breakfast room. The covered rear porch is accessed from the media/family room and the great room warmed by a fireplace. The master suite is a sumptuous retreat highlighted by its lavish bath and two huge walk-in closets. Next door, double doors open to a large study. All family bedrooms feature walk-in closets. Bedrooms 2 and 3 share a bath. Upstairs, Bedrooms 4 and 5 share another hall bath. A home office is located above the three-car garage.

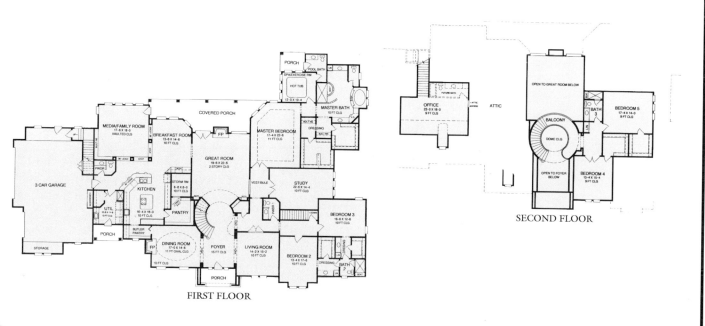

FIRST FLOOR

SECOND FLOOR

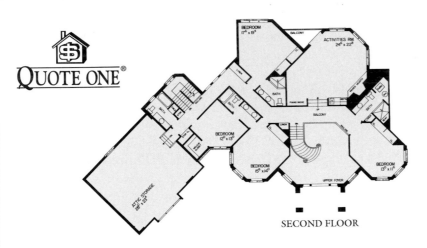

Quote One®

SECOND FLOOR

FIRST FLOOR

plan # HPK0600462

L

STYLE: NORMAN
FIRST FLOOR: 3,736 SQ. FT.
SECOND FLOOR: 2,264 SQ. FT.
TOTAL: 6,000 SQ. FT.
BEDROOMS: 5
BATHROOMS: 5½ + ½
WIDTH: 133' - 4"
DEPTH: 65' - 5"
FOUNDATION: SLAB

SEARCH ONLINE @ EPLANS.COM

The distinctive covered entry to this stunning manor, flanked by twin turrets, leads to a gracious foyer. The foyer opens to a formal dining room, a study, and a step-down gathering room. The spacious kitchen includes numerous amenities, including an island work station and a built-in desk. The adjacent morning room and the gathering room, with a wet bar and a raised-hearth fireplace, are bathed in light and open to the terrace. The secluded master suite offers two walk-in closets, a dressing area, and an exercise area with a spa. The second floor features four bedrooms and an oversized activities room with a fireplace and a balcony. Unfinished attic space can be completed to your specifications.

plan # **HPK0600463**

STYLE: TRADITIONAL
FIRST FLOOR: 3,098 SQ. FT.
SECOND FLOOR: 1,113 SQ. FT.
TOTAL: 4,211 SQ. FT.
BONUS SPACE: 567 SQ. FT.
BEDROOMS: 4
BATHROOMS: 3½
WIDTH: 112' - 0"
DEPTH: 69' - 9"
FOUNDATION. CRAWLSPACE

SEARCH ONLINE @ EPLANS.COM

The magnificent entry of this elegant traditional home makes a grand impression. The soaring ceiling of the foyer looks over a curved staircase that leads to secondary sleeping quarters. The first-floor master suite offers an expansive retreat for the homeowner, with mitered windows and a see-through fireplace shared with the spacious spa-style bath. Formal rooms open from the foyer, and a gallery hall leads to the casual living area, with a two-story family room and French doors to the outside. The three-car garage offers wardrobe space for cloaks.

SECOND FLOOR

FIRST FLOOR

plan# HPK0600464

STYLE: EUROPEAN COTTAGE
FIRST FLOOR: 4,864 SQ. FT.
SECOND FLOOR: 1,215 SQ. FT.
TOTAL: 6,079 SQ. FT.
BONUS SPACE: 854 SQ. FT.
BEDROOMS: 5
BATHROOMS: 5½
WIDTH: 133' - 0"
DEPTH: 63' - 0"
FOUNDATION: BASEMENT

SEARCH ONLINE @ EPLANS.COM

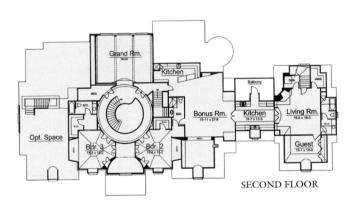

SECOND FLOOR

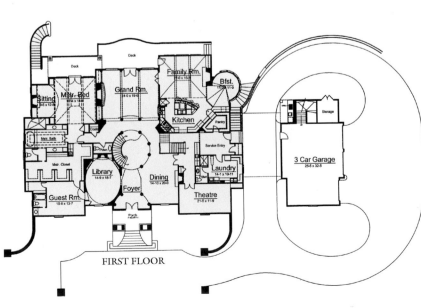

FIRST FLOOR

Introducing the finest in European country estate designs; incredible exterior wood details, stone accents, and smooth stucco create an enchanting facade. Notable features such as the circular staircase, oval library, sequestered home theater, gourmet island kitchen with oversized walk-in pantry, and extensive amentities— including abundant closets—in the master suite create a haven of comfort and refinement. The second level houses two family bedrooms with private baths and walk-in closets, large bonus room with kitchen, and additional fully-outfitted private living space for a live-in nanny.

plan# HPK0600465

STYLE: EUROPEAN COTTAGE
FIRST FLOOR: 2,207 SQ. FT.
SECOND FLOOR: 1,993 SQ. FT.
TOTAL: 4,200 SQ. FT.
BEDROOMS: 4
BATHROOMS: 3½
WIDTH: 74' - 6"
DEPTH: 46' - 0"
FOUNDATION: BASEMENT

SEARCH ONLINE @ EPLANS.COM

Spindle railings and multipane archtop windows distinguish this brick home from others on the block. At the top of the circular front steps, the double doors open to a vestibule with a coat closet. Go through another set of double doors to the main hall, which accesses all the first-floor rooms and a stately staircase to the second floor. The first floor offers a living room with a corner fireplace, an office, a family room that provides a second fireplace, a kitchen with a breakfast area, a powder room, a laundry room, and a formal dining room. The second floor includes a master suite with a private bath, two family bedrooms that share a bath, and a fourth bedroom with a private bath.

SECOND FLOOR

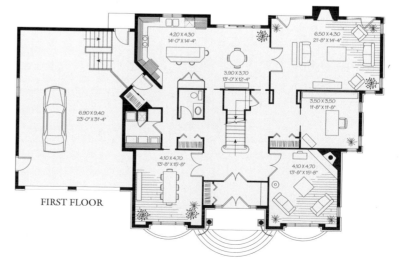

FIRST FLOOR

plan # HPK0600466

STYLE: NORMAN
FIRST FLOOR: 2,267 SQ. FT.
SECOND FLOOR: 2,209 SQ. FT.
TOTAL: 4,476 SQ. FT.
BEDROOMS: 4
BATHROOMS: 3½
WIDTH: 67' - 2"
DEPTH: 64' - 10"
FOUNDATION: CRAWLSPACE

SEARCH ONLINE @ EPLANS.COM

Keystone arches, a wonderful turret, vertical shutters, and decorative stickwork over the entry add to the charm of this fine home. A formal dining room at the front of the plan is complemented by the breakfast bay at the rear. An angled snack bar/counter separates the island kitchen from the gathering room. An adjoining recreation room offers a wet bar and a second flight of stairs to the sleeping quarters. Bay windows brighten the master suite and Suite 2, both with private baths. Two more bedrooms share a full bath that includes a dressing area and twin vanities. The laundry room is on this level for convenience.

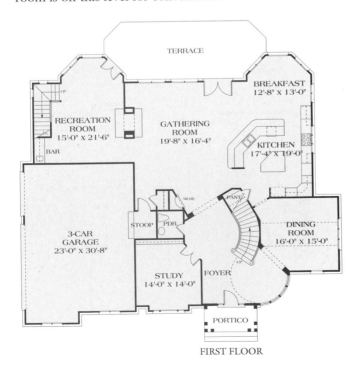

FIRST FLOOR

SECOND FLOOR

plan # HPK0600467

STYLE: EUROPEAN COTTAGE
MAIN LEVEL: 2,961 SQ. FT.
LOWER LEVEL: 2,416 SQ. FT.
TOTAL: 5,377 SQ. FT.
BEDROOMS: 3
BATHROOMS: 2½ + ½
WIDTH: 89' - 0"
DEPTH: 59' - 2"
FOUNDATION: BASEMENT

SEARCH ONLINE @ EPLANS.COM

Stone accents and a charming turret enhance the exterior of this spacious plan. A beamed ceiling highlights the great room, which shares a two-sided fireplace with the foyer; another fireplace can be found in the hearth room, which overlooks a covered rear porch and deck area. A resplendent master suite, with easy access to the laundry area, sits to the right of the plan and boasts a private sitting bay, a dual-vanity dressing area, and a large walk-in closet. The lower level includes media, billiards, and exercise rooms, two bedrooms, and a gathering area that opens to a patio.

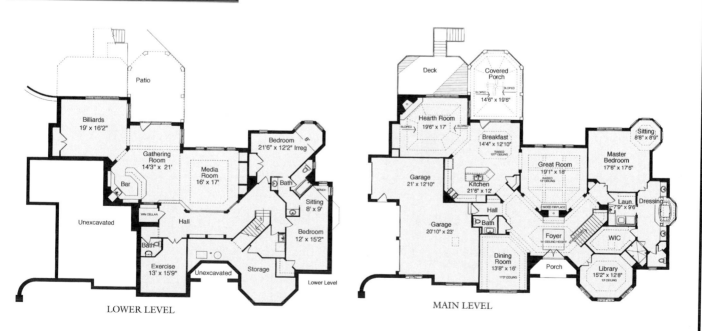

LOWER LEVEL

MAIN LEVEL

plan # HPK0600468

The ornamental stucco detailing on this home creates an Old World charm. The two-story foyer with a sweeping curved stair opens to the large formal dining room and study. The two-story great room overlooks the rear patio. A large kitchen with an island workstation opens to an octagonal-shaped breakfast room and the family room. The master suite, offering convenient access to the study, is complete with a fireplace, two walk-in closets, and a bath with twin vanities and a separate shower and tub. A staircase located off the family room provides additional access to the three second-floor bedrooms that each offer walk-in closets and plenty of storage.

STYLE: MEDITERRANEAN
FIRST FLOOR: 3,568 SQ. FT.
SECOND FLOOR: 1,667 SQ. FT.
TOTAL: 5,235 SQ. FT.
BEDROOMS: 4
BATHROOMS: 3½
WIDTH: 86' - 8"
DEPTH: 79' - 0"
FOUNDATION:
WALKOUT BASEMENT

SEARCH ONLINE @ EPLANS.COM

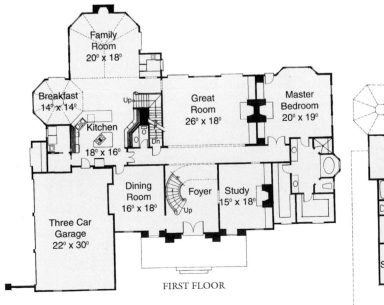

FIRST FLOOR

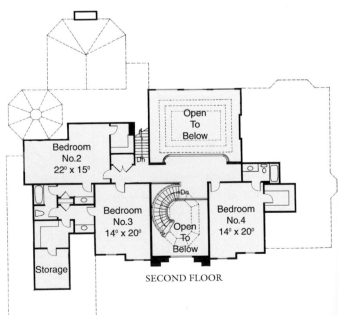

SECOND FLOOR

plan# HPK0600469

STYLE: FRENCH
FIRST FLOOR: 3,874 SQ. FT.
SECOND FLOOR: 2,588 SQ. FT.
TOTAL: 6,462 SQ. FT.
BEDROOMS: 4
BATHROOMS: 5½ + ½
WIDTH: 146' - 8"
DEPTH: 84' - 4"
FOUNDATION: SLAB

SEARCH ONLINE @ EPLANS.COM

An oversized front entry beckons your attention to the wonderful amenities inside this home: a raised marble vestibule with a circular stair; a formal library and dining hall with views to the veranda and pool beyond; and a family gathering hall, open to the kitchen and connected to the outdoor grill. The master suite is embellished with a nature garden, His and Hers wardrobes, a fireplace, and an elegant bath. The second floor offers more living space: a media presentation room and game room. Each of the family bedrooms features a private bath—one suite is reached via a bridge over the porte cochere.

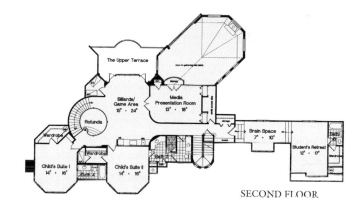

SECOND FLOOR

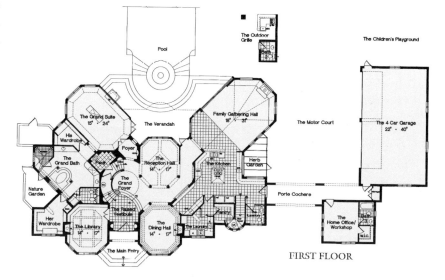

FIRST FLOOR

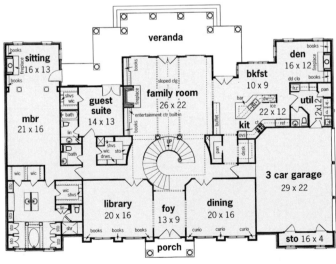

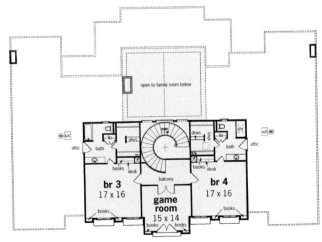

plan# HPK0600470

Two-story pilasters create a sense of the Old South on the facade of this modern home, updating the classic Adam style. The foyer opens through an archway, announcing the breathtaking circular staircase. The formal dining room is situated on the right, and the private library is found to the left. The grand family room is crowned with a sloped ceiling. The angled, galley kitchen adjoins the breakfast nook; the butler's pantry facilitates service to the dining room. The master suite finds privacy on the left with an elegant sitting area defined with pillars. Two bedroom suites, each with walk-in closets, share the second floor with the game room.

STYLE: TRADITIONAL
FIRST FLOOR: 4,208 SQ. FT.
SECOND FLOOR: 1,352 SQ. FT.
TOTAL: 5,560 SQ. FT.
BEDROOMS: 4
BATHROOMS: 4½ + ½
WIDTH: 94' - 0"
DEPTH: 68' - 0"
FOUNDATION:
CRAWLSPACE, SLAB

SEARCH ONLINE @ EPLANS.COM

FIRST FLOOR

SECOND FLOOR

plan # HPK0600471

STYLE: EUROPEAN COTTAGE
FIRST FLOOR: 2,971 SQ. FT.
SECOND FLOOR: 2,199 SQ. FT.
THIRD FLOOR: 1,040 SQ. FT.
TOTAL: 6,210 SQ. FT.
BASEMENT: 1,707 SQ. FT.
BEDROOMS: 5
BATHROOMS: 4½
WIDTH: 84' - 4"
DEPTH: 64' - 11"
FOUNDATION: BASEMENT

SEARCH ONLINE @ EPLANS.COM

Symmetry and stucco present true elegance on the facade of this five-bedroom home, and the elegance continues inside over four separate levels. Note the formal and informal gathering areas on the main level: the music room, the lake living room, the formal dining room, and the uniquely shaped breakfast room. The second level contains three large bedroom suites—one with its own bath—a spacious girl's room for play time, and an entrance room to the third-floor master suite. Lavish is the only way to describe this suite. Complete with His and Hers walk-in closets, a private balcony, an off-season closet, and a sumptuous bath, this suite is designed to pamper the homeowner. In the basement is yet more room for casual get-togethers. Note the large sitting room as well as the hobby/crafts room. And tying it all together, an elevator offers stops at each floor.

SECOND FLOOR

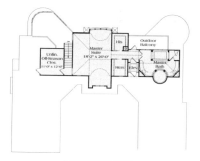

THIRD FLOOR

FIRST FLOOR

BASEMENT

plan # HPK0600472

This majestic storybook cottage, from the magical setting of rural Europe, provides the perfect home for any large family—with a wealth of modern comforts within. A graceful staircase cascades from the two-story foyer. To the left, a sophisticated study offers a wall of built-ins. To the right, a formal dining room is easily served from the island kitchen. The breakfast room accesses the rear screened porch. Fireplaces warm the great room and keeping room. Two sets of double doors open from the great room to the rear covered porch. The master bedroom features private porch access, a sitting area, lavish bath, and two walk-in closets. Upstairs, three additional family bedrooms offer walk-in closet space galore! The game room is great entertainment for both family and friends. A three-car garage with golf-cart storage completes the plan.

STYLE: EUROPEAN COTTAGE
FIRST FLOOR: 3,033 SQ. FT.
SECOND FLOOR: 1,545 SQ. FT.
TOTAL: 4,578 SQ. FT.
BEDROOMS: 4
BATHROOMS: 3½ + ½
WIDTH: 91' - 6"
DEPTH: 63' - 8"
FOUNDATION: CRAWLSPACE, SLAB, BASEMENT

SEARCH ONLINE @ EPLANS.COM

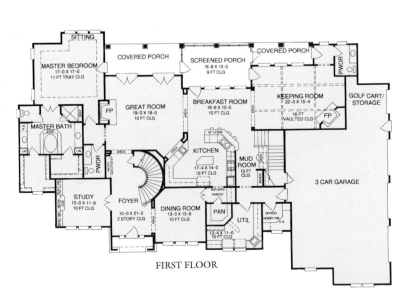

FIRST FLOOR

SECOND FLOOR

plan # HPK0600473

STYLE: FRENCH
FIRST FLOOR: 3,058 SQ. FT.
SECOND FLOOR: 2,076 SQ. FT.
TOTAL: 5,134 SQ. FT.
BEDROOMS: 4
BATHROOMS: 4½
WIDTH: 79' - 6"
DEPTH: 73' - 10"
FOUNDATION: SLAB,
BASEMENT, CRAWLSPACE

SEARCH ONLINE @ EPLANS.COM

This sweeping European facade, featuring a majestic turret-style bay, will easily be a stand-out in the neighborhood and a family favorite. The foyer opens to a spacious formal receiving area. Double doors from the living room open to the rear porch for outdoor activities. The master wing features a sitting area, a luxurious master bath, and two walk-in closets. The spacious island kitchen works with the bayed breakfast room for more intimate meals. The family room offers a warm and relaxing fireplace. A private raised study, three-car garage, and utility room complete the first floor. Upstairs, three additional family bedrooms share the second floor with a music loft, hobby room, and game room.

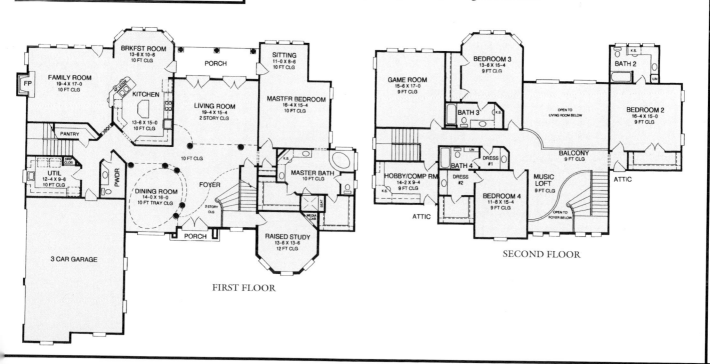

FIRST FLOOR

SECOND FLOOR

© HOME DESIGN SERVICES, INC.
J.N. HANSEN P.T.L.

plan # HPK0600474

Finished with French Country adornments, this estate home is comfortable in just about any setting. Main living areas are sunk down just a bit from the entry foyer, providing them with soaring ceilings and sweeping views. The family room features a focal fireplace. A columned entry gains access to the master suite where separate sitting and sleeping areas are defined by a three-sided fireplace. There are three bedrooms upstairs; one has a private bath. The sunken media room on this level includes storage space. Note the second half bath under the staircase landing.

STYLE: FRENCH
FIRST FLOOR: 2,899 SQ. FT.
SECOND FLOOR: 1,472 SQ. FT.
TOTAL: 4,371 SQ. FT.
BEDROOMS: 4
BATHROOMS: 3½ + ½
WIDTH: 69' - 4"
DEPTH: 76' - 8"
FOUNDATION: SLAB

SEARCH ONLINE @ EPLANS.COM

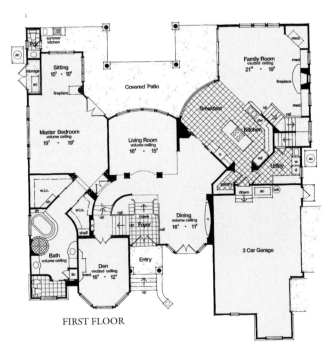

FIRST FLOOR

SECOND FLOOR

OPTIONAL LAYOUT

plan # HPK0600475

STYLE: FRENCH
FIRST FLOOR: 2,559 SQ. FT.
SECOND FLOOR: 2,140 SQ. FT.
TOTAL: 4,699 SQ. FT.
BEDROOMS: 5
BATHROOMS: 4
WIDTH: 80' - 0"
DEPTH: 67' - 0"
FOUNDATION: BASEMENT

SEARCH ONLINE @ EPLANS.COM

Accommodate your life's diverse pattern of formal occasions and casual times with this spacious home. The exterior of this estate presents a palatial bearing, while the interior is both comfortable and elegant. Formal areas are graced with amenities to make entertaining easy. Casual areas are kept intimate, but no less large. The solarium serves both with skylights and terrace access. Guests will appreciate a private guest room and a bath with loggia access on the first floor. Family bedrooms and the master suite are upstairs. Note the gracious ceiling treatments in the master bedroom, its sitting room, and Bedroom 2.

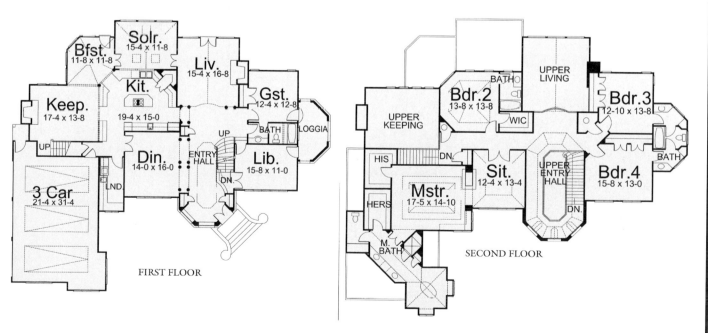

FIRST FLOOR

SECOND FLOOR

plan# HPK0600002

STYLE: FRENCH COUNTRY
FIRST FLOOR: 3,337 SQ. FT.
SECOND FLOOR: 1,292 SQ. FT.
TOTAL: 4,629 SQ. FT.
BEDROOMS: 4
BATHROOMS: 4½
WIDTH: 84' - 10"
DEPTH: 102' - 3"

SEARCH ONLINE @ EPLANS.COM

Dreaming of a home with estate-like elegance and cottage allure? Explore this flexible small-scale chateau. Allow your guests the delight of wandering through the garden courtyard, just off the dining room, before dinner. Retire to the handsome den, with soaring 14-foot ceilings, for a nightcap and conversation. Prepare holiday pastries in the chef's kitchen with friends to keep you company in the comfortable breakfast room. Feel closer without sacrificing space in the open family room fully outfitted with built-ins and a stunning extended-hearth fireplace.

FIRST FLOOR

SECOND FLOOR

plan # HPK0600476

STYLE: EUROPEAN COTTAGE
FIRST FLOOR: 3,118 SQ. FT.
SECOND FLOOR: 1,663 SQ. FT.
TOTAL: 4,781 SQ. FT.
BEDROOMS: 4
BATHROOMS: 3½ + ½
WIDTH: 78' - 0"
DEPTH: 80' - 0"
FOUNDATION: SLAB

SEARCH ONLINE @ EPLANS.COM

Designed for the family who loves individual style and luxurious living, this distinctive estate provides a comfortable home that will elicit "oohs" and "aahs" from everyone who sees it. Enter to a grand foyer within a two-story turret; a gallery hall expands to every room. Columns define the living room and dining area, elegantly arranged for ease of entertaining. The kitchen is a chef's dream come true, and opens to the bright breakfast room and bayed family room. Located in the right wing, the master suite exceeds expectations, with a bayed sitting area, vast bedroom, porch access, and a private bath that will soothe away all of your daily stresses. The upper level allows privacy for all three bedrooms and hosts a game room and expandable area

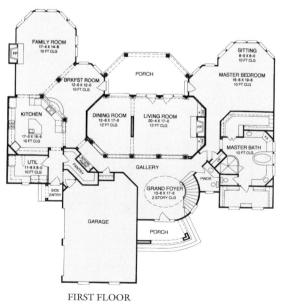

FIRST FLOOR

SECOND FLOOR

plan# HPK0600477

STYLE: FRENCH
FIRST FLOOR: 3,517 SQ. FT.
SECOND FLOOR: 1,254 SQ. FT.
TOTAL: 4,771 SQ. FT.
BEDROOMS: 5
BATHROOMS: 4½ + ½
WIDTH: 95' - 8"
DEPTH: 107' - 0"
FOUNDATION: SLAB

SEARCH ONLINE @ EPLANS.COM

The design of this French Country estate captures its ambiance with its verandas, grand entry, and unique balconies. A spectacular panorama of the formal living areas and the elegant curved stairway awaits just off the foyer. A large island kitchen, breakfast nook, and family room will impress, as will the wine cellar. Plenty of kitchen pantry space leads to the laundry and motor court featuring a two-car garage attached to the main house and a three-car garage attached by a breezeway. The master suite boasts a sunken sitting area with a see-through fireplace, His and Hers walk-in closets, island tub, and large separate shower. A study area, three additional bedrooms, a full bath, and a bonus area reside on the second floor.

FIRST FLOOR

SECOND FLOOR

plan # HPK0600478

STYLE: FRENCH
FIRST FLOOR: 2,608 SQ. FT.
SECOND FLOOR: 1,432 SQ. FT.
TOTAL: 4,040 SQ. FT.
BEDROOMS: 4
BATHROOMS: 3½
WIDTH: 89' - 10"
DEPTH: 63' - 8"
FOUNDATION:
CRAWLSPACE, SLAB

SEARCH ONLINE @ EPLANS.COM

A distinctively French flair is the hallmark of this European design. Inside, the two-story foyer provides views to the huge great room beyond. A well-placed study off the foyer provides space for a home office. The kitchen, breakfast room, and sunroom are adjacent to lend a spacious feel. The great room is visible from this area through decorative arches. The master suite includes a roomy sitting area and a lovely bath with a centerpiece whirlpool tub flanked by half-columns. Upstairs, Bedrooms 2 and 3 share a bath that includes separate dressing areas.

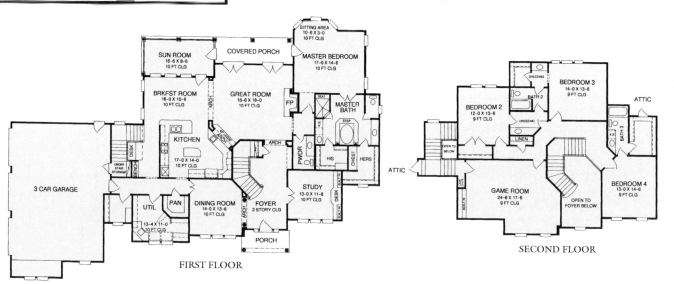

FIRST FLOOR

SECOND FLOOR

© 1991 The Sater Group, Inc.

This home features a spectacular blend of arch-top windows, French doors, and balusters. An impressive informal leisure room has a 16-foot tray ceiling, an entertainment center, and a grand ale bar. The large gourmet kitchen is well appointed and easily serves the nook and formal dining room. The master suite has a large bedroom and a bayed sitting area. His and Hers vanities and walk-in closets and a curved glass-block shower are highlights in the bath. The staircase leads to the deluxe secondary guest suites, two of which have observation decks to the rear and their own full baths.

plan # HPK0600479

L

STYLE: MEDITERRANEAN
FIRST FLOOR: 4,760 SQ. FT.
SECOND FLOOR: 1,552 SQ. FT.
TOTAL: 6,312 SQ. FT.
BEDROOMS: 5
BATHROOMS: 6½
WIDTH: 98' - 0"
DEPTH: 103' - 8"
FOUNDATION: SLAB

SEARCH ONLINE @ EPLANS.COM

QUOTE ONE®

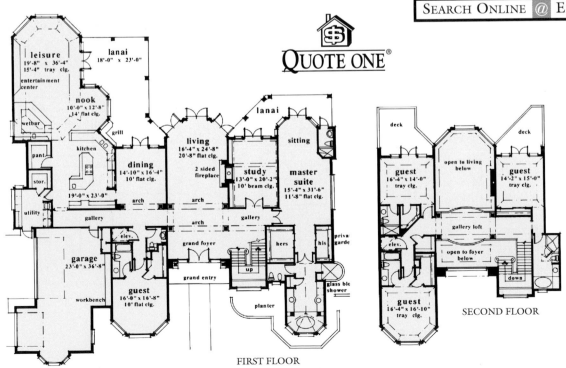

FIRST FLOOR

SECOND FLOOR

plan # HPK0600480

STYLE: ITALIANATE
FIRST FLOOR: 3,734 SQ. FT.
SECOND FLOOR: 418 SQ. FT.
TOTAL: 4,152 SQ. FT.
BEDROOMS: 3
BATHROOMS: 4½
WIDTH: 82' - 0"
DEPTH: 107' - 0"
FOUNDATION: SLAB

SEARCH ONLINE @ EPLANS.COM

Softly angled turrets add sweet drama to this dreamy
Mediterranean manor, as a rambling interior plays function to everyday life. Beautiful interior columns in the foyer offer a fine introduction to open, spacious rooms. A secluded master suite features a beautiful bay window, a coffered ceiling, and French doors to the lanai. Across the master foyer, the private bath satisfies the homeowners' needs by offering a whirlpool tub, separate shower, private vanities, and two walk-in closets. Bedroom 2 includes a sitting bay, a walk-in closet, and a private bath. Upstairs, a spacious loft offers room for computers and books. A wet bar, walk-in closet, and full bath with a shower provide the possibility of converting this area to a bedroom suite.

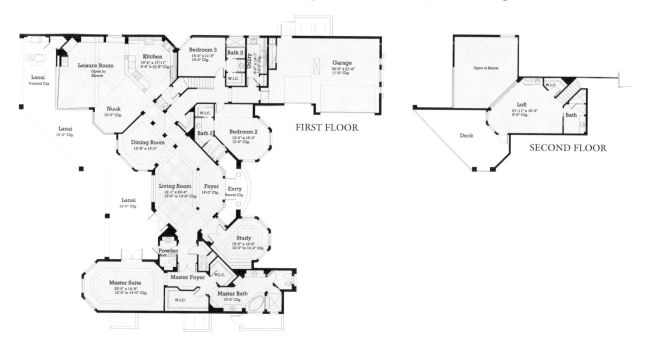

FIRST FLOOR

SECOND FLOOR

Grand arches lend Mediterranean flavor to this contemporary estate. An open interior of decorative columns and stone arches defines the formal living and dining rooms. Leisure space invites relaxation in front of a built-in entertainment center, while the outdoor kitchen encourages dining alfresco. A master suite stretches across the left wing, which includes a quiet study. Among the four additional bedroom suites, one boasts a morning kitchen; two have access to a private deck or veranda.

plan# HPK0630004

STYLE: MEDITERRANEAN
FIRST FLOOR: 4,385 SQ. FT.
SECOND FLOOR: 1,431 SQ. FT.
TOTAL: 5,816 SQ. FT.
BEDROOMS: 5
BATHROOMS: 6
WIDTH: 88' - 0"
DEPTH: 110' - 1"
FOUNDATION: SLAB

SEARCH ONLINE @ EPLANS.COM

FIRST FLOOR

SECOND FLOOR

© The Sater Design Collection, Inc.

plan # HPK0600482

STYLE: ITALIANTE
FIRST FLOOR: 2,850 SQ. FT.
SECOND FLOOR: 1,155 SQ. FT.
TOTAL: 4,005 SQ. FT.
BONUS SPACE: 371 SQ. FT.
BEDROOMS: 4
BATHROOMS: 4½
WIDTH: 71' - 6"
DEPTH: 83' - 0"
FOUNDATION: SLAB

SEARCH ONLINE @ EPLANS.COM

Stone, stucco, and soaring rooflines combine to give this elegant Mediterranean design a stunning exterior. The interior is packed with luxurious amenities, from the wall of glass in the living room to the whirlpool tub in the master bath. A dining room and study serve as formal areas, while a leisure room with a fireplace offers a relaxing retreat. The first-floor master suite boasts a private bayed sitting area. Upstairs, all three bedrooms include private baths; Bedroom 2 and the guest suite also provide walk-in closets.

FIRST FLOOR

SECOND FLOOR

A hint of Moroccan architecture, with columns, arches, and walls of glass, makes an arresting appearance in this home. It allows a diverse arrangement of space inside, for a dynamic floor plan. The foyer spills openly into the immense living area and sunken dining room. A stair encircles the sunken library/great space for a home theater. Beyond is the family room with a two-story high media wall and built-ins, plus the circular breakfast room and island kitchen. A maid's room, or guest room, has a full circular wall of glass and leads to the garage through a covered entry and drive-through area. The master suite is true luxury: circular sitting area, His and Hers facilities, and a private garden. Upstairs is a game room, plus two family bedrooms with private, amenity-filled baths.

plan # HPK0600483

STYLE: MEDITERRANEAN
FIRST FLOOR: 4,284 SQ. FT.
SECOND FLOOR: 1,319 SQ. FT.
TOTAL: 5,603 SQ. FT.
BEDROOMS: 4
BATHROOMS: 4½ + ½
WIDTH: 109' - 4"
DEPTH: 73' - 2"
FOUNDATION: SLAB

SEARCH ONLINE @ EPLANS.COM

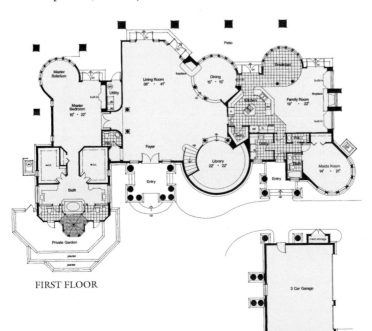

FIRST FLOOR

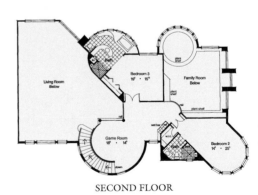

SECOND FLOOR

plan # HPK0600484

STYLE: FRENCH
FIRST FLOOR: 2,901 SQ. FT.
SECOND FLOOR: 1,140 SQ. FT.
TOTAL: 4,041 SQ. FT.
BONUS SPACE: 522 SQ. FT.
BEDROOMS: 4
BATHROOMS: 4½
WIDTH: 80' - 0"
DEPTH: 70' - 0"
FOUNDATION: BASEMENT

SEARCH ONLINE @ EPLANS.COM

This stately French Country home is as magnificent inside as its exterior would suggest. Columns throughout the home are well placed to draw out the spacious grandeur of this plan. The heavenly master suite is a fairy tale come true. His and Hers walk-in closets, a sitting room with a fireplace, and French-door access to the rear veranda guarantee comfort; the extraordinary bath, complete with a huge tub set in a bay overlooking gardens, is sure to pamper. A circular breakfast bay enjoys views of the veranda and the loggia. Upstairs, three bedrooms come with separate lavish baths. Additional space is available to add a guest apartment. A sunken floor separates the downstairs front library from other rooms.

FIRST FLOOR

SECOND FLOOR

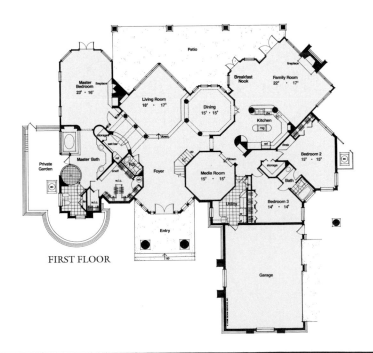

plan # HPK0600485

STYLE: CONTEMPORARY
FIRST FLOOR: 3,770 SQ. FT.
SECOND FLOOR: 634 SQ. FT.
TOTAL: 4,404 SQ. FT.
BEDROOMS: 4
BATHROOMS: 3½
WIDTH: 87' - 0"
DEPTH: 97' - 6"
FOUNDATION: SLAB

SEARCH ONLINE @ EPLANS.COM

This fresh and innovative design creates unbeatable ambiance. The breakfast nook and family room both open to a patio—a perfect arrangement for informal entertaining. The dining room is sure to please with elegant pillars separating it from the sunken living room. A media room delights both with its shape and by being convenient to the nearby kitchen—great for snack runs. A private garden surrounds the master bath and its spa tub and enormous walk-in closet. The master bedroom is enchanting with a fireplace and access to the outdoors. Additional family bedrooms come in a variety of different shapes and sizes; Bedroom 4 reigns over the second floor and features its own full bath.

FIRST FLOOR

SECOND FLOOR

plan# HPK0600486

STYLE: MEDITERRANEAN
SQUARE FOOTAGE: 4,222
BONUS SPACE: 590 SQ. FT.
BEDROOMS: 4
BATHROOMS: 5
WIDTH: 83' - 10"
DEPTH: 112' - 0"
FOUNDATION: SLAB

SEARCH ONLINE @ EPLANS.COM

The striking facade of this magnificent estate is just the beginning of the excitement you will encounter inside. The foyer passes the formal dining room on the way to the columned gallery. The formal living room opens to the rear patio and has easy access to a wet bar. The contemporary kitchen has a work island and all the amenities for gourmet preparation. The family room will be a favorite for casual entertainment. The family sleeping wing begins with an octagonal vestibule and has three bedrooms with private baths. The master wing features a private garden and an opulent bath.

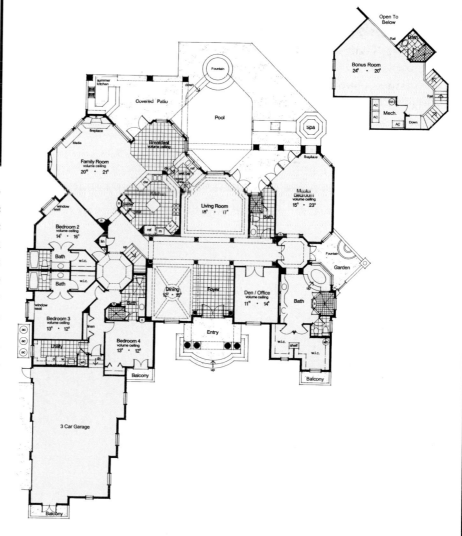

© The Sater Design Collection, Inc.

This stunning Italian Renaissance estate will be the show-piece of your neighborhood. Beautiful brickwork sets off Palladian-style windows and a two-story turret for a romantic treasure you will be glad to call home. Enter past the columned dining room to the great room, with a bowed wall of windows that offers spectacular views, and a two-way fireplace shared with the study. The island kitchen allows plenty of room for two cooks, making meal preparations a joy. The leisure room features a fireplace, built-in entertainment center, and French doors to the veranda. The master suite is an archetype for luxury with a bayed nook, perfect for a sitting area, a spa bath with a corner whirlpool tub, and a secluded master garden. Three upstairs suites enjoy private baths and walk-in closets.

plan # HPK0600487

STYLE: EUROPEAN COTTAGE
FIRST FLOOR: 3,023 SQ. FT.
SECOND FLOOR: 1,623 SQ. FT.
TOTAL: 4,646 SQ. FT.
BONUS SPACE: 294 SQ. FT.
BEDROOMS: 4
BATHROOMS: 4½
WIDTH: 70' - 0"
DEPTH: 100' - 0"
FOUNDATION: SLAB

SEARCH ONLINE @ EPLANS.COM

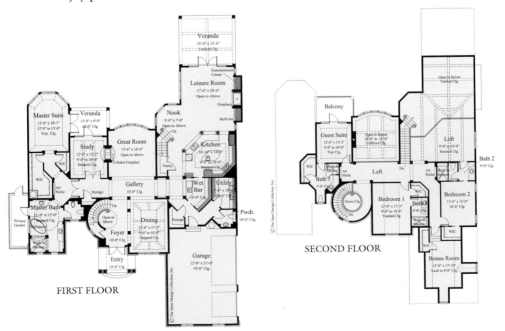

FIRST FLOOR

SECOND FLOOR

OPTIONAL LAYOUT

© The Sater Design Collection, Inc.

plan ⊕ HPK0600488

STYLE: ITALIANTE
FIRST FLOOR: 3,025 SQ. FT.
SECOND FLOOR: 1,639 SQ. FT.
TOTAL: 4,664 SQ. FT.
BONUS SPACE: 294 SQ. FT.
BEDROOMS: 4
BATHROOMS: 4½
WIDTH: 70' - 0"
DEPTH: 100' - 0"
FOUNDATION: SLAB

SEARCH ONLINE @ EPLANS.COM

A Mediterranean masterpiece, this family-oriented design is ideal for entertaining. Double doors reveal a foyer, with a columned dining room to the right and a spiral staircase enclosed in a turret to the left. Ahead, the great room opens above to a soaring coffered ceiling. Here, a bowed window wall and a two-sided fireplace (shared with the study) make an elegant impression. The country-style kitchen is a host's dream, with an adjacent wet bar, preparation island, and space for a six-burner cooktop. Near the leisure room, a bayed nook could serve as a breakfast or reading area. The master suite is a pampering sanctuary, with no rooms directly above and personal touches you will surely appreciate. Upstairs, two bedrooms, one with a window seat, and a guest suite with a balcony, all enjoy private baths and walk-in closets.

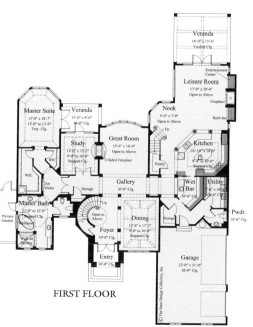

FIRST FLOOR

SECOND FLOOR

OPTIONAL LAYOUT

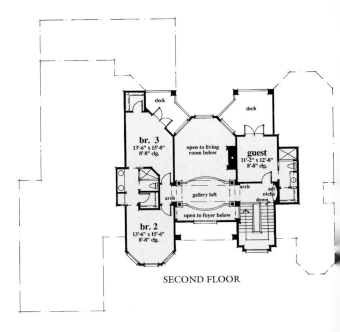

plan # HPK0600489

STYLE: CONTEMPORARY
FIRST FLOOR: 3,027 SQ. FT.
SECOND FLOOR: 1,079 SQ. FT.
TOTAL: 4,106 SQ. FT.
BEDROOMS: 4
BATHROOMS: 3½
WIDTH: 87' - 4"
DEPTH: 80' - 4"
FOUNDATION: BASEMENT

SEARCH ONLINE @ EPLANS.COM

The inside of this design is just as majestic as the outside. The grand foyer opens to a two-story living room with a fireplace and magnificent views. Dining in the bayed formal dining room will be a memorable experience. A well-designed kitchen is near a sunny nook and a leisure room with a fireplace and outdoor access. The master wing includes a separate study and an elegant private bath. The second level features a guest suite with its own bath and deck, two family bedrooms (Bedroom 3 also has its own deck), and a gallery loft with views to the living room below.

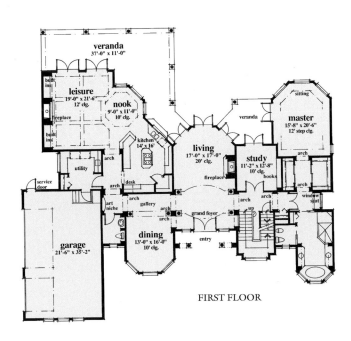

FIRST FLOOR

SECOND FLOOR

plan # HPK0600490

L

STYLE: FARMHOUSE
FIRST FLOOR: 3,166 SQ. FT.
SECOND FLOOR: 950 SQ. FT.
TOTAL: 4,116 SQ. FT.
GUEST HOUSE: 680 SQ. FT.
BEDROOMS: 5
BATHROOMS: 4
WIDTH: 154' - 0"
DEPTH: 94' - 8"
FOUNDATION: SLAB

SEARCH ONLINE @ EPLANS.COM

A long, low-pitched roof distinguishes this Southwestern-style farmhouse design. The tiled entrance leads to a grand dining room and opens to a formal parlor secluded by half-walls. A country kitchen with a cooktop island overlooks the two-story gathering room with its full wall of glass, fireplace, and built-in media shelves. The master suite satisfies the most discerning tastes with a raised hearth, an adjacent study or exercise room, access to the wraparound porch, and a bath with corner whirlpool tub. Rooms upstairs can serve as secondary bedrooms for family members, be converted to home office space, or used as guest bedrooms.

QUOTE ONE®

SECOND FLOOR

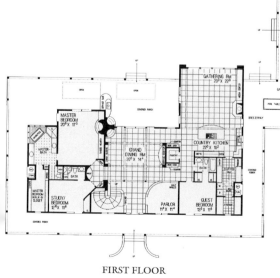

FIRST FLOOR

plan # HPK0600491

STYLE: MEDITERRANEAN
FIRST FLOOR: 3,103 SQ. FT.
SECOND FLOOR: 1,616 SQ. FT.
TOTAL: 4,719 SQ. FT.
BEDROOMS: 4
BATHROOMS: 3½ + ½
WIDTH: 86' - 9"
DEPTH: 84' - 6"

SEARCH ONLINE @ EPLANS.COM

This two-story Southwestern design boasts an exciting layout and great ceilings. The family room soars at the heart of the plan, surrounded by an excellent kitchen and breakfast nook on one side and a turreted stairwell on the other. Octagonal dimensions in these larger rooms create interesting transitional spaces and niches between them and the bedrooms. The master suite commands the left of the plan and features a flow-through design terminating at a very large walk-in closet. The remaining three bedrooms reside upstairs.

FIRST FLOOR

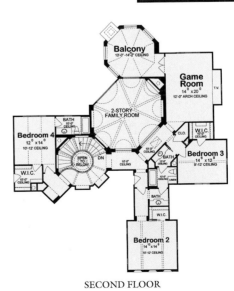

SECOND FLOOR

OPTIONAL LAYOUT

plan # HPK0600492

STYLE: MEDITERRANEAN
FIRST FLOOR: 3,148 SQ. FT.
SECOND FLOOR: 2,055 SQ. FT.
TOTAL: 5,203 SQ. FT.
BEDROOMS: 4
BATHROOMS: 4½
WIDTH: 75' - 4"
DEPTH: 73' - 9"

SEARCH ONLINE @ EPLANS.COM

Sun-washed Mediterranean style offers up a luxurious and intriguing interior and exterior details. An entry porch opens to a long arcade that borders a private courtyard. The spacious gallery greets visitors with a high-style circular staircase and unobstructed views of the formal dining room and attractive study. To the right, relax in solitude and grandeur as the master suite pampers you with ornate ceilings, a sitting bay, His and Hers dressing areas, separate shower and tub, and a room-sized walk-in closet. Splendid open spaces enhance interaction between the family room and large kitchen, which feature an adjoining eating area and planning center. A convenient wine room is a gourmet delight. Generous secondary bedrooms each feature a large walk-in closet, private bath, and access to a flexible game room and tower.

FIRST FLOOR

SECOND FLOOR

Planned Paradise

A truly gratifying landscape design takes cues from the architecture of the home, the owners' sense of style, and the natural properties of the land. Follow these guidelines for planning the perfect landscape for your home.

1. **Perennials and bulbs** used throughout this design establish an overall garden theme and provide cutting flowers for indoor bouquets. But remember that a garden will need a lot of care and constant attention. And a neglected garden will do nothing for a home's curb appeal.

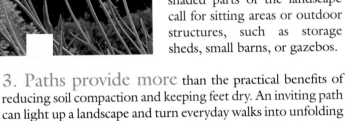

2. **Protected areas** for food gardening and composting are very appropriate in a country-inspired design. More shaded parts of the landscape call for sitting areas or outdoor structures, such as storage sheds, small barns, or gazebos.

3. **Paths provide more** than the practical benefits of reducing soil compaction and keeping feet dry. An inviting path can light up a landscape and turn everyday walks into unfolding journeys. To match the rustic, informal mood of the home in this plan, both the front walkway and driveway cut a curved, unintentional path through the property, which helps create a sense of destination. Use of fieldstones on the walkway adds another rustic touch. A parking spur at the end of the driveway provides extra parking space and room to maneuver vehicles.

4. **What is the topography** of the lot? Are there slopes or irregularities to be worked around?

5. **The stone piers** and picket fence at the entrance to the driveway frame the entry and match the detail and character of the home's stone foundation and porch railing. The choice of plants follows the theme introduced elsewhere in the plan.

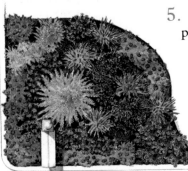

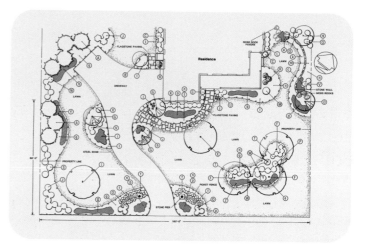

For more information on this landscape plan, turn to page 452.

6. If the plan does not include a tall fence or natural barrier between the lot and the next-door neighbor, place "retreat" areas away from property lines. Resist the natural urge to place quiet areas in only the corners of the yard. With the right design, owners can create a relaxing getaway right in the middle of the plan.

7. What are the growing conditions within the lot and within the region? What plants will flourish naturally?

8. How will the yard be used? Will it be a quiet spot in which to read the Sunday paper, or a secondary spot for guests to gather? Besides personal taste, the amount of space available for the design will constrain the range of options.

9. Use trees, especially deciduous ones, to create a sense of slight separation from the rest of the lawn. An arbor can also add a sense of seclusion, especially with plants growing up and over it.

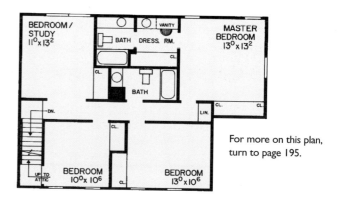

For more on this plan, turn to page 195.

10. Consider how the home can take full advantage of the landscape plan. Porches and decks provide transitions between the outdoor and indoor spaces of the overall design. Will an upstairs master suite be the best way to enjoy views of the gorgeous landscape? Or will a quiet, naturally lit study be in your family's future?

A low deck makes an excellent vantage point for surveying this naturalistic garden, which showcases a beautiful selection of flowers and ornamental grasses.

To integrate the deck more fully with the landscape and to provide light shade, the designer places several low-maintenance trees in planting pockets in the deck. A graceful arbor positioned straight across from the deck stairs beckons strollers to meander along the semicircular path, where they'll encounter a bench inviting them to sit for a spell. The bench supplies respite and a different perspective from which to admire the garden.

An assortment of plants rings the "figure-eight" lawn, which forms the hub of the landscape. Instead of more traditional groundcovers, drifts of blooming perennials and ornamental grasses blanket the ground. The various plants, chosen for a succession of bloom and carefully interspersed to camouflage the dying foliage of dormant spring bulbs, provide a kaleidoscope of color from season to season.

Besides lawn mowing, the only maintenance you'll need to perform is to cut back and remove the dead foliage once a year in late winter. To reduce upkeep further, a low-care groundcover could be substituted for the turf, and a slightly curving, mulched path installed from the deck stairs to the arbor to accommodate foot traffic. The spacious deck offers a comfortable vantage point for enjoying the flowers and foliage. Mulched planting beds keep this garden free of most weeds, and if the optional lawn edging is installed, the only regular maintenance chore will be lawn mowing.

OUTDOOR LIVING

plan # HPK0600503

SHOWN IN SUMMER
DESIGNED BY
DAMON SCOTT

SEARCH ONLINE @ EPLANS.COM

Designed for families who love outdoor living, this backyard features a deck and patio combination that is perfect for entertaining. It features an area for cooking and dining, as well as space for intimate conversations and relaxing in the sun.

ORDER BLUEPRINTS 24 HOURS, 7 DAYS A WEEK, AT 1-800-521-6797

The perfect setting for an outdoor party—or for simply relaxing with family and friends—this backyard features an elegant wooden deck and brick patio that run the length of the house. The deck area on the right (not included in the plans) acts as an outdoor kitchen, featuring a built-in barbecue, serving cabinet and space enough for a dining table and chairs. For those who opt to mingle with the other guests, rather than chat with the cook, a separate area has been provided at the other end.

Built at the same level as the house, and easily accessible from inside, the deck extends the interior living space to the outdoors. Three lovely flowering trees shade the deck and house, while creating a visual ceiling and walls to further reinforce the idea that these areas are outdoor rooms.

Down a few steps from the deck, the brick terrace makes a transition between the house (and deck) and the garden. Open on two sides to the lawn, this sunny terrace feels spacious and open, creating a great place in which people can mingle and talk during a cocktail party or sunbathe on a Saturday afternoon. From here, it's possible to enjoy the garden setting close at hand. The plantings around the perimeter of the yard feature several kinds of tall evergreens to provide privacy. In front of the evergreens, large drifts of flowering perennials are perfectly displayed against the green background. Between the evergreens, masses of shrubbery provide a changing color show from early spring through fall.

OUTDOOR LIVING

plan # HPK0600493

SHOWN IN SPRING
DESIGNED BY
MICHAEL J. OPISSO

SEARCH ONLINE @ EPLANS.COM

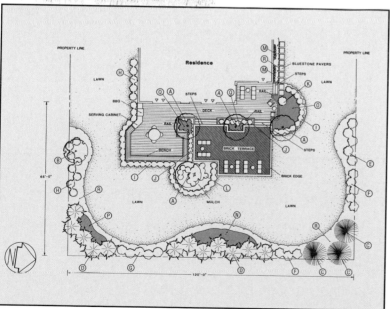

This beautiful Japanese-style garden provides space for outdoor living and entertaining in a tranquil setting. Featuring straight, simple lines, a small lawn, a large deck and extensive plantings of groundcovers and evergreens, the garden practically cares for itself.

When a busy couple wants a landscape that is distinctive and requires little maintenance, the Japanese-style garden and backyard pictured here are a perfect solution. The essence of a Japanese garden lies in emulating nature through simple, clean lines that do not look contrived. The low, tight hedges underscore the plantings behind them, while providing a contrast in form. Looking straight out from the deck, the perimeter planting is a harmony of shades of green, with interest provided from contrasting textures.

Paving stones border the deck because in the Japanese garden, every element has both an aesthetic and a functional purpose. The stones alleviate the wear that would result from stepping directly onto the lawn from the deck, and provide a visual transition between the man-made deck and the natural grass. The pavers act as more than a path; they also provide a sight line to the stone lantern on the left side of the garden.

The deck, like the rest of the landscape, has clean, simple lines, and provides the transition from the home's interior to the garden. It surrounds a viewing garden, one step down. In the Japanese tradition, this miniature landscape mimics a natural scene. The one large moss rock plays an important role—it is situated at the intersection of the stepping-stone paths that lead through the garden. Here a decision must be made as to which way to turn. The stone water basin, a symbolic part of the Japanese tea ceremony, is located near the door to the house, signaling the entrance to a very special place.

OUTDOOR LIVING

plan# HPK0600494

SHOWN IN SPRING
DESIGNED BY
MICHAEL J. OPISSO

SEARCH ONLINE @ EPLANS.COM

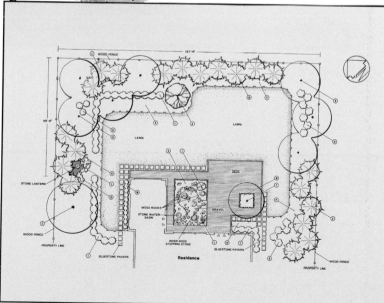

Shaded yards need not be dark and dull, as this backyard design demonstrates. Here, beneath the shadows of seven mature trees, a colorful collection of shade-loving shrubs, perennials, and groundcovers flourishes.

Woe to the gardener who has to deal with established tall trees that cast a great deal of shade—a beautiful, colorful backyard is out of the question, right? Wrong! Nothing could be further from the truth, as demonstrated by this artfully designed shade garden.

The key to working with large existing trees is in using the shade as an asset, not as a liability, and in choosing shade-loving plants to grow beneath them. If the trees have a very dense canopy, branches can be selectively removed to thin the trees and create filtered shade below.

In this plan, the designer shapes the lawn and beds to respond to the locations of the trees. Note that all but one of the trees are situated in planting beds, not in open lawn. Placing a single tree in the lawn helps to integrate the lawn and planting beds, creating a cohesive design. At the right, the deep planting area is enhanced by pavers, a bench, and a birdbath, creating an inviting, shady retreat. Near the house, a small patio provides a lounging spot; its curving shape echoes the curving form of the planting beds.

Throughout the garden, perennials, woody plants, and groundcovers are arranged in drifts to create a comfortable and serene space. The garden is in constant but ever-changing bloom from early spring through fall, as its special plants—chosen because they thrive in just such a shady setting in their native habitats—go in and out of bloom. Fall brings big splashes of foliage color to complete the year-long show. To provide the finishing carpet to this beautiful and cool shade garden, choose a grass-seed variety selected to tolerate shade.

OUTDOOR LIVING

plan # HPK0600495

SHOWN IN SUMMER
DESIGNED BY
MICHAEL J. OPISSO

SEARCH ONLINE @ EPLANS.COM

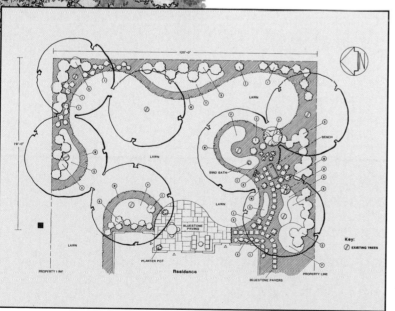

Here is a special backyard designed for both children and adults. The yard offers youngsters their own place to escape into a world of imagination and discovery without compromising the attractiveness of a garden setting.

If there's one thing that can be said about children's play areas, it's that their function usually far outweighs their attractiveness. However, this backyard design presents an excellent solution to a functional children's play yard that is still pleasing to look at. The backyard includes all the fun elements a child would love. On one side of the yard are grouped a play structure for climbing and swinging, a playhouse, and a sandbox enclosed in a low boardwalk. A play mound—a perfect place for running, leaping and holding fort—rises from the lawn on the other side of the yard.

These play areas are integrated into the landscape by their circular form, which is repeated in the sandbox, play mound, boardwalk, and the sand areas under the playhouse and play structure. The curved brick patio and planting border carry through the circular theme. The stepping stones leading to the play areas also follow a circular path—a playful pattern that invites a child to "follow the yellow brick road."

From the house and patio, the views of both the garden and the play areas are unobstructed, affording constant adult supervision from both indoors and out. The border surrounding the yard creates a private setting that offers a changing show of flowers from the masses of shrubs and perennials. Beyond the play structure, a large tree shades the area, providing landscape interest, and perhaps even a place for adventurous young feet to climb.

When the children are grown, this design can be adapted as a playground for older folk by removing the playhouse and play structure and planting lawn, or a flower or vegetable garden.

OUTDOOR LIVING

plan # HPK0600496

SHOWN IN SUMMER
DESIGNED BY
MICHAEL J. OPISSO

SEARCH ONLINE @ EPLANS.COM

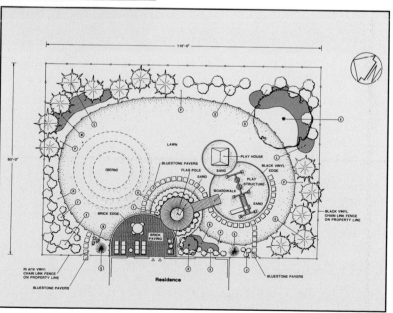

Nature lovers will delight in the abundant number of birds that will flock to this beautiful garden. An attractive collection of berried plants and evergreens offers food and shelter for the wildlife, while creating a handsome, pastoral setting.

There is no better way to wake up in the morning than to the sound of songbirds in the garden. Wherever you live, you will be surprised at the number and variety of birds you can attract by offering them a few basic necessities—water, shelter, nesting spots, and food. Birds need water for drinking and bathing. They need shrubs and trees, especially evergreens, for shelter and nesting. Edge spaces—open areas with trees nearby for quick protection—provide ground feeders with foraging places, and plants with berries and nuts offer other natural sources of food.

The garden presented here contains all the necessary elements to attract birds to the garden. The shrubs and trees are chosen especially to provide a mix of evergreen and deciduous species. All of these, together with the masses of flowering perennials, bear seeds, nuts, or berries that are known to appeal to birds. The berry show looks quite pretty, too, until the birds gobble them up! Planted densely enough for necessary shelter, the bird-attracting plants create a lovely private backyard that's enjoyable throughout the seasons.

The birdbath is located in the lawn so it will be in the sun. A naturalistic pond provides water in a more protected setting. The birdhouses and feeders aren't really necessary—though they may be the icing on the cake when it comes to luring the largest number of birds—because the landscape provides abundant natural food and shelter. Outside one of the main windows of the house, a birdfeeder hangs from a small flowering tree, providing an up-close view of your feathered friends.

OUTDOOR LIVING

plan# IIPK0600497

SHOWN IN AUTUMN
DESIGNED BY
MICHAEL J. OPISSO

SEARCH ONLINE @ EPLANS.COM

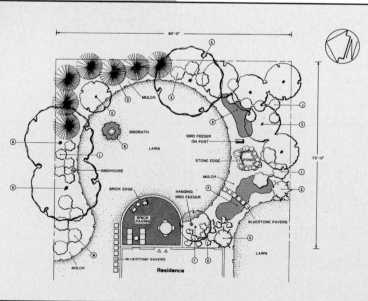

The abundant flowers in this backyard turn it into a paradise for butterflies as well as for garden lovers. Dozens of different kinds of nectar-rich plants, blooming from spring through fall, provide the necessary blossoms to lure the ephemeral beauties not only to stop and pay a visit, but perhaps to stay and set up a home.

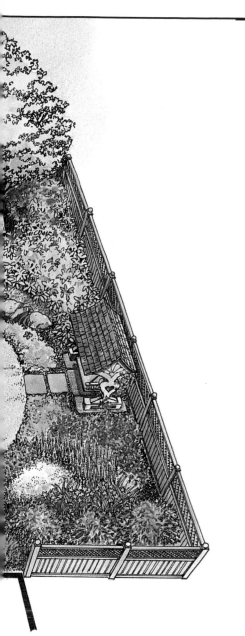

Colorful butterflies will flock to this floriferous backyard, which is planted with flowering shrubs and perennials irresistible to these welcome winged visitors. A butterfly's needs are simple: a sunny spot out of the wind to perch on, a puddle of water to drink from, nectar-rich flowers to sip from and food plants for the caterpillar phase to munch on. The designer incorporates all these needs into this landscape plan, while also providing for human visitors.

The flagstone patio, nestled among the flowers near the center of the yard, brings you away from the house right out where the butterflies congregate. This is a perfect place for a table and chairs, where you can sip coffee during a sunny spring morning or dine during a summer evening, all the while keeping an eye out for a visiting monarch, red admiral or swallowtail feeding on the nearby flowers or perching on the flat rocks near the puddle. The swing and arbor (not included in the plan) provide a cool spot to relax.

Instead of a pure grass lawn, the designer specified a lawn composed of mixed clover and grass. The clover provides nectar for the adult butterflies and forage for the caterpillars. Keep in mind that, as beautiful as they are, butterflies are insects. To enjoy the elusive winged stage, you'll have to tolerate a little feeding damage from the caterpillar stage. It's best to garden organically, steering clear of all insecticides—whether chemical or biological—in this garden, or you're likely to have few butterfly visitors.

OUTDOOR LIVING

plan # HPK0600498

SHOWN IN SUMMER
DESIGNED BY
TOM NORDLOH

SEARCH ONLINE @ EPLANS.COM

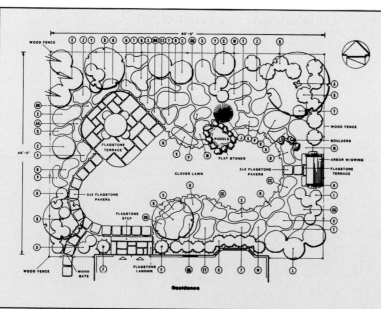

The English perennial border, with its graceful masses of ever-changing flowers, represents the epitome of fine perennial gardening. Planted in a corner of your property, this garden will provide enjoyment for years to come.

The British, being renowned gardeners, boast some of the prettiest flower gardens in the world. Their success in growing perennials to such perfection lies partly in the amenable British climate—cool summers, mild winters, plenty of moisture throughout the year, and very long summer days. Even without such a perfect climate, North American gardeners can achieve a respectable show of perennials by using plants better adapted to their climate. Arrange them into the flowing drifts made popular early in this century by British landscape designers, and you'll have the epitome of a perennial garden in your own backyard.

The perennial border shown here fits nicely into a corner of almost any sunny backyard. Pictured with a traditional evergreen hedge as a backdrop for the flowers, the garden looks equally lovely planted in front of a fence or house wall, as long as the area receives at least six hours of full sun a day.

The designer carefully selected an array of spring-, summer- and fall-blooming perennials, arranging them in artful drifts for an ever-changing display. Spring and summer blooms paint a delightful pink, magenta, and pale yellow color scheme sparked here and there with splashes of white and blue, and autumn brings deeper colors—gold, dark pink, and purple. Patches of burgundy- and silver-hued foliage plants in the foreground help tie the elements of the garden together and play up the flowers. The English perennial border with its graceful masses of ever-changing flowers represents the epitome of fine perennial gardening. Planted in a corner of your property, this garden will provide enjoyment for years to come

plan # HPK0600499

SHOWN IN SUMMER
DESIGNED BY
MICHAEL J. OPISSO

SEARCH ONLINE @ EPLANS.COM

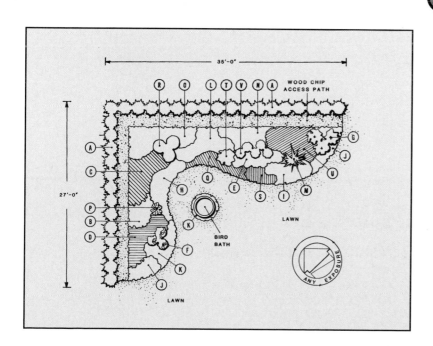

This garden of shade-loving plants flourishes under trees where grass struggles to survive. Be sure to keep the plants healthy by providing plenty of water and fertilizer, especially if the garden plants compete for moisture and nutrients with thirsty tree roots.

If you're constantly complaining that nothing will grow in the shade of the trees in your backyard, consider planting this beautiful shady flower border. Lawn grass needs full sun and struggles to grow under trees, so why not plant something that flourishes in the shade and looks much prettier! This charming flower border features shade-loving perennials and ferns, fits under existing trees, and blooms from spring through fall. In this design, flowering perennials grow through a low evergreen groundcover, which keeps the garden pretty even in winter, when the perennials are dormant.

Also providing year-round interest are rocks and boulders, as well as a bench that invites you to sit and enjoy the pretty scene. The designer shows this garden against a fence along the property border, but you could plant it in front of a hedge or other shrubbery and place it anywhere in your yard. If your property is smaller, you can easily eliminate the corner containing the bench and end the border with the group of three rocks to the left of the bench.

OUTDOOR LIVING

plan # HPK0600500

SHOWN IN SUMMER
DESIGNED BY
MICHEL J. OPISSO

SEARCH ONLINE @ EPLANS.COM

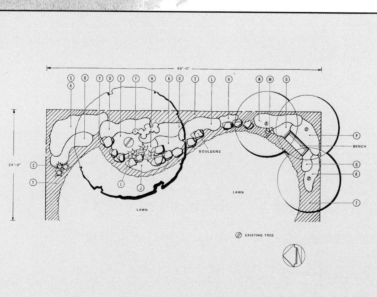

Natural color companions, blue and yellow flowers create a pleasing garden scene that looks great anywhere it's planted. This island bed works perfectly in an open sunny yard, but it could be modified to fit along the side of a house or to the back up against a fence or hedge along a property border.

Blue and yellow flowers planted together reward the gardener with a naturally complementary color scheme that's as bright and pretty as any garden can be. It's hard to err when using these colors, because the pure blues and the lavender blues—whether dark or pastel—look just as pretty with the pale lemon yellows as with the bright sulfur yellows and the golden yellows. Each combination makes a different statement, some subtle and sweet as with the pastels, and others bold and demanding as with the deep vivid hues. But no combination fails to please.

The designer of this beautiful bed, which can be situated in any sunny spot, effectively orchestrated a sequence of blue-and-yellow-flowering perennials so the garden blooms from spring through fall. The designer not only combined the floral colors beautifully together, but also incorporated various flower shapes and textures so they make a happy opposition. Fluffy, rounded heads of blossoms set off elegant spires, and mounded shapes mask the lanky stems of taller plants. Large, funnel-shaped flowers stand out against masses of tiny, feathery flowers like jewels displayed against a silk dress.

Although the unmistakable color scheme for this garden is blue and yellow, the designer sprinkled in an occasional spot of orange to provide a lovely jolt of brightly contrasting color. A few masses of creamy white flowers frost the garden, easing the stronger colors into a compatible union.

plan # HPK0600501

SHOWN IN SUMMER
DESIGNED BY
DAMON SCOTT

SEARCH ONLINE @ EPLANS.COM

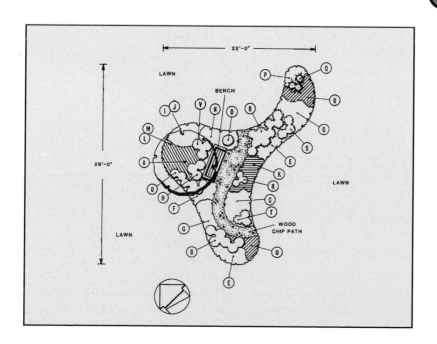

*G*raceful trees, curving lines and bursts of flowers blooming from spring through fall complement this comfortable country retreat. The friendly landscaping creates the perfect finishing touch that says: here's a place to hang up a hammock and relax.

Set in a friendly and homey landscape brimming with flowers from spring through fall, this farmhouse's country atmosphere is now complete. Masses of perennials and bulbs used throughout the property create a garden setting and provide armloads of flowers that can be cut for indoor bouquets. But the floral beauty doesn't stop there; the designer artfully incorporates unusual specimens of summer- and fall-blooming trees and shrubs into the landscape design to elevate the changing floral scene to eye-level and above.

To match the informal mood of the house, both the front walkway and driveway cut a curved, somewhat meandering path. A parking spur at the end of the driveway provides extra parking space and a place to turn around. Fieldstones, whose rustic character complements the country setting, pave the front walk. The stone piers and picket fence at the entrance to the driveway frame the entry and match the detail and character of the house's stone foundation and porch railing. The stone wall at the side of the property further carries out this theme.

Large specimen trees planted in the lawn set the house back from the road and provide a show of autumn color. Imagine completing the country theme in this tranquil setting by hanging a child's swing from the tree nearest the front porch. Also shown here is home plan HPB774 by Home Planners. For information about ordering blueprints for this home, call 1-800-521-6797.

OUTDOOR LIVING

plan# HPK0600004

SHOWN IN SUMMER
DESIGNED BY
DAVID POPLAWSKI

SEARCH ONLINE @ EPLANS.COM

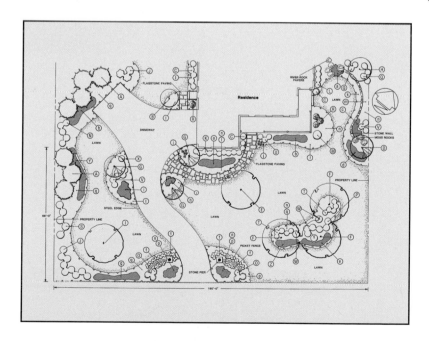

House Plans—
Super Sized

Hanley Wood has compiled the best-selling and most popular home plans into the most extensive home plan resources available. Now delivering more of everything you want—more plans, more styles and more choices—your dream home is right around the corner.

If you are looking to build a new home, look to Hanley Wood first. Pick up a copy today!

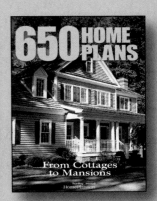

With over 2,500 home plans, finding the right new home to fit

- Your style
- Your budget
- Your life

Has never been easier.

hanley▲wood
SELECTION, CONVENIENCE, SERVICE!

With more than 50 years of experience in the industry and millions of blueprints sold, Hanley Wood is a trusted source of high-quality, high-value pre-drawn home plans.

Using pre-drawn home plans is a **reliable, cost-effective way** to build your dream home, and our vast selection of plans is second-to-none. The nation's finest designers craft these plans that builders know they can trust. Meanwhile, our friendly, knowledgeable customer service representatives can help you every step of the way.

WHAT YOU'LL GET WITH YOUR ORDER

The contents of each designer's blueprint package is unique, but all contain detailed, high-quality working drawings. You can expect to find the following standard elements in most sets of plans:

1. FRONT PERSPECTIVE

This artist's sketch of the exterior of the house gives you an idea of how the house will look when built and landscaped.

3. DETAILED FLOOR PLANS

These plans show the layout of each floor of the house. Rooms and interior spaces are carefully dimensioned, doors and windows located, and keys are given for cross-section details provided elsewhere in the plans.

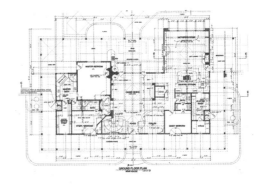

2. FOUNDATION AND BASEMENT PLANS

This sheet shows the foundation layout including concrete walls, footings, pads, posts, beams, and bearing walls, and foundation notes. If the home features a basement, the first-floor framing details may also be included on this plan. If your plan features slab construction rather than a basement, the plan shows footings and details for a monolithic slab. This page, or another in the set, may include a sample plot plan for locating your house on a building site. Additional sheets focus on foundation cross-sections and other details.

4. HOUSE AND DETAIL CROSS-SECTIONS

Large-scale views show sections or cutaways of the foundation, interior walls, exterior walls, floors, stairways, and roof details. Additional cross-sections may show important changes in floor, ceiling, or roof heights, or the relationship of one level to another. These sections show exactly how the various parts of the house fit together and are extremely valuable during construction. Additional sheets may include enlarged wall, floor, and roof construction details.

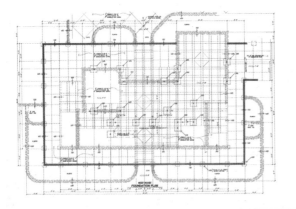

5. ROOF AND FLOOR STRUCTURAL SUPPORTS

The roof and floor framing plans provide detail for these crucial elements of your home. Each includes floor joist, ceiling joist, rafter and roof joist size, spacing, direction, span, and specifications. Beam and window headers, along with necessary details for framing connections, stairways, skylights, or dormers are also included.

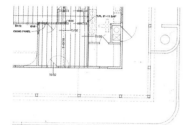

6. ELECTRICAL PLAN

The electrical plan offers a detailed outline of all wiring for your home, with notes for all lighting, outlets, switches, and circuits. A layout is provided for each level, as well as basements, garages, or other structures.

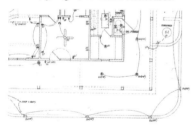

7. EXTERIOR ELEVATIONS

In addition to the front exterior, your blueprint set will include drawings of the rear and sides of your house as well. These drawings give notes on exterior materials and finishes. Particular attention is given to cornice detail, brick and stone accents, or other finish items that make your home unique.

BEFORE YOU CALL

You are making a terrific decision to use a pre-drawn house plan—it is one you can make with confidence, knowing that your blueprints are crafted by national-award-winning certified residential designers and architects, and trusted by builders.

Once you've selected the plan you want—or even if you have questions along the way—our experienced customer service representatives are available 24 hours a day, seven days a week to help you navigate the home-building process. To help them provide you with even better service, please consider the following questions before you call:

■ Have you chosen or purchased your lot?
If so, please review the building setback requirements of your local building authority before you call. You don't need to have a lot before ordering plans, but if you own land already, please have the width and depth dimensions handy when you call.

■ Have you chosen a builder?
Involving your builder in the plan selection and evaluation process may be beneficial. Luckily, builders know they can have confidence with pre-drawn plans because they've been designed for livability, functionality, and typically are builder-proven at successful home sites across the country.

■ Do you need a construction loan?
Construction loans are unique because they involve determining the value of something that is not yet constructed. Several lenders offer convenient contstruction-to-permanent loans. It is important to choose a good lending partner—one who will help guide you through the application and appraisal process. Most will even help you evaluate your contractor to ensure reliability and credit worthiness. Our partnership with IndyMac Bank, a nationwide leader in construction loans, can help you save on your loan, if needed (see the next page for details).

■ How many sets of plans do you need?
Building a home can typically require a number of sets of blueprints—one for yourself, two or three for the builder and subcontractors, two for the local building department, and one or

more for your lender. For this reason, we offer 5- and 8-set plan packages, but your best value is the Reproducible Plan Package. Reproducible plans are accompanied by a license to make modifications and typically up to 12 duplicates of the plan so you have enough copies of the plan for everyone involved in the financing and construction of your home.

■ Do you want to make any changes to the plan?
We understand that it is difficult to find blueprints for a home that will meet all of your needs. That is why Hanley Wood is glad to offer plan Customization Services. We will work with you to design the modifications you'd like to see and to adjust your blueprint plans accordingly—anything from changing the foundation; adding square footage, redesigning baths, kitchens, or bedrooms; or most other modifications. This simple, cost-effective service saves you from hiring an outside architect to make alterations. Modifications may only be made to Reproducible Plan Packages that include the license to modify.

■ Do you have to make any changes to meet local building codes?
While all of our plans are drawn to meet national building codes at the time they were created, many areas required that plans be stamped by a local engineer to certify that they meet local building codes. Building codes are updated frequently and can vary by state, county, city, or municipality. Contact your local building inspection department, office of planning and zoning, or department of permits to determine how your local codes will affect your construction project. The best way to assure that you can make changes to your plan, if necessary, is to purchase a Reproducible Plan Package.

■ Has everyone—from family members to contractors—been involved in selecting the plan?
Building a new home is an exciting process, and using pre-drawn plans is a great way to realize your dreams. Make sure that everyone involved has had an opportunity to review the plan you've selected. While Hanley Wood is the only plans provider with an exchange policy, it's best to be sure all parties agree on your selection before you buy.

CALL TOLL-FREE 1-800-521-6797

Source Key
HPK063

CUSTOMIZE YOUR PLAN –
HANLEY WOOD CUSTOMIZATION SERVICES

Creating custom home plans has never been easier and more directly accessible. Using state-of-the-art technology and top-performing architectural expertise, Hanley Wood delivers on a long-standing customer commitment to provide world-class home-plans and customization services. Our valued customers—professional home builders and individual home owners—appreciate the convenience and accessibility of this interactive, consultative service.

With the Hanley Wood Customization Service you can:

■ Save valuable time by avoiding drawn-out and frequently repetitive face-to-face design meetings

■ Communicate design and home-plan changes faster and more efficiently
■ Speed-up project turn-around time
■ Build on a budget without sacrificing quality
■ Transform master home plans to suit your design needs and unique personal style

All of our design options and prices are impressively affordable. A detailed quote is available for a $50 consultation fee. Plan modification is an interactive service. Our skilled team of designers will guide you through the customization process from start to finish making recommendations, offering ideas, and determining the feasibility of your changes. This level of service is offered to ensure the final modified plan meets your expectations. If you use our service the $50 fee will be applied to the cost of the modifications.

You may purchase the customization consultation before or after purchasing a plan. In either case, it is necessary to purchase the Reproducible Plan Package and complete the accompanying license to modify the plan before we can begin customization.

Customization Consultation $50

TOOLS TO WORK WITH YOUR BUILDER

Two Reverse Options For Your Convenience –
Mirror and Right-Reading Reverse (as available)

Mirror reverse plans simply flip the design 180 degrees—keep in mind, the text will also be flipped. For a minimal fee you can have one or all of your plans shipped mirror reverse, although we recommend having at least one regular set handy. Right-reading reverse plans show the design flipped 180 degrees but the text reads normally. When you choose this option, we ship each set of purchased blueprints in this format.

Mirror Reverse Fee (indicate the number of sets when ordering) $55
Right Reading Reverse Fee (all sets are reversed) $175

A Shopping List Exclusively for Your Home – Materials List

A customized Materials List helps you plan and estimate the cost of your new home, outlining the quantity, type, and size of materials needed to build your house (with the exception of mechanical system items). Included are framing lumber, windows and doors, kitchen and bath cabinetry, rough and finished hardware, and much more.

Materials List . . . .$85 each
Additional Materials Lists (at original time of purchase only) . . .$20 each

Plan Your Home-
Building Process – Specification Outline

Work with your builder on this step-by-step chronicle of 166 stages or items crucial to the building process. It provides a comprehensive review of the construction process and helps you choose materials.
Specification Outline . . . .$10 each

Learn the Basics of Building – Electrical, Pluming, Mechanical, Construction Detail Sheets

If you want to know more about building techniques—and deal more confidently with your subcontractors—we offer four useful detail sheets. These sheets provide non-plan-specific general information, but are excellent tools that will add to your understanding of Plumbing Details, Electrical Details, Construction Details, and Mechanical Details.

Electrical Detail Sheet $14.95
Plumbing Detail Sheet $14.95
Mechanical Detail Sheet $14.95
Construction Detail Sheet $14.95

SUPER VALUE SETS:
Buy any 2: $26.95; Buy any 3: $34.95; Buy All 4: $39.95

Best Value

MAKE YOUR HOME TECH-READY – HOME AUTOMATION UPGRADE

Building a new home provides a unique opportunity to wire it with a plan for future needs. A Home Automation-Ready (HA-Ready) home contains the wiring substructure of tomorrow's connected home. It means that every room—from the front porch to the backyard, and from the attic to the basement—is wired for security, lighting, telecommunications, climate control, home computer networking, whole-house audio, home theater, shade control, video surveillance, entry access control, and yes, video gaming electronic solutions.

Along with the conveniences HA-Ready homes provide, they also have a higher resale value. The Consumer Electronics Association (CEA), in conjunction with the Custom Electronic Design and Installation Association (CEDIA), have developed a TechHome™ Rating system that quantifies the value of HA-Ready homes. The rating system is gaining widespread recognition in the real estate industry.

Developed by CEDIA-certified installers, our Home Automation Upgrade package includes everything you need to work with an installer during the construction of your home. It provides a short explanation of the various subsystems, a wiring floor plan for each level of your home, a detailed materials list with estimated costs, and a list of CEDIA-certified installers in your local area.
Home Automation Upgrade $250

GET YOUR HOME PLANS PAID FOR!

IndyMac Bank, in partnership with Hanley Wood, will reimburse you up to $750 toward the cost of your home plans simply by financing the construction of your new home with IndyMac Bank Home Construction Lending.

IndyMac's construction and permanent loan is a one-time close loan, meaning that one application—and one set of closing fees—provides all the financing you need.

Apply today at www.indymacbank.com, call toll free at 1-866-237-3478, or ask a Hanley Wood customer service representative for details.

DESIGN YOUR HOME – INTERIOR AND EXTERIOR FINISHING TOUCHES

Be Your Own Interior Designer! – Home Furniture Planner
Effectively plan the space in your home using our Hands-On Home Furniture Planner. It's fun and easy—no more moving heavy pieces of furniture to see how the room will go together. The kit includes reusable peel-and-stick furniture templates that fit on a 12"x18" laminated layout board—enough space to lay out every room in your house.
Home Furniture Planning Kit $15.95

Enjoy the Outdoors! – Deck Plans
Many of our homes have a corresponding deck plan, sold separately, which includes a Deck Plan Frontal Sheet, Deck Framing and Floor Plans, Deck Elevations, and a Deck Materials List. A Standard Deck Details Package, also available, provides all the how-to information necessary for building any deck. Get both the Deck Plan and the Standard Deck Details Package for one low price in our Complete Deck Building Package. See the price tier chart below and call for deck plan availability.

Create a Professionally Designed Landscape – Landscape Plans
Many of our homes have a front-yard Landscape Plan that is complementary in design to the house plan. These comprehensive Landscape Blueprint Packages include a Frontal Sheet, Plan View, Regionalized Plant & Materials List, a sheet on Planting and Maintaining Your Landscape, Zone Maps, and a Plant Size and Description Guide. Each set of blueprints is a full 18" x 24" with clear, complete instructions in easy-to-read type. Our Landscape Plans are available with a Plant & Materials List adapted by horticultural experts to eight regions of the country. Please specify your region when ordering your plan—see region map below. Call for more information about landscape plan availability and applicable regions.

LANDSCAPE & DECK PRICE SCHEDULE

PRICE TIERS	1-SET STUDY PACKAGE	5-SET BUILDING PACKAGE	1-SET REPRODUCIBLE *	1-SET CAD*
P1	$25	$55	$145	$245
P2	$45	$75	$165	$280
P3	$75	$105	$195	$330
P4	$105	$135	$225	$385
P5	$175	$205	$405	$690
P6	$215	$245	$445	$750
D1	$45	$75**	$90	$90
D2	$75	$105**	$150	$150

PRICES SUBJECT TO CHANGE   * REQUIRES AN E-MAIL ADDRESS OR FAX NUMBER
                                            ** 3-SET BUILDING PACKAGE

TERMS & CONDITIONS

OUR EXCHANGE POLICY

HANLEY WOOD EXCLUSIVE!

Hanley Wood is committed to ensuring your satisfaction with your blueprint order, which is why we're the only provider of pre-drawn house plans to offer an exchange policy. With the exception of Reproducible Plan Package orders, we will exchange your entire first order for an equal or greater number of blueprints from our plan collection within 90 days of the original order. The entire content of your original order must be returned before an exchange will be processed. Please call our customer service department at 1-888-690-1116 for your return authorization number and shipping instructions. If the returned blueprints look used, redlined, or copied, we will not honor your exchange. Fees for exchanging your blueprints are as follows: 20% of the amount of the original order, plus the difference in cost if exchanging for a design in a higher price bracket or less the difference in cost if exchanging for a design in a lower price bracket. (Because they can be copied, Reproducible blueprints are not exchangeable or refundable.) Please call for current postage and handling prices. Shipping and handling charges are not refundable.

ARCHITECTURAL AND ENGINEERING SEALS

Some cities and states now require that a licensed architect or engineer review and "seal" a blueprint, or officially approve it, prior to construction. Prior to application for a building permit or the start of actual construction, we strongly advise that you consult your local building official who can tell you if such a review is required.

LOCAL BUILDING CODES AND ZONING REQUIREMENTS

Each plan was designed to meet or exceed the requirements of a nationally recognized model building code in effect at the time and place the plan was drawn. Typically plans designed after the year 2000 conform to the International Residential Building Code (IRC 2000 or 2003). The IRC is comprised of portions of the three major codes below. Plans drawn before 2000 conform to one of the three recognized building codes in effect at the time: Building Officials and Code Administrators (BOCA) International, Inc.;

the Southern Building Code Congress International, (SBCCI) Inc.; the International Conference of Building Officials (ICBO); or the Council of American Building Officials (CABO).

Because of the great differences in geography and climate throughout the United States and Canada, each state, county, and municipality has its own building codes, zone requirements, ordinances, and building regulations. Your plan may need to be modified to comply with local requirements. In addition, you may need to obtain permits or inspections from local governments before and in the course of construction. We authorize the use of the blueprints on the express condition that you consult a local licensed architect or engineer of your choice prior to beginning construction and strictly comply with all local building codes, zoning requirements, and other applicable laws, regulations, ordinances, and requirements. Notice: Plans for homes to be built in Nevada must be redrawn by a Nevada-registered professional. Consult your local building official for more information on this subject.

TERMS AND CONDITIONS

These designs are protected under the terms of United States Copyright Law and may not be copied or reproduced in any way, by

any means, unless you have purchased a Reproducible Plan Package and signed the accompanying license to modify and copy the plan, which clearly indicates your right to modify, copy, or reproduce. We authorize the use of your chosen design as an aid in the construction of ONE (1) single- or multifamily home only. You may not use this design to build a second dwelling or multiple dwellings without purchasing another blueprint or blueprints or paying additional design fees. Multi-use fees vary by designer—please call one of experienced sales representatives for a quote.

DISCLAIMER

The designers we work with have put substantial care and effort into the creation of their blueprints. However, because we cannot provide on-site consultation, supervision, and control over actual construction, and because of the great variance in local building requirements, building practices, and soil, seismic, weather, and other conditions, WE MAKE NO WARRANTY OF ANY KIND, EXPRESS OR IMPLIED, WITH RESPECT TO THE CONTENT OR USE OF THE BLUEPRINTS, INCLUDING BUT NOT LIMITED TO ANY WARRANTY OF MERCHANTABILITY OR OF FITNESS FOR A PARTICULAR PURPOSE. ITEMS, PRICES, TERMS, AND CONDITIONS ARE SUBJECT TO CHANGE WITHOUT NOTICE.

CALL TOLL-FREE 1-866-473-4052 OR VISIT EPLANS.COM

IMPORTANT COPYRIGHT NOTICE

From the Council of Publishing Home Designers

Blueprints for residential construction (or working drawings, as they are often called in the industry) are copyrighted intellectual property, protected under the terms of the United States Copyright Law and, therefore, cannot be copied legally for use in building. The following are some guidelines to help you get what you need to build your home, without violating copyright law:

1. HOME PLANS ARE COPYRIGHTED

Just like books, movies, and songs, home plans receive protection under the federal copyright laws. The copyright laws prevent anyone, other than the copyright owner, from reproducing, modifying, or reusing the plans or design without permission of the copyright owner.

2. DO NOT COPY DESIGNS OR FLOOR PLANS FROM ANY PUBLICATION, ELECTRONIC MEDIA, OR EXISTING HOME

It is illegal to copy, change, or redraw home designs found in a plan book, CDROM or on the Internet. The right to modify plans is one of the exclusive rights of copyright. It is also illegal to copy or redraw a constructed home that is protected by copyright, even if you have never seen the plans for the home. If you find a plan or home that you like, you must purchase a set of plans from an authorized source. The plans may not be lent, given away, or sold by the purchaser.

3. DO NOT USE PLANS TO BUILD MORE THAN ONE HOUSE

The original purchaser of house plans is typically licensed to build a single home from the plans. Building more than one home from the plans without permission is an infringement of the home designer's copyright. The purchase of a multiple-set package of plans is for the construction of a single home only. The purchase of additional sets of plans does not grant the right to construct more than one home.

4. HOUSE PLANS IN THE FORM OF BLUEPRINTS OR BLACKLINES CANNOT BE COPIED OR REPRODUCED

Plans, blueprints, or blacklines, unless they are reproducibles, cannot be copied or reproduced without prior written consent of the copyright owner. Copy shops and blueprinters are prohibited from making copies of these plans without the copyright release letter you receive with reproducible plans.

5. HOUSE PLANS IN THE FORM OF BLUEPRINTS OR BLACKLINES CANNOT BE REDRAWN

Plans cannot be modified or redrawn without first obtaining the copyright owner's permission. With your purchase of plans, you are licensed to make non-structural changes by "red-lining" the purchased plans. If you need to make structural changes or need to redraw the plans for any reason, you must purchase a reproducible set of plans (see topic 6) which includes a license to modify the plans. Blueprints do not come with a license to make structural changes or to redraw the plans. You may not reuse or sell the modified design.

6. REPRODUCIBILE HOME PLANS

Reproducible plans (for example sepias, mylars, CAD files, electronic files, and vellums) come with a license to make modifications to the plans. Once modified, the plans can be taken to a local copy shop or blueprinter to make up to 10 or 12 copies of the plans to use in the construction of a single home. Only one home can be constructed from any single purchased set of reproducible plans either in original form or as modified. The license to modify and copy must be completed and returned before the plan will be shipped.

7. MODIFIED DESIGNS CANNOT BE REUSED

Even if you are licensed to make modifications to a copyrighted design, the modified design is not free from the original designer's copyright. The sale or reuse of the modified design is prohibited. Also, be aware that any modification to plans relieves the original designer from liability for design defects and voids all warranties expressed or implied.

8. WHO IS RESPONSIBLE FOR COPYRIGHT INFRINGEMENT?

Any party who participates in a copyright violation may be responsible including the purchaser, designers, architects, engineers, drafters, homeowners, builders, contractors, sub-contractors, copy shops, blueprinters, developers, and real estate agencies. It does not matter whether or not the individual knows that a violation is being committed. Ignorance of the law is not a valid defense.

9. PLEASE RESPECT HOME DESIGN COPYRIGHTS

In the event of any suspected violation of a copyright, or if there is any uncertainty about the plans purchased, the publisher, architect, designer, or the Council of Publishing Home Designers (www.cphd.org) should be contacted before proceeding. Awards are sometimes offered for information about home design copyright infringement.

10. PENALTIES FOR INFRINGEMENT

Penalties for violating a copyright may be severe. The responsible parties are required to pay actual damages caused by the infringement (which may be substantial), plus any profits made by the infringer commissions to include all profits from the sale of any home built from an infringing design. The copyright law also allows for the recovery of statutory damages, which may be as high as $150,000 for each infringement. Finally, the infringer may be required to pay legal fees which often exceed the damages.

BLUEPRINT PRICE SCHEDULE

PRICE TIERS	1-SET STUDY PACKAGE	5-SET BUILDING PACKAGE	8-SET BUILDING PACKAGE	1-SET REPRODUCIBLE*	1-SET CAD*
A1	$470	$520	$575	$700	$1,055
A2	$510	$565	$620	$765	$1,230
A3	$575	$630	$690	$870	$1,400
A4	$620	$685	$750	$935	$1,570
C1	$665	$740	$810	$1,000	$1,735
C2	$715	$795	$855	$1,065	$1,815
C3	$785	$845	$910	$1,145	$1,915
C4	$840	$915	$970	$1,225	$2,085
L1	$930	$1,030	$1,115	$1,390	$2,500
L2	$1,010	$1,105	$1,195	$1,515	$2,575
L3	$1,115	$1,220	$1,325	$1,665	$2,835
L4	$1,230	$1,350	$1,440	$1,850	$3,140
SQ1				$0.40/SQ. FT.	$0.68/SQ. FT.
SQ3				$0.55/SQ. FT.	$0.94/SQ. FT.
SQ5				$0.80/SQ. FT.	$1.36/SQ. FT.

PRICES SUBJECT TO CHANGE

* REQUIRES AN E-MAIL ADDRESS OR FAX NUMBER

PLAN #	PRICE TIER	PAGE	MATERIALS LIST	DECK	DECK PRICE	LANDSCAPE	LANDSCAPE PRICE	REGIONS
HPK0600006	C1	6	Y					
HPK0600007	A3	11						
HPK0600009	A4	12	Y			OLA088	P4	12345678
HPK0600008	A3	12	Y					
HPK0600010	A4	13	Y	ODA013	D1	OLA001	P3	123568
HPK0600011	A3	14	Y			OLA001	P3	123568
HPK0600012	A3	15	Y					
HPK0600013	A3	15	Y					
HPK0600014	A3	16	Y					
HPK0600015	A3	17	Y					
HPK0600016	A4	17						
HPK0600017	A3	18	Y					
HPK0600018	A2	18	Y					
HPK0600019	A4	19	Y					
HPK0600020	A2	20						
HPK0600021	A2	20						
HPK0600022	A4	21	Y	ODA016	D1	OLA001	P3	123568
HPK0600023	A2	22	Y					
HPK0600024	A4	22						
HPK0600025	A3	23	Y	ODA015	D1	OLA003	P3	123568
HPK0600026	A4	24						
HPK0600027	A4	25	Y					
HPK0600029	C1	26	Y					
HPK0600028	A3	26						
HPK0600030	A4	27	Y					
HPK0600031	A3	28	Y					
HPK0600032	A4	29	Y			OLA024	P4	123568
HPK0600033	C1	30	Y					
HPK0600034	A4	31	Y					
HPK0600035	A3	32	Y					
HPK0600036	A3	33	Y					
HPK0600037	A3	34	Y					
HPK0600038	C1	35	Y					
HPK0600039	A3	36						
HPK0600040	A4	37						
HPK0600041	A3	38	Y					
HPK0600042	A4	38	Y					
HPK0600043	A4	39						

PLAN #	PRICE TIER	PAGE	MATERIALS LIST	DECK	DECK PRICE	LANDSCAPE	LANDSCAPE PRICE	REGIONS
HPK0600044	A2	40	Y					
HPK0600045	A2	41	Y					
HPK0600046	A2	41						
HPK0630001	A2	42	Y					
HPK0600048	A3	43	Y			OLA004	P3	123568
HPK0600049	A4	44	Y	ODA003	D1			
HPK0600050	A4	45						
HPK0600051	A4	46						
HPK0600052	A3	47						
HPK0600053	A4	47						
HPK0600054	A4	48	Y					
HPK0600055	C1	48	Y					
HPK0600056	A4	49	Y					
HPK0600058	A3	50	Y					
HPK0600057	A3	50	Y					
HPK0600059	A3	51	Y					
HPK0600061	A2	52	Y					
HPK0600060	A3	52						
HPK0600062	A4	53						
HPK0600063	A3	54	Y					
HPK0600064	A3	54	Y					
HPK0600065	A3	55	Y					
HPK0600066	A3	56						
HPK0600067	A4	56						
HPK0600068	A3	57						
HPK0600070	A3	58	Y					
HPK0600069	A3	58	Y					
HPK0600071	A4	59	Y					
HPK0600073	A4	60	Y					
HPK0600072	C1	60	Y					
HPK0600074	A3	61	Y					
HPK0600075	A3	62	Y					
HPK0600076	A4	62						
HPK0600077	A4	63	Y					
HPK0600079	A4	64	Y					
HPK0600078	A3	64						
HPK0600080	A4	65	Y					
HPK0600081	A3	66						

PLAN #	PRICE TIER	PAGE	MATERIALS LIST	DECK	DECK PRICE	LANDSCAPE	LANDSCAPE PRICE	REGIONS
HPK0600082	A3	66						
HPK0600083	A3	67	Y					
HPK0600084	A4	68	Y					
HPK0600085	A4	69	Y					
HPK0600086	A3	69	Y					
HPK0600088	A3	70						
HPK0600087	A3	70						
HPK0600089	A4	71	Y					
HPK0600091	A4	72	Y					
HPK0600090	A4	72						
HPK0600092	A4	73	Y					
HPK0600093	A3	74	Y					
HPK0600094	A3	74	Y					
HPK0600095	A4	75	Y					
HPK0600096	A4	76	Y					
HPK0600097	A4	76	Y					
HPK0600098	A3	77						
HPK0600100	A3	78	Y					
HPK0600099	A4	78	Y	ODA012	D2	OLA083	P3	12345678
HPK0600101	A4	79	Y	ODA016	D1	OLA093	P3	12345678
HPK0600103	A3	80	Y					
HPK0600102	A1	80						
HPK0600104	A4	81	Y	ODA017	D1			
HPK0600105	A3	82	Y					
HPK0600106	A3	83						
HPK0600107	A4	84	Y					
HPK0600108	A2	85	Y					
HPK0600109	A3	86						
HPK0600110	A4	87						
HPK0600112	A2	88						
HPK0600111	A4	88						
HPK0600113	A3	89	Y					
HPK0600114	A4	90	Y					
HPK0600115	A4	90						
HPK0600116	A3	91	Y					
HPK0600117	A3	92	Y					
HPK0600118	A3	92	Y					
HPK0600119	A2	93						
HPK0600121	C2	94						
HPK0600120	A2	94						
HPK0600122	A3	95	Y					
HPK0600123	A3	96						
HPK0630002	C2	96						
HPK0600125	A4	97	Y					
HPK0600126	A3	98						
HPK0600127	A4	98						
HPK0600128	A3	99	Y					
HPK0600129	A2	100						
HPK0630003	A4	100	Y					
HPK0600131	A3	101	Y					
HPK0600132	A3	102	Y					
HPK0600133	C3	103	Y					
HPK0600134	C3	104	Y					
HPK0600135	A3	105	Y					
HPK0600136	A4	106	Y					
HPK0600137	A3	107	Y					
HPK0600138	C2	108						
HPK0600139	A3	109	Y					
HPK0600140	A4	110						
HPK0600141	C2	111						
HPK0600142	A3	112						
HPK0600143	C2	113						
HPK0600144	C2	114						
HPK0600145	C2	115						
HPK0600146	C2	116						
HPK0600147	C2	117						
HPK0600148	C2	118						
HPK0600149	A4	119	Y					
HPK0600150	A3	120						
HPK0600151	A3	121						
HPK0600152	C4	122						

PLAN #	PRICE TIER	PAGE	MATERIALS LIST	DECK	DECK PRICE	LANDSCAPE	LANDSCAPE PRICE	REGIONS
HPK0600154	C1	128	Y					
HPK0600155	SQ1	129	Y					
HPK0600157	C2	130	Y					
HPK0600156	C3	130						
HPK0600158	A4	131						
HPK0600159	C1	132						
HPK0600160	C2	133	Y	ODA006	D1	OLA004	P3	123568
HPK0600161	C4	134						
HPK0600162	C4	135	Y					
HPK0600163	C3	136						
HPK0600164	C1	136	Y					
HPK0600165	C1	137						
HPK0600166	C1	138						
HPK0600167	C4	139						
HPK0600169	C2	140	Y					
HPK0600168	C1	140	Y					
HPK0600170	C1	141	Y			OLA025	P3	123568
HPK0600171	C1	142						
HPK0600172	C1	143	Y					
HPK0600173	C4	144						
HPK0600174	C2	144						
HPK0600175	A4	145	Y					
HPK0600177	C4	146	Y					
HPK0600176	C4	146						
HPK0600178	C1	147	Y					
HPK0600179	C4	148	Y					
HPK0600180	C4	148						
HPK0600181	A4	149						
HPK0600182	C1	150	Y					
HPK0600183	A4	151						
HPK0600184	C1	152						
HPK0600185	C1	153	Y					
HPK0600186	C2	154	Y					
HPK0600187	C1	155	Y					
HPK0600188	C1	156	Y			OLA001	P3	123568
HPK0600189	C2	157	Y					
HPK0600190	C2	158	Y					
HPK0600191	C1	159	Y					
HPK0600192	C1	160	Y					
HPK0600193	C1	161	Y			OLA001	P3	123568
HPK0600194	C2	162	Y			OLA001	P3	123568
HPK0600195	C2	163	Y	ODA004	D1	OLA020	P4	123568
HPK0600196	C1	164	Y					
HPK0600197	C1	165	Y					
HPK0600198	A4	166	Y					
HPK0600199	C1	167	Y	ODA001	D1			
HPK0600200	C1	168	Y					
HPK0600201	C1	168	Y					
HPK0600202	C1	169	Y					
HPK0600203	A4	170	Y	ODA013	D1			
HPK0600205	C2	171						
HPK0600204	C2	171	Y					
HPK0600206	C4	172						
HPK0600207	C1	172						
HPK0600208	C2	173	Y					
HPK0600209	C4	174						
HPK0600210	C1	175	Y					
HPK0600211	C3	176	Y					
HPK0600212	C1	176	Y					
HPK0600213	A4	177						
HPK0600214	C1	178	Y					
HPK0600215	C1	178	Y					
HPK0600216	SQ1	179	Y			OLA010	P3	1234568
HPK0600217	C1	180	Y					
HPK0600218	C2	181						
HPK0600219	C1	182	Y					
HPK0600220	A4	183	Y			OLA024	P4	123568
HPK0600221	C1	184	Y					
HPK0600222	C2	185	Y					
HPK0600223	A4	186	Y					
HPK0600224	C1	187	Y					

PLAN #	PRICE TIER	PAGE	MATERIALS LIST	DECK	DECK PRICE	LANDSCAPE	LANDSCAPE PRICE	REGIONS
HPK0600225	C1	188	Y					
HPK0600226	A4	189	Y					
HPK0600228	C1	190						
HPK0600227	C4	190	Y					
HPK0600229	A4	191						
HPK0600230	C2	192						
HPK0600231	C2	193	Y					
HPK0600233	A4	194						
HPK0600232	C1	194	Y					
HPK0600234	C2	195	Y					
HPK0600005	C1	195	Y	ODA001	D1	OLA001	P3	123568
HPK0600236	C2	196	Y					
HPK0600235	C1	196	Y					
HPK0600237	C2	197	Y					
HPK0600239	C1	198	Y	ODA012	D2	OLA010	P3	1234568
HPK0600238	A4	198						
HPK0600240	C2	199	Y					
HPK0600242	C1	200	Y					
HPK0600241	C1	200	Y					
HPK0600243	C2	201	Y					
HPK0600245	C3	202						
HPK0600244	C2	202	Y					
HPK0600246	C2	203						
HPK0600248	C1	204	Y					
HPK0600247	C1	204	Y					
HPK0600249	C2	205	Y					
HPK0600250	A4	206						
HPK0600252	C1	207	Y					
HPK0600251	C1	207	Y					
HPK0600253	C1	208	Y					
HPK0600254	A4	208	Y					
HPK0600255	A4	209	Y					
HPK0600003	C3	210						
HPK0600256	C2	210	Y					
HPK0600257	C2	211						
HPK0600258	C1	212	Y					
HPK0600259	C2	212	Y					
HPK0600260	A4	213	Y					
HPK0600261	A4	214	Y					
HPK0600262	C2	214	Y					
HPK0600263	C2	215	Y					
HPK0600264	C3	216						
HPK0600265	C3	216						
HPK0600266	C1	217	Y			OLA004	P3	123568
HPK0600268	C3	218	Y					
HPK0600267	C1	218	Y					
HPK0600269	A4	219	Y					
HPK0600270	A4	220	Y					
HPK0600271	A4	220	Y					
HPK0600272	A4	221	Y					
HPK0600273	C1	222						
HPK0600274	C1	222	Y					
HPK0600275	A4	223	Y					
HPK0600276	A4	224	Y					
HPK0600277	A4	224	Y					
HPK0600278	C1	225	Y					
HPK0600280	C4	226						
HPK0600279	C4	226						
HPK0600281	C4	227	Y					
HPK0600282	C1	228	Y			OLA004	P3	123568
HPK0600283	A4	228	Y					
HPK0600284	C4	229	Y					
HPK0600285	C1	230	Y			OLA001	P3	123568
HPK0600286	A4	231						
HPK0600287	C3	232	Y					
HPK0600288	C3	233	Y			OLA004	P3	123568
HPK0600289	C3	234	Y					
HPK0600290	SQ1	234	Y					
HPK0600291	C2	235						
HPK0600293	C2	236	Y			OLA015	P4	123568
HPK0600292	SQ7	236	Y					

PLAN #	PRICE TIER	PAGE	MATERIALS LIST	DECK	DECK PRICE	LANDSCAPE	LANDSCAPE PRICE	REGIONS
HPK0600294	C3	237	Y			OLA004	P3	123568
HPK0600295	SQ1	238	Y					
HPK0600297	C4	244						
HPK0600298	C4	244						
HPK0600299	C2	245						
HPK0600300	C4	246	Y					
HPK0600301	C4	247	Y					
HPK0600302	C3	248						
HPK0600303	C2	249						
HPK0600304	C3	250	Y					
HPK0600305	C2	250	Y					
HPK0600306	SQ1	251						
HPK0600307	C4	252						
HPK0600308	SQ1	252						
HPK0600309	C3	253						
HPK0600311	C4	254						
HPK0600310	C3	254						
HPK0600312	SQ1	255	Y					
HPK0600313	C4	256						
HPK0600314	C2	257						
HPK0600315	C3	258						
HPK0600316	C2	259	Y					
HPK0600317	C4	260						
HPK0600318	C4	260	Y					
HPK0600319	C4	261						
HPK0600320	L2	262						
HPK0600321	C3	263	Y					
HPK0600322	C3	264	Y					
HPK0600323	C3	265	Y	ODA020	D2	OLA020	P4	123568
HPK0600324	C3	266	Y					
HPK0600325	SQ1	267	Y					
HPK0600326	C4	268	Y					
HPK0600327	C2	269						
HPK0600328	C3	270	Y					
HPK0600329	C2	271						
HPK0600330	C4	272	Y					
HPK0600331	C2	273						
HPK0600332	C4	274						
HPK0600333	C4	274						
HPK0600334	C4	275	Y					
HPK0600335	C4	276	Y					
HPK0600336	C4	277						
HPK0600337	C4	278						
HPK0600338	C4	278						
HPK0600339	C4	279						
HPK0600340	C4	280						
HPK0600341	C2	281	Y	ODA007	D2	OLA012	P3	12345678
HPK0600342	C4	282	Y					
HPK0600343	C4	283	Y					
HPK0600344	C4	284	Y					
HPK0600345	C2	285	Y					
HPK0600346	C4	286	Y					
HPK0600347	C4	287	Y					
HPK0600348	C3	287				OLA024	P4	123568
HPK0600350	C4	288	Y					
HPK0600349	C4	288						
HPK0600351	C2	289	Y					
HPK0600352	C4	290						
HPK0600353	C2	291	Y					
HPK0600354	C3	292	Y					
HPK0600355	SQ1	292	Y					
HPK0600356	C3	293	Y					
HPK0600357	C4	294						
HPK0600358	SQ1	295						
HPK0600360	C4	296	Y					
HPK0600359	SQ5	296						
HPK0600361	SQ5	297						
HPK0600362	C3	298	Y					
HPK0600363	C3	299	Y					
HPK0600364	C3	300	Y					
HPK0600365	SQ1	301						

PLAN #	PRICE TIER	PAGE	MATERIALS LIST	DECK	DECK PRICE	LANDSCAPE	LANDSCAPE PRICE	REGIONS
HPK0600366	C3	302	Y					
HPK0600367	C3	302	Y					
HPK0600368	SQ1	303	Y					
HPK0600369	C2	304						
HPK0600370	SQ1	305	Y					
HPK0600371	SQ1	306						
HPK0600372	C3	306	Y					
HPK0600373	SQ1	307	Y					
HPK0600374	C3	308	Y					
HPK0600375	C4	309						
HPK0600376	SQ1	310	Y					
HPK0600377	C2	311	Y					
HPK0600378	C3	312	Y			OLA001	P3	123568
HPK0600379	C3	313	Y					
HPK0600380	C3	314	Y					
HPK0600381	C3	315	Y					
HPK0600382	C3	316						
HPK0600383	C3	316						
HPK0600384	C3	317						
HPK0600385	C2	318	Y					
HPK0600386	C2	319						
HPK0600387	C4	320						
HPK0600388	C4	321						
HPK0600389	SQ1	322	Y					
HPK0600390	C2	323	Y					
HPK0600391	C2	324						
HPK0600392	SQ1	325	Y					
HPK0600393	C2	326						
HPK0600394	C2	327						
HPK0600396	L1	328						
HPK0600395	C4	328						
HPK0600397	SQ1	329						
HPK0600399	SQ1	330	Y					
HPK0600398	SQ1	330	Y					
HPK0600400	SQ1	331	Y			OLA008	P4	1234568
HPK0600401	C3	332	Y			OLA001	P3	123568
HPK0600402	SQ1	333	Y					
HPK0600403	C2	334	Y					
HPK0600404	C4	335						
HPK0600405	C4	336						
HPK0600406	C2	336	Y					
HPK0600407	C4	337	Y					
HPK0600408	C4	338						
HPK0600409	SQ1	339	Y					
HPK0600410	SQ1	340						
HPK0600412	L1	346						
HPK0600413	L2	347	Y					
HPK0600414	L1	348						
HPK0600415	L3	349						
HPK0600416	C4	350	Y					
HPK0600417	SQ1	351						
HPK0600418	L1	352	Y	ODA002	D1	OLA015	P4	123568
HPK0600419	SQ1	353	Y					
HPK0600420	L2	354						
HPK0600421	SQ1	355	Y					
HPK0600422	SQ1	356	Y					
HPK0600423	SQ1	357						
HPK0600424	L1	358						
HPK0600425	L1	359	Y					
HPK0600426	L1	360	Y					
HPK0600427	SQ1	361	Y					
HPK0600428	C4	362						
HPK0600429	SQ1	363	Y					
HPK0600430	L1	364						
HPK0600431	L1	365						
HPK0600432	L1	366						
HPK0600433	L1	367						
HPK0600434	L3	368	Y					
HPK0600435	C4	369						
HPK0600436	C4	370	Y					
HPK0600437	SQ1	371	Y					
HPK0600438	L2	372	Y					
HPK0600439	L1	373						
HPK0600440	L1	374	Y					
HPK0600441	SQ1	375	Y					
HPK0600442	L1	376						
HPK0600443	SQ1	377						
HPK0600444	SQ1	378						
HPK0600445	L2	379	Y					
HPK0600446	L4	380						
HPK0600447	SQ1	381	Y			OLA017	P3	123568
HPK0600448	L1	382	Y					
HPK0600449	C4	383	Y					
HPK0600450	L1	384						
HPK0600451	C4	385	Y					
HPK0600452	L1	386	Y			OLA008	P4	1234568
HPK0600453	SQ1	387						
HPK0600454	SQ1	388						
HPK0600455	SQ1	389						
HPK0600456	L3	390						
HPK0600457	L3	391						
HPK0600458	SQ1	392	Y					
HPK0600459	L3	393	Y					
HPK0600460	L1	394	Y					
HPK0600461	SQ1	395	Y					
HPK0600462	SQ1	396	Y			OLA028	P4	12345678
HPK0600463	SQ1	397	Y					
HPK0600464	SQ1	398						
HPK0600465	C4	399	Y					
HPK0600466	L1	400						
HPK0600467	SQ1	401						
HPK0600468	L2	402						
HPK0600469	SQ1	403	Y					
HPK0600470	SQ3	404	Y					
HPK0600471	L4	405						
HPK0600472	C4	406	Y					
HPK0600473	L1	407	Y					
HPK0600474	SQ1	408	Y					
HPK0600475	L2	409						
HPK0600002	C4	410						
HPK0600476	C4	411						
HPK0600477	SQ1	412						
HPK0600478	C4	413	Y					
HPK0600479	SQ1	414	Y			OLA008	P4	1234568
HPK0600480	SQ7	415	Y					
HPK0630004	SQ7	416	Y					
HPK0600482	SQ1	417	Y					
HPK0600483	SQ1	418						
HPK0600484	L1	419						
HPK0600485	SQ1	420	Y					
HPK0600486	SQ1	421	Y					
HPK0600487	L2	422						
HPK0600488	SQ1	423						
HPK0600489	SQ1	424	Y					
HPK0600490	L1	425	Y			OLA037	P4	347
HPK0600491	C4	426						
HPK0600492	L1	427						
HPK0600503	P4	430						
HPK0600493	P3	432						
HPK0600494	P3	434						
HPK0600495	P3	436						
HPK0600496	P3	438						
HPK0600497	P3	440						
HPK0600498	P4	442						
HPK0600499	P2	444						
HPK0600500	P2	446						
HPK0600501	P2	448						
HPK0600005	C1	450	Y	ODA001	D1	OLA001	P3	123568

Beauty in Simplicity

Break away from conventional ideas of starter homes. Hanley Wood titles prove that "budget" homes don't have to be boring homes. Elegant, yet affordable plans show how beautiful home design is available at every price range.

NEW!

325 New Home Plans 06/07

The 5th volume in the popular "New Home Plans" series offers all new plans for 2006 and 2007. Every plan is guaranteed to be new and exciting, and updated with the most popular trends in residential architecture.

$10.95 U.S. (*256 pages*)
ISBN-10: 1-931131-65-1
ISBN-13: 978-1-931131-65-0

NEW!

DREAM HOME SOURCE: 350 Two-Story Home Plans

Perfect for families of all sizes and ages, two-story homes offer the universal appeal that has made them among the most popular home plan styles in the country.

$12.95 U.S. (*384 pages*)
ISBN-10: 1-931131-66-X
ISBN-13: 978-1-931131-66-7

NEW!

Big Book of Designer Home Plans

This fabulous compilation profiles ten top designers and reveals dozens of their most popular home plans.

$12.95 U.S. (*464 pages*)
ISBN-10: 1-931131-68-6
ISBN-13: 978-1-931131-68-1

200 Budget-Smart Home Plans

Finally, a collection of homes in all sizes, styles, and types that today's home-owner can really afford to build. This complete selection of houses meets smaller and modest building budgets.

$8.95 U.S. (*224 pages*)
ISBN-10: 0-918894-97-2

The Big Book of Home Plans

Finding paradise at home is even easier with this collection of 500+ home and landscaping plans, in every style.

$12.95 U.S. (*464 pages*)
ISBN-10: 1-931131-36-8

DREAM HOME SOURCE: 350 One-Story Home Plans

A compendium of exclusively one-story homes, for the homeowners that know what they are looking for. Plans run the gamut in both style and size, offering something for everyone.

$12.95 U.S. (*384 pages*)
ISBN-10: 1-931131-47-3

DREAM HOME SOURCE: 300 Affordable Home Plans

There's no need to sacrifice quality to meet any budget— no matter how small. Find stylish, time-proven designs, all in homes that fit small and modest budgets.

$12.95 U.S. (*384 pages*)
ISBN-10: 1-931131-59-7
ISBN-13: 978-1-931131-59-9

DREAM HOME SOURCE: 350 Small Home Plans

A reader-friendly resource is perfect for first-time buyers and small families looking for a starter home, this title will inspire and prepare readers to take the initial steps toward homeownership.

$12.95 U.S. (*384 pages*)
ISBN-10: 1-931131-42-2

Hanley Wood Books
One Thomas Circle, NW | Suite 600 | Washington, DC 20005
877.447.5450 | www.hanleywoodbooks.com

HPH